Sir Gawain and the Green Knight
A Stylistic and Metrical Study

Sir Gawain and the Green Knight

A Stylistic and Metrical Study

by Marie Borroff

Archon Books   1973

Library of Congress Cataloging in Publication Data

Borroff, Marie.
   Sir Gawain and the Green Knight.

   Reprint of the ed. published by Yale University Press, New Haven, which was issued as v. 152 of Yale studies in English.

    Bibliography: p.
    1. Gawain and the Grene Knight. I. Title. II. Series: Yale studies in English.
PR2065.G31B6   1973   821'.1   73-11407
ISBN-0-208-01381-4

[Yale Studies in English, vol. 152]

© 1962 by Yale University
Reprinted 1973 with permission of
YALE UNIVERSITY PRESS
and with a new preface in an unabridged
edition as an Archon Book, an imprint of
THE SHOE STRING PRESS, INC.
Hamden, Connecticut 06514

Printed in the United States of America

to

Louise Cogswell Cushman

Contents

Short Titles	ix
Preface to original edition	xi
Preface to the 1973 reprint	xii

Part One. STYLE

1.	Style and Meaning	3
2.	The Historical Study of Style	27
3.	Style and the Alliterative Tradition	52
4.	The Criticism of Style	91

Part Two. METER

5.	The Phonological Evidence	133
6.	The Metrical Evidence	144
7.	The Alliterative Long Line: The Normal Form	164
8.	The Alliterative Long Line: The Extended Form	190

Notes	211
Bibliography	274
Index of Words	283
Index of Lines and Passages	290
Index of Subjects and Authors	291

Short Titles

EDITIONS

GDS	*Sir Gawain and the Green Knight*, ed. Sir Israel Gollancz, Mabel Day, and Mary S. Serjeantson, Early English Text Society, 210, London, Oxford University Press, 1940.
TG	*Sir Gawain and the Green Knight*, ed. J. R. R. Tolkien and E. V. Gordon, London, Oxford University Press, 1930.

DICTIONARIES

English

BT	*An Anglo-Saxon Dictionary*, ed. Joseph Bosworth, rev. T. Northcote Toller, London, Oxford University Press, 1882.
EDD	*The English Dialect Dictionary*, ed. Joseph Wright, London, Henry Frowde, 1898–1905.
Grein	*Sprachschatz der angelsächsischen Dichter*, ed. C. W. M. Grein, rev. J. J. Kohler, Heidelberg, 1912.
Holthausen	*Altenglisches etymologisches Wörterbuch*, ed. Ferdinand Holthausen, Heidelberg, 1934.
MED	*Middle English Dictionary*, ed. Hans Kurath and Sherman M. Kuhn, Ann Arbor, Michigan, University of Michigan Press, 1954–.
OED	*The Oxford English Dictionary.*
Supplement	*An Anglo-Saxon Dictionary*, ed. Joseph Bosworth, suppl. T. Northcote Toller, London, Oxford University Press, 1921.

Old French

Godefroy	*Dictionnaire de l' ancienne langue francaise*, ed. Frédéric Godefroy, Paris, 1937–38.
TL	*Altfranzösisches Wörterbuch*, ed. Adolf Tobler, rev. Erhard Lommatzsch. Berlin, Wiesbaden, 1925–.

Old Norse

Ordbog — *Ordbog over det gamle norske Sprog,* ed. Johan Fritzner, Oslo, 1886-96.

LP — *Lexicon Poeticum Antiquae Linguae Septentrionalis,* ed. Sveinbjorn Egilsson and Finnur Jónsson, Copenhagen, 1931.

OTHER WORKS FREQUENTLY CITED

Luick — Karl Luick, *Historische Grammatik der englischen Sprache,* Vol. 1, Leipzig, 1921.

Jordan — Richard Jordan, *Handbuch der mittelenglischen Grammatik,* Vol. 1, Heidelberg, 1934.

Oakden — J. P. Oakden, *Alliterative Poetry in Middle English,* 2 vols., Manchester, Manchester University Press, 1930, 1935.

Reaney — P. H. Reaney, *A Dictionary of British Surnames,* London, 1958.

Wells — John Edwin Wells, *A Manual of the Writings in Middle English,* New Haven, Connecticut Academy of Arts and Sciences, 1916. Supplements 1-9, 1919-52.

Plan and Bibliography — *Middle English Dictionary,* with *Plan and Bibliography* by Hans Kurath, Margaret S. Ogden, Charles E. Palmer, and Richard L. McKelvey, Ann Arbor, Michigan, University of Michigan Press, 1954.

Abbreviations of titles of Middle English works are taken from the Title Stencils in *MED, Plan and Bibliography*. For editions used, see Bibliography.

The abbreviations a (*ante*), c (*circa*), and ?, as applied to dates of works and MSS, should be interpreted in accordance with the instructions in *MED, Plan and Bibliography*. Thus c1350 = 1350 or up to a quarter-century earlier or later; a1350 = before 1350, but probably not earlier than 1325; ?a1350 = a1350, but less securely established (and possibly later than 1350). See "Dating the Manuscripts," p. 18.

Preface

THIS BOOK is largely devoted to a single poem, one recognized as the masterpiece of a stylistic tradition. Its purpose is to find the style of the poem in its language and to reveal something of the artistry of the poet. But this book is also concerned with the study of style—specifically, the style of literary texts whose language is remote from our own. Its purpose, more broadly, is to see how the data yielded by philological investigations in Old and Middle English can be used for the study of style, by what methods, and with what results. A good deal of space is therefore devoted to the development of certain conceptual tools: concepts of style, of the relation between style and meaning in language, of the manifestation of stylistic values in the use of language, and of the function of style in poetic narrative.

Limitations of time and space have made it impossible to compare the use of the traditional style in *Gawain* with its use in *Patience*, *Purity*, and *St. Erkenwald*, or the use of elements of the style in *Pearl*. These poems have been disregarded except for consultation on specific points, and the important and interesting problems of authorship posed by them have been left unexplored.

My debts are many and great. The manuscript has been read in whole or in part, and valuable suggestions and corrections made, by Helge Kökeritz, who directed it in its original form as a doctoral dissertation, E. Talbot Donaldson, John C. Pope, Frederick A. Pottle, and R. S. Crane. They are not responsible for any errors which may have interposed themselves between their counsel and the completion of my work. The manuscript has benefited greatly from the astute and kindly editorial supervision of David Horne and June Guicharnaud.

For help in the details of preparation and presentation, I am indebted to Frances R. Lipp, Ann M. Chalmers, and Edith Borroff. Portions of the manuscript were typed by Ann S. Lincoln, Alice L. Durfee, Susan S. Addiss, and Jean J. Andersen. All did excellent work and showed commendable patience with poor copy.

To Louise Cushman, for her unfailing interest and encouragement through the writing of both dissertation and book, my debt is inadequately expressed in the dedication.

MARIE BORROFF

New Haven, Connecticut
December 1961

Preface to the 1973 Reprint

WHEN THIS STUDY was first published, there were only two full-length books in English of direct relevance to the subject: George Lyman Kittredge's *A Study of Gawain and the Green Knight* (Harvard University Press, 1916) and Henry L. Savage's *The Gawain-Poet: Studies in His Personality and Background* (Chapel Hill, North Carolina, 1956). It is pleasant to note that this state of affairs has changed radically. As if in answer to Morton Bloomfield's assessment of what had been accomplished and what still needed to be done ("*Sir Gawain and the Green Knight:* An Appraisal," *PMLA,* 76 [1961], 7-19), a series of books has been published within the last ten years to which the student of *Sir Gawain* and its poet can now turn for information and enlightenment. This study, I hope, is one such. Larry D. Benson's *Art and Tradition in Sir Gawain and the Green Knight* (Rutgers University Press) and John Burrow's *A Reading of Sir Gawain and the Green Knight* (Routledge and Kegan Paul) appeared in 1965; A. C. Spearing's *The Gawain-Poet: A Critical Study* (Cambridge University Press) in 1970. Three collections of essays have also appeared: *Sir Gawain and Pearl: Critical Essays,* edited by Robert J. Blanch (Indiana University Press, 1966), *Twentieth Century Interpretations of Sir Gawain and the Green Knight,* edited by Denton Fox (Prentice-Hall, 1968), and *Critical Studies of Sir Gawain and the Green Knight,* edited by Donald R. Howard and Christian Zacher (University of Notre Dame Press, 1968). Norman Davis's thoroughgoing and valuable revision of the 1925 edition of the poem by J. R. R.

Tolkien and E. V. Gordon (Oxford: Clarendon Press) was published in 1967; the student who is especially concerned with the *Gawain*-poet's use of language now has at his disposal *A Concordance to Five Middle English Poems: Cleanness, St. Erkenwald, Sir Gawain and the Green Knight, Patience, and Pearl*, edited by Barnet Kottler and Alan M. Markman (University of Pittsburgh Press, 1966). It seems appropriate to mention also my own verse translation of *Sir Gawain* (New York: W. W. Norton, 1967), in which I have reproduced the metrical patterns of the original, to at least my own satisfaction, in modern English; a brief critical introduction and an appendix, The Metrical Form, are included.

Two aspects of stylistic theory, the distinction between what I now call words as terms and words as elements of diction, and the conception of a multi-levelled relationship between verbal form and content, were presented in germ in this book, and have since matured. For a fully developed statement, see "Words, Language, and Form," *Literary Theory and Structure: Essays in Honor of William K. Wimsatt*, edited by Frank Brady, John Palmer, and Martin Price (Yale University Press, 1973), pp. 63-79.

MARIE BORROFF

PART I

Style

"As hit is breued in þe best boke of romaunce"

CHAPTER I

Style and Meaning

STYLE may be generally described as the way language is used, the "how" of expressing anything in words as opposed to the "what." To accept this description is to accept also the idea that there *are* different words for the same thing—that what is expressed may remain constant while language varies. But on this point not all will agree. If language is changed, it will be objected, then what it expresses must, always and inevitably, be changed.[1] This position would seem especially difficult to maintain for such a language as English, abounding as it is in pairs of words—*beginning* and *commencement*, for example—which have generally been taken to mean exactly the same thing. We find pairs like these in the Middle English of *Sir Gawain and the Green Knight*, though the words are not identical. Speaking of Gawain's promise to seek out the Green Knight at the end of a year, the poet says,

> Gawan watȝ glad to be-gynne þose gomneȝ in halle,
> Bot þaȝ þe ende be heuy, haf ȝe no wonder . . .
> Þe forme to þe fynisment foldeȝ ful selden.[2]
>
> [495–96, 499]

The modern reader will feel that *ende* and *fynisment* in this passage differ as *end* and *conclusion* differ today, and he will be right —save that ME *fynisment* is a rare word, and modern *conclusion* is not.[3] The difference, at any rate, is one not of meaning, as meaning will be defined here, but of style. If it be maintained that the phrases "the beginning of this book" and "the commencement of this book" have different meanings, we can answer only that they do indeed differ in expressive value, and that the difference is of great importance for the language of poetry. The boundary between meaning and style within the total area of expressive value will be the chief concern of this chapter.

Although we may speak of single words, like *beginning* and *commencement*, as differing stylistically, style properly belongs to language in use. It need not be used correctly or coherently—"Is't possible? Confess! Handkerchief! O devil!" is as likely a subject for stylistic analysis as "Put up your bright swords, for the dew will rust them"—but it must be used *intelligibly* in the sense that it must belong, or seem to belong, to a speaker and an occasion. Understood in terms of speaker and occasion, language produces in its audience the impression of style.

The impression of style is in one sense an impression of source. A series of intelligibly used words, without external identification, may be recognized as a newspaper headline, a business letter, a transcript of a small child's talk. A literary passage may, depending on the qualifications of the reader, be identified as prose of the school of Richard Rolle, alliterative verse as composed by the *Gawain*-poet, prose of the Euphuistic school, Shakespearean dramatic verse. Such identifications must somehow be based on perceptible aspects or features of language. An important part of the stylistic study of literary texts, therefore, is the description and classification of such features. If they are literally present in the language, it ought to be possible, at least to some extent, to handle them as quantities, to point them out and determine their frequency of occurrence. No one imagines that style can be reduced to lists and tables, but the impression of what is characteristic often has factual implications—as when we speak of "simple language" or "heavy use of adjectives"—and it is reasonable to ask that such implications be explored and the impression corroborated or corrected.

The study of style in this descriptive or historical sense need not concern itself with value judgments. To describe the characteristic differences between early and late Shakespearean dramatic verse, for example, is not to say that one or the other is superior. But as a branch of literary criticism, the study of style must deal with questions of effectiveness or lack of effectiveness in the use of language. Here, too, the starting point is an impression, and the attempt must be made to discover the causes of the impression, the features or aspects of language by which it is produced. The study of style in this critical or normative sense cannot be divorced from the study of the work as a whole. We cannot meaningfully speak of the "effectiveness" of a certain trait of style unless we know what the style is supposed to accomplish. If we say, for instance, that clarity of style is effective, we are assuming that the language of the work is designed to communicate. But clarity might be the reverse of effective in the speeches of a dramatic character gone mad or of a comic pedant. For the purposes of stylistic criticism, then, the *features* of language become *devices;* it is necessary to say not only what they are but to what end they are used and with what degree of success.[4]

Returning to the problem of the boundary between style and meaning, let us again consider the synonyms *begin* and *commence*. Can the difference between them, which has been generally described as stylistic, be expressed in more precise terms? One important aspect of it, surely, is that the two words seem appropriate to different kinds of context. *Commence* seems *specifically* appropriate for use in a treatise or other literary form; *begin* would not be inappropriate in a treatise, but it can also be used in a casual conversation, where *commence* would seem inappropriately formal and elevated. Formality in language, then, seems to be associated with the use of words in "works" or structures of which they are the material, as opposed to their use for everyday purposes of communication and self-expression. These verbal structures or "modes of formal discourse" are of many kinds, including laws and the formulas of religious services as well as orations and treatises and those forms, such as poetry and drama, which make up literature in the narrower sense. They are of general significance or value for the culture represented by the language, and it is their recording and transmission that gives rise to literary tradition, whether transmission is accomplished through written or other mechanical means of recording, or through the human memory. Formality of style in language is thus an aspect of cultural tradition, and the appropriateness associated with it is bound up with traditional usage. Language felt to be inappropriate, not formal or elevated enough, for use in a treatise is language that has not traditionally been so used.

Recorded language is not, of course, always formal in this sense. The "modes of informal discourse" include letters, diaries, and the like, which are of private or personal significance and which will be preserved for personal reasons or purely by chance. But because memory and recitation are used less today than in the past for the preservation of literature, it is natural to equate formal discourse, by and large, with written language and informal discourse with spoken language. Nor is formal discourse always recorded or transmitted in an exact verbal form. In such a genre as the primitive folk-tale the work may differ in each presentation. Yet the folk-tale must be classed as a mode of formal discourse. It is of general cultural significance; its narrative structure, if not its verbal form, is preserved by tradition; and its language may include traditional phrases on the order of "Once upon a time" and "They lived happily ever after," which are not used in ordinary speech.

In considering language *as it is used*, we must include mode of discourse as one aspect of the occasion. It affects the choices made among alternatives of verbal expression, and unless we know the mode of discourse, we cannot correctly assess the stylistic effect of language. A man who is angered by a certain political incident will express his ideas and feelings differently in conversation than from the podium.

Mode of discourse exerts a continuous influence on the speaker choosing among verbal alternatives. If we find *commence* used to express the meaning it shares with *begin*, we expect similar choices to be made at other points where similar alternatives of expression are available. In such a statement as "It became known that the union and the company had commenced negotiations," which implies the formal mode of expository prose, the auxiliary verb *had* is used in its full form. One would not write "The union and the company'd commenced negotiations." But if the same content is expressed in the informal style of everyday speech—"They heard the union and the company'd begun to talk things over"—the contracted form may appropriately be used.

It seems truistic at this stage to say that formal discourse and formal language correspond. But if "formal language" is taken to mean language differing markedly from that of everyday speech, the correspondence does not, in fact, always hold. The language of poetry and fiction is not necessarily different from that used on informal occasions, and the style of the informal essay accords with its name. "Formal language," then, properly means the language of formal modes of discourse insofar as it differs traditionally from that of informal modes. The traditional character of the difference must be specified, since clearly not all language departing from ordinary usage is formal. Such alterations of customary idiom as Dylan Thomas' "once below a time," "a grief ago," and "he downed and died" are idiosyncratic and creative rather than traditionally poetic. But it is true that the language of "works," whether these be laws, religious rituals, treatises, or poems, has always tended to differ from that of the informal modes of discourse. This would seem partly due to the conservative character of literary tradition —to its preservation of words and forms originally used, even though they have since become obsolete in the everyday language. And those authors who have attempted to achieve effects of dignity or solemnity, whether in poetry or prose, literature or public oratory, have recognized the value of words free from trivial and familiar associations.

The fact that the language of conversation or personal letters may at times resemble that of formal discourse can be similarly accounted for. Insofar as the speaker's role is public, insofar as he wishes to speak in dignified or solemn fashion, he will tend to adopt formal words and expressions. We speak more correctly, more formally, to a stranger or to one with whom our relationship is official and impersonal than to a friend; we speak more formally to a friend in public than in a private conversation; and so on.

It has been taken for granted so far that the same effect is always produced by language of a given level of formality, that stylistic qualities always depend on an appropriate relationship between language and the context in which it is used. Thus we have spoken of mode of discourse as decreeing certain choices among verbal alternatives, and we have said that the word *commence* produces an impression of formality because it has traditionally been used in formal modes of discourse. But further thought should lead us to see that this way of talking about style, although convenient, involves an oversimplification. The quality of a word may be described in terms of its appropriate use, but use is not in fact always appropriate. Formality in language is traditionally associated with effects of dignity and high seriousness, but if a latter-day Mr. Collins says "commence" rather than "begin" in an informal conversation, his dignity is decreased rather than heightened, and we take him less seriously than before. His use of *commence* is nonetheless stylistic, and if he is a fictional character, the depiction of his use of it is a stylistic device. We cannot, therefore, say that *commence* is a dignified or elevated word; we must say rather that its effect is dignified or elevated *when it is used on an appropriate occasion.* The judgment or perception of style has as its object not language but the act of using language. The nature of the act depends on the occasion. What we are ultimately perceiving or judging is thus the character of the speaker as implied by his language. When language impresses us as appropriate to the mode of discourse in which it is used, we naturally tend to reduce the three elements, speaker, word, and occasion, to the latter two. But in so doing we have tacitly judged the speaker, in that we have taken him seriously: we have inferred that he has the requisite degree of intelligence, education, and decorum for making appropriate choices among alternatives of expression. When language is markedly inappropriate to mode of discourse, the speaker tends to appear ridiculous because of a social deficiency such as ignorance or ill-breeding, or a deficiency of character such as self-importance or rudeness. The level of style considered appropriate in fictional works is determined by convention, and varies from one historical period to another. When, as at present, no one level is decreed, the author has free range in the depiction of manner or personality. The speaker of a poem or novel may be made to seem close and accessible (someone we are or could easily come to be on familiar terms with) or dignified and remote. The effectiveness of such a choice of manner must be judged in relation to the structure of the work as a whole.

Choices among synonymous words or expressions play a part in determining the level of formality of language, whether in literature or in real life. Degree of formality functions as a stylistic device in that it implies the character of the speaker through his linguistic behavior in relation to the occasion of speech. The character of the speaker, whether real or fictional, broadly conceived as including the full range of inherent and socially determined traits, thus becomes the focal concept of the theory of style we are developing here. Not only formality or informality of manner, but emotions, attitudes, knowledge, social class, age, sex, insofar as they can be implied by choices among synonymous words and expressions, are aspects of stylistic effectiveness in this sense. The practice of referring to words as humorous, sentimental, profane, polite, learned, and so on obscures the fact that these qualities belong primarily not to language but to human beings, and are revealed by the act, rather than the content, of speech.[5] The startling effect of *myosotis*, meaning "forget-me-not," in Wallace Stevens' line "I see the myosotis on its bush" derives not from the word itself but from the use of such a word on an occasion traditionally associated with sentimental emotions.

The implications of choices among synonymous words as part of the act of speech are to style what the meanings of words are to content. "Meaning" has been tacitly defined in the foregoing discussion as the power of a word to evoke a certain idea.[6] The implications of this definition must now be examined more closely.

In studying the vocabulary of a foreign language, one may proceed by associating each new word with a native synonym, by learning, for example, that German *Anfang* stands for the same idea as English *beginning*. When a recently memorized foreign word is encountered, the native synonym is consciously recalled and serves as an intermediary between the new word and its meaning. Once the foreign word becomes sufficiently familiar, however, it acquires the power of the native word to evoke the idea directly. Thus it appears that, for practical purposes at least, ideas have an existence independent of any particular verbal formulation, that the power to cause the envisaging of a certain idea may be possessed by more than one word, and that this power may be transferred from one word to another by association. Furthermore, these ideas appear to have distinctive and recognizable identities, since otherwise the judgments of correctness in matters of definition and translation on which cultural intercourse depends would be impossible. But these general statements hold good only on the common-sense level; we have no conception of what such nonverbal ideas may be in reality. In common-sense terms no one would deny that the English word *five* evokes the same idea as the German word *fünf*, or that this idea is distinct from that evoked by the word *four* and its German equivalent. But we do not know in what way the physiological events in separate human brains corresponding to perceiving and understanding words meaning "five" are identical or similar, or how these events differ from those associated with words meaning "four." The simplest and most obvious statements about the meanings of words are based on common opinion rather than on reality in any scientific sense. It is impossible to prove that any word evokes the same idea, or that any two words or expressions evoke the same idea, in more than one mind. We can say only that they seem to do so, that they do so on the practical level of human experience and communication.[7]

It is especially important to recognize the basis in opinion of all statements about the expressive values of language, in order that the goals of stylistic criticism may be realistically defined. Dictionary definitions themselves are merely formulations of authoritative opinion, and in specialized fields the authorities may be few. As in other matters of opinion, "correctness" is determined by agreement among the best judges. The best judges, however, will not always agree. Dictionary definitions are sometimes at variance, and authorities may differ as to whether a new meaning should be accepted. The interpretation of a given word in context is equally a matter of opinion. In literary texts the most reliable interpretation is that of the best critic, and a "correct" interpretation is one on which qualified critics agree. Cleopatra, when she asks, "Dost thou not see my baby at my breast / That sucks the nurse asleep?" is generally taken to be referring to the asp. Such an interpretation of her words may seem too obvious to question. But if it should be maintained that the dying queen believes she is actually holding a child, the opinion could not be proved false in the sense in which the opinion that a certain bacterium causes a certain disease can be proved false. Arguments for the inherent improbability of a literal interpretation of "baby" could be based on the text, but such arguments, though they might convince, would not amount to scientific demonstration. The interpretation of Cleopatra's speech involves a relatively simple choice; the reference to "my baby" may or may not be taken figuratively, but there is no doubt as to its literal meaning. When genuine difficulties of meaning and reference are presented by the words of a statement, as in Hamlet's aside "A little more than kin, and less than kind," the best critics may be expected to differ.

The interpretation of meaning and, a fortiori, the criticism of style are based on opinion. But it does not follow that these disciplines should be dismissed as unprofitable. Some opinions have always commanded more respect or afforded more illumination than others, and the best critics are right most of the time. The very term *disagreement,* moreover, is misleading, since it covers every sort of difference between opinions, from the most extreme to the most minute. It would be difficult to find a generally acceptable equivalent for the word *lufly* in certain lines in *Gawain,* as for example when the poet says, of the beheaded Green Knight, that he "Laȝt to his lufly hed, & lyft hit vp sone" (433). Most students of the poem would probably agree that the word has some such meaning here as "comely" (GDS) or "imposingly handsome," though some might wish to interpret the meaning ironically. But the range of "disagreement" in such a case can scarcely be compared to that associated with one of the few real textual cruces of the poem. In similar fashion, disagreement between two botanists as to the variety to which a certain plant form should be assigned in classification would presuppose agreement as to division, class, order, family, genus, and species.[8]

Having made it clear that this study aspires to the discovery of truth only in a limited sense—that we are interested not so much in what stylistic effects really are as in what they seem to discerning critics to be—we may go on to discuss meaning and its interpretation, with particular attention to the language of poetry. We begin by noting that although meanings are often ascribed to words in abstraction from particular contexts, words can properly be said to *have* meaning only as they are used. Relatively few words are associated with but a single meaning, and even these can be used metaphorically or as part of a code. A word used with any degree of frequency tends to develop new meanings, acquiring in the course of time a range of meaning which may be thought of, when it is considered out of context, as belonging to it potentially. Pairs of words are called synonyms because of a single shared meaning when there is divergence in range of meaning between them. Thus *commencement* shares with *beginning* the meaning "first part," but has in addition the nonshared meaning "graduation exercises." When we read the statement "Commencement is on June 7 this year," the context warrants an interpretation in which this latter idea is evoked by the word and the former is disregarded.

This example might seem to indicate that the context making possible a correct choice among possible meanings must be a context of statement—of words and grammatical structure. But such a verbal context is not required for a correct choice among meanings, nor does its presence necessarily enable the reader to make a correct choice. Consider the word *knight* in the sentence "The knight was captured." Here the potential meanings of all the words in the context are known, and the grammatical structure is understood. We cannot tell, however, whether *knight* means a piece in a chess game or a human being. On the other hand, if the knight in a chess set were visible and someone pointed to it and said the word, or if we read the sequence *king, queen, bishop, knight, rook,* we would without hesitation choose the meaning "chess piece." Interpretations, then, may be based on a context either of words, with or without grammatical structure, or of facts. What we *must* learn from it is the subject of reference in relation to which the word is being used. But we must also know the potential meaning of the word in relation to the subject. If someone points to a piece in chess and says the word *knight,* we interpret it correctly not only because we know the subject of reference is chess, but also because we know that *knight* is the name of a particular piece in that game. Otherwise, we could not tell whether the speaker meant to name the object specifically or generically, or to point out its color or material. One could equally well point to a knight on the chess board and say the word *piece,* or *white,* or *ivory.*[9]

When a word is interpreted in a context of other words, one of the potential meanings of each word is selected to produce the best set of meanings—the group most clearly related to a given subject matter or to associated subjects. In interpreting the sequence *king, queen, bishop, knight, rook* without further context, the meanings of the first four words with reference to human beings, of *queen* with reference to bees, and of *rook* with reference to birds, are disregarded in favor of the set of meanings related to the set in chess. This interpretation is not necessarily correct (it is perfectly possible that a human king, bishop, and knight; an apian queen; and an avian rook might be grouped together in fact or fiction and referred to by this sequence of words); it is rather the most likely interpretation of the sequence without further context.

The interpretation of meaning, then, involves the application of ideas previously associated with words to known or implied subjects of reference. In its application to a subject, a general idea may become more specific. For example, in the statement "The beginning of the poem contains an invocation to the Muse of History" the word *beginning* evokes the idea of part of a literary work. In the statement "The beginning of the poem was postponed because of his time-consuming political activities" it evokes the idea of an action. The word thus has two meanings in the two statements, although the ideas involved differ far less from each other than either differs from the idea of graduation exercises.

This discussion of meaning as the evocation of single ideas is not intended as ruling out the possibility of double or multiple meanings. In cases of double meaning, two acts of interpretation of the sort described above take place simultaneously. The two ideas are evoked within a single context, but they are related to different aspects of the context. When in Shakespeare's sonnet "Poor Soul, the Center of My Sinful Earth" the speaker asks his soul,

> Shall worms, inheritors of this excess,
> Eat up thy charge? Is this thy body's end?

end may be interpreted as meaning both "final state" and "final cause, purpose." The question in which the word appears should thus be answered both "yes" and "no." The first interpretation is warranted by the reference to the physical corruption of the grave in the preceding question. The second interpretation is warranted by the implied subject of the proper relation between the soul and the body (the body is "sinful" and a "rebel"; it must be made a "servant" in order that the soul may attain "terms divine"). The two meanings and the two answers depending on them supplement and corroborate, rather than contradicting or qualifying, each other.[10]

In the lines discussed above, the normal value of a word is multiplied, two different meanings being called simultaneously into play. It can also happen that a single meaning, through its relation to the known subject of reference, is changed; not merely made more specific, as with "the beginning of the poem," above, but "translated"—taken by the reader as having the value of quite another meaning. When Hamlet speaks of "the slings and arrows of outrageous fortune," we take "slings and arrows" to mean the diverse emotional impacts of painful experience. But we do not take this to be their meaning in the sense in which the word *sling* means "catapult." Hamlet is thinking not of the blows of stones and arrows but of "heartache," as the condition of life which makes death desirable. Because a satisfactory interpretation of "slings and arrows" is not yielded by the literal meanings of the two words, we take the ideas they immediately evoke as having the value of analogous ideas in the realm of emotion. These latter ideas, to which no particular verbal form is attached, constitute the goal of the figure; if they are not reached, the figurative meaning has not been interpreted.[11] But the literally signified ideas remain as part of the total expressive value of the words. For an analysis of this aspect of the figure, see below, pp. 19–20.

Double meaning and figurative meaning are similar: both involve the evocation of more than one idea, in context, by a single word. But the two processes are nonetheless distinct. In cases of double meaning a word evokes two ideas directly; in cases of figurative meaning a word evokes an idea from which the reader is impelled to proceed to another idea. The step from idea to idea need not, like that from "slings and arrows" to "emotional impacts," be determined by analogy. Any form of association will serve, and there is accordingly no predictable limit to the modes of figurative expression. The power of taking one idea, in context, as equivalent to another is an important one for the evolution of language, for many meanings now accepted as literal were originally figurative. Once a given act of figurative interpretation has been performed repeatedly, the process is short-circuited. The figurative meaning comes to be evoked directly, as the meaning of a foreign word comes to be evoked directly after repeated association with a native word. What ultimately results is the "dead metaphor," whose literal meaning is disregarded or forgotten. But the dead metaphor may be effectively re-animated. When Regan tells Lear, "I am made of that self metal as my sister, / And prize me at her worth," the modern reader will take the literal meaning of *metal* as having the figurative value of "character," or assume a homonymic pun *metal/mettle* with a literal meaning for the latter word. In Shakespeare's time, however, *metal* and *mettle* were still thought of as two forms of the same word, the meaning "temperament" having developed as a result of repeated figurative use of the meaning "temper (of metal blade)." The original meaning is recalled by the expression "made of" and the subsequent reference to an estimate of value. In *Gawain* there occurs a case of figurative meaning in which the idea directly signified is also relevant to the statement, so that a double meaning, one literal and one figurative, results. After the Green Knight has departed from King Arthur's court, Arthur tells Gawain, "Now, sir, heng vp þyn ax, þat hatʒ in-nogh hewen" (477). Gawain is at this moment holding the ax left behind by the Green Knight. But the expression "to hang up one's ax (or hatchet)" had in Middle English the figurative meaning "to cease from one's labors."[12] This meaning also fits the circumstances, since Gawain has now completed his assigned task of striking the Green Knight a single blow, and has thereby earned the ax for himself.

Figurative expression may be called indirect, since its interpretation involves a step beyond the immediate meaning of a word. But expression may be indirect without being figurative. One sort of literal indirect expression is periphrasis. Pope's "the life that fills the flood" and "that which warbles thro' the vernal wood" are taken, in the context of *An Essay on Man* (Epistle 1, 215–16) to mean "fish" and "birds" respectively. But they do not mean "fish" and "birds" in the sense in which *flood* means "sea" and *vernal* means "in spring." The step from the directly signified ideas to the ideas of "fish" and "birds" does not, as in figurative language, involve the translation of one meaning into another; it is rather a process of identification. The intended subject of reference, which, like "emotional impacts" in Hamlet's phrase, remains nonverbal, is *identified* from directly signified attributes (habitat, behavior) within a general category (living creatures). In both the lines cited above, the attribute-category combination potentially fits more than one subject. "The life that fills the flood" could mean "plankton"; "that which warbles thro' the vernal wood" could mean "the small bird" as opposed to other species. Or again, "the life that fills the flood" could simply mean the activity of the sea on a rough day. In that case there would be no periphrasis; *life*, in the sense of "energy, motion," would express the actual subject of reference rather than an aspect identifying another subject.

Literal indirect expression of this sort, involving the application of a class-meaning to a subject of reference, need not be periphrastic. In *Gawain* 2175 "þe knyʒt kacheʒ his caple & com to þe lawe" the meaning of *knyʒt* is applied to Gawain. But in the statement "The medieval knight at his best embodied both spiritual and secular ideals" the word has its direct meaning only. Another form of literal indirect expression is the pronoun, whose broadly generic meaning is almost always used to identify a particular individual or entity (but cf. the Wife of Bath's "Freletee clepe I, but if that he and she / Wolde leden al hir lyf in chastitee" [D 93–94], where the pronouns do not designate a particular man and woman). Literal and figurative indirect expression may combine when an individual is identified through a meaning expressed figuratively. When Iago calls Othello "an old black ram," *ram* figuratively means not "Othello" but "lecherous man"; the meaning "lecherous man" is taken to refer to Othello.

All these varieties of expression, both periphrastic and nonperiphrastic, may be called modes of reference. In each, the words used have their own direct meanings, and they may also be said to "mean" the subject to which the meaning is applied. But they mean the subject only to the extent that it fits the idea used for purposes of reference. When Gawain is called a *burne* or *freke*, these words indirectly mean not "Gawain" but "Gawain-as-warrior." To use a meaning for purposes of identification is to envisage, under the heading of one out of all its conceivable aspects, a complex unity which exists apart from any particular meaning. The meaning might be compared to a beam of light illuminating a single plane of a many-faceted solid. To use a particular meaning is to compel a particular view of the subject. This is true even when the word used is the most common name for it, the one that would immediately occur to us if we were asked "What is this?" or "Who is this?" To refer to something as a *chair*, for example, compels its being envisaged in terms of its species rather than the genus furniture or the subspecies armchair.[13] The same subject can be referred to as an aggregation of molecules, a structure, a shape, an area of color, an heirloom, an item in an inventory, an antique, a Hepplewhite, father's chair, and so *ad infinitum*.[14] Even the proper name of a person has differing forms. *John M. Jones* is no more a man's real name than *Johnny* or *Uncle John*. Each mode of reference implies a selective view of his identity, a way of grasping it mentally (it is significant that the word *handle* has been used in slang to mean "name"). The implications of naming were understood by Tom Sawyer, who explains to Becky Thatcher that Thomas is "the name they lick me by. I'm Tom when I'm good." It is impossible to say whether the "real" name of the central character of *Sir Gawain and the Green Knight* is *Gawain* or *Sir Gawain;* the narrator uses both.

Like figurative meaning, literal indirect meaning may change its status in the course of time. A descriptive reference, originally intelligible only in context, may, through repeated use, come to mean an individual directly. Such expressions as "The Lone Ranger," "The Rough Riders," "The Wife of Bath," have taken on the value of proper names. The same process is illustrated by originally descriptive surnames such as "Smith" and "White."

The interpretation of meaning is an act of selection. Among the potential meanings of a word, the interpreter takes one or more to be operative in the context of discourse in which the word appears. In cases of double or multiple meaning, two or more meanings are operative simultaneously. In cases of figurative meaning, the directly signified meaning cannot be operative and is therefore translated into a further meaning; the directly signified meaning remains, however, as part of the word's expressive value. In cases of literal indirect meaning, the directly signified meaning is operative as applied to a subject of reference; it both identifies the subject and constitutes a way of viewing it.

In addition to the above, there remains to be described a further mode of meaning which is of particular importance for the language of poetry. A word may have, besides its direct or indirect meaning, a meaning which is inoperative in its immediate context but which is nonetheless suggested by the context of the poem or passage as a whole, and therefore should be included in interpretation as part of its total expressive value. Such a suggested meaning is acquired by the word *scissory* in the context of Louis MacNeice's "Evening in Connecticut." The first stanza runs:

> Equipoise: becalmed
> Trees, a dome of kindness;
> Only the scissory noise of the grasshoppers;
> Only the shadows longer and longer.

The operative meaning of *scissory* is "like scissors (in making a scraping noise by the rubbing together of parts)." (The onomatopoeic character of the word, which obviously makes an important contribution to the effect of the passage, is beyond the scope of this discussion.) But the landscape is visualized by the speaker as subject to an ominous change—he refers later to "the fall of dynasties" and says that "nature is not to be trusted"—so that the idea of severance, both literal and figurative, inevitably comes to mind in a considered interpretation. *Scissory* thus acquires in context the suggested meaning "like scissors (in severing or cutting off)," which, however, is inoperative in relation to *noise*, the modified noun. And this suggested meaning carries a further implication of doom through the association of scissors with the mythical concept of the Fates.

A pattern of suggested meanings may be discerned in an image from Shakespeare's sonnet "When I Do Count the Clock That Tells the Time." [15] The lines in question are "When lofty trees I see barren of leaves / Which erst from heat did canopy the herd." *Barren* here has the operative meaning "bare" (usually with reference to an area of land) which had developed before Shakespeare's time as an extension of the original meaning "childless." But childlessness is the theme of the poem; the tree's change illustrates the effects of time, which the young man addressed by the speaker must combat by begetting children. "Childless" is thus suggested by *barren* and must be included as part of its total expressive value. A further suggestion derives from *lofty, canopy,* and *herd. Lofty* has the operative meaning "tall" with relation to physical height. But it also means "exalted in dignity or rank." *Canopy* has the operative meaning "shade, shelter," figuratively derived from the direct meaning "cover with a hanging." But a canopy in the literal sense is associated with the throne of a king or a dignitary walking in procession. Finally, in addition to its literal meaning, *herd* has the figurative meaning—first cited by the *OED* from Shakespeare —of "the multitude, the common people." The image of the trees, through the particular words used to express the operative meanings involved, thus calls to mind the protective and beneficent functions of a great family in society. The poem expresses a plea to a young man to maintain his family line; the status of the family, explicitly referred to in certain of the other sonnets, is conveyed here by suggestion.

At this point it may be objected that to allow meaning, in poetry or any other form of discourse, to slip the tether of the immediate context is to invite chaos: critical analysis will give way to the description of personal response, and the suggestive power of a word will become "what a word suggests to *me*." Personal response, of course, is always with us; in the realm of meaning there is no appeal from opinion to the scientific verification of facts. But the responsible critic will discriminate between suggestions whose source is his personal—i.e. private—experience, and those which are formally present. The presence of suggestion as an aspect of form depends on a relationship between a word's potential meaning, on the one hand, and the content of the poem in which it appears, on the other. It must not be forgotten that this content is emotional as well as ideational. Logically plausible suggestions must be excluded if they are emotionally false. The word *slings* in "the slings and arrows of outrageous fortune" does not suggest a bandage supporting a broken arm. The emotional force of the figure is too bitter, too painful, to permit inferences related to succour and healing.

The foregoing discussion of the modes of meaning leads us to a more inclusive and satisfactory concept of style than that yielded by a comparison between *beginning* and *commencement*. I originally defined style as the "how" of expressing anything in words as opposed to the "what." Choices among synonymous words are clearly stylistic; here the "what" is the directly signified meaning, which remains constant while the word varies. But meaning may be expressed figuratively—that is, indirectly through another meaning. The choice between the figurative and literal expression of meaning must also be stylistic, since here also the "what"—the indirectly signified meaning of the figure—remains constant. "Slings and arrows," in "the slings and arrows of outrageous fortune," is an indirect way of expressing the meaning "emotionally painful experiences." In cases of figurative versus literal expression, then, the stylistic choice proves to be a choice among meanings—i.e. directly signified meanings—as well as a choice among words. The stylistic effectiveness of figurative language often derives more from the directly signified meanings than from the words expressing them. In the line from Hamlet's soliloquy, the choice of slings and arrows, rather than other sources of injury, as the topic of the figure has important implications with respect to the speaker's thought. Slings and arrows are associated with hostility as well as with harm (cf. "The storms and tempests of outrageous fortune"); the weapons produce bruises and piercing wounds respectively and thus represent a variety, as well as a large number, of injuries; the injuries they produce are more often painful and shocking than incapacitating or fatal, so that they represent prolonged and repeated suffering rather than destruction and the end of suffering. All these associations are preserved when the figure is literally translated.

If the "what" of verbal expression, as opposed to the "how," is conceived as including indirectly signified meaning, then different modes of reference to a single subject must be counted as stylistic alternatives. It seems obvious, on the face of it, that *Gawain* and *þe knyȝt* (where Gawain is intended) are in some sense different ways of saying the same thing, and that the same is true of a periphrasis and its briefer equivalent. We have thus arrived at a concept of style involving not only the relation of word to meaning but the relation of meaning to subject matter. In both relationships style is determined by a series of choices among available alternatives; and these choices may be analyzed as giving to language its characteristic and effective qualities.

We are concerned in this study with verbal style—that is, the expressive values of particular words rather than the larger aspects of literary structure. But in studying the expressive values of words, we find that verbal style in the narrowest sense—that resulting from choices among synonymous words—shades into descriptive style—that resulting from choices among aspects of a given subject of reference, and, more broadly, among the details of a given subject matter. The concept of style in literary works will be narrow or broad according to what is taken as the material with respect to which the artist exercises the power of selection. If we take only directly signified meanings as the material, the "what," of language, we will find ourselves unable to discuss much that is characteristic and effective in a given passage of poetry; on pragmatic grounds alone, therefore, it may be argued that such a concept of style is too narrow. If we include indirectly signified meanings and subjects of reference as part of the material, the discussion of style will tend to impinge on other, broader aspects of literary criticism. It seems clear, however, that this is the lesser of two evils.

The stylistic functions of figurative language and choices among modes of reference have already been discussed in part. In figurative language the directly signified meanings may have implications concerning not only the emotions and attitudes of the speaker but his social class, degree of culture, occupation, and other traits of character. The same is true, more broadly, for the directly signified topics of similes and analogies (cf., in Browning's "The Bishop Orders His Tomb at St. Praxed's Church," "Big as a Jew's head cut off at the nape" and "Blue as a vein o'er the Madonna's breast," and the occupationally determined imagery used by the personae of Joyce Cary's novels). It has already been pointed out that the choice of a mode of reference implies a view of the subject. In the realm of personal names, the choice of name implies the relationship between the person named and the speaker. Here, as with more and less formal synonyms for a given meaning, the stylistically inappropriate choice implies a defect of character or manner (cf. the "glad-hander" who uses a nickname on first acquaintance). The view of the subject may be implied ironically. In the opening speech of *Antony and Cleopatra* the reference to Antony as "our general" implies Philo's consciousness of the disparity between Antony's public role and the "dotage" into which he has fallen.

Mode of reference, like choices among synonyms, may function as a determinant of level of formality. Depending on the circumstances, any mode of reference may be appropriate in informal speech. A description, or a word signifying status, may be used by a speaker to whom the name of the person referred to is not known. Or such a mode of reference may be used, despite the fact that the name is known, when the person referred to figures in the statement in a professional or official capacity. One who knows a doctor by name may nevertheless speak of him as "the doctor" when reporting a professional act or statement. A mode of reference other than the proper name may be determined subjectively by the aspect of the person referred to which is of greatest importance to the speaker or listener. A woman may say of her daughter, "Joan is engaged to Mary Smith's son" when speaking to someone who knows Mary Smith, even though she knows the son's given name. Emotion or attitude may determine such references, in conversation, as "that nice man" or "the fool," when the name would otherwise be used.

Once a person has been introduced as a subject of conversation, however, further references to him will ordinarily take the form of the personal pronoun or, if several people are spoken of alternately, of repetition of the original mode of reference. When a fictional character is designated by a variety of class names and descriptive periphrases which are not necessary for identification or directly related to the context in which they are used, the result is an elevation of stylistic quality. "Son of Laertes" is an elevated mode of reference to Ulysses, and "bearn Ecgþeowes" to Beowulf, when these designations are used by a narrator to whom the proper name is known, at a moment when the fact of paternal relationship is not of immediate consequence. The effect here depends not on language but on the relationship between meaning and subject matter. An effect of formality may be produced also by the inclusion in a reference of pleonastic or logically irrelevant detail. Pope's reference to insects as "the green myriads in the peopled grass" includes the pleonastic adjective "peopled," which in context takes on the character of an epithet. When Gawain begins to participate in the action of the poem, he is referred to as "Gawan, þat sate bi þe quene" (339). Since the fact that he is sitting beside Guenevere has already been stated (109), and since it is not directly relevant to the act described (that of bowing to King Arthur before offering to accept the Green Knight's challenge in his place), its inclusion adds formality to the tone of the passage. "He that sat by the queen," a true periphrasis, would have had much the same stylistic value.

Similar effects are produced by expanded references to objects or beings having in themselves no direct relevance to the subject matter of a passage. Certain correlations can be pointed out in *Gawain*, for example, between the degree of expansion of references to God made in speech by the characters, and the solemnity or importance of the occasion, or the emphasis attached to the statement in which the reference occurs. Thus when Gawain is taking leave of the lord of the castle on the eve of his departure, he uses the polite formula "God repay you," expressed in the words "þe hyʒe kyng yow ʒelde" (1963). But at the conclusion of the episode of the Green Chapel, when the Green Knight and the lord have been revealed as one person, the formula, again used by Gawain, is elaborated in accordance with the solemnity of the moment of culmination, becoming "þe wyȝe hit yow ȝelde / þat vp-haldeȝ þe heuen & on hyȝ sitteȝ" (2441-42). An expanded mode of reference produces an appropriate effect of stasis in the same episode, when the simile "still as a stump," applied to Gawain as he stands awaiting the second stroke of the Green Knight's ax, is cast in the expanded form "stylle . . . as a stubbe . . . þat raþeled is in roche-grounde with roteȝ a hundreth" (2293-94).

The expressive value of words, as we have been considering it here, includes both meaning and implication. The meanings are the ideas evoked, directly or indirectly, by the words, as applied to known or inferred subjects of reference. The implications derive not from the words themselves but from the use or choice of words, *the act* of using words, on a given occasion. What is implied is the character, broadly defined, of the speaker.[16] The study of style is the study of implication rather than of meaning, although implications cannot be fully understood unless meanings are known. Words may have expressive value, however, even though they lack meaning—that is, evoke no ideas. Interjections, for example, may be meaningless—"Wow!" and "Phooey!" are cases in point—but their use, considered in relation to the occasion, will nonetheless have implications about such aspects of the speaker as his degree of surprise, approval or disapproval, humor or solemnity, social class, decorum or the lack of it, and so on. The expressive value of polite phrases of greeting, introduction, leave-taking, and the like consists mainly in implication. *Good-by*, for example, is now purely a verbal act, having lost its original meaning as a wish; variant forms, such as *'by* or *by-by*, differ from it in implication. Expressions like "How do you do?" and "Yours very truly" do have discernible meanings, but these meanings are not literally interpreted in practice. Choices among equivalent phrases—"Good-by" rather than "So long," "Cordially" rather than "Yours very truly"—imply the speaker's attitude, class, or manner. It is characteristic of such "meaningless" expressions that they are best translated by the substitution of the expression, whether similar in content or not, which would be used in the other language on a similar occasion by the same sort of person.

The impression of style is produced not by single words but by language as it is used. In a complete stylistic analysis, not only the words used but such aspects of connected language as syntactic relationships, order, and patterns of rhythm and sound must be considered. Elliptical or fragmentary expression differs stylistically from full or complete expression, and full expression differs stylistically from repetitive or redundant expression. A sequence of words pronounced or punctuated as an exclamation differs stylistically from the same sequence cast as a declarative sentence.

This discussion has for the most part been limited to the basic units of language, the single words and phrases which express meanings. It has become evident that these units, in any linguistic sequence, have implications on two levels which merge indistinguishably in producing the impression of style. Any word has implications *as a word;* these are the implications in terms of which synonyms differ from each other. But it also carries implications deriving from the meaning it expresses. Consider, for example, the lines "Ruin hath taught me thus to ruminate, / That Time will come and take my love away," from Shakespeare's sonnet "When I Have Seen by Time's Fell Hand Defaced." The word *ruin* constitutes a mode of reference to the sights described earlier in the poem. "These ruins" or "these sights" or "these things" could have been used, but *ruin* is more sweeping; it implies more powerfully the effect on the speaker's mind of what he has seen. *Taught,* in the same line, figuratively means "caused"; the meaning could have been expressed literally, but the implications of the direct meaning of *taught*—including the "docility" of the speaker in its root-sense —would then be lost. In the second line there is a play on two meanings of *come;* it expresses literally the change of future time to present, but it also personifies Time through its meaning relative to personal action. This personification is maintained by the expression "take . . . away." The implications of *my love,* as a mode of reference to the person whose death the speaker fears, are obvious. So far as the implications of the words as words are concerned, there is an important and telling contrast between the elevated word *ruminate* and the utter simplicity of diction of the line that follows it.

It will be noted that each of these aspects of style has a determining effect upon the other. The exact meanings used in the line "That time will come and take my love away" could not be expressed in formal diction, since there are no formal synonyms for *time, come, love,* and *away* differing from these words as *commence* differs from *begin*. The general content of the line could be expressed more formally, but only if certain of the meanings were changed, with some such unfortunate result as "That time will ultimately extend its destructive effects to the one I love." Moreover, whether one changes the meanings or the level of diction, the rhythm of the line and its pattern of sound are also changed. The lines present themselves to the critic as a structure in which all aspects of form coexist, each limiting, and limited by, the others.

The effect of style has a multiplicity of causes. Although it is communicated by a single series of words, each of these words participates in many kinds of relationship. The reader, in responding to style, need not distinguish the effect of a word as an element of diction from the effect of the meaning or meanings it conveys, or of its phonetic qualities or accentual value. The critic of style, however, must attempt to analyze the effect into its causes, to discover how the several aspects of verbal form contribute to it and how these aspects relate both to each other and to the work as a whole.[17]

It is because the meanings of the words of a passage play a part in the production of the stylistic effect that it is possible to preserve the effect in part in translating a poem into another language. For the same reason it is possible for the modern reader to sense the stylistic qualities of a Middle English poem, provided that he understands the language fully, without knowing the status of the words in terms of level of formality and other differences among words as words. When the *Gawain*-poet, writing of the Christmas feast at King Arthur's court, says, "Þer tournayed tulkes by tymeȝ ful mony, / Justed ful jolile þise gentyle kniȝtes" (41–42), certain aspects of the style of the lines are readily apparent to the modern reader once the meanings of the words are understood. Their repetitive and expansive character can easily be reproduced in a modern translation, in which *men* or *this company* might be substituted for *tulkes*. Such substitution would of course destroy the pattern of formal alliteration. Less apparent but equally important is the fact that to substitute *men* for *tulkes* would be to substitute an element of common diction for a word of archaic and poetic quality, one of a group of elevated words meaning "man, warrior" whose systematic use was an important feature of the style of Middle English alliterative poetry. But to describe the stylistic value of *tulk* is to presuppose the carrying out of a process of historical investigation which will be the subject of the following chapter.

CHAPTER 2

The Historical Study of Style

The aim of the historical study of style is the recovery of certain lost or obscured expressive values in the language of literary texts. These expressive values are not meanings but implications; they relate not to the capacity of language to evoke ideas but to the *use* or *choice* of language considered as a mode of action.

A work which belongs, as does *Sir Gawain and the Green Knight*, to a period remote in time and to a literary tradition which has not descended, requires historical study as a preliminary to the criticism of style. We cannot intuitively recognize the stylistic qualities of the language of a Middle English poem as we do those of our contemporary language; and while dictionaries of Middle English and the glossaries to individual texts provide information on meanings in almost all cases, they rarely include comments on style. The intuitive impression of style may, in fact, be actively misleading. The vocabulary of *Gawain* is largely remote from our personal experience, and spelling and lettering lends even the familiar words a deceptive aura of the quaint and exotic. Historical study alone can hope to determine the extent to which the language of the poem reflects the ordinary speech of the Northwest Midlands of England in the late fourteenth century,[1] or to identify those elements which would have seemed archaic or elevated to the poet's audience. There is, of course, no guarantee that historical study can achieve these goals, but for a poem of the order of *Gawain* the attempt is surely worth making. The stylistic artistry of the acknowledged masterpiece of Middle English alliterative verse deserves the praise that has been given it,[2] but even more, it deserves a detailed study based on available historical facts. This chapter is devoted to an attempt to discover which historical facts are relevant, how they can be used, and what conclusions can be drawn from them.

Although style and meaning are two quite different aspects of language, a careful study of meanings is indispensable to the historical study of style. Obviously, the way meaning is expressed—whether directly or indirectly—cannot be analyzed unless the meaning is known. Furthermore, a word having a range of meanings usually has a range of stylistic values as well, so that its stylistic status will vary according to the meaning in which it is used. The adjective *fair* in modern English, for example, has a more elevated stylistic value in the meaning "beautiful" than in the meanings "impartial" or "clear (of weather)." For this reason, one must guard against generalizing about the stylistic value of a Middle English word from its value in a single meaning. And not meaning alone, but other aspects of language—such as morphology and phonetic development, which at first blush appear to have little or no bearing on questions of verbal artistry—must be included in the historical study of style. Striking contrasts in stylistic quality between modern variants like *spoke* and *spake*, *yea* and *yeah*, *cherubs* and *cherubim* caution us that the most minor aspect of form may be crucial for stylistic analysis. A Middle English text may present additional complications in that it has passed through the hands of a number of copyists, with occasional or even frequent deviation from the author's original wording as a result. For example, an obviously altered line in *Gawain* is 958 "Chymbled ouer hir blake chyn with mylk-quyte vayles," where *chalk-quyte* is substituted by modern editors.

These considerations are salutary, even sobering. But they need not be discouraging. It was the purpose of the preceding chapter to show that stylistic qualities do not depend solely on those aspects of the language of the past which must be rediscovered by modern students. They are in considerable measure determined by the exact meanings of an author's words, and these meanings are, by and large, available to us today. And in a work of the highest stylistic excellence, such as *Gawain* is universally acknowledged to be, the implications of words as words will further the same artistic purposes as are served by the implications of meanings, syntax, and other aspects of language. We may expect that, through further understanding of its style in the strictly verbal sense, our appreciation of such a work will not be discredited, but enhanced.

The historical study of style must concern itself with the ways in which words as words can be classified, and with the manifestation of these class distinctions on the practical level of usage. One important mode of classification is that according to which words are distinguished as more or less *formal*. The modes of formal discourse include all works of general cultural significance destined for written or mnemonic preservation, such as orations, laws, formulas of religious ritual, treatises, and poems. The modes of informal discourse include the everyday and transient manifestations of language, such as conversation, diaries, and private correspondence.

In terms of this variable we may envisage a range of stylistic values between extremes. Words of the highest level of formality would be those appropriate only to formal modes of discourse, words of the lowest level, only to informal modes, with those appropriate to both kinds of discourse occupying a middle ground.[3] But this account of the matter is oversimplified, since level of formality varies within the formal and informal modes of discourse themselves. The language of essays, public addresses, and other works varies in its degree of resemblance to the language of everyday speech, according to the stylistic conventions of the period, the author's purpose, and other considerations. Conversely, the language of conversation and personal letters varies in its degree of resemblance to the language of literary works, according to the relationship between the people involved, the social status of each, the occasion, and so on. And it must be remembered that stylistic choice, being a mode of human action, is unpredictable and may contradict theoretical principles of appropriate usage.

When one studies level of formality as an aspect of verbal style, it soon becomes clear that the quality of a given passage is not determined by all its words alike. For example, the opening lines of Leonie Adams' "The Walk,"

> A walk above the waters' side,
> None else to hearken there was come,

create an effect of formality, even though many of the words used—e.g. *walk, above, else, there, come*—are appropriate in everyday speech. The effect depends on a group of distinctively formal words and other aspects of language, such as the plural *waters*, meaning "brook"; the inflected genitive; *hearken; none* meaning "no one"; *was* as the auxiliary of the past tense; and the artificial word order. But it depends also on the fact that no distinctively colloquial elements of language are present. Whatever is not literary in the passage is "common" in the sense of being appropriate to both formal and informal modes of discourse.

It appears, then, that distinctive qualities of style are dependent on restriction in range of use. A word used frequently in formal discourse will not have a distinctively formal quality if it is also used frequently in spoken language; a word used frequently in spoken language will not have a distinctively colloquial quality if it is also used frequently in formal discourse. The style of a passage is determined by those words which are restricted in use, the rest forming a stylistically "common" or neutral matrix.

It follows that level of formality should in general be indicated by data on usage, particularly by comparative data on synonyms. If it were possible to collect, over a certain period of time, all occurrences of *beginning* and *commencement*, we should presumably find a statistical distinction between the two groups of occurrences in terms of proportion of formal to informal contexts; corresponding distinctions would appear in similar comparisons between *end* and *conclusion*, and so on.

Since qualities of style result from association primarily or exclusively with certain kinds of contexts, they must be defined in terms of distinctions among contexts. Contexts may be distinguished in terms of the occasion of speech. From this distinction arises the classification into the formal and informal modes of discourse, on which in turn depends the distinction between formal and informal language. Within the realm of formal discourse a word may be associated primarily or exclusively with one form of literature, as for example the "poetic" word, which is excluded not only from spoken language but from literary prose.

On the colloquial level, contexts may be distinguished in terms of the users of language. Stylistic qualities may be defined in terms of any classification of people into groups, and will belong to words or other aspects of language insofar as they are associated exclusively or primarily with a given group. The classification may be based on social level, occupation, national or regional origin, or any other distinction. Thus there are certain words and idioms peculiar to lower-class speakers, to theatrical people, to college students, to Britishers or Americans, to Americans from the South or New England. Any aspect of language associated with a certain group will ordinarily have the stylistic effect of implying a speaker belonging to that group, though it may also be used by a sophisticated speaker for purposes of allusion.

Contexts may be further distinguished in terms of the various spheres of human activity or knowledge. Restriction to one sort of context in this sense results in the technical term, the word associated primarily with the intensive practice of an art, craft, or branch of learning. Words or meanings of a technical nature imply primarily the speaker's knowledge and not the group or class to which he belongs, although the possession of that knowledge may imply other traits, such as social status. The knowledge of the technical terminology of the hunt displayed by the narrator of *Gawain* implies high social status when considered together with his other traits; in itself it might equally well imply the lower status of professional huntsman. Technical terms may be more or less formal, according to the mode of discourse most commonly associated with the activity to which they belong. The technical terms of philosophy, for example, are more literary and elevated than those of carpentry or seamanship.

In addition to these qualities, which derive from restrictions in range of context, frequency and rarity of use in the absolute sense must be counted as determinants of stylistic value: rare words and common words differ as words. As with technical terms, the distinction between them is operative at all levels of discourse. It seems probable that words which are appropriate at both formal and informal levels will in general be used more frequently than either distinctively formal or distinctively colloquial words. The word *bit*, meaning "small part," which is appropriate in both contexts, may be expected to occur more frequently over a given period of time than either the distinctively formal word *particle* or the distinctively colloquial word *smitch*.[4] Another synonym, *scintilla*, is also formal, but occurs comparatively rarely even in literary contexts.[5] And I have heard in local use in Maine a rare colloquial synonym [daɪt] which is apparently a phonetic variant of *doit* (Dutch *duit*) "small coin," hence, "small bit."[6] It is used typically in the phrase "Just a [daɪt]," with reference to second helpings at table. As with this example, one would expect the use of a rare word of distinctively colloquial quality to be geographically limited, since colloquialisms are by definition transmitted directly from person to person via the spoken language. Rare literary words may be known by speakers or readers over a large area, but their use will be restricted within that area to a particular cultural group or to specialists in a particular field of knowledge.

In connection with geographically limited or dialect words, it should be observed that the stylistic significance of such words in Middle English is particularly difficult to interpret. Today, the unselfconscious use of dialect implies a countrified, unsophisticated speaker. But in Middle English there was no nationwide distinction between "Received Standard" and dialect English; all English was equally dialect English. The native of London may have looked down, as Chaucer seems to do, on the speech of regions remote from the capital—"Fer in the north, I kan nat telle wher"—but the modern reader of the poetry composed in those regions ought not, consciously or unconsciously, to set Chaucer up as a standard. The problem will occur later in this chapter in connection with the distinctively Northern vocabulary of *Sir Gawain and the Green Knight*.

Rarity, like other stylistic values, may be associated exclusively with a single meaning. The word *wing*, for instance, is rare in the meaning "process at the side of the nose," whereas the synonym *ala* for this meaning is a rare word absolutely. The rarity of use of a word, therefore, may be connected with the rarity of use of a meaning, as with technical terms, whose meanings, as a rule, require expression only during the practice of the art or study to which they relate. The word *pentangle*, which occurs several times in *Gawain*, is rare in Middle English (in the OED it is cited earliest from *Gawain*, and thereafter not until 1646; *pentacle*, which would presumably have been the earliest Anglicized form of the original ML *pentaculum*, is first cited in 1594). Its infrequent occurrence clearly is bound up with the infrequency of references, in the extant literature, to the design it signifies. It might indeed be argued that the use of such words as *pentangle*—for which there are no synonyms—does not depend on stylistic choice; the word is inevitable, given the meaning to be expressed. However, any meaning can be expressed by periphrasis as well as by a single word. The meaning of *pentangle* is expressed periphrastically in common words in *Gawain* by the phrase "þe endeles knot" (630), and the device is later referred to as *þe knot* (662). Furthermore, a rare word expressing a rare meaning is nonetheless rare as a word, as a phonetic-orthographic structure, and its rarity in this sense is a significant aspect of its stylistic value.

Among words and expressions of common occurrence, those of a stock or formulaic character should be identified as a special class. A stock word is associated with a particular kind of context not because it seldom or never occurs elsewhere, but because it is used with the same meaning and in the same way so frequently as to take on the character of an earmark or mannerism. Stock elements are found on all levels of formality and often tend to become unpleasantly conspicuous. An adjective such as *great* or *swell* may be overworked for certain purposes in the speech of a particular social group; or an author may use certain words so frequently that their effectiveness is diminished (cf. Hemingway's *truly*). A stock element may be a distinguishing feature of a genre, as with the opening "There was a" of the limerick. (Note that part of the formula here is the metrical accent on *was*.) In the stylistic tradition of Middle English alliterative poetry the adjective *good*, among others, must be called stock, for even though it occurs commonly in other contexts in Middle English, it is used with conspicuous frequency for certain set purposes by all the poets, the author of *Gawain* included. Indeed, it is obvious to anyone familiar with the works of the alliterative school that most of the vocabulary and phraseology of *Gawain* is thoroughly traditional both in content and in function. The *Gawain*-poet's audience did not look for—in fact, probably would not have cared for—verbal originality such as we expect in poetry today, and the modern reader must divest himself of this expectation when studying the style of his works.

If the traditional or formulaic use of language represents, with regard to the variable of commonness or rarity, one extreme of stylistic status, the other extreme is represented by the individual speaker's or writer's creative modification of language: the coinage of new words, whether through transference from foreign languages or the use of native elements in new combinations; the figurative development of new meanings for existent words; and the invention or adaptation of words to express new subject matter in the realms of technology or thought. To distinguish the original from the traditional is, of course, one of the goals of historical study, although it is a goal that historical study cannot always hope to achieve. It must always be remembered that the most familiar English word of French or Latin origin had at some time in the past the status of a neologism, and that the most striking image or figure of speech in a Middle English lyric may be traditional.

Given the relationship between stylistic values and usage, certain major problems connected with the historical study of style in Middle English become apparent. The basic data for such study, it goes without saying, must be the available records—the contexts, so far as they have come down to us, in which a particular word appears. Difficulties are presented by both the extent and the nature of these records. First, it is obvious that in all realms of discourse—literary and documentary, poetry and prose—a large proportion of what originally existed has been lost.[7] It is scarcely credible that fourteenth-century alliterative poetry should have developed independently of Old English poetry, which it so strikingly resembles in prosodic structure, vocabulary, and verbal technique. If it did not, a lost continuum of narrative verse in the alliterative form must be assumed for the centuries between the composition of *Beowulf* and that of *Gawain*.[8] Because our knowledge of tradition is perforce incomplete, we can never be sure when a poet is departing from tradition, although we can sometimes be sure when he is following it. The status of *hapax legomenon* or neologism must always, for the same reason, be suspect; the earliest known citation of any word, we must assume, could be antedated if additional records became available.

But more important than the limitation in quantity of the surviving material is its limitation in the range of contexts represented. Since distinctive stylistic values are, as has been shown, dependent on restriction of usage, it follows that negative evidence will be at least as important as positive evidence in determining stylistic status. The use of a word in a number of contexts may for the lexicographer provide adequate evidence of its meaning or meanings. For the determination of stylistic status, however, the presence of a word in a certain kind of context is not enough; it must also be shown to be absent from other kinds of context. A word which appears a number of times in elevated prose is not by virtue of that fact an elevated word, for such a word might have been appropriate also in everyday speech. But of everyday speech in Middle English, we have by definition no written records. The contexts in which a word has come down to us will for the most part be literary, and even when they are not works but records of a relatively inartistic and casual sort—personal letters, inventories, wills, accounts—those which have been preserved will tend strongly in the direction of formal usage. The quality of formality, it will be recalled, belongs above all to the public and dignified occasion of discourse. And it is exactly those records of highest public importance, having to do with persons of high and dignified social status, which are most likely to survive. Even in minor documents we cannot be sure, without additional evidence, that a particular aspect of language does not represent legal, official, or business usage, as distinct from that of ordinary speech.

To object that conversation is after all frequently depicted in the literature of the time, not only in fictional narration but in anecdotal passages of didactic works, is to beg the question. For the extent to which the language of literary works reproduces the language of everyday life is precisely what is to be determined. When the narrator of *Gawain* relates the following speech of the Green Knight,

> Sir Gawan, so mot I þryue,
> As I am ferly fayn
> Þis dint þat þou schal dryue,
>
> [387–89]

it may be that, metrical form and word order aside, the fictional speaker is using words and phrases that the author himself might have used in everyday life. But one cannot argue that *so mot I þryue* is a colloquial idiom because it is found in a fictional representation of speech, any more than one can argue that *ferly* is a poetic word because it is frequently used in *Gawain* and the other alliterative poetry of the fourteenth century.

In determining stylistic value from use in the extant contexts, a combination of positive and negative evidence must be sought. Propitious circumstances for the collection of both kinds of evidence are afforded by certain texts which exist in two or more versions differing significantly in date or dialectical provenience. In comparative studies of such texts, patterns of avoidance as well as of use may be discoverable for particular words. Furthermore, when the records examined are drawn from more than one class of contexts, it is possible to discover certain systematic restrictions in usage which would presumably hold true also for additional material of the same nature if it became available. Thus words found only in poetry can be distinguished from words found also in prose; words found only or chiefly in texts of a certain region can be distinguished from words found in texts of all regions; and so on. It should be emphasized, however, that the significance of such findings is not necessarily self-evident; cf. below, the discussion of stylistic variation among Northern words, pp. 38–40.

We turn now to a discussion of a group of studies in which aspects of the stylistic status of particular words in Middle English have been treated systematically and in detail.

The most important study of regional vocabulary in Middle English is Rolf Kaiser's *Zur Geographie des mittelenglischen Wortschatzes*, Palaestra, 205, Leipzig, 1937. The aim of Kaiser's study was the establishment of a vocabulary criterion of regional origin for Middle English texts which could be used to supplement the criteria derived from historical phonology and grammar.[9] As his primary source of data, Kaiser chose *Cursor Mundi*, a text ideally suited to the purposes of such an investigation.[10] Its vocabulary is extraordinarily large, partly because of its length (over 30,000 octosyllabic or tetrameter lines), partly because it deals with an encyclopedic range of material. It is thought to have been composed at about the end of the thirteenth century in the extreme north of England (or possibly in southern Scotland),[11] but it is extant, partly or as a whole, in MSS of a wide range of provenience. Of the MSS containing all or most of the poem, the two most important are Cotton Vespasian A.iii. (hereafter called C) and R.3.8., Trinity College, Cambridge (hereafter called T). The phonology of T shows consistent and important differences from that of C, which is considered to be closely related to the original. H. Hupe, in "*Cursor* Studies, and Criticism of the Dialects of its MSS," published with the EETS edition of the poem, assigned T to Hereford—i.e. to the Southwest Midland dialect area.[12]

Differences of pronunciation and vocabulary in Middle English between the South and the North—here defined as broadly complementary regions rather than as dialect areas bounded by isoglosses—were apparently so great as to make communication difficult. They are attested to by the *Cursor*-poet himself in a passage adopted by Kaiser as an epigraph.[13] When one compares the C and T texts of the poem in detail, it becomes apparent that the differences in vocabulary between the two are too consistent and too purposeful (they involve the creation of a large number of new rhymes) to be due simply to faulty textual transmission or random scribal substitution of familiar for unfamiliar words. In effect, T represents an adaptation or "translation" of *Cursor* into language that would have been far more intelligible than that of the original in the South of England. The first stages of Kaiser's investigation consisted essentially of a comparison of the original, best represented by C, with the translation, best represented by T.

Kaiser examined the versions of the poem published by EETS, noting those words, presumably belonging to the original, for which entirely different words, and not merely different spellings or inflectional forms, had been substituted in T and its affiliates. A list of the presumably Northern words in the poem was compiled in this manner. From this list were excluded, as a precautionary measure, all words which, though consistently discriminated against in Southern texts of *Cursor Mundi*, nonetheless appeared in works of known Southern provenience.[14] Corroborative data were obtained by Kaiser from comparative examinations of other texts, such as the Northern and the Southern *Passion* and the translations of Robert Grosseteste's *Castel of Love*, in which the same material is treated in regionally different versions. On this basis he was able to identify also a group, considerably smaller in number, of distinctively Southern words.

Kaiser then checked the Northern and Southern words listed in chapter 1 for their occurrence in works of established Northern and Southern origin, such as Rolle's *Pricke of Conscience* and the *Ayenbite of Inwit*. This material is presented in chapter 2. In chapter 3 the criterion of vocabulary is applied to problems of provenience presented by several Middle English texts, including *Gawain*. Kaiser's list of the Northern words in *Gawain* includes over 130 different words occurring over 340 times in all (pp. 154–56), the vocabulary of the poem thus clearly indicating Northern rather than Southern origin. Chapter 4 consists largely of two dictionaries, one of the Northern and one of the Southern words in Middle English. Valuable lists of citations, in which the information available in the *OED* and Middle English dictionaries is supplemented by Kaiser's own researches, are given for each word, showing distribution in religious, legal, and parliamentary prose as well as the poetic texts. From the comparative size of the Northern and Southern word groups (well over 500 Northern words to under 100 Southern) it is clear that most of the regional words in Middle English were Northern. The language of the North was, Kaiser concluded, more vital than that of the South.[15] Its comparative richness was due in part to the exclusively Northern adoption of a large number of Scandinavian loan words (although there are also some Northern words of French origin, e.g. *fylter*; cf. *Gawain* 986), in part to the preservation of native words which were lost in the South, in part to the development of new compounds (e.g. *vmbe-kest, vmbe-lappe*; cf. *Gawain* 1434, 628).

The criterion of vocabulary developed by Kaiser proved of limited value in the determination of regional provenience. By the very nature of his material, he was committed to a broad division of England into "North" and "South," exclusive of an indeterminate Midland area—obviously a much less comprehensive and exact system than that afforded by the study of dialect differences. Although in his discussion of *Gawain* he presented a few vocabulary data suggestive of Western provenience within the Northern area, these were admittedly inconclusive,[16] whereas the Northwest Midland origin of the poem has been definitely established on the bases of phonological and inflectional criteria. Despite its limited utility for the solution of historical problems, however, the material presented by Kaiser is of great intrinsic interest, and the study remains a major contribution to Middle English lexicography.

There remains the problem of the significance of the Northern words as stylistic phenomena. They are clearly a feature of style in the historical sense, since their presence, as an aspect of language aside from meaning, makes possible an identification of source. But how do they function as a device of style in the sense of a contribution to poetic effectiveness? The answer to this question depends on the status of the individual words within the group. A considerable number of them are, as has been pointed out, of Old English derivation. Some of these may have been preserved as part of a native tradition of poetic style which had died out in the South. It is probable too that the Northern vocabulary in part reflects colloquial dialect differences; regional distinctions in official or other classes of formal terminology may also account for a certain number of words. If we consult the groups of citations given for particular items of the vocabulary, we find significant differences in the range of contexts represented. Such a word as *hathel* "man, warrior" (see *OED* s.v. *athel* a. and sb.,² *MED* s.v. *athel* n.) is cited only from poetry; *busk* "hasten" (ON *būask*) is cited from both poetry and prose. But Kaiser was not concerned with this aspect of the status of words. Differences in range of context among his groups of citations remain implicit, and the method used in compiling the citations makes it impossible to be certain of the texts in which a given word does *not* occur.

If certain of the Northern words are poetic, it is this, rather than their regional quality, that will be of primary importance for the criticism of style. If they are colloquial, their stylistic significance depends on their secondary implications: the implications of speaking like a Northerner. The man from the North, as depicted by Chaucer in *The Reeve's Tale*, is verbally uncouth and vulnerable to ridicule. Chaucer can thus play a linguistic practical joke on one of the Northern speakers in the tale, causing him to use the word *hope* in the distinctively Northern sense "believe without desiring" in such a way as to say what he does not mean: "Oure manciple, I hope he wil be deed" (A 4029).¹⁷ But when Gawain says to the Green Knight, with reference to the warriors of Arthur's court, that there are "vnder heuen, I hope, non haȝerer of wylle" (352), the stylistic effect of *hope* would, one assumes, have been independent of the regional character of its meaning. For the audience of *Gawain* the language of the poem would simply have been "our" language, the speaker "one of us." Insofar as cultured speakers of Northern English were linguistically self-conscious, aware of the peculiarly regional elements in their vocabulary, the frequent use of Northernisms might have produced a pleasantly homely effect, a quality similar to that of poetry in Scots for a Scotsman familiar with Standard English.

A source of material of extraordinary value for the study of style in Early Middle English is provided by the two extant manuscript versions of Lawman's *Brut*.[18] The most detailed studies of the vocabulary of the two versions are those of N. Bøgholm and H. C. Wyld,[19] though neither by any means exhausts the potentialities of the material. The value of the *Brut* as a source consists partly in its length: the earlier MS (A version) contains about 32,250 lines equivalent to a half-line of Old English poetry, while the later MS (B version) must have contained originally about 26,960 lines, of which several thousand have been mutilated or destroyed (Madden, *1*, xiii). Moreover, the poem is one of the few surviving literary works of the transitional period between Old and Middle English. It seems to have been completed at about the turn of the thirteenth century, and the manuscripts date from the first quarter and the end of that century respectively.[20] They thus span an interval of seventy-five years or more during a time of rapid change in the vocabulary, as well as the pronunciation and inflectional system, of the language. The manuscripts differ somewhat in dialect, A being Southwest Midland in provenience, B Southwestern.[21] Of greatest importance is the fact that the later version of the text is clearly the product of an attempt at stylistic revision. Both versions are removed by at least one step from an original, X, but B represents a revision and rescension, rather than a transcript, of X. Where B parallels A line for line, it shows considerable alteration of the original vocabulary (as represented by A), often with loss of formal alliteration. It is generally agreed that one of the aims of the B reviser was modernization of the diction of the poem (though not all his revisions, as will be seen, can be explained in this way), and it is with this aspect of the relationship of B to A that we will be chiefly concerned.[22]

The section of Bøgholm's study devoted to Lawman's vocabulary (pp. 17–37) is selective in method. He presents evidence for the contention that "the vocabulary of A bears an older stamp than that of B" and that "the departures of B . . . point toward the future" (pp. 18, 21) in the form of an alphabetical list of words in A which are always or frequently represented by different words in B. The more modern character of the vocabulary of B is tacitly associated with the fact that words in A which have not descended into modern English correspond to words in B which have descended. Thus "æðele, common in A, is replaced by god/bold or other adjectives or disregarded altogether." [23] Of particular importance for our purposes is the fact that Bøgholm takes into account descent into modern dialect English as well as standard. Thus he cites "bæch = valley, B: slade, still current in western counties" (for *slade* cf. *Gawain* 1159, 2147).[24] Finally, Bøgholm indicates that in some cases where B consistently differs from A, the A word had been associated in Old English chiefly or exclusively with poetry. Thus "blancke (OE. blanca is mainly poetical), B: hors." [25]

Wyld's studies were of a more extensive character than those of Bøgholm. He considered Lawman's poem an outstanding work of literature in the native English tradition, one whose value had been greatly underestimated; he ranked it, indeed, as superior to the alliterative poems of the fourteenth century. It was his professed aim in his studies of the poem to demonstrate the variety, richness, and expressive qualities of Lawman's vocabulary.[26] In the first of the essays he presented a list, compiled with the aid of Madden's glossary, of those words in the A version which invariably or frequently correspond to different words in B. This list includes some 150 words and compounds, as compared to about 60 in Bøgholm (ibid., 6, 2–23). The rest of the essays mainly consist of detailed discussions of a series of groups of words of synonymous or closely related meanings, classified in terms of subject matter under such headings as "Words for Human Beings," "Human Form and Features," "Conditions of Life," "Speech and Utterance," and the like.[27] Within each group, the meaning and scope of reference of each word are defined as precisely as possible. Supplementary citations, illustrating usage in Old English poetry and the Middle English alliterative romances, are frequently provided. For example, the discussion, under "Words Expressing Movement," of *buȝen* (OE *būgan* "to bend, bow down, flee," used frequently by Lawman and later by the *Gawain*-poet in the generalized sense "to go") includes citations from *Maldon*, *Juliana*, and *Beowulf*, as well as an analysis of eleven different meanings in Lawman derived from an examination of thirty-two passages (*Language*, *13*, 197–98).

Wyld's studies of particular words touched only rarely and incidentally on style in the sense in which we have been concerned with it here. Yet the words in his groups consistently show differences in stylistic value as well as in meaning, and the poetic or colloquial status of a word may be an important aspect of the "aesthetic value" or "atmosphere" of a word which it was Wyld's purpose to define (*Language*, *9*, 48). To show how meaning may be discussed in combination with style, we will select two of the words used by Lawman in the general meaning "man, warrior": *cniht* and *rink*. The former is discussed by Wyld (ibid., p. 53) under "Words for King, Prince, Noble." Wyld points out that "it is used again and again [by Lawman] in the rather general sense 'noble, warrior,' as an exact equivalent of the old *beorn* and *eorl*, both of which survive," and that it is "by far the commonest word in Lawman" in this sense (ibid.). It also has a specific sense; as an illustration Wyld quotes the line "þa men me dubbede: beiȝene to cnihte" and remarks that "cniht . . . when used specifically, refers to a rank conferred for personal service" (ibid., p. 54). *Rink* is discussed (ibid., p. 50) under "Words Applied to Men." According to Wyld, it "seems only to occur once . . . which is remarkable seeing the frequency of the word in Old English poetry, and the persistence of its use in the later alliterative poems and romances."

The two most common meanings of *cniht* in Old English are "boy, youth" and "attendant, servant" (cf. German *Knecht*). *Cniht* also had the meaning "soldier," in which it was used to translate Latin *miles*. (For these three meanings, see BT and Supplement; passages illustrating the translation of *miles* by *cniht* may be found in Supplement s.v. sense 2a "a man engaged in military service, a soldier.") The meaning "a military servant of the king or other person of rank; a feudal tenant holding land from a superior on condition of serving in the field as a mounted and well-armed man" (*OED* s.v. *knight* sb. sense 4) seems to have developed by the end of the Old English period (see the citations from the Old English Chronicle in the *OED*, and under the corresponding definition, "a soldier of rank, a knight," in BT Supplement s.v. sense 3).

But *cniht* is not found in Old English poetry in the meaning "soldier" or the later meaning "military servant." It is cited 21x in Grein in sense 1 "puer, juvenis" and once in sense 2 "servus"; these are the only meanings given.

Rinc in Old English has only the general sense "man, warrior," and occurs only in poetry. It is described in BT as "a poetical term," and in *OED* (s.v. *rink* sb.¹) as "only poetical."

For Lawman, therefore, *cniht* and *rink* differed radically in stylistic value, the former belonging to the language of real life, the latter to the traditional language of literature. It is significant that another word, probably *man*, corresponds in B to *rink* in the A text (A 5188 has "rinkas feollen," B has "mani m . . þer fulle"; see Madden, *1*, 221). The stylistic difference between the two words was preserved through the Middle English period. *Cniht* continued to be used in a wide range of contexts, both literary and nonliterary, while *rink* retained its exclusively poetic status. Both words appear in *Gawain* (as *kniʒt* and *renk*) and in other alliterative poems of the fourteenth century.[28] But *rink* did not long survive the dying out of the alliterative tradition; it is last cited by the *OED* from sixteenth-century poetry. *Cniht*, as *knight*, descended into modern English. It is not a distinctively poetic word today (compare *swain*) even in its historical sense.

In their studies of the diction of the *Brut*, both Bøgholm and Wyld are concerned with words taken singly. Much can be learned also from a comparison of the phraseology of the two versions. Seyger cites a group of parallel passages in which a phrase in A frequently found in Old English poetry is eliminated in the B revision. In one of these passages a king is referred to in the traditional way as a giver-out of rings: "belan he wes ihaten / bæʒes he dælde" (A 7424–25). In B this appears as: "Belan he was ihote / cniht mid þe beste" (*Beiträge*, p. 3; cf. *Beowulf* 80b, "beagas dælde"). We note that the words used in B have descended into modern English, whereas *bæʒ* in the meaning "(ornamental) ring" has not (it has, however, descended as a nautical term; see *OED* s.v. *bee*² sense 2). Further, although *best* in B alliterates with *Belan*, as does *bæʒ* in A, the position of *bæʒ* in the second half-line as the sole bearer of alliteration is in accordance with the traditional form, whereas that of *best* is not.[29]

Enough has been said, I hope, to show that the potential value of the A and B texts of the *Brut* as source material for the study of the history of style remains largely to be exploited. In drawing conclusions from the use of particular words in the two texts, however, one must proceed with caution. Consistent alteration of a word by the B reviser cannot always be taken to imply obsolescence or archaic-poetic status. A case in point is *argh* "cowardly, ignoble" (OE *earg*), which appears (*Language, 6,* 7, s.v. *earʒh*) in Wyld's list of words in A for which other words are consistently substituted in B. According to Wyld, the word is found once in both texts, and in three instances corresponds to different wording in B. (In Madden's glossary, s.v. *arð*, only three of these uses are cited.) We may note also that the cognate noun, for which see Madden's glossary s.v. *aerhðe(n)*, is found 2x in both B and A, but in four instances is omitted or corresponds to different wording; B has *heiʒe* "awe" once and *drede* once. Despite the apparent discrimination against it by the author of the B revision, *argh* is distributed widely in later Middle English texts, though it is not found in Chaucer. See especially the *MED*, where twenty-eight citations are given as compared to twelve citations prior to 1500 in the *OED*. Of greater importance is the fact that *argh* has descended into modern dialect English in the sense of "cowardly" (see *OED* and *EDD;* according to the latter, its range of distribution includes Sc. Nhb. Dur. Yks. and Lin.). Thus, although *argh* is an unfamiliar word to the modern reader and seems to fall victim to modernization or the attempt to eliminate poetic diction in the B version of the *Brut*, the available facts indicate that it was current in the spoken language in the thirteenth century and later. And it presumably has this same colloquial value in *Gawain* 241, "Þer-fore to answare watʒ arʒe mony aþel freke."

In studying the two versions of the *Brut*, one must be prepared also to recognize different stylistic values for different meanings of a single word. Here an apt illustration is provided by the word *bord*. In its most common modern meaning, "board, plank," OE *bord* occurs both in poetry and in prose; in the meaning "table (used for serving food)" it occurs in poetry and at least once in prose;[30] in the meaning "shield" it occurs only in poetry. A survey, based on the citations in Madden's glossary, of the treatment of the word in the two versions of the *Brut* reveals a clear discrimination between the meanings "plank, table" and the meaning "shield."[31]

In the meaning "plank" *bord* occurs twice in A and is repeated in both instances in B;[32] in the meaning "table" it occurs in A nine times and is repeated by B in all but three instances; in two of these the corresponding line is omitted, in one it has an entirely different content. In the meaning "shield" *bord* occurs four times in A; *sceld* appears in B in two of these passages; in one the corresponding line is omitted, in one it has an entirely different content. Wyld does not include *bord* "shield" in his list of words in A corresponding to different words in B. *Bord* has, of course, survived to modern English in the meanings "plank, table," but not in the meaning "shield." For this latter meaning only four citations are given by the *OED* (s.v. *board* s.b. sense 3), all from poetry; the last is from William Stewart's metrical chronicle of Scotland (1535), where *bourd* is used in a rhyme with *swourd*.[33] The word would thus seem to have had differing stylistic values in the meanings "table" and "shield" from Old English times on.

As a tool for the historical study of style, the two versions of the *Brut* may be expected to provide information mainly on the dying out (perhaps only regionally) of poetic words—e.g. *athel* adj.—or meanings—e.g. *bord* "shield." But the vocabulary of poetry is subject to increase as well as loss, and the transition from Old English to Middle English alliterative verse involved the development of a number of new poetic meanings. An example in point is OE *beonet, bionet*, ME *bent*. The original meaning of *beonet* is "bent-grass"; the word is assumed to have existed as a simplex because of its appearance in compound place (and hence personal) names.[34] In Middle English, *bent* means "field (covered with bent-grass)." (Cf. the compound *bent-feld*, cited by *MED* s.v. *bent* n.[1] sense 1c from thirteenth-century place-names, *Gawain*, and *Wars of Alexander*.) Colloquial status for *bent* "field" is evidenced by the name *Henricus de Bent* and the surname *del Bent*, both cited from the Subsidy Rolls of 1327 by *MED* s.v. sense 2a, and by its descent into modern dialect use (*EDD* s.v. *bent* sb.[2] sense II). *Bent* is common in Middle English poetry. *OED* (s.v. *bent* sb.[1] sense 5) suggests that this is due "partly at least to its alliteration with *battle, bicker, bide . . . bold, bale*, etc." This frequent use results finally in the development of a poetic meaning "battlefield" (since the "fields" referred to in the poetry were inevitably fields of battle), a development obscured by the *OED* entry, in which the senses "battlefield" and "field" are combined. But *MED* distinguishes the two (as 2a and 2b), citing the latter only from poetry. When Gawain says, of the warriors of Arthur's court, that there are under heaven no "better bodyes on bent þer baret is rered" (353), the relative clause is actually superfluous. A modern analogy is *field* in the same two senses; compare "He was valiant in the field" and "He worked hard in the field."

The language of Middle English alliterative verse as a genre has been analyzed by J. P. Oakden in the second volume of *Alliterative Poetry in Middle English*.[35] In a chapter entitled "The Vocabulary of the Poems of the Alliterative Revival" (pp. 175–93), Oakden discusses the words characteristic of these poems under the following headings:

1. The Use of "Chiefly Alliterative" Words
2. Poetic Words
3. Archaic Words
4. The Use of Technical Words
5. Old Norse Words
6. Dialectical Words
7. Rare and Obscure Words

In some general remarks preceding these discussions, he explains that limitations of space and the lack of an authoritative dictionary of Middle English have made a complete study of the problem impossible. His headings, in fact, imply a descriptive rather than an analytical approach. There is a good deal of overlap among them: "practically all the 'chiefly alliterative' words" are poetic words (p. 183); "poetic words are frequently archaic" (p. 187); "the alliterative poets drew largely upon their native dialects for their vocabulary" (p. 192); and so on. Nor is any single principle of classification carried out in full. The category of "Old Norse words," for example, might seem to imply a division of the vocabulary according to the several languages from which it is derived, or an account of the Old Norse element as proportional to the whole. Instead, Oakden gives the total number of "distinct Old Norse words" (as opposed to the number of their occurrences) in several of the poems;[36] the reader interprets these figures on the basis of his knowledge of the length and subject matter of each poem. (The fact that *Piers Plowman* has 180 Old Norse words and *Patience* has 103, for example, will not be taken to mean that *Piers Plowman* has a larger *proportion* of such words.)

The category treated in greatest detail is that of the "Chiefly Alliterative" words, "found but rarely or even not at all, outside the alliterative poems" (p. 175). Under this heading the poems are arranged chronologically and according to type, and a presumably complete list of "chiefly alliterative" words, with line references, is given for each. In "The Gawain group, including St. Erkenwald," Oakden finds fifty such words (pp. 179-80). The discussions of the remaining headings, however, are largely confined to "representative selections," "the most important examples," and similar groups.[37]

Partly because of the overlapping among the seven headings, partly because of the largely selective nature of the material, Oakden's chapter is difficult to use for the stylistic study of the vocabulary of any one poem. One cannot, for example, draw up a list of the poetic words in *Gawain* on the basis of the section devoted to "Poetic Words." If "practically all the 'chiefly alliterative' words" are poetic, it follows that some of them are *not* poetic, and unless a given "chiefly alliterative" word is specifically mentioned in the section on "Poetic Words," it is impossible to be sure whether it is one of the exceptions to the rule. Similar problems arise when one attempts to identify the archaic words, the dialectical words, and so on.

These difficulties can ultimately be traced to the fact that the category of "Chiefly Alliterative Words" is stylistically ambiguous. As defined by Oakden, such words are rarely or never found outside of alliterative poetry. But a positive criterion is also involved, though not stated explicitly: to qualify as "chiefly alliterative," a word must be used by several poets.[38] Insofar, then, as the *Gawain*-poet makes use of the "chiefly alliterative" vocabulary, he is using the traditional style of alliterative poetry. But what *was* the traditional style of alliterative poetry? In order to answer this question, we must know the values—poetic or colloquial, elevated or homely—of the words of which it was composed. And in order to determine these values, we must examine the history of each word individually. Oakden's list of "chiefly alliterative" words in *Gawain* contains *glam* "noise" (from ON *glamm*, with the same meaning), which has descended into modern dialects (see *EDD* s.v. *glam* sb.¹ "talk, noise, clamor"). It also contains *apel* a. "noble," which is avoided by the reviser of Lawman's *Brut*, which has not descended into modern English, standard or dialect, and which is last cited in the *OED* and the *MED* from the alliterative poems of the fourteenth century (see above, p. 41 and p. 225, n. 23). Other examples could be given, but the principle at issue is clear. Oakden's category of "chiefly alliterative words" gives us the characteristic or stock vocabulary-content of Middle English alliterative poetry without further defining the stylistic values of that content. Nor can the values of individual words be learned from the selective discussions under the remaining headings.

No detailed study devoted exclusively to the vocabulary of *Gawain* has appeared since Max Kullnick's *Studien über den Wortschatz in Sir Gawayne and the Grene Knyȝt*, a Berlin dissertation of 1902.[39] Kullnick's work was carried out prior to the publication of the Tolkien-Gordon and Gollancz-Day-Serjeantson editions, and prior to the completion of the *OED*; a number of his explanations of particular words are accordingly no longer accepted.[40] Moreover, the plan of the study and the conclusions to which it leads may be criticized on general grounds, and there are certain inaccuracies and inconsistencies that would seem due entirely to carelessness. The book cannot, therefore, be recommended, either as a source of information or as a guide to the stylistic study of the poem.

Kullnick included in his investigation only the words of the poem which had not descended into modern English. He did not take descent into modern dialects into account, however, and many of the words he discusses may accordingly be found in the *EDD*, although these are not distinguished from words for which there is no record after the Middle English period. In the first section of the study the words are listed alphabetically in groups according to the languages from which they are derived, the ancestral form and the meaning in *Gawain* being given for each. In the second part all the words are listed in one alphabetical series, each word being followed by numbers indicating its occurrence in other Middle English texts. These words are divided into six groups:

I. The oldest Middle English secular poetry (Lawman's *Brut* is included in this group, but no distinction is made between the A and B versions [41])
   II. Metrical romances of the fourteenth century
   III. Alliterating poetry of the fourteenth century
   IV. Chaucer
   V. Sacred poetry of the North (including the York and Towneley Plays)
   VI. Prose

To these six groups Kullnick added a seventh, consisting of works, other than those included in groups I–VI, cited for the words in question in Stratmann, Mätzner, and the volumes of the *OED* then available.

The section on conclusions contains a classification of the words according to their distribution, with tentative statements as to the stylistic significance of each group. The classification runs as follows:

(1) Words found only in alliterative poetry and the early Middle English works (group I and, from group V, the *Ormulum*). These, Kullnick felt, were in all likelihood archaic by the time of the composition of *Gawain*.[42]

(2) Words found only in the North and Northwest. This group was divided into two subgroups: words appearing in Early Middle English works, and words appearing first in the fourteenth century. The former, Kullnick classed as dialect words; the latter, as belonging to the vocabulary of the sacred literature of the North.[43]

(3) Words found only in alliterative poetry and in Chaucer. Kullnick associated these with the treatment of aristocratic subject matter.[44]

(4) Words found in prose as well as alliterative poetry. These words, Kullnick felt, were probably of popular origin and not especially suitable for effects of pathos in poetry.[45]

(5) Words found only in alliterative poetry. Within this group Kullnick distinguished five subgroups:
   (a) Words found only in *Gawain*.

(b) Words found only in *Gawain* and other works ascribed to the same poet.
(c) Words found only in *Gawain* and *Wars of Alexander*.
(d) Words found only in *Gawain*, other works ascribed to the same poet, and *Wars of Alexander*.
(e) Words found in *Gawain* and alliterative poems other than the above.

In assessing the value of Kullnick's conclusions, one wonders immediately why a single system of classification, based on distribution of occurrences, was not used throughout. If the occurrence of a word in the *Ormulum*, for example, was in the final analysis to be considered of special significance, as opposed to occurrence in the other works of Group V, should not the *Ormulum* have been differently classified, or set up as a separate category, at the outset? Moreover, Kullnick's conclusions as to the stylistic significance of his final five groups are at times extremely dubious. Group 1, which supposedly contains words archaic at the time of composition of *Gawain*, includes a number of words which have descended, in the relevant meanings, into Northern dialect use—e.g. *bigge, donke, laþe, tote, þrycche* (see *EDD* s.v. *big* v.², *donk* v., *lathe* v.¹, *toot* v.², and *thrutch* v.). In group 3 (words found only in the alliterative poets and Chaucer), although treatment of aristocratic subject matter may explain such words as *bauderyk* "baldric," *palays* "paling" and *payttrure* (Ch. *peitrel*) "breast-armor worn by warhorses," it can hardly be responsible for *heterly, muckel* n. (Ch. *mochel* adj. and n.), or *stubbe*. In the same group we find *grwe* "grain," which does not occur in Chaucer at all, so far as I have been able to discover, as well as *doser*, which does occur in Chaucer but in a quite different sense. *Doser* in *Gawain* 478 means "ornamental wall-hanging"; aristocratic subject matter might seem to be in question here, but Chaucer uses the word only in the sense "basket carried on the back" (*OED* s.v. *dosser*¹, senses 1 and 2).[46] Finally, although the words of Class 5 are said to have contributed to the unique character of the vocabulary of alliterative poetry,[47] the significance of the five subgroups of that group is left unexplained.

The list of 115 words occurring only in *Gawain* is not wholly consistent with the material presented elsewhere in the study. It includes without comment a number of words listed in the second section as occurring in group VII (citations of additional works in Stratmann, Mätzner, and early volumes of the *OED*). It does not include a group of words followed by a blank, indicating no occurrences other than *Gawain*, in the same section—e.g. *abloy, acole, barlay, baypen*. Oakden states that Kullnick's list "is reduced to about 100 by the references in *OED*, but the number is remarkable" (2, 193). He does not say on what basis the list has been reduced; however, a survey, for a list corrected on the bases suggested above, reveals that at least 70 of the words are considered by the *OED* neither as uniquely occurring in *Gawain* nor as rare.[48] Kullnick's methods of deriving a list of rare or unique words in *Gawain* were unsound, and his lexicographical aids inadequate. The attempt to compile such a list must now await the publication of the remaining volumes of the *MED*.

Although the studies discussed so far have made available a great deal of detailed information about the distribution and use of words in Middle English, none of them develops convincing conclusions with regard to stylistic values, in the sense in which these values concern the critic of poetry. We turn in the following chapter to a study which stands out from others of its kind both in methods used and in results obtained: *Stab und Wort im Gawain* by August Brink.

CHAPTER 3

Style and the Alliterative Tradition

ACCORDING to his introduction to *Stab und Wort im Gawain* (Studien zur englischen Philologie, ed. Lorenz Morsbach, 59, Halle, 1920), August Brink had originally intended a study of the dialect elements of the vocabulary of Middle English alliterative poetry. But he soon came to see that that vocabulary was influenced much less by dialect than by the stylistic art of the poets.[1] Further study enabled him to perceive certain relationships between the use of words in the alliterative line and their stylistic qualities. Taking the vocabulary of *Gawain* as his primary field of investigation, he found that within groups of synonymous words, some invariably alliterated, while others sometimes alliterated and sometimes occurred at the end of the line, where formal alliteration normally is lacking. Moreover, the use of a given word in *Gawain* corresponded strikingly with its use in the alliterative *Morte Arthure, Destruction of Troy, Wars of Alexander,* and other poems. Further patterns appeared. The words used exclusively in alliterating position rarely were found in Chaucer in the relevant meaning, and had failed to descend, in this meaning, into modern standard or dialect English. Brink concluded that the words of high "alliterative rank" (*Rang im Stabe*) were of archaic and elevated stylistic quality, and that they were used in common by the alliterative poets for the purpose of idealizing the persons and subject matter of their narratives. Such artistic aims contrasted with the realistic characterizations and stories, and the more colloquial diction, of Chaucer.[2]

To illustrate the statistical patterns Brink discovered, we may take *lede* and *kniȝt*, two of the many words with the class-meaning "man, warrior" which are used to refer to persons important in the action in *Gawain* and other alliterative poems. *Lede*, according to Brink's figures, occurs in *Gawain* 38x and invariably alliterates. This pattern may be expressed, changing Brink's notation slightly,

STYLE AND ALLITERATIVE TRADITION

as 38a:ona. *Kniʒt* occurs 41x in alliterating position, 27x in non-alliterating position, or 41a:27na.³ In *Morte Arthure* Brink found *lede* occurring 15a:ona, *kniʒt* 22a:99na. *Lede* is not found in Chaucer, nor has it descended into modern English, contrasting in both respects with *kniʒt*. *Lede* is "strongly alliterating" (*starkstabend*); *kniʒt* is "weakly alliterating" (*schwachstabend*).⁴

Approximately half of *Stab und Wort im Gawain* consists of a study of groups of synonymous nouns. The other half is a study of the adjectives (together with their cognate adverbs), differently organized but utilizing the same principles. Verbs are not discussed.⁵ In the section on the nouns, the words for which detailed material is given are grouped under the following headings:

>   Persons
>   People (Nation), Army, Retainers
>   Place
>   Time
>   Weapons, Armor and Clothing
>   Warhorse

A group of strongly alliterating words and a group of weakly alliterating words is discussed under each heading. Briefer treatment is given words whose alliterative rank is questionable, varying from poem to poem, and words of allied but not synonymous meanings. Thus under "Persons," Brink mentions *etayn* "giant," *wodwos* "satyrs, wild men," *God*, and *Kryst*.

Under "Persons," the most important group is that of the words for "man, warrior." To this group belong ten synonyms of high alliterative rank: *burne, freke, gome, haþel, lede, renk, schalk, segge, tulk,* and *wyʒe*. Two of these, *freke* and *schalk*, have descended into modern dialect use in other meanings.⁶ None of the ten is used by Chaucer. It may be added that all are of Old English derivation except *tulk*, from ON *tulkr*.⁷ According to Brink's figures, these ten elevated and archaic synonyms occur in *Gawain* 263a:1na, plus one "questionable" occurrence which will be analyzed later. A survey of the first 2,000 lines of *Morte Arthure*, plus a check of line citations in the glosses to other alliterative poems, gave a total of occurrences 510a:17na or questionable.⁸

The words of low alliterative rank listed by Brink under "Persons" (p. 16) are *king, kniʒt, lorde, mon,* and *syr(e)* (excluding designations for women and words expressing special relationships such as *fere* "companion" and *mayster*). It will be recognized that these words are not so much synonymous with, as similar in meaning to, *burne* and the other words of high alliterative rank—*king, kniȝt, lorde* and *syr(e)* being more specific and *mon* more general. Thus King Arthur may be referred to as a *lede* (cf. line 133) but not as a *kniȝt; lorde* in the plural may be used to mean "warriors, retainers" (cf. line 49), but in the singular it almost always refers to the person of superior rank in a group of warriors (cf. line 316, where the reference is to King Arthur, and 833, where the reference is to the lord of the castle). I prefer to omit *king* from the discussion altogether, since it is used to refer to Arthur in all but line 992 "Þe kyng comaundet lyȝt," where the reference is to the lord of the castle and both TG and GDS emend to *lord*. In *Morte Arthure* the meaning of *king* tends to become generic: it is part of Arthur's magnificence that his "warriors" are kings and fight against kings, as in 600 "Craftyly at Cornett the kynges are aryefede," 608 "The Sowdane of Surry and sextene kynges," and so on. *Syr(e)* was differentiated by Brink from the other words in the group because he found it occurring almost exclusively as a title prefixed to a proper name.[9] For the remaining three words, *kniȝt, lorde,* and *mon,* Brink found occurrences in *Gawain* totaling 117a:72na; in *Morte Arthure,* 50a:199na.[10] All are used by Chaucer and have descended into modern standard English.[11]

The data available for *freke* and *schalk,* the two of the ten elevated synonyms for "man, warrior" which have survived in modern dialects, suggest that both these words may have had different status in different meanings from Old English times. OE *freca* is cognate with the adjective *frec* "desirous . . . audacious, bold" (BT). The only cognate noun in other Germanic languages is ON *freki* "wolf" (see Holthausen). *Freca* has in Old English poetry the generalized sense "man, warrior," as well as the more specific sense "bold man." In both these senses the word is cited in BT only from poetry. It occurs only once in *Beowulf* as a separate word, though it appears also in several compounds which are listed by Klaeber in the glossary under *freca*. He gives the definition "bold one, warrior," labeling the latter but not the former meaning as exclusively poetic. (All the compounds are, as one would expect, exclusively poetic.) The modern Northern dialect meanings given by the *EDD* (s.v. *freak*, sb.¹) are "a strong man, a fighting man" and "a fellow, a fool; an impertinent fellow." Under the first definition there are only two references, one to a collection of Northumberland county words in which no illustration of use is given,[12] and one from a poem by the Scots antiquary and ballad collector Robert Jamieson, published in 1806. The lines in question run "And quhair is ane freik on ground / Darris cry Bo! to me?"[13] A reading of the poem in its entirety reveals that the reference is to "a fighting man" only in the sense of "a belligerent man," and that actually the definition "(impertinent) fellow" might serve equally well as a translation. (A parallel question later in the poem runs "And quhair is ane wyff on ground / Sa leal als Margerie?") The OE adjective *frec* occurs in Old English glosses as well as in poetry (see BT), and has survived in modern dialects (*OED* and *EDD* s.v. *freck* a.) in the original meaning. Evidence for colloquial status for *freke* in Early Middle English is to be found in the *MED* (s.v. *freke* n.), where the surnames *Freke* and *le Freke* are cited from the Pipe Rolls of Winchester (1209) and the Feet of Fine for Oxford (1248) under sense (a) "a brave man, a warrior, a man-at-arms." One cannot be sure of the exact meaning of the name. It may have been an occupational name based on a colloquial meaning "man-at-arms, professional soldier (not of noble rank)." Either would be distinct from the elevated poetic meaning "(noble) warrior." Or it may have simply imputed boldness—cf. the surnames *Bold(e)* and *le Bolde* cited from Kent (1317) and Sussex (1327) in Reaney (s.v. *Bold*). In sum, the available evidence indicates that *freca, freke* had colloquial and elevated meanings in both Old and Middle English, and that the elevated meaning "(noble) warrior" died out soon after the end of the Middle English period, while the colloquial meaning "bold fellow, belligerent man" survived. For the *Gawain*-poet *freke* "man, warrior" must have had associations with the idea of everyday boldness or recklessness which could be exploited in certain contexts. In 703 "& ay he [Gawain] frayned, as he ferde, at frekeȝ þat he met" the persons referred to by *frekeȝ* are not characterized except with respect to their ignorance of the whereabouts of the Green Chapel; the sense remains general. But when, as in 149 and 196, *freke* is used to refer to the Green Knight, its connotations of belligerency and its colloquial application to "fellows" rather than people of refinement make it particularly suggestive.

The data for *schalk* indicate a similar pattern. OE *scealc* had the senses "servant," "rogue," and "man, warrior," all cited by BT exclusively from poetry. Unlike *freke*, it has a group of noun cognates in other Germanic languages, including Goth. *skalk-s* "servant," ON *skalk-r* "rogue," OFris. *skalk* "servant," and OHG *scalch* "servant" (see Holthausen). ME *schalk* "warrior" occurs 10x in the A version of Lawman's *Brut*, to judge from the citations under *scalc* in Madden's glossary. In all cases the passage in B has a different word (usually *cniht*) or an entirely different content.[14] In *Gawain, schalk* has the specific meaning "attendant" in 2061 "His [Gawain's] schalk schewed hym his schelde, on schulder he hit laȝt." The modern Scots dialect meaning is "a servant; . . . a farm-servant" (*EDD* s.v. *shalk*). Again, descent into modern dialect use in the meaning "servant" (which seems, judging from the Germanic cognates, to have been the original sense) implies colloquial status in this meaning, at least in northern England, from Old English times on. The generalized sense was probably acquired as a result of poetic use, since the persons referred to in poetry as "servants" (to their overlords) were usually themselves of high rank. This sense remained exclusively poetic, dying out at the same time as did the elevated sense of *freke*. It would seem, therefore, that *schalk* has a more colloquial quality in *Gawain* 2061 than when it refers to Gawain himself in, for example, 1776 "'God schylde,' quoþ þe schalk, 'þat schal not befalle!'"

So far as the groups of strongly and weakly alliterating words for "man, warrior" are concerned, the principles formulated by Brink appear to hold good. Use in alliterating position only is associated with archaic and elevated stylistic quality, use both in alliterating and final position with colloquial quality. Before discussing the significance of these principles and testing them on other groups of words, we should observe that the large number of words for "man, warrior" and the frequency of their use in alliterative poetry have certain stylistic implications regardless of the value of each of these words as an element of diction. Brink's statistics tell us among other things that reference to persons by a variety of synonymous or nearly synonymous words imputing class-status was a traditional feature of the style of Middle English alliterative poetry, and that the words so used formed part of the traditional diction of that poetry. This device has in itself an elevating effect upon style, since it constitutes a departure from the practice of colloquial speech associated with a particular realm of formal discourse. The distinctively poetic quality of a word used to express the meaning "man, warrior" heightens the effect rather than creating it.

Brink tells us that the proportion of alliterating to nonalliterating uses suggested itself to him as "a formal criterion." [15] It is somewhat surprising, therefore, to find that his tabulations for *Gawain* include uses in the wheels, no distinction being made between such use and use in the long line. It is true that alliteration occurs constantly in the wheels: two of the three important words are almost always linked in this way, and often all three. But such alliteration nevertheless cannot constitute "a formal criterion," because it is not structurally essential in the sense in which alliteration in the long line is essential. The comparable formal criterion in the wheels is end-rhyme. The occurrence of *wyȝe* as a rhyme-word in 249 "Cast vnto þat wyȝe," counted by Brink as "questionable" (p. 15), has therefore exactly the same value as its alliterating occurrences in the long lines, since its use is determined here as there by an aspect of metrical form. But the other words that invariably alliterate in the long lines always appear in alliterating combinations in the wheels as well, so that the distinction has little or no practical consequence for the interpretation of Brink's figures.

The use of the archaic and elevated synonyms for "man, warrior" was explained by Brink as resulting from a conscious attempt on the part of the alliterative poets to idealize and typify their subject matter. It is also possible, of course, to take the purely technical view. The traditional groups of words for the expression of important meanings, each word beginning with a different letter, form an apparatus of obvious value for the practicing poet. Such word-groups were presumably learned by each poet from the works of his predecessors by reading or hearing them in recitation. Now the archaic and elevated synonyms meaning "man, warrior" identified by Brink in *Gawain* and other Middle English alliterative poems correspond strikingly to the group of synonyms for this meaning used in Old English poetry. *Burne, freke, gome, lede, renk, schalk, segge,* and *wyʒe* in *Gawain* have their counterparts in *beorn, freca, guma, leod, rinc, scealc, secg,* and *wiga* in *Beowulf;* and *haþel* in *Gawain* is thought to derive both from OE *hæleþ* n. "warrior" and OE *æðele* a. "noble" (see TG and GDS glossaries). The suggestion of continuity between the two traditions is irresistible, though the documentary evidence for it has been lost, if indeed it ever existed.¹⁶

The only synonym of the ten which does not derive from Old English is *tulk,* from ON *tulkr.* Some light may be cast on this rather obscure word if its history is considered from the point of view of the alliterative tradition. Aside from *Gawain, tulk* is found only in a few alliterative poems: in *Purity, St. Erkenwald, Destruction of Troy,* and *Wars of Alexander.* There is no evidence of its descent into modern English, dialect or standard. ON *tulkr* had the meanings "interpreter, spokesman, middle-man (in commerce)." It does not occur in poetry; its descendants in modern Scandinavian dialects uniformly have the meaning "interpreter," not the generalized meaning "man."¹⁷ The evidence, then, runs counter to an assumption that ON *tulkr* was adopted by Middle English alliterative poets as a literary loan word, and if it was not a literary word, it must have been transmitted into English via everyday speech. Its adoption may, of course, have taken place only within a limited area, and it may never have been a common word even within that area. Limited adoption is indicated by the failure of the word to appear in the extant records (other than alliterative poetry), and by the fact that it has not descended into modern dialects.

At some time prior to the end of the fourteenth century, *tulk* probably suggested itself to one or more poets writing in the alliterative verse form as an additional word for reference to persons, one whose initial consonant made possible a new range of alliterating combinations. Depending on the extent to which the works in which it was originally used were known and admired, other poets would adopt it as well. The transmission of the word would thus proceed on two levels, its history as a literary word becoming distinct from its history as a colloquial word. Generalization to the meaning "man, warrior" may have resulted from its use in poetry, or may have taken place in colloquial speech prior to the adoption of the word into poetry, perhaps as a result of misunderstanding the exact meaning. It should be noted that *tulk* is often, though by no means always, used in alliterative poetry in contexts relating to the specific meaning "speaker." In *Gawain* 638 and 2133 it is combined with *tale;* in 1966 it refers to a guide who is sent along to "teach" Gawain the way to the Green Chapel and who in the last stage of the journey tells him the way rather than accompanying him.[18] But in other cases—e.g. 41 "Þer tournayed tulkes by tymeȝ ful mony" and 1775 "& be traytor to þat tolke þat þat telde aȝt"—no qualification of the general sense "man, warrior" is implied.

The stylistic status of *tulk* "man, warrior" in *Gawain* cannot be positively determined from the available evidence, though it seems likely that the word never took hold in colloquial speech and had become both generalized and elevated by the time of its use in *Gawain* and the other extant alliterative poems in which it appears. From a study of the use of *tulk* we learn also that the general stylistic tradition in which all the alliterative poets participated (that of the common synonyms for "man, warrior" and their use) could be added to by individual poets, such additions attaining a more or less wide currency as the poet's work influenced others. Lack of definite knowledge of the dates and dialect provenience of most of the extant poems, however, makes it impossible for us to trace such lines of influence with any confidence. *Tulk* seems to have been used by three poets, assuming that *Gawain*, *Purity*, and *St. Erkenwald* are the work of one poet, *Destruction of Troy* of another, and *Wars of Alexander* of a third.[19] R. J. Menner has argued that *Wars of Alexander* was influenced by *Gawain*,[20] but no such relationship seems likely for *Gawain* and *Destruction of Troy*. The *MED*, the most recent authority, dates *Gawain* ?c1390, and both *Destruction of Troy* and *Wars of Alexander* ?a1400.[21] The independent use of *tulk* by two contemporary poets as part of the traditional apparatus of synonyms for "man, warrior" strongly suggests that both took it over from one or more earlier poets whose works have been lost. Nor can it be argued that since *tulk* does not appear in the earlier fourteenth-century alliterative poems, it must have been adopted into alliterative verse late in the century, for there is no proof that *Gawain* and *Destruction of Troy* stand in a direct line of descent from, for example, *William of Palerne* or *Winner and Waster*.[22]

The use of archaic and elevated synonyms for "man, warrior" and other meanings can be explained, then, without assuming a conscious idealizing tendency on the part of the poet. These words were a technical aid in the writing of alliterative verse, and for this reason they were preserved as elements of the traditional style, though not used in ordinary speech or formal prose. The fact that words of a more colloquial quality appear at the end of the line, where the poet's choice among synonyms is not influenced by the alliterative pattern, is an argument against the idea that the strongly alliterating words were chosen for their intrinsic stylistic value. But it is nonetheless true that the traditional style of alliterative poetry shows the idealizing and typifying tendency posited by Brink, and to this tendency the archaic and elevated synonyms for important meanings make their contribution. Whatever may be the causal explanation for the presence of words like *burne*, *haþel* and *renk* in the line, they inevitably produce certain effects and must therefore be "explained" not only as technical tools but as stylistic devices.

The exigencies of alliteration do not apply, as a rule, to the last word of importance in the long line,[23] although metrical considerations, such as the favoring of feminine endings and the avoidance of two unaccented syllables at the end of the line, slightly limit the choice of a final word. Brink's figures show that when the meaning "man, warrior" is expressed at the end of the line, an elevated synonym for the meaning is virtually never used. The *Gawain*-poet writes "Þenne þay boȝed to a borde þise burnes to-geder" (481), "Such a fole vpon folde, ne freke þat hym rydes" (196), "Ande al grayþed in grene þis gome & his wedes" (151), and so on through the list of elevated synonyms, but "Justed ful jolile þise gentyle kniȝtes" (42) and "& alle þese fyue syþes, forsoþe, were fetled on þis knyȝt" (656), where the meaning occurs in final position, rather than "þise gentyle burnes" and "on þis gome."

If one examines the use of *kniȝt*, *lorde*, and *mon* in the alliterative line, a pattern not discussed in Brink's study emerges. In *Gawain* and other alliterative poems *kniȝt* is used, both in the singular and in the plural, more frequently in final position than either *lorde* or *mon*. This choice cannot be explained in terms of the stylistic quality of *kniȝt* as compared to *lorde* and *mon*, nor can the choice of the plural *kniȝtes* over *lordes* be explained by the favoring of

STYLE AND ALLITERATIVE TRADITION

feminine endings (which might explain the choice of *kniȝtes* over *men*).²⁴ Of the three, it is likely that *kniȝt* was felt to be the most suitable in scope of reference as a general designation for the persons of the alliterative romances, *mon* being too inclusive and *lorde* —in that it signified pre-eminent social status—too restrictive.

A group of second half-lines in *Gawain*, ending with *kniȝt(es)*, shows striking similarities:

Justed ful jolile þise gentyle kniȝtes	[42]
Oþer sum segg hym bi-soȝt of sum siker knyȝt	[96]
Boþe þe kynges sister sunes, & ful siker kniȝtes	[111]
F[or] to telle of þis teuelyng of þis trwe knyȝteȝ	[1514]
So is Gawayn, in god fayth, bi oþer gay knyȝteȝ	[2365]
Of the chaunce of þe grene chapel, at cheualrous knyȝteȝ	[2399]

This pattern clearly fits the definition of the formula applied originally by Milman Parry to the Homeric poems and later by F. P. Magoun to Old English poetry.²⁵ It is a repeatedly used pattern, of which certain elements are set while others can be varied; it expresses an element of content which appears frequently in the narrative; and it constitutes a metrically satisfactory unit when used in the second half of the line. The pattern consists of the word *kniȝt(es)* in final position preceded by an alliterating adjective; the adjective-noun combination does not have a set grammatical role in the sentence, but it is usually preceded by one or more words (depending on the number of syllables in the adjective) of the less emphatic parts of speech, which serve to complete the half-line.

Examples of the formula can be found in other alliterative poems, such as *Destruction of Troy*, *Morte Arthure*, and *Wars of Alexander*. In lines 1–1000 of *Destruction of Troy* the following examples occur:

Byg ynoghe vnto bed with a bold knight	[397]
With chere for cherys the chiualrus knightes	[509]
Hit sittes, me semeth, to a sure knyght	[530]
Then saide þat semely to þe sure knyght	[560]

A! Jason my ioye & my gentill knight	[867]
Dede ys the dragon and the derffe knightes	[948]

and in lines 1–1000 of *Morte Arthure*, the following:

Appere in his presens with thy price knyghtez	[94]
That Iulius Cesar wan wyth his ientill knyghttes	[115]
Wyrke aftyre the wytte of my wyes knyghttes	[149]
Wyth justicez & iuggez and gentill knyghtes	[246]
On ȝone venemus men wyth valiant knyghtes	[299]
To hostaye in Almayne with armede knyghtez	[555]

In *Wars of Alexander* the pattern is used less frequently, but there are examples: 792 "Felles fey to þe fold many fers knyghtes," and the less typical 52 "Ne ost ordand he nane of na kyd knyȝtis," where the word preceding the adjective alliterates. Many other examples could be cited,[26] but those given here suffice to show that the ending of the second half-line with an alliterating adjective plus the word *kniȝt(es)* was, like the synonyms for "man, warrior," part of the stylistic tradition of alliterative poetry to which *Gawain* belongs. The variety of adjectives alliterating on different letters provides a technical aid for the composition of the first part of the line similar to that provided by the synonym groups.[27] The *Gawain*-poet, we must assume, composed second half-lines of this type in imitation of the alliterative poetry known to him.

It has, of course, long been recognized that the alliterative poems share a common phraseology (though there are different degrees of similarity between different poems), that the same is true of the rhymed romances, and that the two traditions have many phrases in common. A number of valuable compilations of alliterative and other phrases have been published, the most useful for the study of alliterative poetry being that of J. P. Oakden.[28] Oakden's collection of alliterative phrases is presented in seventeen different alphabetical lists, with cross references, beginning with Old English heroic and religious poetry and ending with Chaucer and Gower.[29] Consultation of these lists will show that a number of the alliterative combinations in any passage of *Gawain* occur also in other poems. It is only recently, however, that the repetitive use of words or phrases final in the line has been treated, as it were, with respect.[30] Oakden, in a chapter entitled "The Use of 'Tags' in Middle English Alliterative Poetry," cites a number of the most common second half-lines, e.g. "as the (book, etc.) tells" and "to (carp, etc.) the sooth." These "tags" are viewed in Oakden's discussion as a weakness of the alliterative style.[31] But the method of composition according to which the poet draws upon a traditional stock of phrases cannot in itself be called either good or bad. Such patterns were used by the *Gawain*-poet in the final section of the line as well as in the alliterating sections. The derogatory title of "tag" may justifiably be applied only to a pattern used with disproportionate and hence obtrusive frequency by a given poet. In *Morte Arthure* "as him likes" and its variants become tags; in *William of Palerne*, "witow for soþe"; in *Wars of Alexander*, "as the (boke, etc.) telles."[32] But in *Gawain* "to hondele as hym lykes" (289) and "as the crede telleʒ" (643) are not tags; they merely exemplify the poet's constant adaptation of traditional second half-line patterns to his own purposes.

The repetitive and "set" character of the phraseology of *Gawain* is more than a matter of its relation to the alliterative tradition. The poet also tended to repeat patterns of his own invention. It is dangerous, of course, to attribute the invention of any particular phrase to an alliterative poet, for parallels among the extant poems have yet to be studied exhaustively, and other parallels would undoubtedly be revealed if other poems should come to light. But it is natural to assume that an alliterative poet would have been likely to invent new combinations of words in handling new subject matter and that, having invented them, he would repeat them. Moreover, the history of *tulk* is evidence that the tradition was not static, that individual poets could make their contributions to it. In *Gawain* the combination of *grene chapel* with the traditional pleonastic phrase *on grounde* is used several times in the composition of the long line:

In any grounde þer-aboute, of þe grene chapel   [705]
Of þe grene chapel, quere hit on grounde stondeʒ   [1058]
Þe grene chapayle vpon grounde greue yow no more   [1070]

The same phrase is used also in 417 in the variation "The grene knyʒt vpon grounde grayþely hym dresses." The poet seems to have invented the combination of *hales* (referring to human motion) and *halle dor* for the purpose of describing the entrance and exit of the Green Knight:

> Þer hales in at þe halle dor an aghlich mayster [136]
> Halled out at þe hal-dor, his hed in his hande [458]

The name of Gawain's horse is used in certain repeated combinations:

> Bi þat watȝ Gryngolet grayth, & gurde with a sadel [597]
> Thenne watȝ Gryngolet grayþe, þat gret watȝ & huge [2047]
> Þenne gedereȝ he to Gryngolet with þe gilt heleȝ [777]
> Gordeȝ he to Gryngolet with his gilt heleȝ [2062]
> Thenne gyrdeȝ he to Gryngolet & gedereȝ þe rake [2160] ³³

More examples could be cited, but these suffice to show that the *Gawain*-poet uses new combinations of words in such a way as to supplement, rather than depart from, the traditional phraseology.[34]

Brink's principles, then, explain why *burne* is rarely used in final position, but not why *kniȝt* is used in that position more frequently than *lorde*. The relative frequency of *kniȝt(es)* in final position can be understood only in terms of the traditional patterns of the alliterative line. But Brink was concerned with differences in stylistic quality, and to the study of traditional phraseology as such, stylistic differences are irrelevant. The first half-line "þe fre freke on þe fole" (803) and the second half-line "at cheualrous knyȝteȝ" (2399) are equally traditional. For the reader or audience accustomed to the cadences of Middle English alliterative poetry they have the same repetitive ring; their form satisfies the expectation of the ear in much the same way as the second word in a rhyme. But the fact remains that the diction of "þe fre freke on þe fole"[35] is elevated, while that of "at cheualrous knyȝteȝ" is not. The alliterative combination may involve the linking of two poetic words, such as *freke* and *fole*, or *burne* and *blonk;* of one poetic and one colloquial word, such as *wyȝe* and *world;* or of two colloquial words, such as *king* and *crown*.[36] The alliterative phrases cited from *Gawain* in Oakden's lists include "now or never" (cf. *Gawain* 2216), "hold in (one's) hand"[37] (cf. *Gawain* 444), and others used in colloquial speech today and which must also have been colloquial for the *Gawain*-poet. The study of parallels can supplement, but cannot replace, the study of stylistic differences in relation to metrical structure, as initiated by Brink.

The figures collected by Brink on the use in *Gawain* of the ten elevated synonyms for "man, warrior" show a total of 265 alliterating to 2 nonalliterating uses. Of these two, *wyȝe* in line 249 has already been discussed, and its use as a rhyme-word in the wheel shown to be equivalent to its use as an alliterating word in the long lines. But *freke* in 241 "þer-fore to answare watȝ arȝe mony aþel freke" is a clear violation of the rule. *Freke* does not even alliterate by anticipation, although such alliteration occurs elsewhere in the poem (see below, p. 233, n. 23). In considering this line, we must remember that the "rule" broken by placement of *freke* is in fact nothing more than a description of what the alliterative poets usually do. A poet is always free to depart from traditional practice, and the departures of the best poets are likely to produce special effects which could not have been achieved by the traditional means. It is not surprising, therefore, to find that the *Gawain*-poet's single violation of consistency in the treatment of the synonyms for "man, warrior" has implications of great interest for the interpretation of the passage in which it occurs. The event being described involves a painful discrepancy between the behavior of Arthur's knights and their traditional reputation for courage. At the moment when the narrator is explicitly saying that many of them were afraid to answer the Green Knight, he goes out of his way, so to speak, to refer to them in elevated and idealizing terms. And although *freke*, in combination with the poetic adjective *aþel*, clearly has an elevated meaning, its associations on the colloquial level with boldness and belligerency are part of its total effect. The diction here seems to pay a kind of ironic lip-service to qualities that are traditionally present but which have failed to manifest themselves in response to challenge.

We have so far been discussing the ways in which the stylistic qualities of words determine their use in the long line as if the structure of that line were a matter of alliteration only. But the structure is also one of stress relationships, so that differing metrical use may imply differing degrees of stress. The nature of the connection between stylistic quality and stress should now be explored.

It seems advisable first to study the use of the synonyms for "man, warrior" in the wheels rather than the long lines, since the metrical structure of the former is much less problematic. There is general agreement that the short rhyming lines of the wheels are tripartite in form (see below, p. 155 and p. 261, n. 19). That is, each line has three syllables of greatest importance which will here be called "chief syllables" and labeled "C." The syllables falling between these we will call "intermediate syllables," and the metrical roles of the two kinds of syllables will be described as "chief position" and "intermediate position." A survey of the four hundred odd lines of the wheels shows that the meaning "man, warrior" is expressed in both chief and intermediate position: when it is expressed in chief position, either an elevated or a colloquial synonym may be used; in intermediate position the colloquial synonym *mon* is used almost without exception. Thus an elevated synonym is used in chief position in such lines as:

     C   C   C
Þe *burne* bede bryng his blonk   [2024]

   C   C   C
He ferde as *freke* were fade   [149]

     C   C   C
To þe *gome* he watȝ ful gayn   [178]

A colloquial synonym is used in chief position in such lines as:

    C   C   C
Þat *mon* much merþe con make   [899]

    C   C   C
To *knyȝteȝ* he kest his yȝe   [228]

  C C   C
Þe *lorde* fast can hym payne   [1042]

But in the following lines the meaning is expressed in intermediate position by *mon:*

   C   C   C
Soth moȝt no *mon* say   [84]

     C   C   C
For wonder of his hwe *men* hade   [147]

   C C   C
Þen stod þat stif *mon* nere   [322]

$$\overset{C\qquad C\qquad\quad C}{\text{Bi þat þe bolde }\textit{mon}\text{ boun}} \qquad [2043]$$

The meaning "warhorse" is expressed infrequently in the wheels as compared to "man, warrior," but choice among synonyms seems to follow the same pattern. The meaning is expressed in chief position by both elevated and colloquial words:

$$\overset{C\qquad\quad C\quad\ C}{\text{A }\textit{stede}\text{ ful stif to strayne}} \qquad [176]$$

$$\overset{C\qquad\quad\ C\qquad\quad C}{\text{Þe burne bede bryng his }\textit{blonk}} \qquad [2024]$$

$$\overset{C\qquad\ \ C\quad\ \ C}{\text{His haþel on }\textit{hors}\text{ watȝ þenne}} \qquad [2065]$$

It is expressed once in intermediate position by the colloquial word *hors*:

$$\overset{C\qquad\ C\quad\ \ C}{\text{A grene }\textit{hors}\text{ gret & þikke}} \qquad [175]$$

The interpretation of these examples depends on the recognition of certain characteristics of English verse, not only in the wheels of *Gawain*, but also in Chaucer and the classical tradition as exemplified by Elizabethan and later poets. The structure of the line involves the signalizing of chief syllables by metrical emphasis. Intermediate syllables receive in general less emphasis than chief syllables, and even the most important intermediate syllables (those causing what are described as spondees in iambic or trochaic meter) are in general less emphatic than the adjacent chief syllables with which they are linked in phrase groups. The degree of emphasis which may be given words in intermediate position is thus limited or controlled by the meter; it is in this sense that such words may be called "subordinate." For example, in *Gawain* 58 "Hit were now gret nye to neuen" and in the first line of *The Book of the Duchess* "I have gret wonder, be this lyght" the intermediate syllable *gret* receives slightly less emphasis than the chief syllable it precedes, although it might receive equal emphasis if the lines were read as prose. *Most* is similarly treated as an important intermediate syllable both in *Gawain* 638 "As tulk of tale most trwe" and the line "For such a gest most mete" from Thomas Vaux' "The Aged Louer Renounceth Loue." [38]

But in the wheels of *Gawain* as well as in Chaucerian verse the majority of the intermediate syllables are actually such as to demand little emphasis in a natural prose reading; that is, they consist of conjunctions or prepositions, or the unaccented syllables of polysyllabic nouns. In the first of the wheels in *Gawain*, for example,

    C   C   C
  Where werre & wrake & wonder
  C   C C
  Bi syþeʒ hatʒ wont þer-inne,
   C   C   C
  & oft boþe blysse & blunder
  C   C   C
  Ful skete hatʒ skyfted synne   [16–19]

only three intermediate syllables—*where*, *boþe*, and *ful*—receive a degree of emphasis comparable to that of the chief syllables.[39] The normal pattern of the line—weak intermediate syllables falling between strong chief syllables—is thus varied by the occasional use of heavier intermediate syllables which prevent the verse from falling into a monotonous "dog-trot" rhythm, and may also, in the hands of the skilled poet, enhance the effectiveness of particular passages through an appropriate relationship between emphasis and meaning.

 If, then, we do not find words of elevated quality in intermediate position, but do find synonymous words of colloquial quality in that position, the reason would seem to be that colloquial words can more readily undergo the limitation of stress which is imposed on important intermediate syllables. The elevated word is by definition the emphatic word, one used in place of the everyday word for the sake of a heightened effect. One would not expect to find it, therefore, in a metrically subordinate position.

 The issue is clouded slightly by the fact that phonetic constitution, as well as stylistic value, may play a part in determining whether or not a word will be used in intermediate position. A word such as *kniʒt*, in which nonhomorganic consonant combinations precede and follow the vowel, becomes conspicuous in intermediate position by virtue of its sheer phonetic weight; "Bi þat þe bolde mon boun" is metrically smoother than "Bi þat þe bolde kniȝt boun." Unless something were to be gained by a marked departure from the normal accentual pattern or by emphasizing the noun in relation to the adjectives *bolde* and *boun*, one would expect *mon* rather than *kniȝt* to be the poet's choice. But certain of the elevated synonyms for "man, warrior," although phonetically suitable for intermediate position, are avoided by the poet in favor of *mon*. When the poet writes "Bi þat þe bolde mon boun" rather than "Bi þat þe bolde wyȝe boun," it seems reasonable to conclude that *wyȝe* would be disproportionately emphatic for stylistic reasons. *Mon*, in contrast to *wyȝe*, is the colorless word, the expected word for the meaning which can easily be slurred over; in context "þe bolde mon" is almost equivalent to "the bold one." It was in fact as a result of just such de-emphasized use that its unaccented doublet, the pronoun *mon* "one," must originally have developed.[40] Where the meaning to be expressed was "warhorse," the poet could as well have written "A grene fole gret & þikke" as "A grene hors gret & þikke," so far as the phonetic structure of *fole* and *hors* are concerned. Here again, however, emphasis falls on the adjectives imputing qualities—on *grene*, *gret*, and *þikke*—and the everyday word *hors* is metrically subordinated.

As with the use of the synonyms for "man, warrior" in the long lines, there is in the wheels one exception to the rule, and here again, curiously enough, the word exceptionally used is *freke*. In lines 1315–16 the poet writes "W[atȝ] neuer freke fayrer fonge / Bitwene two so dyngne dame." The reference, of course, is to Gawain as guest of the lord of the castle. In the first of these lines rhetorical emphasis seems to demand that *neuer* be read as a chief syllable. In that case *freke* must be an intermediate syllable. In the passage of the narrative in which the line occurs (as with "Þer-fore to answare watȝ arȝe mony aþel freke") there is a striking disparity between the attributes traditionally associated with the word *freke* and the circumstances in which the man to whom it refers actually finds himself. He is "captured" not on the field of battle but in the hall, by ladies toward whom his conduct must perforce be affable and courteous rather than belligerent or bold. The extraordinary conspicuousness of *freke* as a heavy intermediate syllable is appropriate both to the ironic implications of the word itself and to the highly emphatic cast of the statement in which it appears.

Before summarizing the remaining discussions of groups of synonymous nouns, and assessing the value of the principles developed by Brink for the historical study of style, we must consider one additional problem. In the use of the nouns designating place and time, Brink (pp. 18–24) found patterns inconsistent with those presented by the "man, warrior" group. Among those included under the heading "earth, world, field," the poetic and archaic word *erde* (OE *eard* "[native] land") [41] occurred, as expected, exclusively in alliterating position. The expected contrast in use was shown by the colloquial word *erþe* (modern English *earth*), which occurred exclusively in final position in *Gawain* (0a:13na) and preponderantly in final position in *Morte Arthure* (6a:18na). The expected pattern of exclusively alliterating use was found also in two other poetic words in the group, *folde* and *molde*. (The latter is poetic in the meaning "the world on which we dwell; the earth," for which see *OED* s.v. *mould* sb.¹ sense 6; it survives in modern dialect use in the meaning "loose, broken, or friable earth," for which see *OED* s.v. sense 1, *EDD* s.v. *mould* sb.¹ sense 2.) But *world*, certainly not a distinctively poetic or elevated word, proved to have the same high alliterative rank as *erde*, *folde*, and *molde* (*Gawain* 14a:0na; *Morte Arthure* 13a:0na). We should note that the "earth, world, field" group resembles the "man, warrior" group in that the words it contains differ somewhat in meaning. *Erde* is more narrow than *erþe*, *folde*, and *molde*, which refer to the whole terrestrial globe *on* which we live, and these in turn differ from *world*, originally a composite of *wer* "man" plus *ald* "time, life" (see Holthausen s.v. *weorold*, and *OED*), which refers to the conditions of existence, the realm *in* which we live.

In attempting to explain why *world* behaved like an elevated word in the long line, Brink noted that it was often used in pleonastic phrases, resembling in this respect the elevated words *erde*, *folde* and *molde*. It could thus be looked upon as a poetic word in *Gawain* (pp. 19–20). Brink was, I feel, essentially right, although *world* cannot be called a poetic word in the sense in which "poetic" has been used in this study. An important distinction is involved: that between the intrinsic quality of a word (in a certain meaning) and the quality taken on by the word as a result of the relationship of its meaning to the statement in which it is used (see above, pp. 22–23). A true pleonastic phrase—one that is genuinely superfluous in a statement—is elevated by virtue of being pleonastic, whether or not it is elevated as diction. In *Gawain* 196–98,

> Such a fole vpon folde, ne freke þat hym rydes,
> Watȝ neuer sene in þat sale wyth syȝt er þat tyme,
>   with yȝe,

the phrases *wyth syȝt* and *with yȝe* are pleonastic. *Vpon folde* is also pleonastic if, as seems proper, it is read as an adjectival phrase dependent on *fole* rather than an adverbial phrase dependent on *watȝ . . . sene:* the location it imputes is of no importance for the content of the statement as a whole. But *in þat sale* is not pleonastic; the limitation it imposes on the verb is relevant. Such a sight had never been seen *in that hall*. I should like to digress momentarily to point out that the three pleonastic phrases function effectively as a device of style in this passage and cannot with justice be condemned as "meaningless tags," although such phrases are ineptly used by certain of the alliterative poets. The retardation of narrative pace produced by *vpon folde*, *wyth syȝt*, and *wyth yȝe*, together with the emphasis upon "seeing," enhance the description of the suspended activity, the virtual stupefaction, produced by the spectacle of the Green Knight on his green horse.

The pleonasm as a legitimate device of elevated style produces effects of emphasis and retardation of pace because of its tautological character. A given phrase may or may not be pleonastic, depending on its relation to the content of the statement in which it is used. The device cannot, therefore, be as easily identified as a simile or apostrophe, and the status of a phrase in a particular line may be subject to dispute. Pleonasms become flaws of style or "meaningless tags" only when the effects they produce are inappropriate. Wholesale condemnation of "tags," however, usually rests on the assumption that every detail in a narrative statement must add information or qualify meaning in order to be effective, and the history of style does not bear out this assumption. Such condemnation is akin to the "common sense" condemnation of the elevated periphrasis. "This is as muche to seye as—it was nyght!" says Chaucer as narrator of *The Franklin's Tale*, after an expanded statement in the tradition of classical rhetoric. Certain of the pleonastic phrases in *Gawain* seem neither particularly effective nor particularly ineffective, but neutral. *With syȝt* in 1705 "& quen þay seghe hym with syȝt, þay sued hym fast" (referring to the hounds following the fox) cannot be defended on the same grounds as *wyth syȝt* and *with yȝe* in the passage discussed above, but neither is its expletive quality obtrusive.

The expansion of statement in formal discourse to include repetitive or redundant material must be distinguished from the colloquial use of idioms in which the primary or literal meaning of a particular word is lost. Consider the difference between such a statement as "In those days our Lord walked on earth among men" and "What on earth d'you mean?" or "I don't know what on earth I'm going to do about it." "In þis worlde" in *Gawain* 2321 "Watȝ he neuer in þis worlde wyȝe half so blyþe" cannot but remind us of such modern colloquial constructions as "I never in this world thought she would do it." Where such phrases are combined with pronouns like *alle* or *no* (as in *Gawain* 238 "al þe wonder of þe worlde" and 1275 "no freke vpon folde") or with an adjective in the superlative degree (938 "þe welcomest wyȝe of þe worlde," 2098 "þe worst vpon erþe"), it seems reasonable to assume that they are less elevated in quality than when they are used absolutely.

The words designating time and place, as the above examples indicate, occur chiefly in phrases as the objects of prepositions, and rarely as the subjects or direct objects of verbs. In contrast, the nouns meaning "man, warrior" are often the subjects of verbs, this grammatical role being the obvious corollary of their role as performers of the actions described in the narrative. In studying the use in the long line of such words as *erde, erþe, world,* it is necessary, therefore, to study the phrases in which they occur. If we compare the phrases used in final position in *Gawain* with those used in alliterating positions, a general pattern of difference emerges. The phrases occur in all positions, but they are more often pleonastic in alliterating position than at the end of the line. This difference is reminiscent of the treatment of the elevated and colloquial synonyms for "man, warrior," where again the more elevated element is favored in alliterating position. The two words of this sort most often used at the end of the line are *erþe* and *grounde,* the latter of which is not discussed by Brink. Both words are used by the alliterative poets generally in traditional end-of-line patterns, often referring to the surface of the earth or ground as a place to which something extends or falls (e.g. the body of the warrior in battle scenes), rather than as a location. Thus *erþe* and *grounde* are final in *Gawain* in such lines as 427 "Þe fayre hede fro þe halce hit to þe erþe," 1928 "He were a bleaunt of blwe þat bradde to þe erþe," and 526 "Þe leueʒ laucen fro þe lynde & lyʒten on þe grounde"; cf. also, in *Morte Arthure*, 2079 "The stede and the steryn mane ["man"] strykes to þe grownde" and 2794 "The renke relys abowte and rusches to þe erthe"; in *Siege of Jerusalem* 117 "Þe secunde persone, þe sone, sent was to erþe" and 1073 "Fellen doun for defaute [f]latte to þe grounde."[42] *Grounde* is also used pleonastically in *Gawain*, but only in alliterating position, as in 1070 "Þe grene chapayle vpon grounde greue yow no more."

The *Gawain*-poet's use of *erþe* and *erde* shows that the two words differed for him both in meaning and in stylistic quality, although in *Wars of Alexander* and other poems of more Northern provenience than *Gawain*, they had become confused. The *Gawain*-poet uses them in the phrases *(up)on erþe* and *in erde*; both phrases may be pleonastic, and in such use are virtually synonymous. The use of *in* shows that *erde* is thought of as meaning "(geographically bounded) region," rather than "the globe *on* which men live."[43] *(Up)on erþe* is, as Oakden points out, used at the end of the line in *Morte Arthure* and other poems. In most of the examples he cites, the phrase is combined idiomatically with superlatives, or with *alle* or *no;* thus "þe doughtyeste þat duellyde in erthe" (219, 3321). In this example it is the verb "þat duellyde" rather than *in erthe* which is the redundant element, since "þe doughtyeste on erthe" would express the meaning fully. In *Gawain*, *upon erþe* in final position has almost the effect of a pleonasm in certain lines, e.g. 1137 "By þat any day-lyʒt lemed vpon erþe" and 1854 "For he myʒt not be slayn for slyʒt vpon erþe." But in the latter example one could substitute "no slyʒt upon erþe," and in the former the narrator seems to be describing the striking of the earth by the sun's rays at dawn (cf. 1180 "Lurkkeʒ quyl þe day-lyʒt lemed on þe wowes"). Where a true pleonastic phrase is used, and the line alliterates on vowel or *h*, the poet prefers *in erde*: 27 "For-þi an aunter in erde I attle to schawe," 140 "Half etayn in erde I hope þat he were," and 881 "Alle of ermyn in erde, his hode of þe same." Except for the fact that *erþe* never occurs within the line, the discrimination between *erde* and *erþe* thus resembles that between *lede* and *lorde*.

The more closely we examine the words meaning "earth, world, field" as they are used in *Gawain*, the more apparent it becomes that this group differs essentially from the "man, warrior" group. When the poet uses *kniʒt* at the end of the line and either *kniʒt* or *burne* within the line, a pattern of discrimination among synonyms of different stylistic quality can be distinguished. But the phrases in which such words as *erþe* and *grounde* occur may have different meanings in different positions, and their stylistic quality is not constant even in a single meaning, but depends on the relationship of the meaning to context.

The use of *erþe* and *grounde* in final position, therefore, need not represent a choice of either of these words in preference to *world*, since the meaning to be expressed may be "the surface of the earth" rather than "the realm of human existence." The use of *world* exclusively in alliterating position does not indicate that it is a poetic or elevated word; its quality will depend on the use made of its meaning in the passage. *Grounde*, used in a pleonastic phrase, will be as elevated as *world* in the same use. Where *(up)on erþe* is equivalent in meaning to *in þe world* and is preferred at the end of the line, the difference in usage would seem to be based on something other than level of style. It may be that metrical considerations were originally involved—a sounded final *-e* in *erþë* (OE *eorðe*, inflected *eorðan*) perhaps provided a desired feminine ending at a time when the old inflectional *-e* of *worlde* (OE *w[e]orold*) as the object of a preposition had become silent (see below, Part II, pp. 140–41). In the absence of a full understanding of the metrical structure of Middle English alliterative verse, however, we cannot attempt to explain why the tradition took shape as it did, but can only say that *(up)on erþe* is traditional at the end of the line, whereas *in þe worlde* is not.

To *world* we may add *court* (Brink, p. 20) and *sesoun* (p. 23) as words of colloquial quality which traditionally occur only in alliterating position. According to Brink's figures, *court* occurs in *Gawain* 17a:0na, in *Morte Arthure* 6a:0na; *sesoun* occurs in *Gawain* 5a:0na. The words equivalent to *court* in final position are most commonly *place* and *halle*, as in 252 "& sayde, 'wyʒe, welcum iwys to þis place,'" 495 "Gawan watz glad to be-gynne þose gomnez in halle," and occasionally *sale*, as in 349 "þer such an askyng is heuened so hyʒe in your sale." Since two of these are of

OF derivation, the high alliterative rank of *court* cannot be explained by the fact that it is a Romance word. Brink points out (p. 20) that *heuen* invariably alliterates in *Gawain*, occurring 7a:0na, but that it has low alliterative rank in *Morte Arthure*, occurring 1a:7na. The meaning "sky, heaven" is expressed in final position by *welkyn* in *Gawain* 1696 "& ful clere c[a]steȝ þe clowdes of þe welkyn."

The apparent inconsistency shown by *frythe* "wood," which occurs in *Gawain* 4a:0na, and which, according to Brink's findings, always alliterates in other poems as well, seems to be based on a confusion between two meanings of different stylistic value. The *EDD*, which Brink consulted for information on dialect descent, gives "wood" as a modern meaning (s.v. *frith* sense 1), the complete definition being "a wood, plantation, coppice; a clearing in a forest or wood"; sense 2 is "unused pasture-land." Both are cited from Northern dialects. It would seem logical on the face of it that the latter part of the definition given for sense 1 should actually belong to sense 2. The *OED* (s.v. *frith* sb.²) distinguishes the meaning "a wood of some kind . . . esp. in poet. phrases associated with fell, field" (sense 1) and "a piece of land grown sparsely with trees or with underwood only. Also, a space between woods; unused pasture land . . . Now only dial." (sense 2). When one notes further that in the *EDD* the only uses clearly illustrating the sense "wood" are from poetry (e.g. "the shady frith"), it seems clear that *frith* was poetic in Middle English when it meant "forest" without suggestion of openness or sparse growth. The citations in the *OED* for sense 1 are all from poetry after the twelfth century, and the *MED* cites only poetry in senses 2a "a park, a woodland meadow" and 2b "any wooded area, woodland."[44] In *Gawain* the meaning is clearly "forest" in all instances: for example, when the attendant who is to show Gawain the way to the Green Chapel leaves him to continue his way alone, he says he will not accompany him "þurȝ þis fryth" any further (2151); the next line is "Bi þat þe wyȝe in þe wod wendeȝ his brydel."

The rest of Brink's findings on the nouns bring up no further problems and may be summarized briefly.[45] ("High alliterative rank" means use exclusively in alliterating position in all poems examined by Brink, unless otherwise noted.) In the group "Designations for People (Nation), Army, Retainers" *douth* and *here* have high alliterative rank, as opposed to *meny*, which alliterates weakly (pp. 17–18). *Folk* has high alliterative rank; Brink suggests that it had in Middle English a poetic sense "retainers at a court" as distinguished from "people, persons" and "servants."[46] Brink also includes the archaic and poetic word *þede* under this heading, but *þede* means "country" rather than "people" in its single occurrence in *Gawain* (see *OED* s.v. *thede* senses 1 and 2). Under the heading "Earth, World, Field," in addition to *erde, folde, molde, world, heuen,* and *frythe,* Brink classes *bent* "battlefield," *berȝ, burȝ,* and *teld* as words of high alliterative rank (pp. 18–21). Of low rank in this group, in addition to *erþe* and *place,* are *gate, hill, home, londe, syde, toun, way, wod,* and *won* (pp. 21–22). Under "Designations of Time," *sesoun* has high alliterative rank, as opposed to *day, ȝer, morn(yng), niȝt, siþes, tyme, tyde, þrow, whyle, winter,* and *stounde* (pp. 23–24). Under "Designations for Weapons, Armor and Clothing," words having high rank are *bront, bronde,*[47] *schafte* "spear,"[48] and *scharp* "sword," the latter apparently unique in *Gawain* (pp. 24–25); words of low rank are *armes, arwes, cloþes, cote, gere, harnays, helme, lance, scheld, sword,*[49] *tole, wede, weppen,* and *yrnes.* Under "Designations for Warhorse," words of high rank are *blonk* and *fole* of which the latter has descended in a nonpoetic meaning "offspring of a horse";[50] words of low rank are *hors* and *stede.* A survey of the list makes it clear that the colloquial synonyms in general outnumber the elevated synonyms in a given group, even though this is not true of the words meaning "man, warrior."

Before turning to the adjectives, we may assess the value, for the historical study of style, of the principles developed by Brink from the nouns. The concept of alliterative rank unquestionably furnishes the investigator with a valuable tool to use in conjunction with other methods and data. Certain of its limitations, however, must be borne in mind: (a) The determination of high alliterative rank should be tentative if a word occurs only two or three times in the poem; a single alliterating occurrence is of little significance. (b) High alliterative rank, even when determined with certainty for a word of frequent occurrence, does not necessarily mean elevated stylistic value (cf. *world*), although words of elevated value generally have high alliterative rank. However, low alliterative rank would seem to be a clear sign of colloquial value, provided that

STYLE AND ALLITERATIVE TRADITION 77

other evidence does not conflict. (c) Poets vary in the rank they accord certain words, so that a survey of use in several poems is always advisable. The *Morte Arthure* poet, for example, as noted by Brink, p. 13, treats *beryn* (*burne*) as a word of low rank, perhaps owing to confusion with *baron* (see p. 231, note 6).

Brink's study of the adjectives (including cognate adverbs), the other major part of *Stab und Wort im Gawain*, differed from his study of the nouns in its organization.[51] Instead of dividing the adjectives according to meaning, he divided those having high alliterative rank into three groups (pp. 30-49), putting into a fourth group all those of low rank (pp. 49-53). The first three groups consisted of (I) those which did not survive the Middle English period, (II) those which descended into modern standard English, and (III) those which descended into modern dialects. The adjectives of the first three groups were, Brink maintained, elevated and poetic in stylistic value, while those of the fourth were of colloquial value.[52] As with the nouns, certain adjectives were found to vary in rank from poem to poem and were classed separately (p. 49). For many of the words Brink added data on use in Old English poetry, in the OS *Heliand*, and in Middle English poetry other than the alliterative school.

The adjectives in the four groups are listed below with indications of the number of occurrences of each in *Gawain*. I have altered the classification of a few words, as noted, and have omitted variant spellings. For *wlonk* (I), *bare, clere, gentyle, grymme* (II) and *bayn* (III), I have disregarded single occurrences in the wheels listed by Brink as na or "questionable."

GROUP I.[53] *aþel* (6a), *brayn(wod)* (3a), *broþe(ly)* (2a), *cofly* (1a), *ʒederly* (4a), *haʒer* (2a), *methles* (1a), *rapely* (1a), *runisch(ly)* (3a), *selly* (*sellokest, sellyly*) (5a:1na),[54] *skete* (1a), [w]*eterly* (1a),[55] *wlonk* (6a), *wynne(lich)* (4a).

GROUP II.[56] *bare* (11a), *big(ly)* (5a), *bold(ly)* (14a), *bryʒt* (27a:3na), *kene(ly)* (5a), *chef(ly)* (8a), *clere* (13a), *coynt(ly)* (5a), *comly(-lych,-lokest,-lyly)* (24a), *cortays(ly)* (9a), *dere(ly)* (25a:1na [57]), *duʒty* (3a), *fayn* (4a), *felle (felly)* (5a), *fersly* (3a), *fre(ly)* (10a:1na [58]), *gay(ly)* (18a), *gentyle* (5a), *glad(ly, -loker)* (9a), *grymme* (1a), *hardy(ly)* (4a), *liʒt* "bright" (cf. *lyʒt* adj.[1] in TG glossary) (4a), *lyʒtly* "quickly" (7a), *lufly(ly)* (18a), *mery*(*ly*) (23a:2na⁵⁹), *pertly* (*apert*) (4a), *prestly* (2a), *proud* (7a), *pure*(*ly*) (9a), *redly* (5a), *rogh* (8a:1na⁶⁰), *sadly* (4a).

GROUP III. *bayn* (1a), *borelych* (3a), *boun* (5a), *breme*(*ly*) (12a), *brent* (1a), *derf*(*ly*) (6a), *derne*(*ly*) (3a), *dryʒe*(*ly*) (6a), *farand* (1a), *ferly*(*ly*) (5a), *feye* (1a), *grayþe*(*ly*) (9a), *ʒep*(*ly*) (7a), *heterly* (7a), *lel*(*ly*) (7a), *lodly* (1a), *mayn* (4a), *mensk*(*ful, -ly*) (6a), *queme* (2a), *rad*(*ly*) "quick(ly)" (8a), *rad* "cowardly" (1a), *ronk* (1a), *seme*(*ly, -lyly*) (13a), *sere* (*serlepes*) (8a:1na⁶¹) *schene* (3a), *schyr*(*ly*) (14a), *styf*(*ly*) (23a), *stor* (2a), *styply* (1a), *tene* (3a), *tor* (2a), *þro* (8a⁶²), *wale* (4a), *war*(*ly*) (7a), *wene* (1a), *wrast* (1a), *wyʒt*(*ly*) (5a).

ADJECTIVES OF LOW RANK.⁶³ *best* (14a:8na), *better* (2a:1na), *biliue* (7a:2na), *bliþe*(*ly*) (10a:3na), *bothe* (17a:13na), *clene*(*ly*) (6a:10na), *erly* (2a:3na), *fayr* (25a:7na), *first* (9a:17na), *god*(*ly*) (51a:15na), *gret* (10a:12na), *ʒern* (3a:ona in *Gawain*, but 2a:6na in Langland, etc.), *ʒong* (4a:2na), *hard* (5a:2na), *heʒ*(*ly*) (46a:9na), *huge* (6a:4na), *long* (10a:4na), *lyttel* (4a:ona, but 18na in *Morte Arthure*, etc.), *loude* (3a:3na), *loʒe*(*ly*) (5a:3na), *mony* (6a:45na), *noble* (2a:11na), *neʒ* (3a:2na), *quik*(*ly*) (3a:2na), *riche*(*ly*) (22a:14na), *ryʒt* (8a:7na), *same*(*n*) (2a:3na), *smal* (1a:2na), *soft*(*ly*) (5a:2na), *sore* (3a:ona, but 10a:4na in Langland, etc.), *swete*(*ly*) (4a:3na), *þik* (2a:10na), *wel* (21a:17na), *wylde* (6a:3na).

Brink also lists a number of adjectives of indeterminate status which are differently used by different poets (p. 49). These are: *fele, holde, hende, lef, siker, trwe, worþ, gayn, brode, deþ,* and *soþ*.

The above groups do not by any means exhaust the adjectival vocabulary of the poem, nor did Brink intend them as exhaustive. But the stylistic principles governing the poet's use of adjectives can be amply demonstrated from them.

It will be observed that among the adjectives of high alliterative rank, there are certain inconsistencies in the form of occurrences in nonalliterating position in the long lines, "high alliterative rank" having so far been taken to mean use in alliterating position only. Such inconsistencies are limited to groups II and III—i.e. to the adjectives which have descended into modern standard or dialect English. Similar inconsistencies are found in *Wars of Alexander* and other poems; see, e.g., *bold*(*ly*) in group II and *breme* in group

III, Brink, pp. 35, 43. In attempting to explain these inconsistencies, I shall examine the principles underlying Brink's classification in terms of a somewhat more flexible concept of stylistic value.

In studying those adjectives of high alliterative rank which have descended into modern English, Brink found it necessary to explain the fact that many of them occurred in Chaucer. This was a genuine difficulty. Brink had previously accounted for the use of archaic and poetic words by the alliterative poets in terms of their "idealizing and typifying" treatment of narrative material. Such words were avoided by Chaucer, who used a more colloquial diction suitable to his more realistic narrative art. Since the adjectives of groups II and III were assumed to be elevated and poetic, their presence in Chaucerian verse was unexpected. Brink solved the problem to his own satisfaction by showing that a given adjective occurring both in alliterative verse and in Chaucer tended to have more realistic and colloquial meanings as used by the latter poet, or in certain cases was used by him only as a rhyme word or in alliterative combinations of a traditional character.[64]

As an example, let us take *stiff* (group III), which, according to Brink's figures (pp. 47–48), occurs 23a:ona in *Gawain*, 1a:ona in *Morte Arthure*, 7a:ona in Langland, 16a:ona in *Wars of Alexander*, etc. The adjective also occurs in Chaucer, the *Concordance* giving four citations including two from the *Romaunt of the Rose* Fragment A. OE *stīf*, from which *stiff* is derived, is exemplified only once, in a gloss where *stifne* corresponds to L *rigentem* (see BT; cf. *OED* s.v. *stiff* a.). Old English has the related verbs *stīfian*, *ā-stīfian* "to stiffen," and the adjective has a number of cognates in the Germanic languages (see Holthausen). These, together with such non-Germanic cognates as L *stipes* "post, treetrunk," indicate that the original meaning was "hard, solid, rigid (like wood)." The "idealizing and typifying" meanings of *stiff* in Middle English alliterative poetry have to do with human attributes of strength (see *OED* s.v. sense 12) and resolution (sense 8). When the Green Knight, speaking to Arthur of the fame of his court, says that

> þy burȝ & þy burnes best ar holden,
> Stifest vnder stel-gere on stedes to ryde, [259–60]

stifest means both "strongest" and "most resolute," these attributes being equally relevant to the circumstances expressed by the phrases "vnder stel-gere" and "on stedes to ryde." Taken together, these phrases mean something like "in knightly array, on knightly enterprises," and *stifest* is thus virtually equivalent to *best* in the preceding line—i.e. best in knightly virtues. The reputation which the Green Knight has come to test is a matter of tradition, and it is appropriate that the line in which he refers to it should be highly traditional in phraseology. "Stiff on steed" is one of the most common of the alliterating phrases in which *stiff* appears,[65] and "stif(est) vnder stel-gere," though apparently original with the *Gawain*-poet, is modeled on such stock combinations as OE "heard under helme" and ME "worthy under weed."[66] *Ride* is a verb frequently used in final position in Middle English alliterative poetry; cf. lines 142, 160, 196, etc., in *Gawain* and citations from other poems below, p. 249, n. 35 (s.v. 142).

Stiff has this same idealizing and typifying meaning in the *Romaunt of the Rose* Fragment A 1270 "The knyght was fair and styf in stour," the linking with *stour* being again formulaic.[67] (Its other occurrence in this poem, where it describes the current of a stream, need not concern us here.) But in *The Canterbury Tales*, it is used quite differently. It has its OE meaning "rigid" in *The Summoner's Tale* D 2267-68 "Thanne shal this cherl, with bely stif and toght / As any tabour, hyder been ybroght." In *The General Prologue* A 673 "This Somonour bar to hym a stif burdoun," it has the obsolete meaning "of voice, sound: powerful, loud" (*OED* s.v. sense 15).[68] In *The Wife of Bath's Prologue* D 380 "Baar I stifly myne olde housbondes on honde," it expresses strength and resolution, to be sure, but not on the high plane of the alliterative romances. Here we are reminded of such modern colloquial uses of the adjective as "What he needs is a good stiff talking-to." We may note, further, that among the Northern dialect meanings listed by *EDD* are "sturdy, strong" (sense 4) and "firm, resolute, unyielding" (sense 5), both illustrated from Yorkshire.

The history of *stiff* thus shows it developing new meanings from Old English times on, in application—originally figurative—to new subjects of reference. It comes to signify attributes not only of inanimate substances but of motion and sound, the human body, actions, and moral character. These developments take place at all stylistic levels, the resultant meanings ranging from the distinctively elevated and poetic to the distinctively colloquial. The fact that in "Baar I stifly myne olde housbondes on honde" *stifly* may be translated "stoutly, resolutely" should not be allowed to obscure the essential difference between its meaning in this use and its traditional idealizing meaning in alliterative poetry. The latter would be more accurately paraphrased as "strong, resolute (in heroic actions or circumstances)." We may compare the contrasting meanings and stylistic values of *great* in modern English in the expressions "a great guy (or fellow)" and "a great man." In both these uses, *great* might be defined as "excellent, commanding esteem," but the "excellences" referred to are of different sorts and are manifested on different planes, while the implied "esteem" is familiar and affectionate in the former, solemn and reverent in the latter.

Examining now the *Gawain*-poet's use of *stiff*, we find that the adjective has not only its idealizing and typifying poetic meaning but the literal meaning found in Chaucer and in present-day speech. It is used with reference to Gawain's helmet in 606 "Þat watȝ stapled stifly, & stoffed wythinne." It is used with reference to the beheaded Green Knight, who "styþly . . . start forth vpon styf schonkes" (431)—i.e. his legs did not buckle (cf. 846 "Sturne, stif on þe stryþþe on stal-worth schonkeȝ," where the reference is to the lord of the castle). It has its figurative meaning "powerful" with reference to sound in 1364, where the hunters are said to start homeward "strakande ful stoutly mony stif moteȝ."

Brink made an important distinction between the use of adjectives in alliterative poetry and their use in Chaucer, but he did not fully realize the implications involved. If *stiff* as used by Chaucer is a less elevated word than *stiff* "(heroically) resolute," then it is less elevated in *Gawain* also in the meanings "rigid" and "loud (of sound)." As used by the *Gawain*-poet, it has not one value but a range of values depending on its meaning and reference in a given context. In all meanings and stylistic values, however, its alliterative rank remains high.

As with the group of elevated synonyms for "man, warrior," the use of strongly alliterative adjectives in *Gawain* can be explained technically without appealing to conscious idealizing aims on the part of the poet. Within Brink's classes I, II, and III, groups of adjectives can easily be identified which express synonymous or allied meanings of a qualitative nature.⁶⁹ In general these adjectives serve to intensify; referring to the persons and scenes viewed sympathetically by the narrator, they impute qualities of moral excellence and material splendor; referring to hardships or dangers with which the heroes are confronted, they impute qualities of dreadfulness, fierceness, and strangeness.⁷⁰ Thus beauty and splendor are imputed to persons or things by *apel, mere, wynne,* and *wlonk* (group I), *bryȝt, clere, comly, dere, gay, lufly,* and *mery* (group II), and *queme, semly, schene, schyr, wale* and *wene* (group III). Courage and prowess are imputed by *big, bolde, kene,* and *hardy* (group II) and *derf, dryȝe, stiff, þro,* and *wyȝt* (group III). Qualities of quickness and promptness, often implying courtesy or readiness to serve on the part of an attendant, are imputed by *cofly* and *ȝederly* (group I); *chef(ly), prestly,* and *redly* (group II); and *boun, ȝep(ly),* and *rad(ly)* "quickly" (group III). Other examples could be added. The frequent use of adjectives such as these is, like the variation in mode of reference to persons, a traditional feature of the alliterative style. Since the relevant qualities belong, as it were, by definition to the persons and scenes of the narrative, the use of a given adjective need not be restricted to occasions on which the trait it expresses is actually being demonstrated. It may be so used, of course, as in *Gawain* 1633 "Þenne hondeled þay þe hoge hed, þe hende mon hit praysed," where Gawain—referred to as "þe hende mon"—is actually showing his courtesy at the moment. But since the quality of courtesy is traditionally his, the adjective can always be applied to him. It follows, therefore, that the qualitative adjective in the alliterative style tends to appear as an epithet. Since the epithet, like the pleonasm, is a device of elevated style, the effect of an adjective so used will be independent of its status as diction. *White* is not an elevated word, but may produce an effect of elevation, as in the phrase "white snow" (cf. *Gawain* 2088 "Þe quyte snaw lay bisyde"). The effect of the epithet may in turn be ironic if the quality imputed is actually contradicted in the behavior or situation of the person described. Gawain is certainly not "Gawayn þe blyþe" in 1213, where he is maneuvering as best he can within the difficult and confining circumstances imposed on him by the lady of the castle.⁷¹

Because of their large number, their groups of near-synonymous meanings, and the freedom with which they can be used, the qualitative adjectives furnish the poet with an important technical resource in the composition of the alliterative line. To this the adjectives of low rank, as well as those of the first three groups, make their contribution. A number of these express the same qualitative meanings as were exemplified above; thus beauty and splendor are imputed by *best, clene, fayr, god, godly, gret, noble, rych,* and *swete;* promptness and readiness by *biliue, ȝern,* and *quyk,* all of which belong to Brink's fourth group.

All these adjectives, in their qualitative meanings, have an idealizing and typifying function in the traditional style of alliterative poetry. Many of them have a history similar to that of *stiff,* in that an elevated qualitative meaning, originally figurative, exists side by side with an objective meaning expressing physically measurable properties such as size or hardness. The objective meaning as a rule is found in the present-day spoken language and must have been colloquial in Middle English also; the elevated qualitative meaning, in certain cases, dies out with the alliterative tradition itself. A number of these adjectives doubtless had distinctively colloquial—perhaps unrecorded—meanings in Middle English, but such meanings will be disregarded in the present discussion, since they are not part of the traditional alliterative style.

As examples we may take *gret* and *hyȝe,* two adjectives of low alliterative rank which are similarly used by the *Gawain*-poet, though differing in their histories prior to the Middle English period. OE *grēat* had the objective meanings "coarse (of particles or texture)" (cf. the cognates *groats* and *grit*) and "big, bulky (of persons and things)." (See BT and Supplement.) It was also used with reference to abstract concepts; cf. "greate heahnisse" (BT) and "great yfel" (Supplement). Grein cites only one occurrence in poetry; here the adjective has the meaning "massive" and modifies *grindlas* "bolts, bars." [72] Old English *hēah* had the objective meanings "tall (of persons)" and "lofty (of things)"; its Germanic and non-Germanic cognates have such meanings as "hill," "tumor," and "protuberance" (Holthausen). It also had the originally figurative qualitative meanings "noble," "exalted," "of superior kind." (See BT, Supplement, and Grein.) It is of frequent occurrence in its objective and qualitative meanings in both prose and poetry. We find it, for example, in *Beowulf* in such alliterating combinations as "heah Healfdene" (57a) and "heah hlifian (with reference to the barrow)," and in such compounds as *heah-cyning, heah-gesceap*, and *heah-setl* (see Klaeber's glossary).

As used by the *Gawain*-poet, *gret* and *hyȝe* have a variety of meanings, both factual and qualitative, the latter idealizing in function and elevated in stylistic value. What is of greater importance, these adjectives have only their objective meanings when used in final position; in contrast, their qualitative meanings are restricted to use in alliterating position. The objective meanings, however, are not restricted in use to final position; they alliterate as well. Thus *gret* occurs in final position in 139 "& his lyndes & his lymes so longe & so grete," 1441 "For he watȝ b[ronde] bor alþer-grattest," and 2005 "& drof vche dale ful of dryftes ful grete," in all of which it has the meaning "of large size." We find it occurring in alliterating position in 2014 "& grayþeȝ me sir Gawayn vpon a grett wyse" and 2469–70 "& I wol þe as wel, wyȝe, bi my faythe, / As any gome vnder God, for þy grete trauþe." In the former it may be translated "noble, magnificent"; in the latter it has much the same qualitative meaning as *great* has in modern English in the phrase "a great love." We also find *gret* occurring in alliterating position in the meaning "of large size"—e.g. in 1171 "& þe gre-houndeȝ so grete, þat geten hem bylyue." In the sole exception to the rule, where the qualitative meaning "eminent (of persons)" occurs in final position, *gret* is used not as an adjective but as a noun: "Þer wakned wele in þat wone when wyst þe grete / Þat gode G[awayn] watȝ commen, gayn hit hym þoȝt" (2490–91). It also alliterates by anticipation.

The same patterns appear in the poet's use of *hyȝe*. He writes "On ["One"] þe most on þe molde on mesure hyghe" (137) and "& innermore he be-helde þat halle ful hyȝe" (794), but "Hit watȝ Ennias þe athel & his highe kynde" (5) and " 'Of such a selly soiorne as I haf hade here, / Your honour at þis hyȝe fest, þe hyȝe kyng yow ȝelde!' " (1962–63). *Hyȝe* is used in its factual meaning in alliterating position in, for example, 2199–2200 "Þene herde he of þat hyȝe hil, in a harde roche / . . . a wonder breme noyse."

In all the lines discussed so far, the two adjectives have full emphasis. But they also occur within the line as nonalliterating words. In many cases, such use seems to be attended by reduction of stress. *Gret* in nonalliterating use within the line sometimes merely indicates large amount or high degree with respect to the noun it modifies, the noun receiving the greater emphasis:

> With gret bobbaunce þat burȝe he biges vpon fyrst [9]
> Þe does dryuen with gret dyn to þe depe sladeȝ [1159]
> Þat oþer stif mon in study stod a gret whyle [2369]

Compare, in the wheels, 1149 'Gret rurd in þat forest" and 1259 "Scho made hym so gret chere," where *gret* is an intermediate syllable. *Hyȝe* sometimes occurs in idiomatic combinations such as *hyȝe table*, *hyȝe dece*, with alliteration falling on the noun. Here again emphasis on the noun seems to be indicated. Examples are:

> Talkkande bifore þe hyȝe table of trifles ful hende [108]
> Driuande to þe heȝe dece, dut he no woþe [222]

But compare 250 "Þenn Arþour bifore þe hiȝ dece þat auenture byholdeȝ." An adequate discussion of such lines as these would trespass on the domain of metrical study. Neither the structure of the long line in terms of the number and placement of emphatic syllables nor the relation between formal alliteration and emphasis has yet been discussed, nor is such discussion possible within the scope of the present chapter.[73]

The fact that Brink considers all occurrences of *gret* and *hyȝe* together obscures the actual variation in meaning and stylistic status, and consequently in metrical treatment, revealed by a careful study of their use in *Gawain*. In their qualitative idealizing meanings, these adjectives are elevated words and their alliterative rank is high. But they are not elevated in their objective meanings, and in these meanings their alliterative rank is low.

We return now to the inconsistent occurrences in final position in the long lines of certain of Brink's adjectives of high alliterative rank. As examples for brief discussion we will take *bryȝt* and *mery*, both in Brink's group II, which occur in final position in the long lines of *Gawain* three times and twice, respectively. In addition, Brink cites for *mery* one occurrence in nonalliterating position from *Piers Plowman*. This is doubtless line 10 of the Prologue: "I slombred in a slepyng, it [the *borne*] sweyued so merye" (B-Text);

cf. the now obsolete meaning "of sound or music: pleasant, sweet" cited below.

OE *beorht*, from which ME *bryȝt* is derived, had the objective meanings "luminous, shining, gleaming (by intrinsic or reflected light)." These are found in Old English prose and poetry (see BT and Grein; cf. the non-Germanic cognates meaning "dawn," "white," etc., cited by Holthausen). The objective meanings have of course descended into modern English, where they are used in speech as well as in formal contexts. OE *beorht* also had such qualitative meanings as "fair, lovely," "splendid," and "divine, holy" (BT). It is cited by Grein in the phrases "seo beorhta mægð" and "þæt beorhta bold" s.v. sense 1 "splendidus . . . formosus," and "beorht fæder [i.e. God]" s.v. sense 4 "clarus . . . divus, sanctus"; cf. "beorhtran saule þonne snaw," cited from the *Blickling Homilies* in Supplement. The use of these meanings in poetry and religious prose suggests that they were elevated as compared to the objective meanings; similar qualitative meanings, having elevated stylistic value, are familiar to the modern reader in poetic use (cf. A. E. Housman's simultaneous exploitation of objective and qualitative meanings in "They carry back bright to the coiner the mintage of man, / The lads that will die in their glory and never be old"). In alliterating position in *Gawain*, *bryȝt* is used in both its objective and its qualitative meanings, as in 520 "To bide a blysful blusch of þe bryȝt sunne" and 853 "[They] broȝt hym to a bryȝt boure, þer beddyng watȝ noble," respectively. But in its three occurrences in final position, it has the objective meaning "gleaming, reflecting light"; it is used in each case as an adverb in combination with a verb expressing this meaning:

þen grene aumayl on golde [g]lowande bryȝter [236]
A schelde & a scharp spere, schinande bryȝt [269]
Hit watȝ no lasse, bi þat lace þat lemed ful bryȝt [2226]

Mery had in Old, Middle, and early modern English a number of meanings unfamiliar to the modern reader. The Germanic precursor of OE *myrge*, from which ME *mery* is derived, evidently meant "short" (see the cognates cited by Holthausen s.v. *myrge* and *OED* s.v. *merry* a., and the suggested explanation in the latter of the change in meaning). In Old English there is no trace of the meaning "short"; the definition given in BT (s.v. *mirige* adj.) is "pleasant, delightful, sweet." The adjective is used with reference to natural surroundings (cf. "Him [i.e., to the birds] þa twigu þincaþ swa merge" and "an myrige dun," cited in BT and Supplement respectively) and to music (cf. "myrige leoþ," glossing *dulce carmen;* the citation s.v. *mirige* adv. with reference to singing; and *mirig-ness*, glossing *musica;* all in BT). The general meaning "of things: pleasing, agreeable" (*OED* sense 1) continued to be used in Middle English with a wide range of reference and in a wide range of contexts. Cf. in *OED* senses 1b "of a place or country: pleasant, delightful"; 1c "of sound or music: pleasant, sweet"; and 1f "of herbs, drugs, etc.: pleasant to the taste or smell"; all cited from prose as well as poetry. The meaning "of looks or appearance: pleasant . . . hence, expressive of cheerfulness" (sense 2), first cited from a1225, gradually became obscured in modern English, merging with the current meaning "full of animated enjoyment" (sense 3); this latter is first cited from 1320. A similar development is shown by the adverb *merrily;* cf. the definition in *OED* s.v. sense 1: "in early use: pleasantly . . . cheerfully, happily. In mod. use: with exuberant gaiety . . . mirthfully." The earliest citation for the adverb in this sense is *Gawain* 2295 "Þen muryly efte con he mele, þe mon in þe grene," where the speech that follows is "pleasant" (though mockingly so) rather than "exuberantly gay" or "mirthful."

Because of its meanings, its wide range of reference, and the large number of common words (such as *man, mind,* and *make*) with which it could be linked, *mery* was admirably suited to the purposes of the traditional adjectival apparatus of alliterative poetry. Within the tradition it may be said to have "idealizing" functions in that it frequently imputes praiseworthy qualities, but for the most part, its qualitative meanings are nonelevated, and hence lack the solemnity of tone of *stiff* "heroically resolute" and *hyȝe* "noble." Thus, we find citations from sixteenth-century prose in *OED* for the meaning "of looks or appearance: pleasant, agreeable" (cf. "þe myry mon," *Gawain* 1263) and "of weather: . . . pleasant, fine" (sense 1d; cf. "miry watȝ þe mornyng," *Gawain* 1691). But there are signs of the adjective's having developed at least one poetic meaning in alliterative verse. In *OED*, sense 1e "of dress: handsome" is cited only once, in the phrase "a mery mantill" in

Wars of Alexander. The same phrase occurs in *Gawain* at least once and probably twice (see below, pp. 239–40, n. 53). In *Gawain* 142, the meaning "most handsome" for *myriest*, with reference to the physique of the Green Knight, is clearly indicated by the explanatory lines that follow (see below, the discussion of the passage, p. 114).

The modern meaning "full of animated enjoyment," from which implications of praise are largely or entirely absent, is found in alliterating position in 497 "For þaȝ men ben mery in mynde quen þay han mayn drynk" (cf. 899–900 "Þat mon much merþe con make, / For wyn in his hed þat wende"). It is in this meaning exclusively that *mery* appears at the end of the line in *Gawain*, once as an adjective and once as an adverb:

> Þe lorde let for luf lotez so myry [1086]
>
> Þe lorde ful lowde with lote laȝed myry [1623]

It has this meaning also in its single occurrence in the wheels, where it neither alliterates nor rhymes: "Þus myry he watȝ neuer are" (1891).

The seeming inconsistencies presented by *bryȝt* and *mery* can, then, be clarified to a considerable extent by the analysis of meanings and stylistic values. *Bryȝt*, in its elevated idealizing meanings, resembles *stiff* in that it has high alliterative rank. But unlike *stiff*, it has low rank in its objective meanings. *Mery*, in its qualitative meanings, has high alliterative rank, but it is not an elevated word in most of these meanings. It has low rank in the meaning "mirthful," in which it has descended into the modern language.

The principles accounting for the metrical treatment of adjectives in the alliterative tradition are, in general, clear. Of those adjectives which are frequently used and which have descended into modern English, each may be expected to have a complicated history involving a variety of meanings and stylistic values. In studying the use of such an adjective by the *Gawain*-poet, we must consider the available information on its meanings and their contexts of use prior to, during, and subsequent to the Middle English period. In a given occurrence in *Gawain* we must consider its value in the accentual structure of the line, so far as this can be determined, and the relationship of its meaning to the general content of the statement in which it appears. We must be prepared, too, to find that, as with *freke*, inconsistent use—the breaking of stylistic habit or "rule"—is attended by a heightening of emphasis which is in some way contributive to the passage as a whole. But this is only because in *Gawain* we are dealing with the stylistic artistry of an acknowledged master. Claims for such subtleties in the style of, e.g., *Cheuelere Assigne* would rightly be considered suspect unless the accepted estimate of that poem's artistic value (see Oakden 2, 41) were first revised upward.

Although the qualitative meanings of *gret, hyȝe, bryȝt*, and other similar adjectives are restricted to use in alliterating position, the traditional alliterative style does provide for the expression of qualitative meanings at the end of the line. One of the adjectives most frequently used for this purpose is *noble*, which, in the ten occurrences I have noted in the long lines, alliterates only once (118). In final position immediately following the noun it modifies, it is formulaic:

& quy þe pentangel apendeȝ to þat prynce noble	[623]
Þat þou, leude, schal be lost, þat art of lyf noble	[675]
& þe teccheles termes of talkyng noble	[917]
Rises & riches hym in araye noble	[1873]

With the adjectives as with the nouns, traditional usage cannot always be explained. One cannot say, for example, why *stiff* does not occur at the end of the line in its factual meanings. If it is discriminated against because its use would result in a masculine ending, then why are *gret* (OE *grēat*), *fayre* (OE *fæger*), and *hyȝe* (OE *hēah*) not restricted to use within the line? In similar fashion the overwhelming preponderance of occurrences in final position of *mony* (6a:45na) and *noble* (1a in the long line: 11na) can be "explained" only by saying that these words have a strong tradition of use at the end of the line. It does seem in general to be true, however, that figurative meanings alliterate and do not occur in final position. The qualitative meaning of *noble* is not, like that of *gret* or *hyȝe* or *bryȝt*, figurative in origin. The same tendency can be illustrated from the verbs. Thus in 2178 "Þenne he boȝeȝ to þe berȝe, aboute hit he walkeȝ" *walkeȝ* is used literally, whereas in 1521 "Your worde & your worchip walkeȝ ay-quere" it is used figuratively. From the technical point of view, this results from the fact that the poet tends to "force" the meanings of words in order to obtain the needful alliteration. In the hands of the inept poet the extended meaning appears awkward. Oakden speaks of the ineffective and strained use of the alliterating adjectives in *Alex. Maced. (Alexander A)*, giving such examples as "in a ferce place" (2, 27). In the hands of the skilled poet the same process results in effective creation of metaphorical meaning.

Finally, as with the nouns, the adjectives whose "high alliterative rank" is determined by a single occurrence vary in stylistic status, ranging from such an archaic and rare word as *methles* (Brink, p. 32) in group I to such a distinctively colloquial word as *farand* in group III (Brink, p. 44; *EDD* s.v. *farrand* a. sense 2 "well-behaved, decent, becoming"). Each adjective of infrequent occurrence must be studied as a special case.

The language of *Sir Gawain and the Green Knight* is thoroughly traditional. Where he is original, the poet may rather be said to add to the tradition than to depart from it. The store of stock phrases, of set patterns, of ways of building the line, of modes of reference, of qualitative adjectives, which was drawn on by the *Gawain*-poet was drawn on equally by the other poets. These characteristic features of style are historically determined: the *Gawain*-poet was born into the tradition in which he wrote. But from the point of view of the criticism of style, features become devices. The superiority of *Gawain* over other poems belonging to the same tradition consists not in the devices themselves but in what they accomplish. In the hands of the mediocre poet the technical resources of the alliterative style merely make possible the construction of the line. In the hands of the *Gawain*-poet these resources take on poetic power: the technical problems of the line are not merely solved but transcended. The result is "þe best boke of romaunce."

CHAPTER 4

The Criticism of Style

THE PRECEDING CHAPTER was concerned with certain words and phrases used by the author of *Sir Gawain and the Green Knight*—that is, with certain elements of style. Each of these elements, it is true, was studied in relation to the group of contexts in which it occurs in the poem. The stylistic values of words, like their meanings, are determined in use; conversely, it is from the use made of words, especially by the skilled poet, that their stylistic values can best be determined. But though the words studied were taken in context, the focus of attention nevertheless was on the words themselves, isolated from the text and grouped for purposes of comparison. The criticism of style, however, is ultimately concerned not with words but with poetry—with passages such as the successive stanzas of *Gawain*, to which every aspect of language contributes: the meanings expressed, the kinds of words used to express meanings, their syntactic relationships, their order, and their metrical and phonetic patterns. More particularly, it is concerned with the coalescence of the aspects of language to produce an impression both of the characteristic quality of the passage and of its effectiveness as part of a narrative poem. This impression is experienced intuitively and immediately rather than as an analytical or deductive process, and in a sense it is prior to criticism. The work of criticism is the attempt to relate the impression to its causes in the passage, to describe factually and in sufficient detail those aspects of language and meaning which contribute to it—as a scientist might attempt to identify the chemical conditions of a recognizable flavor or scent.

The impression of style is, properly speaking, an impression of the use of language rather than of language itself. The use of language in turn, considered in relation to the occasion or mode of discourse, implies the character, in the broadest sense, of the speaker.[1] In works of narrative poetry the speaker figures as the "I" through whose consciousness the events making up the plot are mediated to us. This narrating "I" is, like the persons of the action, a fictional being, and he is created by the implications of the poet's language. His character includes such traits as his formality or informality of manner, his social class and degree of culture, his technical knowledge, and the attitudes—approval or disapproval, sympathy or detachment, humor or solemnity, and so on—which he exhibits toward the subject matter of his narration. The style of the poem is thus the characteristic or effective way in which the story is told, and for the purposes of stylistic criticism, the broad outline of events is the material with relation to which stylistic choice is exercised. It does not matter that the poet may in fact have invented or modified some of the events themselves. Thus, even if the *Gawain*-poet was not the first to combine the "temptation" and "beheading game" stories, he seems to have originated that alternation of temptation and hunting scenes which contributes importantly to the effectiveness of the poem.[2] Given an event as material, the poet must devise a succession of details as a means of narrating it. As an example we may take the coming of the lady of the castle to Gawain's bedroom on the first morning. This event could have been treated in four or five lines; actually, it takes up sixteen (1179–94). Gawain lies in a fine bed, under a handsome coverlet; it is late, and daylight shines on the walls; he hears in half sleep a little noise at the door; he lifts his head, opens the curtain, and peers warily out; he sees that it is the lady; she closes the door after her stealthily and moves toward the bed; he becomes embarrassed; he lies down and pretends to sleep; she steps silently to the bed, lifts the curtain, comes inside, sits softly down, and stays there, waiting for him to awaken. These details, aside from the words and metrical patterns in which they are expressed, constitute an aspect of the style of the passage; they are characteristic and effective both in their abundance and in their content. The narrator envisages the action with characteristic interest and intensity, dwelling imaginatively on it as a series of precisely differentiated stages. This mode of perception results in a retarded pace, which in turn brings about an appropriate enhancement of suspense. It is, further, both characteristic and effective that the narrator sees the action from two complementary points of view: first, that of Gawain inside the curtains (1182-90); then that of the lady, whom Gawain can no longer see (1191-94); then again that of Gawain (1195 ff.). The skill of the poet can thus be appreciated in part if the details of narrative content are understood. And the historical study of style will have justified itself if through its findings we can see something of the artistry of the language in which that content is expressed.

Our study of words and phrases in *Gawain* included a survey of their use in other alliterative poems belonging to the same stylistic tradition. As a result of this comparative examination, we can distinguish two aspects of the personality and character of the narrating "I." Certain traits—those implied by the traditional features of the style of alliterative poetry—are his by convention, *qua* narrator of an alliterative romance. Other traits—those implied by the poet's modification of the traditional style and his use of it for the purposes of this particular poem—are his as an individual. As we have seen, the traditional practice of referring to the persons of the narrative by now one, now another of a group of synonyms expressing class status tends in itself to elevate the style, regardless of the value of the particular words of the synonym group. This effect manifests itself for the reader as the narrator's dignity of manner, the solemnity of his attitude toward his subject. This manner and this attitude, then, are among his traits, but they are common to all narrators of alliterative romance and are expected of him by virtue of his role. The narrator's traditional attitude is further implied by his frequent use of adjectives imputing extraordinary, larger-than-life qualities—of excellence and splendor, joy and grief, courtesy and prowess, courage and strength, danger and hardship, according to the subject matter of the passage in question. Again, the effect of this feature of style is independent of the stylistic status of the particular adjectives used. Finally, the archaic and poetic elements of the traditional vocabulary of alliterative poetry serve to elevate the style further. Since such words are remote from the familiar and trivial associations of everyday life, they imply the speaker's idealization of the subject matter. To call Gawain a *hapel* or a *burne*, rather than a *kniʒt* or *lorde*, is to envisage him in lofty terms. The use of the archaic and poetic vocabulary also serves to make the character of the narrator more impressive, for it implies his knowledge of the tradition and its values, his status as an authority.

Both the traditional and the individual in the style of *Sir Gawain and the Green Knight* may be illustrated by a passage from the opening section of the poem, stanza 3 of Part I:

> Þis kyng lay at Camylot vpon kryst-masse,   37
> With mony luflych lorde, ledeȝ of þe best,
> Rekenly of þe Rounde Table alle þo rich breþer,
> With rych reuel oryȝt & rechles merþes.   40
> Þer tournayed tulkes by tymeȝ ful mony,
> Justed ful jolile þise gentyle knyȝtes,
> Syþen kayred to þe court, caroles to make;
> For þer þe fest watȝ ilyche ful fiften dayes   44
> With alle þe mete & þe mirþe þat men couþe a-vyse;
> Such glaum ande ³ gle glorious to here,
> Dere dyn vp-on day, daunsyng on nyȝtes;
> Al watȝ hap vpon heȝe in halleȝ & chambreȝ,   48
> With lordeȝ & ladies, as leuest him þoȝt.
> With all þe wele of þe worlde þay woned þer samen,
> Þe most kyd knyȝteȝ vnder Krystes seluen
> & þe louelokkest ladies þat euer lif haden,   52
> & he þe comlokest kyng þat þe court haldes;
> For al watȝ þis fayre folk in her first age,
>   on sille;
> Þe hapnest vnder heuen,   56
> Kyng hyȝest mon of wylle,
> Hit were now gret nye to neuen
> So hardy a here on hille.

In this passage diction and phraseology, the placement of words and phrases in the line, the alliterating combinations, the use of synonyms for "man, warrior," the adjectives implying idealized qualities, and the archaic and poetic words—all are thoroughly traditional. Parallels abound both in the rest of *Gawain* itself and in the other extant alliterative poems.[4] Among the archaic synonyms for "man, warrior," *lede* 38 and *tulk* 41 occur in alliterating position in accordance with traditional usage, while *knyȝtes* 42 occurs in traditional fashion, preceded by an alliterating adjective, at the end of the line.[5] Other elevated words characteristic of the tradition are *kayre* 43, poetic in the meaning "to go," [6] and *kyd* 51, poetic as an adjective in the meaning "renowned";[7] these occur in the expected alliterating position. *Sille* 55, in the bob, is elevated in the meaning "floor (in a hall)" (see discussion below), the archaic word *here* 59, meaning "army" (see Brink, p. 17), occurs in ornamental alliterative combination with *hardy* and *hille* in the wheel. Most of the adjectives in this passage are common in alliterative poetry, and a number of them are discussed by Brink. *Luflych* 38 (*louelokkest* 52), *gentyle* 42, *dere* 47, and *comlokest* 53, as well as *hardy* 59 in the wheel, are assigned by Brink to his group II—adjectives of high alliterative rank which have descended into modern standard English—and all alliterate here. *Best* 38, *rych* 39 and 40, *mony* 41, *samen* 50, and *fayre* 54, as well as *hyȝest* 57 and *gret* 58 in the wheel, are classed by Brink as low in alliterative rank. Of these, *best*, *mony*, and *samen* occur in final position, while *hyȝest* and *gret* occur in intermediate (relatively unemphatic) [8] position in the wheels and do not alliterate. *Leuest* 49 varies in alliterative status, according to Brink (p. 49), among the poems of the tradition. It alliterates here and, so far as I have noted, elsewhere in *Gawain*. *Jolile* 42 and *kyd* 51 are omitted by Brink, unaccountably, since both are common in alliterative poetry and seem to be used consistently in alliterating position, as they are here.

An additional feature of the traditional style of both the alliterative and the rhymed romances is the frequent use of pleonastic phrases expressing location, such as "on earth," "in (battle)field," "in hall." [9] Two phrases of this sort, *on sille* 55 and *on hille* 59, occur in the bob and wheel. *Vnder heuen* 56, which is frequently used pleonastically in poetry (see Oakden, 2, 390) is not so used here but provides the range of reference for the superlative adjective. The alliterating phrase "semely appon sille" is cited by the *OED* from *Duke Rowlande and Sir Ottuel* to illustrate the poetic meaning "floor" of *sill*, literally "timber . . . serving as the foundation of a wall" (s.v. *sill* sb.¹, sense 1). *On sille* thus has the same force as *vpon flet* (cf. *Gawain* 832), its figurative meaning "on floor" being further extended to the meaning "in hall." [10] I have not found *on hille* used pleonastically elsewhere in the romances, but its figurative meaning here resembles that of *mote* (cf. *Gawain* 635, 2052), "a mound or eminence . . . esp. as the seat of a camp, city, castle . . . ," which had in poetry the figurative sense "castle" (*OED* s.v.

mote sb.², senses 1 and 1b). The original French word also had both meanings; Godefroy, for example (s.v.¹ *mote*) cites it in the sense "castle" from Wace. The traditional association of the two meanings indicates that *on hille* can here be taken to mean "in a castle (located on a hill)."

The style of the passage is elevated in accordance with tradition. It also has a simplicity and straightforwardness which, though possible within the tradition, are not necessitated by it. There are no significant problems of meaning or syntax, variant interpretations having been proposed for only two lines: *ful* 44 is taken by GDS as referring to *fest* and by TG as referring to *fiften dayes;* the manuscript reading *glaumande* 46 is retained by GDS, but altered by TG to *glaum ande*. In both cases, however, the difference between variant interpretations is slight, and neither line can really be called obscure either in diction or in syntax. With only two exceptions—*rekenly* 39 and *glaum* 46, which will be discussed separately below—the passage is made up entirely of common words, some common only within the romance tradition, the rest common in Middle English generally; and the words are used in meanings which themselves are common either within the tradition or generally. An exception here is *a-vyse* 45, which is comparatively rare in the meaning "devise," though common in the totality of its meanings.[11]

The level of diction of the passage contributes to its simplicity of style. Words and meanings of traditional elevated character are infrequent in comparison with those which, so far as we can judge, were used both in literature and in everyday speech. Thus *ledeʒ* 38 and *tulkes* 41 make up a total of two occurrences of the archaic synonyms for "man, warrior," as opposed to six occurrences of *lorde* (38, 49), *kniʒtes* (42, 51), and *mon* (45, 57). Colloquial status can be assumed for those words which have descended into modern speech in the meanings they have in the passage, or which appear in modern dialects. *Hap* 48 "(good) luck," *wone* 50 "live," and *nye* 58 "trouble" have survived in these meanings (*EDD* s.vv. *hap*. sb.¹, *won* v., and *noy* sb.²). *Rechles* 40, a variant form of *reckless*, was, according to *OED* (s.v. *reckless* a.), in common use from c1375 to 1650. *Wele* 50, in the sense "welfare, prosperity," survives to the present day, although its use is largely restricted to the alliterative phrase "weal and woe."[12] *Samen* 50 "together" has not descended, but its colloquial status is indicated on several counts. First, it is frequent in alliterative poetry at the end of the line. Second, it is cited by the *OED* (s.v. *samen* adv.) from a prose text of c1400, the English translation of Mandeville's *Travels*. Third, the cognate verb *sam* "to bring together" survives in modern dialects (see *EDD* s.v. *samm* sense 1).

Colloquial status may also be argued for *hapnest* 56. The adjective *happen* seems to be a blend of *hap* (ON *happ* "good luck") and ON *heppinn* "lucky" (from *happ* with front mutation of the vowel).[13] The colloquial status of *hap* is indicated by its dialect descent. *Heppinn* was not a distinctively poetic word in Old Norse;[14] its influence in the formation of *happen* would therefore presumably have been exercised through the ordinary language rather than through literary tradition.[15] Although *happen* a. is cited by the *OED* only from two poetic texts other than *Gawain* and has failed to descend into modern standard or dialect English, its lack of general currency seems due simply to the competition of *happy*, also based on *happ*, which is first cited by the *OED* from Rolle's *Pricke of Conscience* and *Cursor*. There is no metrical or phonetic reason for the *Gawain*-poet's choice of *happen* rather than *happy* in line 56; it seems reasonable, therefore, to assume that *happen* was the form of the adjective he ordinarily used.

Neuen 58 "to name" (ON *nefna* "to name") presents somewhat the same picture as *hapnest*, with the all-important difference that it is a rhyme-word. ME *neuen* had a competing synonym in *nemn* (OE *nemnan*), although neither word has descended into modern dialect or standard use.[16] For poetic purposes, *neuen* offered the great advantage of rhyming with such useful words as *heaven*, *seven*, and *steven* in the sense of "voice" and "appointed time" (*OED* s.v. *steven* sb.¹ sense 1 and *steven* sb.² sense 2). In the meaning "to name" it is cited by the *OED* (s.v. *neven* v. sense 2) from *Cursor Mundi*, Brunne's *Chronicle*, Chaucer's *House of Fame*, Lydgate's poems, and Douglas' *Aeneis*, in every case as a rhyme-word. According to the *OED*, "the form *nemen(e)* is occasionally found in MSS where the rime-word shows that *neven* is intended." *Neven* may nonetheless have been in use in speech, at least in the *Gawain*-poet's locality. It occurs in *Gawain* in the long line as well as in rhyme (cf. line 10), and it occurs in final position in *Wars of Alexander* at least once and probably twice.[17] In the sense "to appoint" *neven* is cited by the *OED* (s.v. sense 2b) from the Rolls of Parliament 1442.

Rekenly 39 is problematic in meaning rather than in stylistic status. OE *recenlīce* adv. was a derivative of *recen* a.; there was also an adv. *recene* and a v. *(ge)recenian*. According to *OED* (s.v. *reken* a.), the adjective occurs "in English only as a poetic word of very lax application." In most of its uses, however, OE *recen* seems clearly to mean "prompt" or "swift."[18] *Recenlīce*, defined by BT as "quickly . . . straightway," occurs several times in the OE prose gospels, corresponding to L *cito, protinus, continuo*.[19] *Recenian* is defined as "to arrange, dispose, reckon," and *gerecenian* as "to explain," in BT; the Supplement adds "to pay" for the former, and "to arrange, set in order" for the latter. The OE nouns *(ge)recu* f. and *gerec* n. appear to be related to *recen* and its derivatives (see Holthausen s.v. *ge-rec*). These nouns have such meanings as "guidance, correction, rule . . . decree, orderly condition" (see BT and Supplement); the derivative *gereclīce* adv. is defined by the Supplement as "in an orderly manner, (of movement) smoothly, quietly." It seems significant in this connection that the MLG and OFris. cognates of OE *recen* had the meanings "orderly" and "in order" respectively (see Holthausen s.v. *recen*).

Neither *reken* nor *rekenly* survives Middle English. *Reken* is last cited by *OED* from *Morte Arthure, Purity*, and *St. Erkenwald; rekenly* from *Purity, Gawain*, and *Wars of Alexander*. Both words can therefore be assumed to have been poetic and archaic for the *Gawain*-poet. In some of the uses of *reken(ly)* in Middle English alliterative poetry, the meaning "prompt" or "swift" seems to be preserved, e.g., in *Wars Alex.* *794–95 (Dublin MS only; EETS ed., p. 29) "And he [the wild horse] als rekyndly [20] ran rolland hym vnder,/ As he þe sadyll had sewyd seuenten wynter." In *Morte Arth.* 4081 "The rekeneste redy men of the rownde table," the combination with *redy* may indicate that promptness or speed in action is meant. But it is also possible that *rekenly* in *Wars Alex.* *794 means "in orderly or docile fashion," and that *rekeneste* in *Morte Arth.* 4081 means "best arrayed or ordered." And there are other uses, in which the idea of swiftness or promptness is clearly ruled out. *Reken* occurs several times in *Pearl*. It refers, e.g., to the sides of the pearl, which are said to be "So rounde, so reken in vche araye" (5). In *Purity* 737–38 it corresponds to L *justus* in Abraham's question to God, "What if fyve faylen of fyfty þe noumber, / And þe remnaunt be reken?" In *Gawain* 251 "& [Arthur] rekenly hym [the Green Knight] reuerenced, for rad was he neuer," *rekenly* may mean either "promptly" or "politely, in a seemly or correct manner."

The evidence, then, indicates that *reken* and *rekenly*, which originally expressed swift, prompt, or orderly qualities in a continued action, became generalized in reference and meaning through use in poetry. In the line "Rekenly of þe Rounde Table alle þo rich breþer" it is probably best simply to translate the adverb as "fittingly." Its grammatical reference, too, seems generalized: the *rich breþer* are "fittingly" enrolled as members of the Round Table, and they are "fittingly" present as guests at the Christmas festivities at Camelot. The elevated stylistic quality of the word is presumably enhanced in its meaning and use in this line.

One additional word, *glaum* 46, warrants separate discussion. The MS reading *glaumande gle* is emended by TG, correctly I think, to "glaum ande gle," while GDS allow it to stand. Whether noun or verb, *glaum* is derived from Old Norse *glaumr* n. "noise, gaiety" (see TG and GDS glossaries; not in *OED*). A closely similar word, *glam* "noise" (ON *glam(m)* "noise"), occurs in *Gawain* 1652 in alliterative combination with *gle:* "Much glam & gle glent vp þer-inne." GDS object to "glaum ande gle" in 46 on the ground that it "makes the metre defective, as it is in 1652, while the present participle ending *-ande* is dissyllabic" (p. 97). But the fact that the ending *-ande* was originally dissyllabic does not mean that it is dissyllabic in the long alliterative line as composed in the Northwest Midlands toward the end of the fourteenth century.[21] Neither the structure of the alliterative line nor the relation of that structure to syllable count has been determined satisfactorily, and it seems unwise to object to "glam & gle" in 1652 on the basis of an assumed rule to which the poet would hold without exception. One might rather argue from the use of "glam & gle" that the metrical pattern of "glaum & gle" was admissible. TG point out, further, that "there is no evidence of a verb formed from Old Norse *glaum*" (p. 81). The alliterative coupling of the nouns *glaum* and *gle* has a close parallel in Old Norse in the phrase "glaumr ok gleði" "gladness,"[22] and a further parallel in English in the common alliterative phrase "gamen and gle," which goes back to early Middle English[23] and perhaps even to Old English (cf. "gamen ond gleodream," *Beowulf* 3021a). Granting that *glaum* is a noun, its stylistic status has yet to be discussed. We should note that *glam* occurs in modern dialect use (*EDD* s.v. *glam* sb.[1]), so that its status must have been colloquial. *Glaum* has not descended, but neither is there any reason for considering it a poetic or elevated word. It does not show the generalization from the original Old Norse meaning that we find in such poetic words of the same derivation as *tulk* or *kayre*. *Glaumr* was not a poetic word in Old Norse,[24] and the alliterative phrase "glaumr ok gleði" apparently occurs only in Old Norse prose.[25] It seems probable, therefore, that *glaum* was used in spoken language by the *Gawain*-poet, though it too was probably a less common word than *gamen* or *gle*, perhaps differing from these latter somewhat as in modern English *sprint* differs from *run*.[26]

Although its vocabulary is largely of an everyday character, the effect of the passage is nonetheless one of elevation and dignity. The few elevated words and meanings it contains serve to enhance this effect, but are not in themselves sufficient to cause it. Of greater importance for the criticism of style is the group of qualitative adjectives, which also expresses the most important meanings. Examination of the content of the passage shows that the subjective preponderates over the factual throughout. In twenty-three lines we learn that King Arthur held a Christmas feast at Camelot with the knights of the Round Table and their ladies; there were jousts and carols; the feast lasted fifteen days, with joyful clamor by day and dancing by night. The rest is idealization, much of it taking the form of explicit judgments expressed by the narrator with intensity and conviction. Statements of fact are expanded by repetition and emphasis rather than by a variety of illustrative detail. Lines 37–42 may be contrasted, for example, with *Morte Arthure* 64–68 and 74–77:

> Þis kyng lay at Camylot vpon kryst-masse,   37
> With mony luflych lorde, ledeʒ of þe best,
> Rekenly of þe Rounde Table alle þo rich breþer,
> With rych reuel oryʒt & rechles merþes.
> Þer tournayed tulkes by tymeʒ ful mony,
> Justed ful jolile þise gentyle kniʒtes

. . .

CRITICISM OF STYLE

> Thane aftyre at Carlelele a Cristynmesse he haldes,   64
> This ilke kyde conquerour & kende hym for lorde,
> Wyth dukez & dusperes of dyuers rewmes,
> Erles & ercheuesqes and oþer ynowe,
> Byschopes & bachelers & banerettes nobill
> . . .
>
> Thus on ryall araye he helde his rounde table,   74
> With semblant & solace & selcouthe metes;
> Whas neuer syche noblay in no manys tym[e]
> Mad in mydwynter in þa weste marchys.

In the passage from *Gawain*, *lordes*, *ledeʒ*, *breþer*, *tulkes*, and *kniʒtes* refer alike to all the members of a single group; the poet emphasizes their community of spirit as "brethren" of the Round Table, and the qualities of excellence in which all share alike. In the passage from *Morte Arthure* the *dukez*, *dusperes*, *erles*, and so on are different groups, and the number and importance of these groups serve to demonstrate in a logical way the *noblay* of the feast, over which the narrator exclaims a few lines later. This more realistic technique is used elsewhere in *Gawain*, but it is alien to the lines under discussion here.

Because of the idealizing tendency in the treatment of narrative content, a number of words, mostly adjectives, having a range of objective and qualitative meanings and a corresponding range of stylistic values (see above, pp. 83–88), are taken in their least objective, most elevated senses. *Rekenly* 39 is, as we have seen, wholly devoid of its factual implication of speed. But *rekenly* is presumably a poetic word in all its meanings, unlike *rych*, 39 and 40, which can mean "costly" but must here have its more elevated meaning "noble, splendid." (Compare 590–91 "When he watʒ hasped in armes, his harnays watʒ ryche, / Þe lest lachet ouer loupe lemed of golde," where *ryche* occurs in final, nonalliterating position.) Material aspects of the content are played down rather than emphasized. *Rych reuel* is linked with *rechles merþes* (40), and *mete* 45 is linked with *mirþe*. (The phrase "mete and mirþe" is infrequent in Middle English as compared to such phrases as "mete and mele," "mirth and melody," "mirth and minstrelsy," in which the two associated concepts are equivalent or closely related.[27]) *Vpon heʒe* 48, *hyʒest* 57, and especially *wele* 50 resemble *ryche* in the relation of meaning and stylistic value to subject matter. For comparison we may cite *hyȝe* in 524 "Fro þe face of þe folde to flyȝe ful hyȝe" and *wele* in 1820 "Wyt ȝe wel, hit [the ring] watȝ worth wele ful hoge." Compare also *vpon hyȝt* in 332 "Þe stif mon hym bifore stod vpon hyȝt [i.e. erect]." *Jolile* 42 has no purely objective meanings, but the qualities it imputes can be more or less dignified; here it must mean "gallantly" rather than "cheerfully" or "in lively fashion" (compare *joly* 86).[28] *Rechles* 40 and *dyn* 47 seem to have had mildly derogatory implications which are here neutralized by the context.[29] Both are adapted by the poet to serve as alliterating words.

The passage comes to a climax of intensity in lines 50–55. The narrator affirms that the court lived at Camelot "with all þe wele of þe worlde"—not all the goods of the world but all that is good, as defined in the preceding lines. The *þay* of line 50 is expanded in the three lines that follow into *knyȝteȝ*, *ladies*, and *kyng*, each preceded by a stock epithet of compliment traditionally linked with it in alliteration. The suspension of syntax and the elaborate parallelism of lines 51–53 give the lines elevation and dignity, while at the same time they retain their quality of simple and direct affirmation. In assessing the total effect, here as elsewhere in the poem, we cannot overlook an additional point. For the ear educated in the stylistic tradition of alliterative poetry, the closing of each line with a word traditionally used in final position constitutes a recognizable cadence, a satisfaction of conscious or unconscious expectation similar to that produced in rhymed verse by the second rhyming word.

The sequence of long lines reaches its conclusion in another summarizing statement, in which the youth of the court is now emphasized, with implications that will be discussed later. The wheel recapitulates the content of the preceding group of lines in terse and dignified fashion. It concludes with a pleonastic linking of qualitative adjective and phrase expressing place which appears thoroughly traditional and might easily be passed over without a second glance. But so far as I have been able to discover, "hardy on hille" 59 does not occur elsewhere in the alliterative and rhymed romances. On reflection, the reason for this is obvious: "hardiness" is not properly demonstrated "on hill"—i.e. in castle; it is demonstrated in the field. One is reminded of Sir Thopas, who was "fair and gent / In bataille and in tourneyment." But the effect here is certainly not parody; neither is it clearly ironic. The *here* is called *hardy*, as the *ledeȝ* are said in line 38 to be "of þe best," not in contradiction to particular actions or events, but in abstraction from them. The narrator does not question the traditional hardihood of Arthur's knights; his affirmation in lines 58–59 is straightforward. But there remains a nuance that seems inescapable. The traditional warlike virtues of the group of retainers exist in isolation, at least for the moment, from external hostility or challenge.

In the stanzas that follow (60–129), the narrator proceeds to a more circumstantial account of the New Year's festivities at Camelot. Even here, however, the details are such that there is little or no emphasis on material luxury or splendor. Stanza 5 is devoted entirely to a description of Arthur's behavior, his refusal to eat "vpon such a dere day, er hym deuised were / Of sum auenturus þyng an vncouþe tale" (92–93). Much of stanza 4 is concerned with such acts as the crying of "Noel," the giving of unspecified New Year's gifts, and washing before sitting down at meal (a traditional detail). Stanza 6 describes the order of seating and the music that accompanied the first course, and it is the music, rather than the banquet, that is said to cause "many a heart to heave full high" (120). The poet does not attempt to overwhelm the reader with catalogues of factual detail, as the other alliterative poets often do. Guenevere, we are told, wears "þe best gemmes / Þat myȝt be preued of prys wyth penyes to bye" (78b–79), but no gems are mentioned by name, and the wheel, which follows immediately, is devoted entirely to her beauty of person. To take a single example from the rest of the literature, the ornaments worn by Youth in *The Parlement of the Three Ages* include diamonds, a carbuncle, bezants, beryls, chalcedony, sapphires, emeralds, amethysts, and rubies.[30] With the "good ber & bryȝt wyn boþe" referred to in line 129 may be contrasted *Morte Arthure* 200–205:

> Þane clarett and Creette clergyally rennen
> With condethes full curious, all of clene siluyre;
> Osay a[n]d algarde and oþer ynewe,

>   Rynisch wyne and Rochell, richere was neuer;
>   Vernage of Venyce vertuouse and Crete
>   In faucetez of fyn golde: fonode who so lykes!

King Arthur's refusal to take his place at the table is reported by the narrator in a way that deserves close attention. The gesture itself is, of course, part of the tradition. The narrator does not simply explain it, he overexplains it, giving it two motives, the first of which is not traditional. The youthful king is active and restless, even a little childish; he does not like to remain seated for a long time.[31] The second motive, the traditional one, is carefully differentiated from the first: "& also anoþer maner meued him eke, / Þat he þurʒ nobelay had nomen." His behavior is also a sort of grand gesture, but its impressiveness as a gesture is diminished by its previous association with sheer boyish temperament. The treatment of the same material in *La Queste del Saint Graal* affords an illuminating contrast. Here, owing to his happiness at the return to the court of Sir Gawain, Sir Bors, and Sir Lionel, Arthur forgets that he must wait for an adventure to present itself before joining in the feast. He is reminded by Sir Kay that he should not sit down. The custom is thus depicted as involving a degree of self-denial on the king's part, rather than according with his natural inclinations.[32]

The combination of the traditional qualitative adjective *stif* and the phrase *in stalle*, used both in line 104 of the wheel "He stiʒtleʒ stif in stalle" and in the first of the long lines of stanza 6 "Thus þer stondes in stale þe stif kyng his-seluen," appears to have been devised by the *Gawain*-poet for use in this episode. It is modeled on a number of traditional phrases. "Stif in stalle" is reminiscent of "stiff in stour" (with variants "stithe, sterne in stour"), which in turn has parallels in other phrases such as "bolde in batell," "felle in fight."[33] *In stalle* is also parallel in position with *in halle* (102), with which it rhymes. These parallels suggest that *in stalle* means "in (his) place" rather than, or perhaps as well as, "in a standing position." Thus "stif in stalle" also suggests the traditional phrase "still in stede" ("stead, place").[34] (With 104 "He stiʒtleʒ stif in stalle," we may compare 2213a "Who stiʒtleʒ in þis sted?") The use of *stif* in combination with *stalle* and *stonde* insidiously robs it of its force as a traditional adjective of compliment to warlike virtues. Even more insidiously, it results in suggestions of unheroic woodenness and rigidity. As an epithet in the phrase "þe stif kyng," imputing qualities known to be characteristic of the person, *stif* adds solemnity of tone; in this context the solemnity of tone is meaningless. The traditional attitude of the narrator toward Arthur, as implied by the adjective, is maintained, one might say, solely "by courtesy." Whatever implications of boldness and inflexibility of will the descriptive reference might have carried are considerably diminished by the line that follows, in which we learn that the king was "talkkande bifore þe hyʒe table of trifles ful hende" (108).

The fact that Arthur was "bifore þe hyʒe table" rather than at it is to have important consequences for the behavior of the Green Knight. The description of the latter's entrance in the stanza that follows should now be discussed in some detail:

>Þer hales in at þe halle dor an aghlich mayster,   136
>On þe most on þe molde on mesure hyghe;
>Fro þe swyre to þe swange so sware & so þik,
>& his lyndes & his lymes so longe & so grete,
>Half etayn in erde I hope þat he were;   140
>Bot mon most I algate mynn hym to bene,
>& þat þe myriest in his muckel þat myʒt ride;
>For of bak & of brest al were his bodi sturne,
>Bot[h] his wombe & his wast were worthily smale,
>& alle his fetures folʒande in forme þat he hade,   145
>   ful clene;
>For wonder of his hwe men hade,
>Set in his semblaunt sene;
>He ferde as freke were fade,
>   & ouer-al enker grene.   150

This passage resembles stanza 3 in certain important respects. First, it too reflects the traditional style of alliterative poetry in diction, phraseology, and the placement of words in the line.[35] The use of words referring to persons is of particular interest and will be discussed in some detail below. Here we may note that *mayster*, though it is used nowhere else in *Gawain*, does occur as a noun of low alliterative rank in other poems in the general meaning "man, citizen" as well as in such specific meanings as "teacher" (cf. *Wars of Alexander* 1545 "Doctours & diuinours & othire dere maistris" and 1920 "With all þe hathils & þe heris & þe hiʒe maistris"). Of the traditional synonyms for "man, warrior" there are two occurrences: *mon* alliterates in 141 and *freke* occurs in the wheels in alliterating combination with *ferde* and *fade* (149). Of the verbs expressing some aspect of the general meaning "to go," *hales* 136 alliterates as it does in *Gawain* and elsewhere in alliterative poetry, and *ride* 142, a verb frequently used at the end of the line, occurs in final position here (cf. 160b "þere þe schalk rides," 196b "ne freke þat hym rydes," 260b "on stedes to ryde," etc.). Only one of the adjectives in the passage, *myriest* 142, is classified by Brink as strongly alliterating; it alliterates here. *Worþi*, according to Brink, varies in alliterative rank in the tradition; *worthily* alliterates here, but *worþy* occurs also in final position in *Gawain* (cf. line 1848). *Hyghe* 137, *þik* 138, *longe* 139, *grete* 139, and *smale* 144 are classified by Brink as low in alliterative rank; of these, *hyghe, þik, grete,* and *smale* occur here in final position. Neither *most* 137, 141, nor *sturne* 143 is discussed by Brink. *Most*, in the meaning "greatest,"[36] occurs in final position in *Gawain* 914 as a fourth alliterating syllable; it alliterates here. *Sturne* is frequent as a qualitative adjective and has high alliterative rank;[37] its occurrence here at the end of the line is metrically atypical, and it is used also in a nontraditional meaning, as will be shown later.

Two of the traditional poetic words for "earth, world, land"—*molde* 137 and *erde* 140—occur in the passage, both in alliterating position. *On þe molde* is not pleonastic, since it completes the superlative; *in erde* is pleonastic, however, as it almost always is in *Gawain*.[38] Of the remaining words in the passage, *mynn* 141 appears to be poetic and *myriest* 142 is elevated by virtue of its meaning. *Swyre* 138 may be poetic (see the discussion that follows).

ON *minna*, from which *mynn* 141 is derived, was used both in poetry and prose. It had the meanings "to mention, refer to" (cited from prose only), "to remind," "to remember" (reflexive and impersonal), as well as other extended and figurative meanings such as "visit."[39] After Rolle, it is cited by the *OED* (s.v. *min* v.²) only from poetry. It usually occurs in alliterating position or as a rhyme-word, and in alliterative poetry seems to have taken on in English the extended poetic meaning "to say, tell . . . record, relate." The second half-line "as mynes vs þe writtis" (*Wars of Alexander* 1249) may be compared with the formula "as þe [boke, etc.] tells"; presumably, *þe writtis* are informing us of what we do not already know rather than reminding us. In *Gawain* the best translation

CRITICISM OF STYLE   107

often appears to be "think," with implications of the original sense "remind oneself, remember." This too is apparently a poetic sense-development. "Think" seems an appropriate translation for, e.g. 1681 "Make we mery quyl we may, & mynne vpon joye" and 1800 "Þat I may mynne on þe, mon, my mournyng to lassen." But *mynn* 141 cannot mean "think (reflect upon)," and one hesitates between "remember" and "relate, affirm." Perhaps the latter is best, since the narrator is more likely to express (or refuse to express) opinions about the events he describes than to describe himself as recollecting them. Cf. 1010 "Bot ȝet I wot þat Wawen & þe wale burde," etc. and 1991 "Ȝif he ne slepe soundyly, say ne dar I."

Myriest 142 is not used here in any of the senses given in the *OED* under *merry* a. The context makes it clear that neither the now archaic meaning "pleasant, agreeable (with reference to facial expression)" (sense 2) nor the current meaning "full of animated enjoyment" (sense 3) is intended. The meaning "of things: pleasing, agreeable" (sense 1) is not cited with reference to the human body. The phrase "a mery mantyle" occurs in *Gawain* 1736 and *Wars of Alexander* 2864 (sense 1e). In *Morte Arthure* 3239 a meadow is described as "The meryeste of medill-erthe, that men myghte beholde" (sense 1b). As a qualitative adjective of high alliterative rank, *merry* was apparently used by the poets to refer to various subjects as needed; the application of *myriest* 142 to the shapeliness of the Green Knight is thus consistent with traditional practice.

Swyre 138 is cited by the *OED* (s.v. *swire*, sense 1 "the neck") only from poetry and usually as a rhyme-word. It is used by Chaucer only in Fragment A of the *Romaunt of the Rose* 325, rhyming with *ire*. The phrase "swete of swyre" is cited by the *OED* from *Siege of Milan*, and Oakden cites "swete of sware" from *Bone Florence de Rome* (2, 339). The phrase "a suetly swyre" occurs in "Blow, Northerne Wynd," [40] and the line "Hire swyre is whittore þen þe swon" occurs in "Alysoun." [41] In all these phrases the reference is to the neck of a woman. So far, *swyre* certainly looks poetic but, curiously enough, it appears in alliterative poetry as a word of low rank, in reference both to women and to men (cf. *Destruction of Troy* 3301 "[If you had drunk as much as you have wept] Thou faithfully were fillid vnto þi faire swyre" (ref. to Helen); 9136 "All abouen on hir brest & hir bright swire" (ref. to Polyxena); *Wars of Alexander* 779 "Has a helme on his hede & honge on his swyre"; *Siege of Jerusalem* 363 "Suþ knyt ("knit") with a corde to eche knyȝtes swer" (variant readings *nekke, corps*); and *Gąwain* 957 "Þat oþer wyth a gorger watȝ gered ouer þe swyre"). This is the only instance I have discovered in which a word of presumably poetic status is consistently (rather than exceptionally) used at the end of the line. The variant readings of *Siege of Jerusalem* 363 indicate that a dialect difference may be involved. The MSS substituting *nekke* and *corps* belong to the East Midland group (as does a third MS in which the meaning of the line is changed entirely), whereas the poem itself is thought to be of Northwest Midland derivation.[42] Certainly the combination of *swyre* 138 with the inelegant word *swange* "groin" would tend to neutralize any elevated connotations the word might have had.

The unusual word *fade* 149 has been the subject of a good deal of dispute, although there has been general agreement that it is a poetic word. The *MED* points out (s.v. *fad[e]* pred. adj.) that it occurs only in Northern texts and, except for the phrase *fad as fas* in *Cursor* 5539 (C), only in rhymes. The *MED* suggests that the word is a participle based on *fa*, the Northern form of *foe*, and translates as "hostile." Whatever the derivation of the word may be, this meaning is far more plausible than the meaning "elfin, like a supernatural being," implied by the recently suggested derivation from a late Latin *fadus* < *fatus* "fay."[43] The reason for the Green Knight's supernatural appearance, his greenness, has not yet been mentioned; it is introduced in the line that follows as an additional point: "& ouer-al enker grene." The possibility that the Green Knight is enchanted is not explicitly discussed until four stanzas later, and the poet does not usually digress in such fashion.

The sequence of long lines plus the bob contains only one unusual word, *swange* 138, the stylistic value of which is discussed below. *Hale, myriest,* and *sturne* are common in themselves, though their meanings in the passage are unusual. *Aghlich* 136 (*OED* s.v. *awly* a.) is comparatively rare as a derivative of *awe*, but the poet's choice of this derivative in preference to *awful*, which is cited from the thirteenth century on by the *OED*, is not motivated by meter or rhyme, and it seems reasonable to assume that *aghlich* was in general use in his locality. At least two unfamiliar words, however, appear in the wheel. These are *fade* and *enker*, the latter of which has the look of a rare colloquialism (see below). I should like also to suggest a third, *forwonder* 147. There is no positive evidence, so far as I know, for the existence of such a noun; the poet would presumably have created it himself on the basis of the participial adjective *forwondered* (cf. line 1660 and the citations in the *MED* s.v. *forwondred* ppl.). This would not be surprising, considering that he also created a verb *schaft* by conversion from the noun (see line 1467). But the best argument in favor of uniting *for* with *wonder* is the fact that in all other cases the conjunction *for* in its modern meaning is used with precision—that is, what follows it explains what precedes it (cf. 1870-71 "Thenne lachcheʒ ho hir leue & leueʒ hym þere, / For more myrþe of þat mon moʒt ho not gete"; 1922 "& þenne þay helden to home, for hit watʒ nieʒ nyʒt"; 2414-16 "Bot hit is no ferly þaʒ a fole madde . . . For so watʒ Adam in erde with one bygyled"; etc.).

The remaining words in the passage are colloquial. Of those that have not descended, in the relevant meanings, into standard English, *lyndes* "loins" 139 and *wombe* "belly" 144 have come down as dialect words (*EDD* s.v. *lend* sb.², *womb*). *Smale* 144 is used in modern dialects in the meaning "slender" (*EDD* s.v. *small* a. sense 3). *Etayn* 140 survives in the different but perhaps relevant meanings "a 'boggle,' a hobgoblin" (*EDD* s.v. *ettin*). *Folʒande* 145 is a use of *follow* v. similar to that of the expression "to follow on," which is cited by the *EDD* (s.v. sense 6) from Gloucestershire in the meaning "to resemble, match." *Muckel* 142 is a phonetic variant of *mickle*, which survives in dialect use in the meaning "size" (*EDD*), and *sware* is a variant of *square*; cited by the *OED* in the meaning "solid, sturdy (of limbs, the body, etc.)" into the nineteenth century (s.v. *square* a. sense 4; cf. modern *square-built*).

The meaning of *enker* 150 has been disputed. GDS gloss the word "vivid" and derive it from OF *encré* in the phrase *vert encré* "deep green," with possible influence from ON *einkar-*. TG gloss "very" and derive from *einkar-*. With this latter interpretation, the *MED* is in agreement. In Old Norse, compounds of *einkar* "particularly, specifically" with adjectives occur both in poetry and prose. In skaldic poetry it is combined with *breiðr* "broad," *tíðr* "attractive," *fúss* "ready," etc.; in prose, with *hátt* "high," *litill* "little," *fagrt* "fair," *mjök* "much," *vel* "well," and *hræddr* "afraid." Such compounds were not, therefore, distinctively poetic, and influence from skaldic poetry, the complex techniques of which were alien to Middle English verse, seems wholly unlikely. Nor is there any evidence for even a limited tradition of *enker-* compounds in English alliterative poetry. *Enker grene*, therefore, seems likely to have been a distinctively colloquial expression, its use here adding vividness to the diction as well as emphasis to the meaning "green."

Finally, *swange* "groin" 138 must have been a colloquial word. It shows no change of meaning from the Old Norse original *svangi*, which does not occur at all in poetry. It was used by the alliterative poets, chiefly in combination with *sword* and *swap* "strike," in such passages as *Morte Arthure* 1129–30 "Swappez in with the swerde, þat it þe swange brystedde;/ Bothe þe guttez and the gorre guschez owte at ones," where the style is graphic and realistic.

The entrance on the scene of the Green Knight is brilliantly handled. Lines 136–50, like the lines analyzed earlier, are composed in the traditional style of alliterative poetry, although they are somewhat less conventional in phraseology.[44] The words used in the two passages are similar; the proportion of traditional poetic words is small in both, and there is in both a small group of obscure words which turn out to be either distinctively poetic (*rekenly, fade*) or distinctively colloquial (*glaum, enker*), so far as the available evidence enables us to determine. But the two passages differ significantly in effect, and the tradition is utilized in the later passage in a different way.

We may think of the poet, at the moment he is about to introduce the Green Knight, as faced with a problem of reference. The point of view in the narrative has so far been that of the company at Arthur's court, who are about to be confronted with a being of a sort completely unfamiliar and unpredictable. To refer to this being as a "Green Knight" at the outset would be to forego part of the suspense, part of the dramatic excitement which attends the gradual revelation of his identity and nature. What the poet does is to refer to him at first obliquely, as a *noise*. (He uses the same device in a more literal way at the moment of the Green Knight's second entrance: "Þene herde [Gawain] of þat hyȝe hil, in a harde roche, / Biʒonde þe broke, in a bonk, a wonder breme noyse," 2199–2200.) In doing this he takes advantage of the now rare meaning "an agreeable or melodious sound" (*OED* s.v. *noise* sb. sense 5). *Þe noyce* referred to in line 134 is the music of trumpets, pipes, and drums accompanying the serving of the first course, which, though loud, was delightful (cf. line 120). The *noyse* associated with the Green Knight, however, is of a different sort; it is indeed *ful newe*, so far as the life at court depicted in the earlier stanzas of the poem is concerned, and the implications of discord in the word will soon be fully realized.

In the first description of the Green Knight the poet creates a minor effect of climax by withholding the word naming the stranger's color until the end of the last line of the wheel. Thereafter, *grene* is used again and again. The word *kniʒt*, however, is not used with reference to him by the narrator until line 377, or about 140 lines later, and even here he is called "þe knyʒt in þe grene," the phrase "þe grene knyʒt" appearing first in line 390. Actually, there is justifiable doubt whether the visitor *is* a knight in the specific sense of that word. He is not dressed as one (cf. lines 203–204), nor is he carrying shield or spear (205). In 228 "To knyʒteʒ he kest his yʒe" he seems to be differentiated from the group of actual knights, and the synonyms used to refer to him (*freke* 149, 196, *gome* 151, *haþel* 221, 234, *wyʒe* 249, 252, etc.) thus mean "man, warrior" in a very general way, *freke* being of course especially ambiguous. The court's difficulty in identifying him is clearly brought out in the interchange between him and King Arthur. At first, Arthur addresses him simply as *wyʒe* (252) and invites him to dismount and stay, while obviously not knowing what sort of person he is or what he wants. The Green Knight in answering brings out the fact that he does own knightly weapons and could have brought them if he had wished to (268–70). Arthur, as if to remedy the error of identification, at once addresses him as "sir cortays knyʒt" (276). At the same time he attempts to place him within the world of the court by suggesting that he is seeking single combat in the traditional sense, this having been one of the possibilities suggested earlier in the poem (96–99).

In the first direct reference to the Green Knight (136) both the noun and the verb have implications of great interest. A priori, the logical choice for the noun might have seemed to be *wyȝt*. In Middle English this word had not only the meaning "a human being, man or woman" (*OED* s.v. *wight* sb. sense 2)—it is used by the poet to refer to the lady in line 1792—but "a living being in general" (s.v. sense 1); and it was often applied to supernatural beings (sense 1b). But *mayster,* the poet's actual choice, is certainly much better.[45] As was pointed out above, *mayster* is used in alliterative poetry to refer to men, as a rule to men who are not warriors. But in addition to this general meaning, it has a host of more specific meanings which *wyȝt* does not have and which give it positive suggestions of great value. It differs, in fact, from all other words referring to persons in its associations with practical superiority, authority, and dominating or manipulating roles of various sorts in the real world. *Master* was used in the language of everyday communication to refer to persons having authority or competence not only in learning (*OED* s.v. *master* sb.¹ sense 12) but in such realms as government (sense 1), seamanship (sense 2), carpentry (cf. sense 14), and so on. (Cf. also sense 7: "One who has the power to control, use, or dispose of something at will.") The word thus leaves the Green Knight's identity open to doubt as *kniȝt* would not have done, while strongly implying the domineering role he is to play in the episode that follows.

The use of *hales* in this line, as in line 458, is comparatively rare in alliterative poetry. Of the meanings cited by the *OED* (s.v. *hale* v.¹), the closest is "to move along as if drawn or pulled . . . hasten, rush; spec. of a ship, to proceed before the wind with sails set" (sense 4). *Gawain* 136 is cited; the other uses all refer to ships.[46] *Hale* also had the meaning 'to flow, run down in a large stream," as in *Pearl* 125, and in this meaning survives in modern Scots and Northern dialects (s.v. sense 4b). Colloquial status for the nautical meaning is evidenced by the seventeenth- and eighteenth-century quotations in the *OED*. The metaphorical use of *hale* for the coming of the Green Knight on his horse thus suggests powerful and continuous motion.

The third word in the line that describes the Green Knight, the adjective *aghlich,* does not belong to the traditional diction of alliterative poetry; hence it does not have an established elevated meaning like that of, for example, *kyd*. As with other words expressing fearfulness, its quality will depend directly on the context in which it is used (cf. "a dreadful cold," "a dreadful catastrophe";

"an awful thought [of Doomsday]," "an awful thought [of having left theatre tickets at home]," etc.). Since the noun it modifies refers to real people rather than to monsters or supernatural beings, and since the diction of the line in general is colloquial, *aghlich* suggests the startling or even frightening impact of a powerful presence suddenly appearing out of nowhere; but it does not imply stark terror or solemn awe.

The statement of the Green Knight's entrance is thus made in realistic rather than grandiose or exaggerated terms, and the poet's method in describing the person of the Green Knight in the lines that follow is a realistic and direct method. The passage contrasts in this respect with that analyzed earlier, and the difference between them is revealed with particular clarity if one examines the metrical use of the descriptive adjectives in each. Compare, for instance, lines 50–54 of stanza 3:

> With all þe wele of þe worlde þay woned þer samen,
> Þe most kyd knyȝteȝ vnder Krystes seluen,
> & þe louelokkest ladies þat euer lif haden,
> & he þe comlokest kyng þat þe court haldes;
> For al watȝ þis fayre folk in her first age

with lines 137–41 of stanza 7:

> On þe most on þe molde on mesure hyghe;
> Fro þe swyre to þe swange so sware & so þik,
> & his lyndes & his lymes so longe & so grete,
> Half etayn in erde I hope þat he were;
> But mon most I algate mynn hym to bene

In the first group of lines only one adjective occurs in final position, and this adds little to the content of the line. The assertions of ideal quality are parallel and categorical; the essential meanings are carried by alliterating qualitative adjectives. In the second group of lines three adjectives occur in final position; two of these, *hyghe* and *grete*, although they do have abstract and idealizing meanings, are here used concretely to refer to physical dimensions. The specific details in lines 138–39 systematically bear out the general statement in line 137. The size of the Green Knight's torso is measured from throat to groin; then the size of "his lyndes & his lymes" is described. In view of the carefully managed ordering of the details, *lymes* should be interpreted as meaning "legs" (the word is cited by the *OED* in this meaning from Mandeville's *Travels*, c1400, s.v. *limb* sb.¹ sense 2b), since the gigantic stature of the Knight would depend on the combined length of his torso and his legs.

But the narrator does not depend, as in the earlier passage, on the sheer intensity of his statements to impress the reader. The details he presents validate a clause of result, and the judgment is carefully qualified: "Half etayn in erde I hope þat he were; / Bot mon most I algate mynn hym to bene" (140–41). Again one is reminded by contrast of *Morte Arthure*, in which the description of the giant concludes with the statement

> Who þe lenghe of þe lede lelly accountes,
> Fro þe face to þe fote [he] was fyfe fadom lange.
> [1102–03]

If the *Gawain*-poet does not wish to make the Green Knight monstrous in size, neither does he wish to make him repellent. He now praises his comeliness of form, but it should be noted that *myriest*, which here alliterates in an extended meaning, is substantiated by the details that follow as the superlatives in stanza 3 are not. The *OED* cites an entry from *Promptorium Parvulorum* (s.v. *stern* a. sense 4b) which seems almost designed as a gloss for *sturne* 143: "sterne, or dredful in syghte, terribilis, horribilis." Perhaps "formidable" would be a good modern equivalent. *Clene* 146 is not qualitative; it merely intensifies the meaning of *folȝande* 145 (see the *OED* s.v. *clean* adv. sense 5, "wholly"). The style of this passage is thus much more direct and down to earth than that of stanza 3. The meanings of most of the poetic and elevated words it contains are peripheral—*on þe molde, in erde*. The important meanings are expressed in colloquial and graphic language. The result is that the Green Knight materializes for us as the "kyd knyȝtes" and "louely ladies" did not. And his presence looms physically upon the scene with far more force as a result of a description tied to reality than it would have if the poet had presented him in grandiose and absolute terms.

The same technique is used again and again. As the Knight awaits the blow from Arthur's hand, he stands "herre þan ani in þe hous by þe hede & more" (333). His fearfulness as a potential

CRITICISM OF STYLE

opponent is expressed in relative terms: "Hit semed as no mon myȝt / Vnder his dyntteȝ dryȝe" (201–202). The phrasing is of course peculiarly appropriate to the ordeal Gawain must later undergo at his hand. The poet, in fact, seems to have inverted the traditional phrase "dele a dint" (Oakden, 2, 277) and created a formulaic linking of *dryȝe* and *dint* for the purposes of this poem. When Gawain is about to depart, the court grieves that one as worthy as he should "wende on þat ernde, / To dryȝe a delful dynt, & dele no more / wyth bronde" (559b–61). The most triumphant taunt the Green Knight utters takes the same comparative form. After Gawain has flinched at the first feint of the ax, the Green Knight exclaims that he had not flinched under the same circumstances, "Wherfore þe better burne me burde be called / þer-fore" (2278–79).

Assuming that style in narrative poetry manifests itself as the narrating "I"—the fictional being, implied by the language of the poem, by whom the events are reported—let us assess the role of the narrator of *Gawain* in the Challenge Episode, beginning with a summary of the events themselves. The Green Knight rushes into the court during the banquet and opens parley rudely, demanding to know which of those present is the king. The court is frightened at his supernatural appearance, but Arthur speaks. The challenge is presented and at first the court is silent. At this the Green Knight jeers; then Arthur accepts the challenge, but Gawain requests that he be allowed to take his place. The request is granted and he beheads the Knight, who picks up his head and departs, after explaining how Gawain is to go about finding him in a year's time.

Given these events as the material of the story, the particular form they will take—and this is true of all reporting, whether in life or in fiction—will depend on who is narrating them, his attitudes, his interests, and his sympathies. In addition it will depend on the way his mind and imagination work: any story can be told by one person methodically, by another in random fashion, by one person in detail, by another sketchily, and so on. The events, as mediated by the narrator, cease to be material; they are realized. Story becomes plot. The story of the Challenge Episode could be made into a number of different plots. It could, for example, be treated as an adventure in which the courage and courtesy of

Arthur's court were demonstrated in an encounter with the supernatural. This statement, however, would constitute an inaccurate summary of the plot as we have it in *Gawain*. Rather, the Challenge Episode appears to us as a series of humiliations and discomfitures for the court which we feel as more comic than tragic. Despite the fact that the challenge is successfully met, the Green Knight departs from the scene as the victor in a kind of psychological warfare.

His overwhelming presence throughout the episode results in part from the simple fact that whereas he is described at length and in the minutest detail, neither Arthur nor any of his knights is described at all. The only detail of personal description prior to the entrance of the Green Knight is the reference to Guenevere's *yȝen gray* (82). Five lines plus the bob are devoted to the canopy and carpets surrounding her, and a little later on, nine lines plus the bob to the dishes served at the banquet. But the narrator goes into a lavish account of the Green Knight's size, figure, dress, accouterments, horse, coiffure, beard, and ax. It is much as if, in a group painting, one figure were drawn in the style of a Dürer engraving and the others sketched in a few lines. The Green Knight continues to receive the largest share of the narrator's attention throughout the events that follow. The fact that he has much more to say than anyone else aids in making his presence powerfully felt. This, of course, is not the narrator's responsibility (he reports all speeches verbatim); but the actions and gestures of the Green Knight are also given much more space than those of Arthur and the court.

After the challenge is delivered, for example, the narrator begins by telling of the reaction of the assembly:

> If he hem stowned vpon fyrst, stiller were þanne
> Alle þe hered-men in halle, þe hyȝ & þe loȝe   [301–02]

There follow six lines of description, leading to the jeering speech which in a sense constitutes the climax of the episode: we are told how the Green Knight rolled his eyes, bent his brows, and wagged his beard and coughed as a preliminary to speaking. When Arthur accepts the challenge, two lines describe his handling of the ax (330–31), but these are followed by six lines plus the bob, describing the Green Knight's bold confrontation of the expected blow.

When Gawain in his turn takes the ax and accomplishes the beheading, four lines are devoted to the Green Knight's gestures of preparation (417–20), six to Gawain's act of striking (421–26), but thirty-three (427–59) to the Green Knight's actions after the head falls. The picking up of the head, the final instructions, and the departure could have been dealt with in half as much space; instead, the narrator tells us of the rolling of the head among the beholders' feet, the glistening of the blood on the green clothing, the "ugly body that bled," and the head's lifting up its eyelids and "speaking with its mouth." The Green Knight continues to dominate the scene ("Moni on of hym had doute," 442) even though the blow he requested has been struck; and the loss of his head is, in fact, dealt with in the narration in such a way that through it he becomes more terrifying than ever. The king and Gawain begin to laugh (463–64) only after the sound of the green horse's hoofs has died away.

The material of the narrative, from the beginning of the poem on, is presented in such a way that certain relationships are tacitly emphasized, those which in another treatment of the same material might have been played down or suppressed altogether. One such relationship appears in what may be considered the first discomfiture of the court by the Green Knight, a discomfiture made possible by the fact that the king is not in his place at table. The narrator's account of the reasons for this behavior has been discussed in detail, and it has been shown that he takes pains to emphasize the part played in it by sheer youthful restlessness. Because Arthur is not in his place, the Green Knight can ask "Wher is þe gouernour of þis gyng?" (224–25) instead of greeting the head of the household as a preliminary to the delivery of the challenge. His question implies, moreover, that the king does not stand out from the rest in appearance or manner. And it is ambiguously, if not rudely, worded (*gyng* is cited by the *OED* from early Middle English on not only in the meaning "the retinue of a great personage" but "in depreciatory sense: a crew, rabble," s.v. *ging*, sb. senses 2, 3c). The minor humiliation undergone by Arthur in not being recognized is thus tacitly presented as deserved. It is the appropriate outcome of his youthful behavior, his *child-gered* mannerism. And this behavior in turn is a manifestation of the youthfulness of the court itself, which was earlier described as being in its "first age." The ironic reversal of this detail of the opening description is fully accomplished when the Green Knight, scoffing at the idea of meeting any one of them in single combat, says "Hit arn aboute on þis bench bot berdleʒ chylder" (280).

In a sense the coming of the Green Knight is the exact fulfillment of Arthur's desires as stated earlier. Here indeed is "sum mayn meruayle, þat he myʒt trawe" (94), and it is later "breued . . . ful bare / A meruayl among þo menne" (465–66). But what Arthur had been waiting for was not the marvel itself, but "of sum auenturus þyng an vncouþe tale . . . of alderes, of armes, of oþer auenturus" (93, 95). (*Alder* here surely is the traditional archaic-poetic word meaning "chief, prince or ruler" rather than the more colloquial word "elder."[47]) If someone actually came to the court, it was to be a warrior asking to "join in jousting" with one of his knights. With these expectations the Green Knight is utterly at variance, and his coming produces all the discord foretold by the initial reference to him as "anoþer noyse ful newe." His uncouth appearance and attire have already been discussed, and his manners are unconventional as well. The *gomen* he proposes is unheard of as a mode of knightly combat. It deprives Gawain of the use of sword and shield and involves a humiliating passivity, an inhibition of natural response and action. The Green Knight does in fact descend upon the court with all the irresistible force of a torrent or a ship in full sail, as the metaphorical verb *hales* implies. The implications of the reference to him as *an aghlich mayster* are fully realized. The physical paralysis and silence of the court, even the courteous behavior and quiet courage of the king and Gawain, are overwhelmed by the blustering, rude speeches, the overbearing manner and vigorous gestures, the loud laughter, and the undaunted self-possession, even when headless, of the Green Knight.

With all this, the narrator continues to play his time-honored role, to express, in the words and phrases in which the details are presented, the traditional attitudes of respect and solemnity. Arthur's knights are referred to as *siker knyʒtes* (96), as *aþel frekes* (241), as *burnes* (337), as *renkkeʒ* (432), as the *fre meny* (101), as the *ryche* (362); Arthur himself is "þe stif kyng" (107) and "þe derrest on þe dece" (445). Whatever the relationship between these appellations and descriptions and the facts being narrated, they keep their face value, so to speak, in implying the narrator's manner. At one point, indeed, he explicitly defends the court against the imputation of cowardice. "I deme hit not al for doute" (246), he says, when the court is too frightened to answer the question as to the whereabouts of their king:

> Bot sum for cortaysye
> Let hym þat al schulde loute
> Cast vnto þat wyȝe.[48]   [247–49]

But their silence, prior to this statement, has been the subject of an expanded and emphatic description (242–45), and the form of the defensive statement makes the element of opinion intrusive. "I am sure some of them refrained out of courtesy" is actually less emphatic than "Some of them refrained out of courtesy."

It has already been seen that in the interaction between narrative material and narrative style, the traditional alliterative phraseology is sometimes significantly modified. "Bold on bent" becomes "hardy on hille"; "stif in stour" becomes "stif in stalle." But the traditional phrases themselves may take on an enhanced value as a result of the circumstances of the narration. Such a phrase, in the Challenge Episode, is "burne on bench." This is listed by Oakden as traditional in alliterative poetry (2, 268, s.v. "baroun upon benche"). In origin it is a conventional mode of reference to the retainers at a banquet, and as such doubtless antedates the Middle English period (cf. *Beowulf* 1013a "Bugon þa to bence"—i.e. "went to the banquet-hall"). The phrase is alluded to in the Green Knight's statement "Hit arn aboute on þis bench bot berdleȝ chylder" (280). The knights are literally seated, as is brought out in 242–43 "& al stouned at his steuen, & stonstil seten / In a swoghe-sylence þurȝ þe sale riche." It is Arthur, the only one standing, who answers the challenge, and when he prepares to strike the Green Knight with the ax, the latter awaits him as calmly as if "any burne vpon bench hade broȝt hym to drynk / of wyne" (337–38). Gawain then tacitly defends the posture of the court by asking permission to rise: "Wolde ȝe, worþilych lorde . . . Bid me boȝe fro þis benche & stonde by yow þere . . . I wolde com to your counseyl" (343–44, 347). And Gawain defends his fellow knights by alluding to another phrase, phonetically similar but of contrasting significance. It is not seemly, he continues, that the king should undertake the adventure "whil mony so bolde yow aboute vpon bench sytten" (351); there are none stouter of purpose under heaven, "ne better bodyes on bent þer baret is rered" (353). But Gawain's courtesy does not serve entirely to dispel the passive implications of the former phrase.

The narrator of *Gawain*, we may safely say, is richly conscious of the disparity between the reputation for valor and warlike prowess of Arthur's knights and what actually takes place when the Green Knight thrusts himself upon them. But this does not imply that his attitude toward them involves either hostility or contempt. Because he has avoided emphasis on material luxury and worldly power in his depiction of the life of the court, the Challenge Episode is not seen as a rebuke to arrogance or sensual self-indulgence. Arthur and his knights are charmingly youthful and joyous; their pleasures are innocent. And although it is overshadowed by the more conspicuous presence of the Green Knight, Gawain's behavior is exquisitely courteous. His self-possession in requesting that the adventure be allotted to him and in actually dealing the blow indicates clearly that he, at least, had refrained from speaking "for cortaysye" (247) rather than out of fear. In such a passage as 366–71,

> Þen comaunded þe kyng þe knyȝt for to ryse;
> & he ful radly vp ros, & ruchched hym fayre,
> Kneled doun bifore þe kyng, & cacheȝ þat weppen;
> & he luflyly hit hym laft, & lyfte vp his honde,
> & gef hym Goddeȝ blessyng, & gladly hym biddes
> Þat his hert & his honde schulde hardi be boþe,

there is no ironic disparity between the implications of the traditional adverbs *radly* "with (courteous or befitting) promptness" and *luflyly* "graciously, in a manner worthy of approval" and the circumstances of the action. Gawain's manner here fully validates the epithet "þe hende," bestowed on him by the narrator when he is talking to the Green Knight a moment later.

There remain to be discussed certain aspects of the fictional narrator which, though manifested in his language, belong to descriptive style rather than to verbal style in the narrowest sense (see above, p. 20). A full discussion cannot be attempted here, but some remarks may be made, and examples given, under the main headings of 1. actions, 2. space, and 3. descriptive detail.

1. The narrator tends to see actions, whether major or minor, as reciprocal, giving explicit attention to the reciprocating or responding agent even when the response is of no importance to the story line or could be omitted as obvious. The germ of such a tendency may be discerned in the traditional style of alliterative poetry, which provides for the expression of qualities of promptness and readiness in response to commands or requests (see above, pp. 82–83). But the tendency is sufficiently consistent and systematic in *Gawain* to distinguish that poem from the works of other alliterative poets.[49] The following passages are typical:

Þen comaunded þe kyng þe knyʒt for to ryse;
& he ful radly vp ros, & ruchched hym fayre,
Kneled doun bifore þe kyng, & cacheʒ þat weppen;
& he luflyly hit hym laft, [366–69]

Þe fayre hede fro þe halce hit to þe erþe,
Þat fele hit foyned wyth her fete, þere hit forth roled; [427–28]

Þe freke calde hit a fest ful frely & ofte,
Ful hendely, quen alle þe haþeles re-hayted hym at oneʒ
  as hende, [894–96]

With care & wyth kyssyng he carppeʒ hem tille,
& fele þryuande þonkkeʒ he þrat hom to haue,
& þay ʒelden hym aʒay[n] ʒeply þat ilk;
Þay bikende hym to Kryst, with ful colde sykyngeʒ.
Syþen fro þe meyny he menskly de-partes;
Vche mon þat he mette, he made hem a þonke
For his seruyse & his solace & his sere pyne
Þat þay wyth busynes had ben aboute hym to serue;
& vche segge as sore to seuer with hym þere
As þay hade wonde worþyly with þat wlonk euer. [1979–88]

In its interplay of action and response, the account of Gawain's reception at the castle of Bertilak de Hautdesert contrasts strikingly with a similar passage in *Destruction of Troy:*

Þay let doun þe grete draʒt & derely out ʒeden
& kneled doun on her knes vpon þe colde erþe
To welcum þis ilk wyʒ, as worþy hom þoʒt;
Þay ʒolden hym þe brode ʒate, ʒarked vp wyde,

& he hem raysed rekenly & rod ouer þe brygge;
Sere seggeȝ hym sesed by sadel, quel he lyȝt,
& syþen stabeled his stede stif men in-noȝe.
Knyȝteȝ & swyereȝ comen doun þenne
For to bryng þis buurne wyth blys in-to halle;
Quen he hef vp his helme, þer hiȝed in-noghe
For to hent hit at his honde, þe hende to seruen,
His bronde & his blasoun boþe þay token.
Þen haylsed he ful hendly þo haþeleȝ vch one,
& mony proud mon þer presed, þat prynce to honour; [817–30]

Þai [Jason and his company] bowet to the brode yate or þai bide wold.
The Kyng [Æetes] of his curtessy Kayres hom vnto,
Silet furthe of his Citie seriaunttes hym with,
Mony stalworth in stoure as his astate wold;
Than he fongid þo freikes with a fine chere,
With hailsyng of hed bare, haspyng in armys,
And led hom furthe lyuely into a large halle,
Gaid vp by a grese all of gray marbill,
Into a chamber full choise (chefe) on þere way,
Þat proudly was painted with pure gold ouer,
And þan sylen to sitte vppon silke wedis,
Hadyn wyn for to wale & wordes ynow. [362–73]

Animals and even, in one instance, the inanimate "meat" or food awaiting Gawain become responsive agents in the narrator's imagination:

He [the boar] hurteȝ of þe houndeȝ, & þay
Ful ȝomerly ȝaule & ȝelle. [1452–53]

Bot quen þe dynteȝ hym [the boar] dered of her dryȝe strokeȝ,
Þen, brayn-wod for bate, on burneȝ he raseȝ,
Hurteȝ hem ful heterly þer he forth hyȝeȝ,
And mony arȝed þerat & on lyte droȝen. [1460–63]

Þe wylde watȝ war of þe wyȝe with weppen on honde,
Hef hyȝly þe here, so hetterly he fnast,
Þat fele ferde for þe freke, lest felle hym þe worre; [1586–88]

[The lord] hit hym vp to þe hult, þat þe hert schyndered,
& he ȝarrande hym ȝelde, [1594–95]

CRITICISM OF STYLE

> Thenne watz Gryngolet grayþe, þat gret watz & huge,
> & hade ben soiourned sauerly & in a siker wyse,
> Hym list prik for poynt, þat proude hors þenne; [2047–49]
>
> His schalk schewed hym [Gawain] his schelde, on schulder he hit lazt,
> Gordez to Gryngolet with his gilt helez,
> & he startez on þe ston, stod he no lenger . . . [2061–63]
>
> & þenne he meued to his mete þat menskly hym keped, [1312]

(In view of this tendency, the meaning "awaited" given for *keped* in GDS' glossary seems preferable to TG's "occupied.")

2. The narrator tends to see a given object or agent in relation to other objects or agents within a limited space. The resultant effect is one of fullness or crowding, with, at times, a stereoscopic projection and depth in the imagined scene.[50] Again, the tendency is sufficiently marked to distinguish *Gawain* from the works of the other alliterative poets. There is a striking example of it in the description of the New Year's banquet at Arthur's court. The narrator, telling us in traditional fashion of the abundance of the food, says that there was

> Foysoun of þe fresche, & on so fele disches
> Þat pine to fynde þe place þe peple bi-forne
> For to sette þe sylu[eren] þat sere sewes halden,
>   on clothe; [122–25]

Here the effect depends partly on a realistic limitation in the size of the banquet table. But it depends also on the narrator's explicit reference to *disches, peple, sylueren, sewes,* and *clothe* (cf. "So many dishes that there was scarcely space to set them down"). This passage may be compared with the account in *Morte Arthure* of the entertainment of the Romans, where the narrator lists one delicacy after another, including

> Flesch fluriste of fermyson with frumentee noble,
> Therto wylde to wale and wynlyche bryddes,
> Pacokes and plouers in platers of golde,
> Pygges of porke-despyne, þat pasturede neuer;
> Sythen herons in hedoyne, hyled full faire;
> Grett swannes full swythe in silueryn chargeour[e]s,
> Tartes of Turky: taste whan þem lykys! [180–86]

In the *Morte Arthure* passage the effect aimed at is one of overwhelming splendor, the means being the accumulation of descriptive references without spatial definition (cf. the passage describing the wines served at the same banquet, discussed on pp. 103–04 above).

The same technique is used in the description of the forest into which Gawain rides on his quest for the Green Knight. Here the narrator frames the scene with hills on either side, and then fills it, moving in imagination from far to near, with the great oaks, the hazel and hawthorn bushes tangled together, the rough, hanging moss, and the birds perched in rows on the twigs below which Gawain is riding:

> Hiȝe hilleȝ on vche a halue, & holt-wodeȝ vnder
> Of hore okeȝ ful hoge a hundreth to-geder;
> Þe hasel & þe haȝ-þorne were harled al samen,
> With roȝe raged mosse rayled ay-where,
> With mony bryddeȝ vnblyþe vpon bare twyges,
> Þat pitosly þer piped for pyne of þe colde.
> Þe gome vpon Gryngolet glydeȝ hem vnder. . . .
>
> [742–48]

3a. Descriptive details in *Gawain* are frequently circumstantial, expressing temporary conditions or relationships—e.g. the presence of onlookers—as opposed to attributes inherent in the agent or object. As with the narrator's interest in responsive action, such a tendency can be seen in embryo in the traditional style; specifically, in the stock of alliterative combinations linking persons or qualities with phrases expressing position or place, e.g. "burne on blonk" (Fuhrmann, p. 18) and "bold on bent" (Oakden *2*, 268 s.v. "bachelors on bent"). But even such phrases as these are often given a specific relevance to circumstances in the style of *Gawain* which is not decreed by tradition, as in "His haþel on hors watȝ þenne" (2065)—i.e. his servant had mounted and was ready to leave with him—or the Green Knight's admonishment to Gawain, "Bolde burne, on þis bent be not so gryndel" (2338).

In each of the following lines one of the strongly alliterating synonyms for "man, warrior" is used in a descriptive detail referring to a group of onlookers or participants who need not have been explicitly mentioned. The result, as with the narrator's treatment of space, is to people or crowd the scene.

CRITICISM OF STYLE 125

> & ru[n]yschly he raȝt out, þere as renkkeȝ stoden, [432]
> & hem to-fylched as fast as frekeȝ myȝt loke, [1172]
> Þay ferden to þe fyndyng, & frekeȝ hem after; [1433]
> & he vnsoundyly out soȝt seggeȝ ouer-þwert, [1438]
> Syȝ hym byde at þe bay, his burneȝ bysyde; [1582]
> Here he watȝ halawed when haþeleȝ hym metten, [1723]

A relative clause or prepositional phrase expressing a circumstantial attribute may combine with its noun to form a periphrastic reference:

> Þe gome vpon Gryngolet glydeȝ hem vnder [748]
> Þe burne bode on bonk, þat on blonk houed, [785]
> Þe leude lystened ful wel, þat leȝ in his bedde, [2006]

The specific relevance of descriptive detail in the poem often makes for the sort of rhythmic continuity or momentum characteristic of the restrictive relative clause, as in the following passages:

Þe bores hed watȝ borne bifore þe burnes seluen
Þat him for-ferde in þe forþe þurȝ forse of his honde
                so stronge; [1616–18]
& went on his way with his wyȝe one
Þat schulde teche hym to tourne to þat tene place
Þer þe ruful race he shulde re-sayue. [2074–76]

Certain lines in which prepositional phrases or relative clauses are separated from the main clause with a comma by GDS could equally well be read without a pause:

> Gawan gotȝ to þe gome with giserne in honde, [375]
>
> In-to þe comly castel þer þe knyȝt bideȝ
>   ful stille; [1366–67]

(TG omit punctuation in 375.)

There is, of course, no question of the *Gawain*-poet's avoidance of descriptive details expressing inherent attributes. Beside those of the type quoted above, we find numerous lines like the following:

> Þat broȝt hym to a bryȝt boure, þer beddyng watȝ noble [853]

> 'bi Kryst, hit is scaþe
> þat þou, leude, schal be lost, þat art of lyf noble!' [674–75]
>
> Thenne watȝ Gryngolet grayþe, þat gret watȝ & huge, [2047]
>
> Hade hit dryuen adoun as dreȝ as he atled,
> Þer hade ben ded of his dynt þat doȝty watȝ euer. [2263–64]

But the style of *Gawain* involves a larger admixture of the circumstantial than that of the other alliterative poets.

3b. Descriptive detail in *Gawain*, more often than in the works of the other alliterative poets, expresses what is observed or perceived from a locus within the scene. The relation between descriptive detail and perception may be explicit, as in Gawain's first sight of the lady of the castle, where, after describing her in traditionally superlative terms, the narrator adds the more telling detail that she was "wener þen Wenore, as þe wyȝe þoȝt" (945). Compare, in the Challenge Episode, "Þe stif mon [the Green Knight awaiting a blow from Arthur] hym bifore stod vpon hyȝt, / Herre þen ani in þe hous by þe hede & more" (332–33), and the discussion above of realistic technique in the portrayal of the Green Knight, pp. 113–15. On the morning of her first visit to Gawain, the lady is described as she sits on his bed; Gawain, who had been feigning sleep, has just decided to open his eyes:

> Wyth chynne & cheke ful swete,
> Boþe quit & red in blande,
> Ful lufly con ho lete,
> Wyth lyppeȝ smal laȝande. [1204–07]

Here, chin, cheek, gracious looks, and lips imply the face seen at close range. It is the lips, parted in laughter, to which the hero's gaze is finally drawn, and on which it lingers.

The narrator's adoption of the visual perspective of the central character frequently enhances dramatic suspense, as in the Episode of the Green Chapel when Gawain is awaiting the second stroke of the Green Knight's ax:

> Bot Gawayn on þat giserne glyfte hym bysyde,
> As hit com glydande adoun on glode hym to schende,
> & schrank a lytel with þe schulderes for þe scharp yrne. [2265–67]

Here the blade is described as Gawain sees it from below. Compare, in an otherwise dramatic account of the battle between Gawain and Modred in *Morte Arthure*, "He schokkes owtte a schorte knyfe, schethede with siluere" (3852), where neither combatant would presumably be looking at the sheath. The effectiveness of the above-quoted lines from *Gawain* is heightened by the expansive reference to the descent of the blade. The content of the adverbial clause, which occupies an entire line, is superfluous, but the drawing out of the instant of suspense is psychologically valid from the point of view of the person concerned.

In the account of the third and final stroke in the same episode, there are, as one might expect, a number of verbal parallels to the beheading of the Green Knight in the Challenge Episode. "He [the Green Knight] lyftes lyȝtly his lome & let hit doun fayre" (2309) echoes "Let hit doun lyȝtly lyȝt on þe naked" (423), and "þe scharp schrank to [Gawain's] flesche þurȝ þe schyre grece" (2313) echoes "Þat þe scharp of þe schalk schyndered þe bones, / & schrank þurȝ þe schyire grece, & sc[h]ade hit in twynne" (424–25). There is a further parallel in that the narrator in both passages refers to the sight of blood, but it is a parallel with a difference. In the beheading scene the Green Knight's blood is said to have "blykked on þe grene" (429) of the headless trunk—i.e. it is seen by the spectators. In the Episode of the Green Chapel, Gawain sees his own blood as it falls to earth over his shoulders to "blenk on þe snawe" (2315).

The choice of a particular word to express the content of the descriptive detail is sometimes important in effects of this kind. On the morning of her second visit to Gawain, we are told that the lady "commes to þe cortyn & at þe knyȝt totes" (1476). *Toten* had in Middle English the meanings "to protrude, stick out" (see *OED* s.v. *toot* v.¹ sense 1) and "to peep, peer" (sense 2). The figurative meaning "to look inquisitively; to pry" (sense 2b) is earliest cited from Gower. The word has descended into Northern dialects in the meanings "to peep and pry about" (see *EDD* s.v. *toot* v.² sense 1) and "to jut out; to project; . . . to shoot above the ground, as corn, etc." (sense 3). Its meanings make it particularly apt for the line in question. Gawain is awake, ready to greet the lady when she arrives (see line 1477). *Totes* expresses the thrusting in of her head through the curtains as seen by the man in the bed; it also suggests her intrusiveness, her unwelcome "peeping" at Gawain in the privacy of his bedchamber. Compare the use of *loke* "to look" in similar position in the line in 478–79 "& hit [the ax] watȝ don abof þe dece, on doser to henge, / Þer alle men for meruayl myȝt on hit loke."

The same precision is shown in the use of *lyft* and *kay*, both meaning "left (side or hand)," in two lines in neither of which the choice of word is compelled by the alliteration. In describing Gawain's journey in quest of the Green Chapel, the narrator tells us that "Alle þe iles of Anglesay on lyft half he haldeȝ" (698). Here, *lyft* (as opposed to *west*) expresses Gawain's point of view. But when Gawain prepares to strike the beheading blow, we are told that "Þe kay fot on þe folde he be-fore sette" (422). Here, *lyfte* could equally well have been used. But *kay*, like *toten*, must have been a colloquial word for the *Gawain*-poet; it has descended into Northern dialects in such compounds as *key-fisted* "left-handed," and *key-neive* and *key-paw* "the left hand." (See *EDD* s.v. *key* adj. senses 1(3), (6), and (8); cf. *OED* s.v. *kay*, *key*, a.) "Þe kay fot" thus has the immediacy of the language one would use to refer to one's own hand or foot in everyday situations. Compare the use of *lyfte* in alliterating position in the description of the green girdle as worn by Gawain: "& þe blykkande belt he bere þeraboute, / A-belef as a bauderyk, bounden bi his syde, / Loken vnder his lyfte arme" (2485–87). Here the point of view is not Gawain's own, but that of one looking at him.

The above-discussed features of style manifest themselves in the poem as what might be called the characteristic mode of imagination of the narrating "I," who is here also the narrating "eye." In general, the narrator of *Gawain* tends to imagine agents and objects as they assume particular relationships within a limited space (and in limited time). He tends also to adopt the point of view of the character central in a given narrative passage as that character responds to the circumstances of the action. The result is vividness, but it is vividness of a special kind. When it is visual, it depends as much on the exact appropriateness of what is seen, by whom, and from where, as on the color, texture, or other intrinsic sensory or aesthetic qualities of the object. It is the vividness of the frozen stream that "henged heȝe ouer [Gawain's] hede in hard ysse-ikkles" (732), rather than of those streams that "thro' wavering lights and shadows broke, / Rolling a slumbrous sheet of foam below" in the landscape of "The Lotos-Eaters." In recognizing the dramatic implications of the successive details of the narrative, the reader is pulled in imagination into the world of the poem, and experiences it as a reality.

In the Challenge episode, as later in the poem, the narrator's attitude toward the hero is one of affection. And in this episode Gawain shows himself superior to the rest of the court (the king excepted) in his response to an unfamiliar, trying, and seemingly dangerous situation. As a result of this response, he is to be singled out for sore trials of chastity, of courtesy, and finally of courage. In the first there is no real question of failure. The second, conducted concomitantly by the lady in the bedchamber scenes, is the more subtle, the more suspenseful, and the more amusing of the two, though the hero's courtesy, like his chastity, is successfully maintained throughout. It is in the third that, showing himself less hero than human, he falls short, and as a result, abandons courtesy too for a few moments in an acrimonious outburst of antifeminism. In the account of these trials, as in that of the Challenge episode, the elements of discomfort, frustration, and annoyance inherent in each situation will be realized to the full, and the extent to which Gawain falls short of the ideal, by implication, clearly defined. But through it all, the narrator's time-honored attitudes of solemnity and deference—mixed with a genuinely felt affection—will be maintained.

This story and the way it is told—the "what" and the "how" of the narration—must, for the purposes of a study of style, be considered as two different things. The historical study of style reveals that in *Sir Gawain and the Green Knight*, the verbal expression of the story is thoroughly traditional, to an extent that is more and more fully apparent as one becomes more familiar with the other extant works belonging to the same tradition. But in *Gawain* the traditional features of style do not serve the traditional purposes. They become devices for the production of an effect in which the narrator—the presiding, interpreting "I," with his emotions and attitudes, his manner, and his particular mode of imaginative perception—is all-important. In the last analysis what this narrator has to tell and the way in which he chooses to tell it are one.

PART II

Meter

"Wylde werbles & wyȝt wakned lote,
 Þat mony hert ful hiȝe hef at her towches"

CHAPTER 5

The Phonological Evidence

A METRICAL TEXT presents a written record of patterns that are essentially auditory—expressed by the voice and understood by the ear. This generalization—with a few exceptions [1]—applies even to the present age, when poetry is far more often seen than heard. It is certainly true for a Middle English poem such as *Sir Gawain and the Green Knight,* which was, according to its own testimony, designed to be recited aloud. "If ȝe wyl lysten þis laye bot on littel quile," says the poet, "I schal telle hit as tit, as I in toun herde, / with tonge" (30–32), and considerably later, "& ȝe wyl a whyle be stylle, / I schal telle yow how þay wroȝt" (1996–97). In embarking upon a metrical analysis of *Gawain,* therefore, it is necessary to invoke the aid of historical phonology, which tells us, given the time and place of its composition, how the words of the poem were presumably pronounced by the poet.

The historical phonologist must at times distinguish between the pronunciation used by the author and that implied by the spelling of the manuscript, which in a Middle English text is usually separated from the autograph copy by at least one or two removes. In the *Gawain* MS, for example, initial *wh* (OE *hw*) and *qu* (OE *cw*, OF *qu*) are interchanged: e.g. *whyle* is spelled *quyle* (814, 1115) and *quene* is spelled *whene* (74, 2492). But such spellings cannot be taken to mean that the initial consonants of *whyle* and *quene,* in the speech of the *Gawain*-poet, were similar enough to alliterate. *Wh* words and *qu* words are never, in fact, used in alliterative combination by that poet, as they are by the authors of *Morte Arthure* and *Destruction of Troy.* The orthography of the MS of *Gawain* is thus misleading with respect to the poet's pronunciation of *wh* and *qu.*[2] This aspect of pronunciation does not affect metrical analysis. But orthography may obscure the metrically important aspect of syllable count, as will be seen later.

The two problems of historical phonology of greatest importance for the metrical analysis of *Gawain* are the accentuation of Romance words³ and the pronunciation of final *-e, -es,* and *-ed.*

The assimilation, during the Middle English period, of a large vocabulary of OF loan words was attended by the accentual remodeling of certain groups of these words according to the native system. The results of this remodeling are to a large extent reflected in the modern English accentuation of words derived from Old French, but many variant forms have been lost, and the nature of the variants and the chronology of the process in Middle English have been subject to dispute.⁴ As with other problems in the history of pronunciation, it is more profitable to think in terms of "tendencies," varying in extent of influence and at times mutually opposed, than of "rules" affecting alike all words in a given group. Such tendencies reflect the practice of speakers of different cultural levels, some proficient in French, some ignorant of it, during a period in which there was little or no concern for standardization in the modern sense. They can be presented most clearly by starting with the original OF words, grouping these according to syllabic composition. Syllables containing the final unaccented vowel of neutral quality, [ə], spelled *-e* in Old French as in Middle English, will be disregarded in the grouping of OF words.⁵ These syllables were retained in Middle English, but were never accented in either language.

The first group consists of monosyllabic words and dissyllables ending in unaccented *-e*. It is exemplified by OF *bref, court, front, age, lettre, table, prove* v., *truble* v.⁶ It presents no problem, since the accent in Old French fell uniformly on the stem and remained on the stem in Middle English.

The second group, dissyllabic words ending in a consonant or accented vowel and trisyllables ending in unaccented *-e*, consists for the most part of stem-suffix and prefix-stem derivatives. The two kinds of derivatives showed differing accentual tendencies and will therefore be discussed separately.

In stem-suffix derivatives, exemplified by *prisun, mirour,* ONF *castel, bataille, manere, miracle, raisonne* v., *querele* v., *damage* v., the second syllable—i.e. the suffix—predominated accentually in

Old French.[7] English speakers tended to shift the accent in these words to the first syllable. This tendency was apparently due to the influence of familiar native words and inflectional forms such as *moder, gomen, sadel, felawe, millere, brighteste, singende, hondes,* and *mannes,*[8] in which the first syllable received the predominant accent.

In prefix-stem derivatives the second syllable—in this case the stem—again dominated accentually in Old French. English speakers tended to retain the accent on the stem in words with light prefixes resembling unstressed native prefixes. Thus ONF *arei* "array," *debat, destresse, ensample, entente, avoue* v., and *repaire* v. followed the pattern of such native derivatives as *aboute, again, another, beginnen, bestowen,* and *undon.* But heavier prefixes, in which the analogy with native practice was less clear, could sometimes attract the accent. Words formed from *com-/con-, per-/par-,* and similar prefixes thus showed conflicting accentual tendencies which are reflected in the inconsistent modern accentuation of *pardon, pertain, comfort, command, conscience, contrive,* etc. (For the systematic accentual distinction in modern English between *portrait* and *portray, conflict* n. and *conflict* v., etc., see below, pp. 136–37.)

The accentual treatment of these words in Middle English was determined largely by their resemblance in phonetic structure to native words. The modern reader proceeds similarly in accenting Lewis Carroll's nonsense-words *brillig* and *slithy* on the first syllable; he applies to them the accentual pattern familiar to him in *silly, brilliant, slimy, writhing,* etc., without consciously thinking of the unaccented syllables in any of these words as suffixes. Shift of accent from the second syllable to the first could and did take place in Middle English in OF words of uncertain morphology whose second syllables sounded like suffixes. Thus OF *baril* "barrel" and *barain* "barren," words of obscure origin (see *OED*), shifted the accent together with *burel* "woolen cloth" (dim. of *bure;* see *OED*) and *villein* "base, low-born" (from L *villa;* see *OED*). Words which had originated as compounds tended to develop variant accentual forms, according as they were felt to resemble one or another class of words. OF *travaille* v. (originally from a compound meaning "three-stake") and *mainteine* v. (originally a compound meaning "hold in hand") could be accented in Middle English on either the first syllable or the second (for etymologies see *OED*).

The pronunciation of certain Romance prefixes as nonemphatic in Middle English corresponds to an apparent lack of logical force; they could be and often were interchanged or dropped from words altogether by aphaeresis, with little or no effect on meaning.[9] Aphaeretic tendencies in Middle English were doubtless favored by the prior existence of pairs of verbs, with and without prefixes, differing little or not at all in meaning, such as native *arise(n)/ rise(n)*, *abide(n)/bide(n)*, and the ME derivatives of OF *avoue/ voue* and *endure/dure*. Aphaeretic variants and derivatives indicating confusion among prefixes are frequent both in late Middle English and in Anglo-French. Some of these Middle English variants have survived into the modern language, familiar examples being *esquire/squire* and *defence/fence*. But there were many more; such groups as *achesoun/anchesoun/encheason/chesoun* "occasion," *acounter/encounter/counter*, and *amay/esmay/demay/dismay* are typical (Middle English citations for all these words may be found in the *OED*).

Certain unusual forms found in *Gawain* and the other poems of the same MS may be attributed to these tendencies. *Enfoubled* "muffled," *Gawain* 959, has the stem of OF *afubler*, which had developed in Anglo-French the aphaeretic variant *fubler* (see Pope, No. 1137). *E(n)n(o)urned*, *Gawain* 634, 2027,[10] *Pearl* 1027, has a complicated history even for a ME word; it seems to be an altered form of *anorn*, which is itself a new derivative of *orn* "adorn" (see *OED* s.vv. *enorn*, *anorn*, *orn*, *adorn*). *Pearl* has *endorde* (368) for *adored*; and the latter was itself confused both with *adorn* and *anoure* "to honor" (see *OED*). All these variants are important for our purposes as indicating the accentual dominance of the stem over the prefix. It will be noted that the prefixes most frequently involved are *a-*, *de-*, *dis-*, and *en-*.

In modern English verbs with prefixes of Romance and Latin origin are often distinguished from cognate nouns or adjectives by accent, the noun or adjective being accented on the prefix while the verb is accented on the stem.[11] We say *cómpound* a. but *compóund* v., *pórtrait* n. but *portráy* v., *rébel* n. but *rebél* v., and so on. Such a tendency appears in the language as early as Old English, in which *ándgiet* "intelligence" corresponds to *ongíetan* "to understand," *ófer-geong* "crossing" and *ófer-genga* "traveler" to *ofer-gángan* "to cross."[12] In Middle English also, certain nouns and adjectives of Old English derivation could be accented on the prefix, e.g. *by-spell* (OE *bīspell*, with accented *bī-* corresponding to unaccented *be-* in verbs), *forward* "agreement" (OE *foreweard*, with *fore-* corresponding to *fore*, prep. and adv.). These native practices must have had a share in determining the modern treatment of Romance noun or adjective and verb cognates. But it is difficult to say how early such accentual distinctions as that between *rébel* n. and a. and *rebél* v. became fixed or "correct."[13] According to Kökeritz (*Shakespeare's Pronunciation*, p. 335) they were "not yet fully established or fixed" in Elizabethan English. Where there was diversity of practice in 1600, we should expect still more in 1350–1400.

Words of three or more syllables ending in a consonant or accented vowel and words of more than three syllables ending in unaccented -*e* may be classed together as a third group. They are of comparatively infrequent occurrence and need be discussed here only briefly. The two most important groups are those in which the first syllable is the stem, e.g. *cortesie, prisonnier,* and *raisonnable,* and those composed of prefix-stem-suffix, e.g. *desirous, aventure,* and *convenable.* All these had in Old French a secondary accent on the first syllable in addition to the primary accent on the third.[14] Words of the first group were regularly accented in Middle English on the first and third syllables, with the primary accent shifting to the first. This pattern is reproduced in modern English. Words of the second group showed conflicting tendencies in Middle English. Some had forms with accent on the prefix and suffix in contradiction to modern usage, e.g. *desirous* (see *OED*), which has since been reaccented to conform to the cognate noun and verb. Here again, aphaeresis may provide evidence for accent on the stem, as in *despitous*, of which the reduced form *spitous* (see *OED*) appears in *Gawain* 209 as *spetos*.[15] Most of these words doubtless had two accentual forms, of which one has since been lost. Thus OF *aventure* n. and v. developed in Middle English two reduced forms, *venture* and *aunter*,[16] the former presupposing accent on the stem, the latter on the prefix. Varying developments are also shown by originally tetrasyllabic words such as *commandement* and *commencement*. The former word had the reduced form *comament*, of frequent occurrence in the Cotton MS of *Cursor Mundi* (for metrical interpretation see below, pp. 153–54), which implies accent on the prefix in contradiction to modern usage. *Commencement* had a similar reduced form *comsement*, which occurs in the stanzaic *Morte Arthure;* this development may have been influenced by the reduced form *comse* of *commence* v., which is fairly frequent in Middle English (for the latter see *OED* and *MED;* cf. *comsing* vbl. n., cited as a separate word in the *MED* and in the *OED* s.v. *comse*). *Pearl* has both *adubbement* (OF *ado[u]bement*) and the reduced form *dubbement*. The latter may have existed in Old French or Anglo-French; cf. the reduced forms *dobëor* n., *dober* v. in TL.

The chronology of the accentual shifts in words of Romance derivation remains to be discussed. Aside from metrical usage, which will be taken up separately below, there are two kinds of phonological evidence for believing that OF words were made to conform to native accentual patterns very soon after their introduction into English, at least by speakers who did not know French.

1. Final *-e* was lost very early in Middle English in originally accented OF suffixes, as indicated by such spellings as *manner, mesur* (OF *manerë, mesurë*) in thirteenth-century MSS. An example of particular interest is *riches* (OF *richessë*), found in the A text of Lawman's *Brut* (line 8091). The word seems clearly to be used as a plural with the meaning "articles of great value."[17] If so, a pronunciation is implied in which the OF suffix has fallen together with native unaccented *-es*. This loss, which considerably antedates the loss of *-e* in *place, age,* and the like, implies weakening of accent on the preceding syllable.[18]

2. As early as the fourteenth century there are spellings indicating the reduction, presumably to [ə], of originally accented suffix-vowels, notably diphthongs. In the Cotton MS of *Cursor Mundi* we find *batel(l)* 471, 3463 (OF *batailë*) and *trauel(l)ing* 3487, 4694 (OF *travail-*). *Pearl* has *saffer* "sapphire" 118, 1002 (OF *safir*). The significant reversed spellings *chapayle* "chapel"

(OF *chapele*) and *grauayl* "gravel" (OF *gravele*) occur in *Gawain* 1070 and *Pearl* 81 respectively.[19] Such reductions imply that loss of accent in the suffixes in question had taken place at a considerably earlier date.[20]

Although the reduced forms cited above developed out of full forms, this does not necessarily mean that the full form was replaced by the reduced form. In most, if not all cases, the reduced and full forms must have existed in Middle English side by side. Thus although *comament* "commandment" represents a further reduction of a trisyllabic form *commandment,* accented on prefix and suffix, in which the syllabic -*e*- of OF *commandement* has been lost, a tetrasyllabic form with accent on the stem has survived into modern dialect English (see *commandement* sb., "also written *commandiment,*" in the *EDD,* cited from w. Yks. and Oxf.).[21] So *commence,* with accent on prefix, doubtless continued to be used in Middle English beside *comse,* with the stem-accented form as a further variant. A modern analogy may be found in *travel* and *travail,* both from OF *travailler.* The first syllable is "accented" in both words, but there is an obvious difference in the degree of accentual predominance of the first syllable over the second. *Travel* is descended from the ME reduced form cited from the Cotton MS of *Cursor* (see above, p. 138); in the second syllable of *travail,* the modern vowel corresponding regularly to the ME diphthong *ai* has been reintroduced as a spelling-pronunciation since Shakespeare's time.[22] The two were not distinguished as separate words with separate meanings until the eighteenth century (see *OED* s.v. *travel* v. sense 2, "to make a journey," where the spelling *travail* is cited as late as 1714). Most of the originally accented suffix-vowels of Romance words exist today in reduced form; the vowels of the suffix-syllables of *certain, prison,* and *raisin* are alike neutral and unaccented. But it is highly probable that in late Middle English there existed, for all such words, two forms corresponding to modern *travail* and *travel,* both showing shift of accent, one with further reduction of the accentually subordinate syllable. The reduced and full variants of Romance words in Middle English doubtless represented different stylistic tendencies, the reduced forms being associated with the less educated speakers—those less influenced by French modes of pronunciation—and with the more casual uses of language, the full forms with speakers of higher cultural level and with the language of literature (cf. *is not* and *isn't, something* and *somethin'* in modern English).

The second phonological problem to be discussed is the pronunciation of final *-e*. This problem is of importance in a metrical study because final *-e*'s may count as syllables in Middle English rhymed verse, the most familiar example of this practice to the modern reader being the verse of Chaucer.

In native words *-e* is derived primarily from unaccented final vowels. In some OE nouns and adjectives, such as *talu* "tale," *flota* "sailor," and *mete* "meat," there was a final vowel in all forms of the word; in others it was present only in inflected forms, as in the d.s. *stāne* of *stān* "stone," the g.d.i.s. *mēde* of *mēd* "reward," and the weak declension *gōda, gōde,* etc., of *gōd* "good." OE adverbs in *-e* often corresponded to adjectives ending in a consonant, as with *dēope* "deeply" and *dēop* "deep," *sōþe* "truly" and *sōþ* "true." Almost all verb-forms had final unaccented vowels, e.g. *helpe,* 1st pers. sg. pres. indic. of *helpan* "to help," *brōhte,* 1st and 3rd pers. sg. pret. indic. of *bringan* "to bring"; *maca,* imp. sg. of *macian* "to make." Final *-a, -u,* and *-e* fell together at the end of the Old English period as an unaccented vowel of neutral quality which came always to be spelled *-e*. OE inflectional endings consisting of vowel plus *m* or *n* fell together in Middle English as *-en;* this *-en* was frequently reduced further to *-e*. In *Gawain* the infinitive ending (OE *-an*) appears almost exclusively as *-e* (see GDS, p. lviii). To these *-e*'s of native origin were added the *-e*'s—of similar phonetic quality—of such Romance words as *age, manere, digne, honeste,* and *commence*.[23]

In theory every word or form whose Old English or Old French ancestor had *-e* should also have *-e* in Middle English, but there are inconsistencies in practice. For example, the inflectional *-e* of the d.s. of *stān* and many other OE masculine nouns was dropped early in Middle English, presumably by analogy with the other forms of the singular, which lacked *-e*. But the n.s. of *mēd* and many other OE feminine nouns tended to acquire an *-e*, presumably by analogy with the other forms of the singular, in all of which *-e* was present. Adverbs originally lacking *-e*, such as *oft*, could acquire it in Middle English by analogy with other adverbs.[24]

The history of -*e* in Middle English is a history of attrition resulting finally in its loss, as a sounded vowel, in all words and forms. This is a phonological process and must be distinguished from the loss (and acquisition) of -*e* by analogy referred to above. The history of the process is complicated; in summarizing it, it is necessary to distinguish both among groups of words and among dialect regions.

In certain groups of words, -*e* was lost early in Middle English in all regions. Such loss took place in original trisyllables when the preceding syllable bore a secondary accent, presumably after weakening of this accent. Thus Orm (ca. 1200) drops the -*e* of *laffdiȝ* (OE *hlǣfdige*) "lady" and *almess* (OE *ælmesse*) "alms," though he retains it in such words as *wise* (OE *wīse*) "manner" and *pride* (OE *þridda*) "third." The same process is illustrated by the loss of -*e* in Romance words with originally accented suffixes ending in -*e*, such as *manere* and *mesure;* shift of the accent back to the first syllable was presumably followed by weakening of the suffix (see above, pp. 138–39). Similarly, inflectional -*e* in dissyllabic adjectives such as *wurði* was subject to early loss. Association with weakening of accent in the preceding syllable is shown also by the early loss of -*e* in words receiving little accent in phrase groups, e.g. *hir* "her" (OE *hire*), *sir* when used as a title (OF *sire*) beside *sirë* used independently, and *when* (OE *hwænne*) beside stressed *whennë*.[25]

Final -*e* was retained longest following the stem in words accented in phrase groups, e.g. in *sone* "son" (OE *sunu*), *grene* "green" (OE *grēne*), *place* (OF), and *large* (OF). In these words silencing of -*e* took place earliest in the North (here as in other respects the least conservative dialect area) and spread gradually toward the South. It is generally agreed that -*e* had ceased entirely to be pronounced by the end of the thirteenth century in the North, by the mid-fourteenth century in the North Midlands, and by the early fifteenth century in the South Midlands and South.[26] In comparing the treatment of -*e* in the verse of *Gawain* with its treatment in Chaucer, therefore, it is important to remember that the former belongs to the Northwest Midland, the latter to the Southeast Midland, dialect region. We should expect Chaucerian verse to be the more conservative of the two.[27]

Metrical evidence bearing on the pronunciation of -*e* will be discussed below. Orthographical evidence for loss of -*e* is of course provided by its omission where originally present; thus in the Cotton MS of *Cursor* we find such spellings as *hert* 43 "heart" (OE *heorte*), *herth* 71 "earth" (OE *eorðe*), *tell* 12 "[I] tell" (OE *telle*), and *wyn* 72 "[to] win" (OE *winnan*). In later MSS we find that -*e* is not only omitted where originally present, but added to words in which it could never have been sounded.[28] Such "irrational" treatment of -*e* is common in the MS of *Gawain*, as in *wroʒt* 3 "[he] wrought" (OE *worhte*), *laye* 30 "lay, song" (OF *lai*), and *Gawayne* 1619 (OF -*wain*, -*vain*).[29] Loss of -*e* is indicated also by rhymes between words originally having -*e* and words lacking it. Numerous rhymes of this sort appear in *Cursor Mundi*, e.g. from the Cotton MS, *Adam: nam* "name" (OE *nama*), 405–406; and *for-þi* (OE *for þȳ*): *dri* "[to] dry" (OE *drȳgan*), 309–10. It should be observed that the evidence of the rhyme itself may or may not be reflected in the spelling. The monosyllabic pronunciation of *name* implied by the rhyme with *Adam* cited above is indicated also by the spelling *nam* in Cotton, but Fairfax has *adam: name*, and Trinity has *Adame: name* (for the dates of these MSS, see below, p. 257, n. 1). Rhymes linking words originally having -*e* to words lacking -*e* are found also in the wheels of *Gawain*, and will be discussed in a later section.

Final -*es* in Middle English occurs chiefly in the pl. and poss. sg. of nouns, in the 3rd pers. sg. pres. indic. of verbs in the North Midlands, and in the 3rd pers. sg. and pl. pres. indic. of verbs in the North.[30] Final -*ed* occurs chiefly in the pret. and pa. ptc. of weak verbs. These endings, unlike -*e*, were preserved until the end of the fourteenth century in all regions in nouns and verbs when immediately preceded by the syllable bearing primary accent, e.g. in *stones, werres, takes, blames, lerned, gained, bihestes, bicomes*, and *avised*. The vitality of the syllables is shown by the fact that the quality of the vowel underwent certain phonetic developments. In the North the spellings -*is* and -*id* became widespread after the thirteenth century; in the West Midlands, -*us* and -*ud*.[31] Sporadic loss of -*es* and -*ed* as syllables in originally dissyllabic words seems to have occurred from the end of the fourteenth century on in phrases like *by Goddes soule*.[32] This phenomenon is comparable to the loss of the vowel of *not* in *isn't, can't*, and so on. Final -*es* and -*ed* continued to be sounded under certain conditions in the modern period. Unlike -*e*, -*ed* is common as an unaccented syllable in sixteenth-century and later verse; it is still heard today as an archaism in poetic and biblical diction. Final -*es* sometimes counts as a syllable in Shakespearean verse, as in *St. Colmes Inch* (*M* 1.2.61), *whales bone* (*LLL* 5.2.332).[33]

Loss of -*ed* and -*es* took place comparatively early in original trisyllables when the preceding syllable bore secondary accent (as in *ladies*) or was unaccented (as in *loveres, answered*). Like -*e*, these syllables were also subject to early loss in words receiving little accent in the phrase, such as *elles* and *whennes*. These processes are thought to have taken place in or by the beginning of the fourteenth century, still earlier in the North.[34]

CHAPTER 6

The Metrical Evidence

MIDDLE ENGLISH rhymed verse provides evidence for the accentuation of Romance words and the treatment of final *-e, -es,* and *-ed*. Metrical evidence depends on scansion, and scansion in turn depends on consistent metrical principles. Such principles can be found in as early a Middle English rhymed poem as *Cursor Mundi*, composed at about the end of the thirteenth century.[1] The verse of *Cursor* makes a particularly appropriate point of departure for the purposes of this study, more so than the relatively familiar verse of Chaucer. This is partly because *Cursor* is regionally closer to *Gawain* than Chaucer, and partly because its time of composition precedes that of *Gawain* by more than half a century, so that it may be expected to illustrate something of the metrical tradition from which the rhymed verse of the wheels of *Gawain* is derived. It has the additional advantages of being roughly 30,000 lines long, thus containing abundant material for generalization, and of being extant in a number of MSS, so that textual corruption in one version can frequently be demonstrated from the others.

In general, meter in English results from the recurrence of syllables distinguished by emphasis at what are perceived as rhythmically regular intervals of time. These will here be called chief syllables, and the syllables from which they are distinguished, intermediate syllables; chief and intermediate syllables will be said to occupy chief and intermediate position in the line. This terminology is designed to avoid the difficulty that arises from calling chief syllables "accented" and intermediate syllables "unaccented," when the analysis of particular passages of verse makes it obvious that intermediate syllables may in fact be strongly accented. But the degree of accent they receive in relation to adjacent chief syllables is controlled or limited by the reader's sense of their metrical rank, as it would not be if they were read in a prose passage. It is in this sense that they may be called "subordinate."[2]

The form assumed by Middle English rhymed verse can best be explained as a compromise between native and continental metrical principles. Native verse, as exemplified by Old English poetry and such early Middle English texts as Lawman's *Brut* and *The Proverbs of Alured*, was characterized by a fixed number of chief syllables in the line, with allowance for considerable variation in the number of intermediate syllables. Chief syllables could be directly juxtaposed (as in Sievers' OE metrical types C and D, when the first stressed syllable was long[3]) or separated by one, two, or more intermediate syllables. The resultant fluctuation in syllable count is illustrated by the following lines from the *Brut*:

> Þa loh Arður   ludere stefene.
> Iþonked wurðe drihtene   þe alle domes waldeð.
> [A text, 20825–26][4]

The principles of Old French and accentual Latin verse contrasted sharply with those of native English verse. Adherence to a strict count of syllables was essential in both. In the OF octosyllabic line as written by, for example, Chretïn de Troyes, syllabism was the sole constituent of form, there being, properly speaking, no chief syllables.[5] As adapted into English, this line became quadripartite or tetrameter. Medieval Latin accentual verse was also syllabic, but it differed from Old French octosyllabic verse in having a regular number of chief syllables. It insisted also on alternation between chief and intermediate syllables within line or half-line units; in other words juxtaposition of chief syllables was avoided. In iambic or trochaic meters chief syllables were separated by one intermediate syllable, in anapestic or dactylic meters by two.[6] As an example of accentual trochaic meter in medieval Latin verse, we may take the opening of an anonymous English poem of the twelfth century on the martyrdom of St. Thomas of Canterbury:

> Summo sacerdotio / Thomas sublimatus
> est in virum alium / subito mutatus.[7]

Both Old French and accentual Latin verse are of course characterized by end-rhyme, which corresponds as a formal constituent to alliteration in Old English verse.

The rhymed couplets of *Cursor Mundi* resemble Old French octosyllabic couplets; the poet is known to have used at least one Old French source having this form.[8] But the verse owes something also to Latin accentual iambic and trochaic meters, and it has a flexibility in syllable count that is reminiscent of the native tradition. A metrical survey of the poem, disregarding all lines containing phonetically problematic words—i.e. Romance words whose accentuation is in doubt and words in which final -*e* may or may not be pronounced—makes possible the identification of a normal or statistically preponderant accentual-syllabic pattern, together with variants of more or less frequent occurrence.[9] The normal pattern may be expressed in metrical notation as x C x C x C x C, C indicating chief syllables and x intermediate syllables. Occasionally there is an unaccented syllable at the end of the line providing a feminine ending. In this normal pattern and its variants one observes that as a rule juxtaposition of chief syllables is avoided. There is, however, a pattern, exemplified fairly frequently, in which such juxtaposition does occur. The chief syllables involved are the second and third, and the omission of an intermediate syllable between them is, as it were, compensated for by the presence of an additional intermediate syllable in the next unit of the line.[10] This is the "reversed foot" of traditional metrical terminology; the pattern is x C x C C x x C (x). A reversed foot may also begin the line, the pattern then being C x x C x C x C (x), or the initial unaccented syllable may simply be omitted, producing the pattern C x C x C x C (x). This last is the "headless line" which is found also in Chaucerian tetrameter.

The first chief syllable of the line is never preceded by more than one intermediate syllable. But two intermediate syllables may fall between chief syllables even if an intermediate syllable has not previously been omitted in the line. The additional syllable usually comes after the second chief syllable, less frequently after the first. The patterns are x C x C x x C x C (x) and x C x x C x C x C (x). A headless variant of the former, with the pattern C x C x x C x C (x), occurs fairly frequently. The conditions under which an additional intermediate syllable can be admitted between chief syllables are, however, strictly limited. The sequence C x x is usually made up of a dissyllabic word plus an unaccented monosyllable

METRICAL EVIDENCE   147

such as a preposition or the definite article. The first syllable of the former may or may not be long; the second is as a rule phonetically light in that it is unaccented and ends in a vowel (e.g. -*ly*, -*y*) or a single consonant (e.g. -*er*). Certain words, such as *fader*, *oþer*, and *bodi*, recur in such sequences with conspicuous frequency. The suffix-syllables -*y*, from OE -*iʒ*, LOE -*ī*, and -*ly* in adjs. and advs., from OE -*līc*(*e*), ON -*liʒ*(*e*), became short in Middle English in words like *any*, *holy*, and *gladly* (see *Historische Grammatik*, No. 443). Such syllables are presumably unaccented in *Cursor* in intermediate position, though they sometimes receive the accent in rhyme (see, e.g. 7432, 11659, where the second syllable of *weri* "weary," OE *weriʒ*, rhymes with *melodi* and *bi* "by" respectively; cf. Luick, n. 1). As a result, the time intervals between chief syllables in C x x C sequences do not differ significantly from those in C x C sequences. In cases where the second intermediate syllable begins with a vowel, the first should perhaps be elided; the possibility of alternative scansions with and without elision will be indicated below where relevant.

The following lines, all quoted from the Cotton MS, illustrate the normal form and its most common variants:

```
    x   C x C x  C  x C
Man yhernes rimes for to here 11              [1]
    x C  x  C  x  C   x Cx
To win þe blis he had forlosin                [714]
    C  x    x C   C x x C
Al þat scho badd gladli he did                [20137]
    C  x   x C   C   x  x C
Sum in þe air, sum in þe lift                 [495]
    C x x   C    x  C x  C
Mast es it wroght for frankis man             [239]
    C x   C  x C x  C
Selden was for ani chance
    C x  C  x   C   x  C
Praised Inglis tong in france                 [245–46]
    C x C  x   C   x    C  x
Ne þe nedder was noght bittur                 [697]
```

```
   x   Cx    Cx  ⎡ xC    xC
   Of July Cesar ⎨ þe emparour                    [3-4]
                 ⎢  C    xC
                 ⎣ þe‿emparour

   x  Cx   Cx  x    C  x   C
   Mi moder bodi kep wel to me              [20688]

   x  Cx  x   C    x   C    x  C
   Mi bodi þou kepe fra þaim, i sai         [20333]

   C   xCx    x   Cx   C
   O mi fader þat þus es dight              [11854]

   C   x   x   Cx   x   C    x  C
   Ar þat þi broiþer be commen in            [3642]

   C  x    x ⎡ C x  x   Cx     Cx
   þou art my⎨ sister and i þi broþer        [2410]
             ⎢  C   x
             ⎣ sister‿and

   Cx x    C    x  x   Cx   C
   Naked and hungri sco cled & fede         [20121]
```

The tendency to avoid juxtaposition of chief syllables, except where compensation follows to form a "reversed foot," [12] may be further illustrated by lines in which normal word order is reversed to avoid such juxtaposition, e.g.:

```
   x   C  ẋC   x Cx    C
   For qua bigin wil ani thing               [4379]

   x  C  x   Cx   CxC
   To planted be in paradise                [11715]
```

A study of the *Cursor* MSS is instructive with regard to the relationship between meter and the scribal transmission of texts in Middle English. In Cotton, generally considered the closest to the original poem of the four MSS printed in parallel columns by EETS, there are many lines in which the inflectional ending of the genitive singular or the plural of monosyllabic nouns is spelled -*s* rather than -*es*. Since *Cursor* was composed at about the end of the thirteenth century, such forms must have been pronounced as dissyllables in the spoken language of the poet (see above, pp. 142-43). The omission of the unaccented syllable results in many

METRICAL EVIDENCE

cases in a metrical pattern which violates the principles described above as governing the juxtaposition of chief syllables. An example is 904 "In soru þou sal þi berns [children] ber," in which the orthography implies the inadmissible pattern x C x x C x C C. The missing syllable is in fact supplied in the other three MSS of the EETS edition; F has *barnys*, G *childer*, and T *children*. In 528 "And mans hefd has thirls seuen" the ending of the genitive singular is omitted in *mans*, that of the plural in *thirls*. F has *mannes, þirlis*, G has *manys, thirlis*, and the wording of T is altogether different. The inflectional ending of the genitive singular is entirely omitted in 266 "In crist nam our bok be-gin"; F and G have *cristes*, T has *cristis*. The ending of the 3rd pers. sg. of the pres. indic. is omitted in 548 "O thyng man liks, il or welle"; G has *likis*, T has *likeþ*; F omits the line. The *-ed* of the weak preterite is omitted in 6278 "And drun mani hundreth score"; F has *drowned*, G *drenklid*, and T *drenched*. These spellings are to be accounted for in terms of the date of the Cotton manuscript, which reflects the pronunciation of a period later than the composition of the poem.

In the lines discussed above, orthography implies fewer syllables than one would expect in terms either of metrical principles or historical phonology. But orthography may in certain cases imply more syllables than were originally intended. In 100 "Was neuer hir mak, ne neuer sal be" a reading of both instances of *neuer* as dissyllabic results in the unusual pattern x C x x C x C x x C. Although the spelling in all four MSS is *neuer*, it is possible that the poet intended the monosyllabic pronunciation reflected in *nerþe-less* (21247) and found also, with the spelling *ner*, in the A version of the *Brut* (see *OED* s.v. *ne'er*). In 4696 "Tilmen [plowmen] oueral þe land a-boute" a reading of *oueral* as trisyllabic results in the pattern C x x x C x C x C, which to my knowledge is never found elsewhere in the poem. Here the reduced pronunciation *o'erall* is certainly intended. (G has "Plomen ouer all þe land aboute," T has "Plowemen ouer al þe lond aboute," F diverges with "til alle men in lande a-boute," perhaps misunderstanding *tilmen*.)

It is possible, then, to apply to the orthography of a Middle English text principles developed through a study of nonproblematic lines, and to assume failure of the orthography to reflect the pronunciation intended by the poet, where such an assumption does not conflict with findings of historical phonology. This will be found true also in the metrical analysis of *Gawain*.

It will be obvious from the above discussion that a metrical text such as *Cursor* has certain limitations as a source of evidence for accentual practices in Middle English. First of all, scansions can at best indicate the relationship C x, that is, the accentual predominance of one syllable over another, without specifying the *degree* of predominance. The C x relationship is exemplified equally by the two syllables of *goddhed* in 561 "His goddhed es in trinite" and the two syllables of *thinges* in 563 "Minning and þat o thingës thrin." Second, the variant metrical patterns of *Cursor* are such that only occurrences in certain positions in the line can be used as evidence. Occurrences in initial position must be ruled out, since the first two syllables may scan either C x or x C; such a line as 1520 "Musik, þat es þe sune o sang" does not tell us which syllable of *musik* is accentually predominant. Occurrences in mid-position are usually questionable because of the existence of the patterns x C x C x x C x C and C x C x x C x C. Such a line as 551 "For þis resun þat ȝee haue hard" (551) might strike the reader initially as having the pattern x C x C x C x C, with the second syllable of *resun* occupying chief position, but

C x C x x C x C
For þis resun þat ȝee haue hard

certainly cannot be ruled out and in fact comes to seem the more likely possibility after prolonged study of the poem.

Discounting these metrically ambiguous cases, one can find throughout the poem numerous clear scansions indicating the accentual predominance of one syllable over another. Although *musik* in line 1520 is ambiguous, it must clearly be scanned C x two lines later in 1522 "He drou þan oute o musik neu," since otherwise an inadmissible pattern x C x C x x C C results. Although *resun* is ambiguous in 551, it is clearly scanned C x two lines later in 553 "Bot resun yett, al herd ȝee noght," since otherwise there results the inadmissible pattern x x C C x C x C.

A full account of the metrical treatment of the Romance words in *Cursor* could, considering the size of the text, take up a volume in itself. The material that follows is drawn partly from a detailed study of sections of the poem, partly from the line references given for particular words in the glossary.

With regard to Romance words composed of stem plus suffix, the evidence is clear and consistent. When they occur *within* the line, these words regularly scan C x; that is, the suffix is subordinated to the stem. At the *end* of the line they scan x C, the suffix providing the rhyming syllable. The same word may be scanned both ways in successive lines, as with *merci* and *sarmon* in the following passages:

Fra ful hei he [Lucifer] fell fullaw
. . .
Þar he ne has merci neuermare;
For god aght noght gif þam mercy
Þat þar efter wil not cri.   [481, 484–86]

Þan bicom cristen al þat tun,
Þat petre soght wit his sarmon,
O sarmon wald he nawight [G na wight; T no wey] blin.
        [19795–97]

Passages in which the same word is repeated a number of times are especially indicative. *Castel*, for example, in "The parable of the Castle of Love and Grace" (9877 ff.) is scanned C x within the line in 9877, 9879, 9881, 9893, 9911, 9931, 9933, 9963, 10006, and 10066, but x C in rhyme in 10015 and 10035. *Angel*, in the story of the birth of John the Baptist (10935 ff.), scans C x within the line in 10956, 10958, 11016, 11089, and 11155; it does not appear in rhyme. *Baptize*, in the episode of the baptism of Jesus by John (12828 ff.) is scanned C x within the line in 12846, 12847, 12849, 12854, and 12857 but x C in rhyme in 12867.

Since the pattern x C would be as useful within the line as C x, its consistent avoidance in that position indicates that it represents an artificial mode of accentuation used solely for purposes of rhyme. Further evidence for its artificiality may be found in the treatment of native stem-suffix derivatives, which were certainly accented on the stem in the spoken language; these native words too are scanned C x within the line and x C in rhyme. Thus *maidan* 78 rhymes with *nan*, *drightin* "God" 179 with *vyn*, *duelland* "dwelling" (pr. ptc.)

392 with *stand*, and *weri* "weary" 7432, 11659, with *melodi* and *bi* "by," respectively. The practice of rhyming on the suffix, using both native and Romance words, is familiar to us from the verse of Chaucer. It undoubtedly reflects the influence of Old French verse, in which similar rhymes were of frequent occurrence. Compare, for example, the following lines of Robert Grosseteste's *Chasteau d'amour* with the parallel lines of *Cursor*:

Grosseteste 245–46:	Cursor 9557–58:
Kar dautre rien neurent envie	For he ne had neuer sa gret envie
Fors kavoir li en lur baillie.	Als þis man for to be baillie.[13]

It is important to note that this artificial shifting of the accent in rhyme implies a pronunciation preserving the full form of the suffix. In such a pronunciation the difference in degree of accent between the two syllables is slight and the balance can readily be tilted in favor of the syllable which is normally subordinate. It would be difficult for a modern speaker to shift artificially the accent of *battle* or *travel*, words in which the original suffix has been reduced. But such a shift can easily be made in *travail*. Similarly, in Wallace Stevens' line "When amorists grow bald, then amours shrink" ("Le Monocle de mon Oncle"), *amours* can be read C x, as the meter suggests, by one who pronounces the word in accordance with its original French form, giving the initial vowel its distinct quality rather than reducing it to the indeterminate sound. A similar balance between syllables is required for the sort of accentual fluctuation which occurs in, for example, *uphill* in the phrases "an úphill walk" and "a walk uphíll," discussed by Jespersen in his "Notes on Metre."[14] We say "Fórward march" but not "to march forwárd"; the reduction of the second syllable of *forward* prevents it from receiving the predominant accent. In *Cursor* the prefix *un-* in 11815 "Þat caitif vn-meth and vn-meke" seems to exhibit this sort of accentual fluctuation (cf. *unmade* in modern English "to leave an únmade bed" and "to leave a bed unmáde").

It is possible also that certain Romance and native words should be scanned x C, with an artificial shift of accent to the suffix, in mid-line. Typical cases are *wengeance* in 1928 "O þis

METRICAL EVIDENCE   153

wengeance þat i haue tan" and *wirscip* in 11478 "For wit wirscip
i will him se." If these words are scanned C x, the pattern
C x C x x C x C results, as in 9877 "In a castel als here es tald,"
where C x for *castel* is strongly indicated by its treatment elsewhere in the passage. But the syllables *wengeance þat* and *wirscip i*
form considerably heavier C x x sequences than *castel als*, heavier
than the meter usually allows. Perhaps, then, *wengeance, wirscip,*
and other words with heavy suffixes should be scanned x C in
lines of this type. Native stem-suffix derivatives seem to be scanned
x C in mid-line occasionally in Chaucerian verse; thus we should
perhaps scan *-ness* as a chief syllable both in *Cursor* 11331 "And
for gladnes he gaf a cri" and *TC* 1:116 "Of his goodnesse he
gladede hire anon."

The metrical treatment of words composed of prefix plus stem
shows, as one would expect, less uniformity than that of stem-
suffix derivatives. On the whole there is more shift of accent back
to heavy prefixes than is reflected in modern English, especially in
words beginning with *com-* or *con-*. In addition to *counseil* n. and
v., which are scanned C x (2216, 13151) in accordance with modern usage, the scansion C x is shown by *comand* v. (6809, 10649),
confund (730), and *consail* "concealed" (27411; see glossary). So
far as I have observed, the prefix *de-* never occurs in chief position. *Defaut* (13354), *denunced* (29251), *desired* (15066), and
deuised (9960) have the scansion x C (x). *Despit* (2610, 7825)
scans x C but *respit* (21508) scans C x. Variant forms are indicated for *puruai* "purvey," which scans both C x (8311) and x C
(8777). There are a few instances of x C scansions differing from
modern usage, e.g. *prophet* (706) and *conquest* (2540).

Romance words of three syllables or more are comparatively
infrequent in *Cursor*, and usually occur at the end of the line in
rhyme, so that the possibility of an artificial shift of stress must be
reckoned with. Metrical evidence for the accentuation of these
words is therefore scanty. Dissyllabic *aunters*, scanning C x,[15] is
both implied by the spelling and metrically permissible in 12 "Þat
aunters sere I here of tell." *Purueance* clearly scans C x C in intralinear position in 11677 "Vr water purueance es gan," as does
contenance in 3368 "Sco tint na contenance wit þis." *Commandment*, which probably occurs more frequently than any word of
this class in the text, presents difficulties because of the variety of

its forms. It seems clearly to scan C x C in intralinear position in 340 "All his comament was don." The spelling *comament* implies reduction of the stem, presupposing accent on prefix and suffix (see above, p. 139). But one cannot infer from the spelling the pronunciation intended by the poet. A tetrasyllabic form *comandëment*, with accent on the stem, would result in the scansion C x x C x C x C; this pattern is admissible in the metrical system of the poem, so that *comandëment* cannot be ruled out on metrical grounds. F has the spelling *comandement*, G has *comandment*, T has *biddying*. In 11720 "His comanment was noght vndon" the same ambiguity presents itself. Here F has the same wording as C, but G and T have "His comandement was done." This last must be scanned as a headless line with the tetrasyllabic stem-accented form. The most one can say is that trisyllabic *commandment*, with accent on prefix and suffix, is always a *possible* reading in C.

It was pointed out above, in connection with the phonology of -*e*, that rhymes between words originally having -*e* and words originally lacking -*e* are of frequent occurrence in *Cursor*, and that the pronunciation implied by such rhymes may or may not be reflected in the spelling. Our concern here is with the intralinear treatment of -*e*, insofar as it can be deduced from the metrical principles of the text. Sounding of -*e* within the line is indicated where otherwise such patterns as x C C x C x C, x C x C x C C, etc., would result. The validity of the metrical principles involved is shown by the fact that in these lines the relevant word originally had -*e*, whether or not this -*e* is orthographically represented. As examples, we may cite 1014 "Flours þar es wit suetë [OE *swēte*] smelles" and 11375 "Wit richë [OE *rīce*, OF *riche*] giftës þat þai broght,"[16] 479 "Fra þan his nam[ë] [OE *nama*] changed was," and 6236 "Þe egypcien to seruë þar." The -*e* of the weak adjectival declension is sometimes to be sounded, as in 6270 "Þe brad[ë] wai he did him in" (F has *brade way*, G *brod watir*, T *brode watir*), 6808 "Þe first[ë] child þat þe es born," 9979 "Þat sco hir ches þe first[ë] dai,"[17] and others.

But although such lines can be found throughout the poem, they are infrequent, particularly in comparison with the sounding of -*e* in Chaucerian verse.[18] Thus in "The Passage of the Red Sea," lines

6199–300, there are only two cases in which sounding of -*e* is metrically necessitated (see above, 6270, 6236). In certain lines the poet (or the scribe) inserts an unaccented word where -*e* might have been used, e.g. in 11567 "Tua yeir or less, i tel it yow" (cf. Chaucer, "How high, I can not tellë yow," *HF* 547).

We may now turn to the wheels of *Gawain*, which provide an ideal gateway to a metrical study of the long lines. It is possible to take for granted the basic structure of the short line—one of three chief syllables [19]—and the metrical patterns present fewer difficulties than the alliterative verse of the poem. From the wheels, one may hope to learn something about the accentuation of Romance words and the treatment of final -*e*; this information in turn will be useful in studying the long lines. With regard to the treatment of -*e*, the short lines, including the bob, have the further advantage of containing about three hundred rhymes. It is with a survey of these rhymes that our examination of the wheels will begin.

There are at least two cases in which -*e* is unquestionably sounded in rhyme in *Gawain*, once when *forsoþe* "forsooth" (OE *for sōþe*, with inflectional -*e* preserved in a "petrified dative" [20]) rhymes with *to þe* "to thee" (413, 415), and once where *waþe* "danger" (ON *vaði*) rhymes with *ta þe* "take thee," imper. sg. (2355, 2357). The reader will recall similar rhymes in Chaucer, e.g. *Troye: joie: fro ye*, *TC* 1.2, 4, 5. But whereas -*e* was still sounded in the spoken language in the second half of the fourteenth century in Chaucer's London, it had ceased to be sounded in the Northwest Midland dialect region of the *Gawain*-poet by the middle of the century—i.e. several decades before the presumed time of composition of *Gawain*. For the *Gawain*-poet, then, these rhymes must have represented an obsolete mode of pronunciation. They were doubtless traditional in phraseology, inherited from the period when -*e* was still sounded in the spoken language.

These two rhymes seem to indicate that -*e* is to be sounded in other rhyme-words as well. But there is evidence to the contrary in the form of rhymes between words originally having -*e* and words lacking it. The presence of such rhymes, as well as regional provenience, suggests that the verse of the wheels of *Gawain* is more closely connected in metrical tradition with *Cursor* than with Chaucerian verse. In the rhyme system of the latter, words having

-*e* regularly rhyme with other words of the same category, and the same is true for words lacking -*e*. Significant exceptions occur in *The Tale of Sir Thopas*, where, in such rhymes as *Thopas : gras* (OF *grace;* normally dissyllabic in Chaucer), similar combinations in the popular metrical romances appear to be parodied.[21]

In compiling from the wheels of *Gawain* a list of rhymes between words having -*e* and words lacking -*e* it is necessary to proceed with caution. Each rhyme-word must be a clear case, the various possibilities for analogical acquisition or loss of -*e* being ruled out. The first rhyme in *Gawain, wynne : þer-inne,* seems at first to qualify for inclusion in such a list (*wynne* comes from OE *wynn, þer-inne* from OE *þær-inne*). But *wynne* might have had a sounded -*e* in Middle English (the -*e* of the MS is of course not phonetically conclusive). It is derived from an OE feminine noun of the class that often acquired -*e* in Middle English by analogy (see above, p. 140). And it is the object of a preposition, so that it could conceivably have a sounded -*e* as a "petrified dative," like *soþe*, in a traditional phrase. In general, nouns whose Old English ancestors were feminine, and those which, whatever their ancestry, are used as the objects of prepositions, must be ruled out as examples of words lacking -*e*. Nor are adverbs eligible as -*e*-less words, since any adverb could acquire -*e* in Middle English by analogy (see above, p. 140). Adjectives are ruled out if used in the plural or even as the objects of prepositions, although the survival of -*e* in the dat. sing. of the adjective in late Middle English is highly improbable.

Despite these difficulties and despite the small number of rhymes in the text, as compared to the 15,000 odd rhymes of *Cursor*, it is possible to compile a list of respectable size (cf. the examples cited by TG, p. xxi). There are, first, eight rhymes between originally m. or n. nouns or proper names, whose ancestors lacked -*e* and which are not used as the object of prepositions, rhyming with verb forms whose endings are derived from -*an*, -*en*, and -*e:*

1. *day : say* (infin.), 298, 300
2. *Gawan*[22] *: frayn* (infin.), 487, 489
3. *lyȝt* (OE *lēoht,* n.) *: diȝt* (3rd sg. pret. indic., or infin., obj. of *con*, 993), 992, 994
4. *payne* (infin.) *: Gawayn,* 1042, 1044

5. *graunte* (infin.) : *seruaunt* (OF *servant*, ref. to a man), 1841, 1845
6. *rewarde* (3rd pl. pres. indic.) : *Reynarde* (with scribally added *-e* [23]), 1918, 1920
7. *grone* (infin.) : *tone* (with scribally added *-e;* variant, with southern vowel, of *tan,* contr. of *taken;* cf. 1811), 2157, 2159
8. *lorde* (with scribally added *-e;* OE *hláford*) : *acorde* (infin.), 2403, 2405

There are three rhymes between words lacking *-e* and nouns or adjectives originally having *-e* in all cases:

9. *haste* (OF *haste*) : *blaste* (with scribally added *-e;* OE *blǽst* m.), 780, 784
10. *done* (with scribally added *-e;* OE *don,* pa. ptc.) : *sone* (OE *sōna*), 1287, 1289
11. *al one* (OE *eall āna*) : *tone* (see above, 7), 2155, 2159

There is one rhyme between the name *Gawain* and an adjective in the plural:

12. *Gawayn : fayn* (mod. *frekeʒ*), 838, 840

There is one rhyme between a verb in the infinitive and an adjective, originally lacking *-e,* in the ns:

13. *strayne : gayn* (ON *gegn*), 176, 178

What can be inferred from these rhymes? Whereas the rhymes of Chaucerian verse imply that *-e,* if present, ought always to be sounded (else why supply each rhyming word in *-e* with a partner of the same category?), the rhymes of *Gawain,* like those of *Cursor,* imply the opposite: that *-e* is not to be sounded at all, even when it is present in both words of a rhyming pair.[24] The two exceptions to this rule involve not a pair of words having *-e* but one word of that category and a phrase ending in an unaccented pronoun. No principle can be invoked as decreeing the sounding of *-e* in such a rhyme as *aboute* (OE *on-būtan*) : *doute* (OF *dute*), 440, 442, or *þonk[e]* (infin.) : *wlonk[e]* (pl.), 1975, 1977. To appeal to Chaucerian verse is to assume what has not been proved: that the *Gawain*-poet and Chaucer composed according to the same metrical principles. It also disregards what historical phonology tells us about the differing treatment of *-e* in the spoken language of the two poets. A priori, we should expect *-e* to be sounded much less frequently in the verse of *Gawain* than in that of Chaucer.

Aside from the fact that the line is shorter by one chief syllable, the lines of the wheels are similar in their metrical patterns to the four-part lines of *Cursor*. Surveying those lines in which the words do not present problems of pronunciation, we find that the normal or most frequently exemplified pattern is x C x C x C, with an occasional additional syllable as a feminine ending. Additional intermediate syllables forming anapestic feet are proportionately more frequent than in *Cursor*, and sometimes are found at the beginning of the line. Many lines have two such syllables. The line has the headless forms C x C x C and C x C x C x. The pattern C x x C x C (x) also occurs; in relation to the normal pattern, the first two syllables of such lines may be said to constitute a reversed foot.

The patterns so far described may be exemplified by the following lines:

    x C x   C x   C
He stiȝtleȝ stif in stalle   [104]
    x C x   C x   C x
As hit is stad & stoken   [33]
    x x   C x   C x   C
To þe gome he watȝ ful gayn   [178]
    x C   x x C x   C
I deme hit not al for doute   [246]
    x C x   C x x   C
Þat vgly bodi þat bledde   [441]
    x x C   x   x C x C
I be-seche now with saȝeȝ sene   [341]
    x C x x C x x C
& comlyly kysses his face   [1505]
    C x C x C
Cast vnto þat wyȝe   [249]
    C x C   x C x
Gladly, sir, for soþë   [415]
    C x   x C x   C
Vnder his dynetteȝ dryȝe   [202]

METRICAL EVIDENCE   159

The question now arises whether juxtaposition of chief syllables is admissible in the metrical patterns of the wheels, and if so, under what conditions. There are certain lines in which an intermediate syllable seems to be omitted between the first and second chief syllables, with an additional intermediate syllable as compensation in the next unit of the line. The result is a "reversed second foot," with the pattern x C C x x C (there is no headless form of this type). Conclusive examples are scarce; in some cases scansion depends on rhetorical subordination of one word to another, as in 1042 "Þe lorde fast can hym payne," where *fast* seems to call for more emphasis than the auxiliary verb *can*. 1975 "Þe lorde Gawayn con þonk" is a clear example of the pattern if we assume, as there is every reason for doing, that *Gawayn* is accented on the first syllable (for the accentual treatment of the name, see below, p. 165). In these two lines the *-e* of *lorde* (OE *hlāford*) is orthographic only, so that juxtaposition of chief syllables cannot be avoided by reading dissyllabic *lordë*. If the possibility of x C C x x C is admitted, the pattern applies also to certain lines in which the first important word originally had *-e*. The reversed second foot makes the sounding of this *-e* unnecessary. Examples are 365 "& gif [infin.] Gawen þe game," 1043 "To holde lenger þe knyȝt," 1122 "To bed [cf. Chaucerian *to beddë*; McJimsey, p. 69] ȝet er þay ȝede," 1124 "Þe olde lorde of þat leude," and 1556 "Hir leue [OE *lēaf*, f.] fayre con scho fonge." In the last three, alliteration between *ȝet* and *ȝede*, *lorde* and *lede*, and *fayre* and *fonge* should be noted as reinforcing rhetorical emphasis.

Juxtaposition of chief syllables without compensation in the form of an additional intermediate syllable seems to occur in eight lines. In all of these, however, an *-e* is present in the original form of the first word receiving chief emphasis. If we assume sounding of *-e* in these words, such patterns as x C C x C and x C x C C are consistently avoided throughout the poem, and the treatment of *-e* in the rhymed lines of *Gawain* proves to be similar to its treatment in *Cursor*. The eight lines in question follow, with the etymologies of the relevant words: [25]

       x   Cx   C   x   C
1. Til *meȝel-mas*[*se*] mone   [532]
    The *-e* of *masse* (OE *mæssan*, g.s. of *mæsse*) has been scribally omitted.

```
         x   C  x  C  x  C
2. Wyth ryche cote-armure                                      [586]
         OF riche, OE rīce.
         x  C x  C  x C
3. He made non abode                                           [687]
         OE macode, contracted in early ME to madë.
       x  x   C  x  C   x  C
4. Bitwene two so dyngne dame                                 [1316]
         OF digne.
     x C x   C  x C
5. Bi þat on prynne syþe                                      [1868]
         LOE prinna, from ON prinn-r; see OED s.v. thrin
         and BT s.v. prinna.
        C  x  x C   x  C
6. Thus to þe derk[e] nyȝt                                    [1177]
         The inflectional -e of the wk. adj. decl. has been scrib-
         ally omitted (OE deorc).
      x   C  x  x  C  x   C
7. Þaȝe he be a sturn[e] knape                                [2136]
     x    x C
   þaȝe he be
         The -e of sturne (OE styrne; see TG and GDS glos-
         saries) has been omitted.
      x C  x   x C  x C  x
8. & þer-for þat tappe ta þe                                  [2357]
         OF tape, not OFris. tap; for the two alternatives, see
         TG and GDS glossaries.
```

There is a single anomalous line: "Þe knyȝt wel þat tyde" (736) Here it is possible that a metrically awkward headless form, with *þe* as the first chief syllable, should be imposed, or that we are to reckon with a pseudo-archaic form *knyȝtë*, such as is occasionally implied by the meter in the stanzaic *Morte Arthure*.[26] I prefer to think, however, that the line, like some of the long lines, is missing a word or otherwise corrupt. Corruption may be indicated by the fact that alliteration is lacking, since this is unusual in the wheels.

There is observable also a countertendency in the short line to avoid sequences of more than two intermediate syllables. Where

METRICAL EVIDENCE

three intermediate syllables seem to occur in sequence, it is regularly possible to reduce them to two by contraction. The *-ed* of the preterite of weak verbs and the verbal and nominal *-es* are the syllables most frequently suppressed (see above, p. 142); similar contractions are occasionally found in Chaucerian verse, e.g. *CT. Prol.* A 589 "His heer was by his erys ful round yshorn," *CT. Fkl.* F 946 "He seyde he lovede, and was biloved no thyng." Typical examples from the wheels are:

    x C   x x C x C
He *sayned* hym in syþes sere   [761]

    x C   x x C   x x C
He *hurteʒ* of þe houndeʒ, & þay   [1452]
    Perhaps we should also read *houndeʒ* as monosyllabic.

    x x   C xC   x C
To *Goddeʒ* wylle I am ful bayn   [2158]

    x C   x   x C x C
He *lened* with þe nek & lutte   [2255]

    C   x x   C   x   C
Leteʒ me ouer-take your wylle   [2387]
    Here *ouer* is read as *o'er* as in *Cursor* 4696 (C), cited above.

Elision is called for in 147:

    x   C (x)   x   x C   x   C
Forwonder[27] of his hwe men hade

An exception to the rule seems to occur in 83:

    x C   x x   x C(x)   x C
A *semloker* þat euer he syʒe

and another in 2478:

    C x   x   x C(x)   x   C
Whider-warde-so-euer he wolde

although *warde* may not have been in the line as originally composed.

   Metrical evidence for the accentuation of Romance words in the wheels is limited mainly to stem-suffix derivatives. The treatment of these is again reminiscent of *Cursor*. As rhyme-words, they must be scanned with chief emphasis on the suffix, but in intralinear position the metrical evidence consistently shows chief emphasis on the stem. One can cite a number of lines in which the scansion x C of stem-suffix derivatives would result in inadmissible metrical patterns such as x C x C C and x C C x C; no such patterns result from the scansion C x. Examples are the following:

C x x C x C Set in his *semblaunt* sene	[148]
x C x C x C & sayd, 'sir *cortays* knyȝt'	[276]
x C x C x C Þe kyng & *Gawen* þare	[463]
x C x C xC A *porter* pure plesaunt	[808]
x C x C x C 'Graunt *mercy*,' quoþ Gawayn	[838]
x C x C x C Your *seruaunt* be, & schale	[1240]
x Cx C x C Much *solace* (OF *solas*) set þay same	[1318]
x C x C x C When *Gawayn* wyth hym mette	[1370]
x C x C x C x Sir *Gawayn* lis & slepes	[1686]
x C x C x C On bent much *baret* bende	[2115]
x C x C x C x Quoþ *Gawayn*, 'I schunt oneȝ'	[2280]

From these instances we may infer the scansion C x also for stem-suffix derivatives such as *batayl* (OF *bataille*), in which the suffix originally had -*e*. The accentuaton of derivatives of this category cannot be deduced from the meter of the lines in which they occur, since suffix accentuation plus sounding of -*e* would result in metrically admissible patterns. In 897 "Þis penaunce now ȝe take" it would be metrically possible to read *penáuncë*, the resultant pattern being x x C x C x C. In 277 "If þou craue batayl bare" it

METRICAL EVIDENCE 163

would be possible to read *batáyl[lë]*; the pattern would then be x x C x C x C, with chief emphasis falling on *craue*. These metrically ambiguous lines can be resolved, however, with the aid of the evidence for stem-accentuation cited above; we will prefer to scan:

   x C x   C   x C
Þis *penaunce* now ȝe take
   x C   x   Cx   C
If þou craue *batayl* bare,

and so on.

In view of the treatment of Romance stem-suffix derivatives in intralinear position, it may be concluded that the suffix-accent they receive in rhyme was not used in the spoken language. Similar artificial shift of accent to the suffix in rhyme is exemplified in the wheels for native derivatives, e.g., *talkyng* in 927 "Schal lerne of luf-talkyng" and *laȝande* in 1207 "Wyth lyppeȝ smal laȝande."

CHAPTER 7

The Alliterative Long Line: The Normal Form

THE NATURAL STARTING POINT for a study of the accentuation of Romance words in the long lines is their use in the formal alliterative patterns, since chief emphasis and alliteration may in general be expected to correspond.[1]

Looking first at the Romance derivatives composed of stem and suffix, we find that the alliteration uniformly falls on the stem. This fits with the metrical evidence of the wheels, which shows chief emphasis on the stem for words used in intralinear position in contrast to the artificial suffix-accent of the rhymes. The following words which scan C x in the wheels (see above, p. 162) alliterate on the stem in the long lines:

>   baret, 21, 353, 752
>   cortays, 469, 539, 1511, 2411
>   porter, 813, 2072
>   semblaunt, 468, 1273, 1658
>   seruaunt, 976, 1971
>   solace, 1085, 1624, 1985

Certain other words which occur in the wheels in rhyme but not in intralinear position are found in the long lines alliterating on the stem:

> chapelle (2186 *rh.* spelle), 63, 451, 1674, 2399; elsewhere in the long lines it occurs in the phrase *grene chapel*, alliterating on *g;* cf. 705, 1058
> forest (1149 *rh.* kest); 741
> honours (1813 *rh.* youreʒ); 1038, 1228, 1806, 1963, 2056
> plesaunt (808 *rh.* erraunt); plesaunce 1247
> raysoun (227 *rh.* doun), 392, 1344, 1804

Of particular interest because of the frequency of its occurrence is the proper name *Gawain;* it scans x C as a rhyme-word in 487, 838, 1044, 1619, 1948, and 2156, and C x in intralinear position in the wheels in 463, 1370, 1686, 2280, and also, if we admit the possibility of a reversed foot, in 365 and 1975 (see above, p. 159). In the long lines it uniformly alliterates on *g,* e.g. in 109, 375, 381, etc.; or in the Norman form *Wawan,* on *w,* e.g. 559, etc.

Words composed of prefix plus stem do not show the same consistency of pattern. A word or two closely related words may alliterate on the prefix in one line and on the stem in another. Thus *deserve(d)* alliterates on *d* in 452 and on *s* in 1803; *re-hayte(d)* on *h* in 895 and 1422, on *r* in 1744. *Demay* "dismay" v. alliterates on *d* in 470; *dismayd* alliterates on *m* in 336. Alliteration on the prefix often implies a mode of accentuation contradicting modern usage, as with *deserve.* Additional examples are listed below.

1. Words with *com-* or *con-*,

    a. alliterating on the prefix:

    comaunded "commanded" 366
    comaundeʒ "present my compliments, salute" 2411 [2]
    comended 1629
    comfort n. 1011, 1221, 1254
    comfort v. 1099, 2513
    compas n. 944
    compast v. 1196
    confessed 2391
    conueyed 596
    coundutes 1655
    counseyl n. 347
    counseyl v. 557

    b. alliterating on the stem:

    constrayne 1496
    coundue "conduct" v. 1972

2. Words with *de-, di-,* and *dis-,*

    a. alliterating on the prefix:

    de-liuerly 2009
    de-partyng 1798

deuayed "refused" 1493 (TG read *denayed*, but cf. 1497)
deuised 92
disserued 452
disert n. "that which is deserved" 1266

b. alliterating on the stem:

de-bated 68, 2179
defence 1282
de-fende 1156, 1551
degre 1006
delyuer v. 851
de-paynt 620
de-prece "disemprison" 1219
deprece(d) "oppress, subjugate" 6, 1770
de-vaye 1497
displese 1304, 1839, 2439
dispoyled 860
disport 1292

3. Words with *re-*,

a. alliterating on the prefix:

re-chatande "sounding the recheat" 1911
rechated 1466
rehersed 392, 1243
relece "release" v. 2342
remorde 2434
renay(ed) 1821, 1828
renoun 313, 2434, 2458, 2519
re-sayue 2076
resayt 1168
reuel n. 40, 313, 538, v. 2401
rewarde n. 1804, 2059

b. alliterating on the stem:

refourme 378
repreued 2269
resette 2164

Meschaunce 2195 alliterates on the stem, *meschef* 1774 on the prefix (cf. *bonchef*, alliterating on *b* in 1764; there may have been a tendency to accent *bonchief* and *mischief* on the first syllable to emphasize the opposition of meaning between them [3]).

Words having the prefixes *a-* and *en-*, in contrast to the groups discussed above, alliterate, with one exception, on the stem. Examples with *en-* are: *enbaned* 790, *enbelyse* 1034, *endured* 1517, and *enfoubled* 959; with *a-*: *achaufed* 883, *acheue* 1081, 1107, 1838, 1857, *acole* 1936, 2472, and *a-corde* n. 1384. But *anamayld* "enameled" 169, from OF *enamailler, enameler*, with AF *an-* corresponding to CF *en-*, alliterates on *m*. For information on this verb, the noun from which it is derived, and their variants in ME, see *MED* s.v. *enamelen* v., *enamel* n., and *amal* n.; *OED* s.v. *enamel* v. and sb. and *amel* sb. Cf. the variant *aumayl* in *Gawain* 236, which does not participate in the alliterative pattern.

Among dissyllables of Romance derivation which originally were compounds, alliteration on the first syllable is the rule. Examples are: *maynteines* 2053, *trauayl* n. 2241, *toruayl* n. 1540 (a hybrid form, with influence from ON *torveldi;* see TG, GDS glossaries), and *trauayled* v. 1093; *hawbergh* (<OHG *halsberg* "neckguard") 203, 268; *kerchofes* (OF *cuevrechef*, AF *courchief*) 954.

Among Romance derivatives of three or more syllables, those in *com-* or *con-* alliterate consistently on the prefix. Examples are: *comaundement* 1303, 1501; *compayny* 556, 1011, 1099, etc.; *concience* 1196; *conysaunce* 2026; *countenaunce* 100, 335, 1490, etc. *Conable* 2450, alliterating on *c*, is a Northern reduced form of *covenable*, itself a variant of *convenable* (see TG glossary and the *OED*). Among words in *de-*, *deuocioun* 2192 and *destine* 1752, 2285 alliterate on *d*, but *debonerte* 1273 alliterates on *b*. *Ex-ellently* 2423 seems to show vowel-alliteration; *enterludeȝ* 472 alliterates on *l*. *Remnaunt*, a reduced form of *remenant*, alliterates on *r* in 2342, 2401, but *recreaunt* 456 alliterates on *c*. Among words in *a-* there is proportionately more alliteration on the stem. *Aunter* n., a reduced form of *aventure*, alliterates on the vowel in 27, 2522, 2527, as do *awenture* 29, *auenture* 250, *auenturus* pl. 491, and *auenturus* a. 93. But the aphaeretic form *venture* occurs, with *v*-alliteration, in 2482 (so GDS; TG read *mony aventure*). *A-vanters* 1342, *apparayl* 601, and *a-quoyntance* 975 alliterate on the stem.

For many of the words listed on the preceding pages, reduced forms in Middle English and metrical use in *Cursor* and Chaucer provide evidence for accentual variants in the spoken language which have not descended into modern English but which seem to be implied by the alliteration in *Gawain*. Some of the relevant material is presented below:

> Prefix-accent in Middle English in *command* v., *commandment* has already been discussed. The evidence cited has consisted of scansions in *Cursor* and the reduced form *comament*. Chaucerian scansion regularly indicates accent on the stem for both words, but *RRose* 2307 (Frag. B) "Do it goodly, I comaunde thee," implies a C x scansion for *comaunde*.
>
> *Confess* v. regularly scans with emphasis on the stem in Chaucer; cf. *CT.Squ.* F 494 "Myn harm I wol confessen er I pace." But *confessour* scans C x C in three lines in *CT.Sum.*; cf. D 2239 "Unto my confessour to-day he spak"; also D 2260, 2265.
>
> *Conveyed* scans C x C in *CT.Kn.* A 2737 "And conveyed the kynges worthily." (But accent on the stem is implied in *LGW* F 2305 "And hym conveyeth thourgh the mayster-strete.")
>
> *Debonair* and its derivatives had aphaeretic forms in Middle English presupposing accent on the second syllable; see *OED* s.v. *bonair, bonairly, bonairty*. *Bonerli* "debonairly" is found in *Cursor* 23872 (F) "bonerli to teyche his broþer." Cf. also *BD* 986 "Had as moche debonairte" and *Comp.L.* 102 "Your gentilesse and your debonairtee," in both of which the scansion x C x C is implied.
>
> *Mayntein* scans C x in *CT.Kn.* A 1441 "And gaf hym gold to mayntene his degree." *Mayntene* appears to scan x C x in *CT.Kn.* A 1778 "That wol mayntene that he first bigan," but a headless line with scansion C x is also possible.[4]
>
> ME *creant* a. seems to be an aphaeretic variant of *recreant* (see *OED* s.v. *creant* a.[1]); such a development would presuppose accent on the stem.
>
> *Relees* n. "release" scans C x in *RRose* 4440 (Frag. B) "Shulde ay be relees to my woo." The same scansion for *reles* v. is exemplified in a variant of *Cursor* 20633 (B.M. Additional) "I schal hem reles sone anone" (EETS, 68, p. 1645).

There are five instances of C x scansions of *renon* in Chaucer, e.g. "Ne renoun in this cas, ne veyne glorie," *CT.Kn.* A 2240; cf. also *HF* 1406, *LGW* 1054, *Pity* 63, 86, and *RRose* (Frag. B) 2880. There are also two instances of x C; cf. *Pity* 88, *HF* 1736.

Reward n. scans C x in *LGW* F 375 "That han no reward but at tyrannye"; cf. also *PF* 426 and *RRose* (Frag. B) 3254. There are also instances of x C; cf. *LGW* 1622, *TC* 2.1133, 5.1736.

The above material on prefix-stem derivatives and their treatment in the long lines of *Gawain* gives rise to certain tentative generalizations:

1. For words in *com-* or *con-*, the accentual forms in modern English, together with the Middle English variants which have not descended, indicate that alliterative use in *Gawain* is consistently based on accentual forms existing in the spoken language. In reading the poem we should thus accent the prefix in *comaunded, confessed, comfort* n. and v., *conveyed,* and other words alliterating on *c,* but the stem in *constrayne* and *coundue,* which alliterate on the stem-consonant (see above, p. 165).

2. For words in *re-* the picture is similar, though not as conclusive. We should certainly follow the alliteration in accenting the prefix in *relece, renon, revel* n. and v., and *rewarde* n., and the stem in *refourme, repreued,* and *resette* (modern *receipt;* for the spelling see *OED*). Prefix-accented variants may also have existed for other words in *re-* alliterating on *r* (see lists above), but compare the discussion of the relationship between alliteration and accent, below, pp. 170–71.

3. For words in *de-* or *dis-* there is little or no evidence of forms with prefix-accentuation. Both in *Cursor* and in Chaucer, the metrical treatment of *de-* words seems exclusively to imply accent on the stem. The only exception I have observed is *desert* "wilderness," which scans C x in *HF* 488 "In the desert of Lybye." Similar evidence may be cited from those lines of *Pearl* which can be scanned with fair certainty. Whereas accent on *com-* is implied by 55 "Þaȝ kynde of Kryst me comfort kenned" and 1072 "What schulde þe mone þer compas clym," accent on the stem in words with *de-* or *dis-* is implied in 15 "Þat wont watȝ whyle deuoyde my wrange," 124 "Fordidden my stresse, dystryed my payneȝ," 280

"My grete dystresse þou al todrawez," and 1021 "As John deuysed ʒet saʒ I þare." It should be observed, further, that words in *com-* or *re-* alliterate more frequently on the prefix than on the stem in *Gawain*, and that the reverse is true for words in *de-* or *dis-*.

If the words in *de-* which alliterate on *d-* did not have prefix-accented forms in the spoken language, are we to assume that they received an artificial accent for purposes of alliteration, comparable to that placed on normally unaccented suffixes in rhyme? The answer to this question depends on the relationship between alliteration and accent. It can be shown that the two do not necessarily correspond.

In the first place there is a good deal of latitude in the number and placement of alliterating syllables in the long lines. Although the patterns a a / a x and a a a / a x are statistically preponderant, the variants a x / a x and x a / a x are by no means infrequent; they occur in *Gawain*, according to Oakden's figures (*1*, 190), a total of 99 times. Only one emphatic alliterating syllable, then, is necessary in the first half-line. A second alliterating syllable need not be present at all; it follows that if present, it need not receive chief emphasis. Thus in 1216a "& þat is þe best, be my dome" the alliteration on *be* is not essential to the form, so that there is no need to give the preposition more than the emphasis it would normally receive in relation to other parts of speech. In other first half-lines one of the alliterating syllables is the unaccented native prefix *be-*, as in 1741a "Hir brest bare bifore." Here again, an artificial degree of emphasis is not metrically necessary. These principles may be extended to first half-lines in which the second or third alliterating syllable is *de-*, e.g. 1798 "Now, dere, at þis de-partyng, do me þis ese" and 2009 "De-liuerly he dressed vp er þe day sprenged." Emphasis on the stem in *de-liuerly, de-partyng* is both phonologically probable and metrically permissible.[5]

The second half-line is less varied in form than the first, both in syllable count and in alliteration. An alliterative link with the first half-line is essential.[6] As a rule, the number of alliterating syllables in the second half-line is restricted to one; in a small minority of cases there are two. In a number of lines the single alliterating syllable is a word or prefix which was certainly not emphasized in the spoken language, e.g. the preposition *with* in 987 "Er me wont þe wede, with help of my frendez" and the auxiliary verb *mot* in 2053 "Þe mon hem maynteines, ioy mot he haue." Sometimes it is the prefix *be-*, as in the second half of 1216 "& þat is þe best, be my dome, for me by-houeʒ ⁷ nede" and in 1741 "Hir brest bare bifore, & bihinde eke," of which the first half-lines were cited above. More important, there are lines which are intelligible to the ear only if a nonalliterating syllable in the second half-line receives emphasis at least equal to that on the alliterating syllable:

& layte as lelly til þou me, lude, fynde	[449]
For I haf hunted al þis day, & noʒt haf I geten	[1943]
He myntez at hym maʒtyly, bot not þe mon ryneʒ	[2290]
Wherfore þe better burne me burde be called	[2278]

There is accordingly no need to stress the prefix *de-* even when it is the sole alliterating syllable in the second half-line. Accent on the stem of *disserued* in 452 "Such a dunt as þou hatʒ dalt, disserued þou habbeʒ" corresponds to accent on the stem of *bi-gineʒ* in 112 "Bischop Bawdewyn abof bi-gineʒ þe table," 1571 "He gete þe bonk at his bak, bigyneʒ to scrape," and elsewhere.

It appears that, at least insofar as accentuation is concerned, the alliterative line is closer to the spoken language than the short rhyming line. The relation between accent and rhyme (considering alliteration as "initial rhyme") is more flexible; we do not find an artificial mode of word-accent brought systematically into play. It remains to be seen whether this colloquial character appears also in the treatment of final *-e*.

It has been shown that in the short rhyming lines of *Gawain* -e normally remains unsounded. It functions as a syllable twice to provide a rhyme with an unaccented word, and about a dozen times in intralinear position to avoid uncompensated juxtaposition of chief syllables. Its sporadic sounding is thus warranted by principles of rhyme and meter, and analogous principles must be established to warrant its sounding in the long alliterative lines. But there is no justification for assuming that the metrical principles of the short lines will hold true for the long lines as well. The two belong to different, and in certain respects opposed, traditions. Juxtaposition of chief syllables has been a common phenomenon in native verse from Old English times on, and the regularity in syllable count on which the convention of the reversed foot depends has never been a feature of the native tradition. The metrical principles of the alliterative lines must be determined, so far as possible, from the lines themselves.

In studying the short lines of the wheels, it was possible to assume a basic structure of three chief syllables or metrical units to the line. Unfortunately, no such assumption can be made for the alliterating lines. Their structure has long been a subject of dispute, the two major views being that there are seven stresses, with four in the first half-line and three in the second,[8] and that there are four stresses, with two in each half-line. Since metrical principles cannot be formulated apart from a concept of metrical structure, it will be necessary to consider the four-stress and seven-stress theories before taking up the problem of final -*e*.

The seven-stress theory has in fact been allowed to lapse during the past four decades; it was last defended at length by William Ellery Leonard, whose study "The Scansion of Middle English Alliterative Verse" appeared in 1920.[9] The four-stress theory had been upheld by Luick and Skeat, among others; its twentieth-century adherents include Menner, Sisam, Tolkien and Gordon, and Oakden.[10] The dispute between the two theories has its roots in a similar dispute about Old English verse. But even if a four-stress structure for the OE line could be demonstrated, this structure would not necessarily apply to its ME descendant. The differences between the two are as marked as their similarities, and the ME line is obviously the longer in count of syllables.

Leonard was himself a poet of repute, and to his attack on the four-stress theory he brought the authority of a practitioner of the craft of versification. He can, I believe, be answered in his own terms.

Leonard felt, and rightly, that the problems involved in the dispute over the structure of the ME line could be illustrated as well from modern as from Middle English verse.[11] The meter of "Þat pitosly þer piped for pyne of þe colde" (*Gawain* 747), whatever it may be, differs little or not at all from the meter of "That piteously there pipèd for pain of the cold." The differences between the four- and seven-stress readings of these and other lines can best be made clear with the aid of certain metrical terms and definitions which must now be presented in some detail.

Metrical structure depends on the predominance and subordination of emphasis rather than the presence or absence of emphasis as a fixed quantity. In the English metrical tradition with which we are most familiar, there is one relationship of emphasis, the C x relationship, and there are two grades or ranks of syllables, here called chief and intermediate. The number of metrical units to the line is determined by the number of chief syllables; the normal iambic pentameter line, for instance, may be expressed in metrical notation as x C x C x C x C x C. In practice chief syllables vary in intensity, as do intermediate syllables, and there is variation also in the degree to which intermediate syllables are subordinated to their neighboring chief syllables. But in terms of form all chief syllables alike are C, all intermediate syllables x, and all sequences of chief and intermediate syllables C x.

However, there are certain simple and obvious verse rhythms in English, whose structure involves more than a single relationship of form, and thus more than two grades of syllables. A nursery rhyme (such rhythms often occur in nursery rhymes, jump-rope jingles, and other traditional popular verses) will furnish a convenient example:

> There was a crooked man,
> And he went a crooked mile,
> And he found a crooked sixpence
> Upon a crooked stile.

It is possible to scan the first and fourth lines of this stanza in traditional terms as iambic trimeter—i.e. as having three chief syllables or metrical units. The second and third lines can be scanned in traditional terms as trochaic tetrameter, with a syllable lacking in the final foot of the second line—i.e. as having four metrical units. While these scansions are possible if we take the lines singly and out of context, they are clearly false to the movement of the stanza as a whole, in which two syllables in each line predominate over all the rest, thus:

> There *was* a crooked *man*,
> And he *went* a crooked *mile*,

>And he *found* a crooked *six*pence
>U*pon* a crooked *stile*.

But these two syllables do not account completely for the metrical structure of the lines; the syllable *crook-* cannot be dismissed as wholly subordinate. In the first line, though it receives less emphasis than *was* or *man*, it predominates in emphasis over *a* and *-ed*, and its role in the other lines is similar. In addition *crook-* is perceived as regularly falling midway in time between *was* and *man*, *went* and *mile*, and so on. The structure of the lines can be described by calling the most important syllables major chief syllables and the three occurrences of *crook-* minor chief syllables. If the stanza is recited in the chanting fashion we associate with nursery rhymes, then *And* in lines 2 and 3 and *-pence* in line 3 become minor chief syllables also; *And* is perceived as falling midway in time between *man* and *went*, and so on. We may represent this structure by using C for major chief syllables, c for minor chief syllables, and x, as before, for intermediate syllables:

>   x C x c x C
>There was a crooked man
>c x C x c x C
>And he went a crooked mile,
>c x C   x c x C c
>And he found a crooked sixpence
>x C x c x C
>Upon a crooked stile.

This sort of metrical structure may be called "compound," again borrowing a term from William Thomson's *The Rhythm of Speech*.[12] It involves not one but two relationships of emphasis, and not two but three grades of syllables: major chief, minor chief, and intermediate.

Lines which, taken out of context, are susceptible of more than one scansion may be called metrically ambiguous. The ambiguity of line 2 of "There Was a Crooked Man" is shown by transplanting it into a stanza of William Blake's:

>"Piper, sit thee down and write
>In a book, that all may read."

So he vanished from my sight
And he went a crooked mile.

The Blake stanza clearly has a structure of four simple units to the line; in traditional terms its meter may be described as trochaic tetrameter, the second syllable of the final foot being consistently omitted.

Let us apply to these two stanzas, whose metrical structure is clear, the question that must be decided about the long lines of *Gawain:* what is the "correct" number of metrical units to the line in each? The answer obviously depends on one's definition of a metrical unit. If we scan:

   c x C x c x C
   And he went a crooked mile,

and count both major and minor chief syllables as constituting metrical units, then this line, like the lines from Blake, has a structure of four units. But if we count only *major* chief syllables as constituting metrical units, then the lines of "There Was a Crooked Man" have a structure of two units. Neither method of description is wrong, but it seems reasonable to prefer the latter, which reflects the perceptible difference in movement between the two passages.

Further experiments in transplantation reveal a significant difference between simple and compound structure, as applied to the same number of syllables in a series. It will be observed that "And he went a crooked mile," read in the context of the stanza from Blake, is slower as well as more emphatic (heightening of emphasis takes place in reading *And* and *crook-* as major chief rather than minor chief syllables) than the same line in its proper context. Conversely, "And he pluck'd a hollow reed" would become more rapid as well as less emphatic in the context of "There Was a Crooked Man." Emphasis and retardation of pace are natural corollaries in the rhythm of speech as well as in meter. Thus, if one should say "Come on!" three times with increasing impatience, the two syllables might at first be pronounced almost as one ("C'mon!"), the second time less rapidly, as an iamb ("Come *on!*"), the third time slowly, as a spondee (*"Come on!"*).

Metrically ambiguous lines are read in context according to a previously established structure. But how is metrical structure established? The answer immediately suggests itself: there must in every poem be certain lines which are metrically clear, admitting of but one scansion. These lines are the key to the structure; once it is established, ambiguous lines are adapted to it.

The distinction between clear and ambiguous lines is not itself always clear; that a line admits of but one scansion may in practice be a matter of dispute. But in many cases the attempt to impose scansions other than the most obvious one results in distortion of natural emphasis and pace to the degree that the scansion will universally be felt as wrong. If one attempts to read "Piper, sit thee down and write" according to the meter of "And he went a crooked mile," with *pip-* and *down* as minor chief syllables, the subordination of *piper* to *sit* contradicts the natural tendency to emphasize the noun in the vocative case, while the rapidity with which the first three syllables must be read contradicts the natural pause after the vocative, indicated typographically by a comma. The first three syllables of the line thus clearly resist the attempt at compounding, although the remainder of the line, "sit thee down and write," lends itself naturally to a reading as C x c x C.

Distortion, then, is not a uniform quantity which is either present or absent but a matter of degree, and its perception depends on aesthetic judgment. If it is sufficiently obvious, all will agree in rejecting the scansion. (Presumably no one would accept a reading of "Piper, sit thee down and write" according to the meter of "[I am] monarch of all I survey.") But in almost any passage of verse there will be borderline cases. "In a book, that all may read," for instance, may be read with very little distortion as c x C x c x C. One might argue that in such a reading *all* demands a degree of rhetorical emphasis at least equal to that accorded to *book* and *read*, and therefore ought not to be subordinated as a minor chief syllable. But if the line were considered out of context, it would be difficult to adjudicate between a compound two-part and a simple four-part structure.

The lines from Blake resist compounding because the resultant reading is more rapid and less emphatic than that demanded by syntax and rhetorical emphasis. Resistance of an opposite sort may be illustrated from the first stanza of Thomas Hood's "The Bridge of Sighs":

> One more Unfortunate,
> Weary of breath,

Rashly importunate,
Gone to her death!

The structure of these lines is clearly one of two simple units, with chief syllables separated either by two intermediate syllables or a temporally equivalent pause. In traditional terms the passage scans as dactylic dimeter, the two final syllables being omitted in the second and fourth lines. The first and second or third and fourth lines may be compared with the compound meter of

C   c x   C   x c
Pease porridge in the pot

C   c   C
Nine days old.

This meter may be imposed on Hood's lines, which will then scan as follows:

C   c   x C x c
One more Unfortunate,

C c x   C
Weary of breath,

C c x   C x c
Rashly importunate,

C   c x   C
Gone to her death!

The alternative here is not between four simple and two compound but between two simple and two compound units. The latter scansion appears "incorrect" because it results in a reading which is clearly overemphatic and retarded in pace. *Weary*, as a sequence of a major and a minor chief syllable, must be pronounced more slowly than is natural; *-y* cannot well bear even minor emphasis. The same is true of the second syllable of *rashly* and the fourth syllables of *unfortunate* and *importunate*. But "Gone to her death" is metrically ambiguous; in a context of two compound units it could be adapted without distortion to that structure.

The distinction between simple and compound meter is of great importance for the long lines of *Gawain*. This is partly because the adherents of the seven-stress theory have counted both primary and secondary stresses in the determination of metrical units. A succession of alternating primary and secondary stresses produces compound meter, the primary stresses appearing as major chief syllables, the secondary stresses as minor chief syllables. Thus the seven-stress line

    C x   c x C c   C   c x C
    Four and twenty blackbirds, baked in a pie

is cited by Leonard as a modern analogue to the alliterative long line in Middle English.[13] It will be noted that this line contains four *major* chief syllables. Counting only these, its structure may be described as one of four (compound) units. The difference between the seven-stress and four-stress theories thus resolves itself into the difference between uniformly compound and uniformly simple meter, the seven-stress theory decreeing the regular alternation of minor with major chief emphasis. As was shown earlier in the discussion of "The Bridge of Sighs," compound units are both slower and heavier than simple units. The tacit rejection of the seven-stress theory in recent years indicates that the resultant reading has been felt to be unnatural in the same way that a reading of "One more unfortunate, / Weary of breath" according to the compound meter of "Pease porridge in the pot, / Nine days old" is unnatural.

Coming now to test the four- and seven-stress theories on the long lines of *Gawain*, we expect a priori that a given line will fall into one of three groups:

1. Metrically clear lines indicating a four-stress scansion
2. Metrically clear lines indicating a seven-stress scansion
3. Metrically ambiguous lines which can be read without distortion according to either scansion

If the four-stress scansion is "correct," lines of groups 1 and 3 will be the rule and those of group 2 the exception; if the seven-stress scansion is correct, 2 and 3 will be the rule and 1 the exception. No proportion, however large, of ambiguous lines can be counted as evidence on either side.

For reasons that will become clear later, we will begin with an analysis of the second half-lines. Surveying the first verse-para-

ALLITERATIVE LONG LINE: NORMAL

graph of *Gawain*,[14] we find that a number of these half-lines are metrically ambiguous. They can be read naturally with three stresses—i.e. as compound, with a minor chief syllable falling between major chief syllables:

$$\begin{array}{ccc} C & c & C \\ \text{of tresoun} & \text{þer} & \text{wroȝt} \end{array}$$

$$\begin{array}{ccc} C & c & C \\ \text{lyftes} & \text{vp} & \text{homes} \end{array}$$

$$\begin{array}{ccc} C & c & C \\ \text{he biges} & \text{vpon} & \text{fyrst} \end{array}$$

But they do not serve to *establish* the compound structure, because they can equally well be read in terms of two simple units:

$$\begin{array}{cc} C & C \\ \text{of tresoun} & \text{þer wroȝt} \end{array}$$

$$\begin{array}{cc} C & C \\ \text{lyftes} & \text{vp homes} \end{array}$$

$$\begin{array}{cc} C & C \\ \text{he biges} & \text{vpon fyrst} \end{array}$$

In other words the syllables *þer*, *vp*, and *-pon* do not necessarily take secondary stress; they can be subordinated completely without distortion. If these ambiguous half-lines are to be interpreted as compound, the structure must be established by half-lines whose structure is clearly compound, half-lines for which a reading in terms of two simple units is not sufficiently emphatic. But such examples are lacking. And conclusive evidence of the opposite sort is provided in the passage by second half-lines clearly indicating a structure of two simple units:

$$\begin{array}{cc} C & C \\ \text{to brondeȝ} & \text{\& askeȝ} \end{array}$$

$$\begin{array}{cc} C & C \\ \text{\& teldes} & \text{bigynnes} \end{array}$$

$$\begin{array}{cc} C & C \\ \text{Felix} & \text{Brutus} \end{array}$$

Read as compound, these half-lines are unnaturally heavy and slow.

A similar analysis, with the same results, could be made for any verse-paragraph of *Gawain*. The three-stress compound structure can be imposed on a number of the second half-lines, but it is not established by unambiguous examples. The two-stress structure is clearly established and can be imposed on all the second half-lines uniformly without distortion.

We now proceed to test the four- and seven-stress theories on the first half-lines. Here it becomes necessary to take into account a variant form of the first half-line recognized by the adherents of the four-stress theory, which is usually interpreted as having three chief syllables of equal rank—i.e. a structure of three simple units. This "extended" form has been associated specifically with the first half-lines containing three important alliterating words.[15] Conspicuous examples of this form in the first verse-paragraph of *Gawain* are "þe borȝ brittened & brent," "Fro riche Romulus to Rome," and "& fer ouer þe French flod."

A survey of the first half-lines of the first verse-paragraph reveals, as before, the presence of a group of metrically ambiguous lines. These can be read naturally in terms of four stresses—i.e. as compound, with two major and two minor chief syllables:

$$\overset{c\qquad C\ c\qquad C}{\text{Siþen þe sege & þe assaut}}$$

$$\overset{C\ c\qquad C\ c}{\text{Watȝ tried for his tricherie}}$$

$$\overset{c\qquad C\qquad c\quad C}{\text{On mony bonkkes ful brode}}$$

But these lines can be read equally well as simple, with subordination of all but the two major chief syllables:

$$\overset{C\qquad\qquad C}{\text{Siþen þe sege & þe assaut}}$$

$$\overset{C\qquad\qquad C}{\text{Watȝ tried for his tricherie}}$$

$$\overset{C\qquad\qquad C}{\text{On mony bonkkes ful brode}}$$

Here again, the interpretation of ambiguous lines as compound depends on the establishment of the four-stress compound structure by metrically unambiguous lines, and such lines are lacking.

As evidence on the opposite side, there are certain first half-lines for which a four-stress reading is unnaturally slow and heavy, for example:

$$\begin{array}{cc} \text{C} \quad \text{c} & \text{C} \quad \text{c} \\ \text{þe tulk þat} & \text{þe trammes} \end{array}$$

$$\begin{array}{cc} \text{C c} & \text{C c} \\ \text{Ticius to} & \text{Tuskan} \end{array}$$

These half-lines seem clearly to indicate a reading in terms of two stresses or two simple units. First half-lines of this type recur throughout the poem, e.g. in the second verse-paragraph: "Þat a selly in siȝt" (28) and "I schal telle hit as tit" (31); in the third: "Þer tournayed tulkes" (41) and "Justed ful jolile" (42); and so on. And finally, there is the extended form mentioned above in which three chief emphases appear to be demanded by three important alliterating syllables.

The first half-line, then, seems to have either a two-stress or a three-stress form; this conclusion accords with the four-stress theory, which allows for a five-stress variant. The proportion of ambiguous examples is larger in the first half of the line than in the second.

At this point, the two halves of the line must be put together, as of course happens in the actual reading of any passage. If this is done, the evidence for the two-stress reading of ambiguous first half-lines becomes conclusive. The second half-lines, as Luick saw, are the key to the meter of the poem; it is they that clearly indicate its structure. Each first half-line—except the very first of the poem—is read in a context of two second half-lines whose structure is one of two simple units. Isolated from its context, "Watȝ tried for his tricherie" might be scanned as compound, with *for* and *-ie* as minor chief syllables. But the actual sequence is "of tresoun þer wroȝt / Watȝ tried for his tricherie, þe trewest on erthe." In the movement of the passage as a whole, "Watȝ tried for his tricherie" will inevitably be influenced by the half-lines that precede and follow it, and will therefore be read in terms of a structure of two simple units. There are, it is true, certain lines of which both halves are metrically ambiguous, lines on which a seven-stress reading may be imposed without distortion. But

Leonard argues unfairly when he prefaces a line of this type (from *Piers Plowman*) with a line of his own invention clearly establishing a seven-stress structure (p. 73):

There was junketing o' midnight, a jump down and up!
There was laughing and lowering and "let go the cup!"

Two can play at that game; the four-stress structure of the same line could equally well be "demonstrated" as follows:

There was music and mirth, both downstairs and up,
There was laughing and lowering and "let go the cup!"

The seven-stress and four-stress theories have now been tested on the long lines, and the latter found to result in the more acceptable reading. The choice between the two readings, it should be observed, has important consequences with regard to the treatment of final -*e*. The four-stress reading is the more rapid and less emphatic. Chief emphasis is placed on only four syllables in most of the lines and on five in the rest, whereas the seven-unit theory decrees the placement of major chief emphasis on four syllables and minor chief emphasis on three in every line. Where emphasis is proportionately frequent, it is natural to read with as many syllables as possible, choosing full in preference to contracted forms when both exist. If "There was laughing and lowering" is read with minor chief emphasis on the -*ing* of *laughing* and *lowering* as well as major chief emphasis on *laugh-* and *low-*, it is natural to pronounce *lowering* with three syllables. If chief emphasis is placed only on *laugh-* and *low-*, it is natural to contract *lowering* to two syllables. This tendency corresponds to the increasingly full syllabication, occurring simultaneously with increased emphasis and slowing of pace, in the series "C'mon!" "Come *on!*" and "*Come on!*" A priori, then, we may expect that -*e* will be pronounced as a syllable less frequently by those who read the alliterating line as one of four simple units than by those who read it as compound throughout.[16] (It should be recalled also in this connection that -*e* was lost comparatively early in Middle English in words which did not receive accent in the sentence.) In view of the fact that sounding of -*e* in the short rhyming lines has been shown to occur only in a few exceptional cases, there is every reason to proceed on the assumption that -*e* in the long lines is similarly treated: that it is *not* to be sounded unless metrical principles decreeing its sounding can be formulated. As with the short lines, the treatment of -*e* in intralinear position and its treatment in final position must be distinguished as separate problems.

The most detailed and authoritative statements on the treatment of -*e* in the ME alliterative line, read according to the four-stress theory, are those of Karl Luick. Luick's earliest study, "Die englische Stabreimzeile im XIV., XV., und XVI. Jahrhundert," has been referred to previously; it appeared as a two-part article (*Anglia*, 11, 392–443, 553–618) in 1889. Luick began this study with an examination of the metrical patterns of the late fourteenth-century alliterative poem *Destruction of Troy*.[17] Taking only the second half-lines, as perceptibly more regular and uniform in structure than the first, he surveyed the accentual-syllabic patterns of those (in lines 1–2000) composed of words none of whose ancestral forms had final -*e*. In this way he arrived at a classification of the half-line into seven types, named from those formulated for the OE half-line by Sievers. The seven types were presented, with statistics on the comparative frequency of their occurrence, in schematized form beside the OE types from which they had presumably evolved (p. 404).[18] The most common ME type, called A by Luick, was schematized (x) ´ x x ´ x; the second most common type was called C and schematized x x ´ ´ x. The third most common type, called BC and schematized x x ´ x ´ x, was derived by Luick, as its name implies, from certain forms of the OE B and C types.[19] Of the four remaining types, three—A₁ (x ´ x x ´), A₂ (´ x x ´), and C₁ (x x ´ ´)—were viewed as variants lacking a final unstressed syllable; the development of such variants was attributed to the gradual loss of -*e* in the spoken language.[20] The seventh type, that of lowest frequency of occurrence, was called B and schematized x x ´ x ´.

Luick next raised the question of the sounding of final -*e*. Adopting, on the basis of the spellings of the MS of the poem, the view—more conservative than that expressed later in *Historische Grammatik* (see below, p. 255, n. 26)—that certain -*e*'s, such as those of nouns and verbs, were sounded in the spoken language of the poet, he concluded that these -*e*'s were in general to be sounded in the verse as well. This sounding had the desirable result of maintaining the same overwhelming proportion of feminine to masculine endings as had been found previously in the examination of -*e*-less lines.[21] In Luick's scansions, therefore, the -*e* of *name* (OE *nama*) is sounded in, for example, "Colchos by name" (*Destruction of Troy* 152), which thus belongs to the A type rather than A_1; the -*e* of *grace* (OF *grace*) is sounded in "as hym grace felle" (76; the -*e* of *felle*, OE *fēoll*, is scribal only), which thus belongs to the B type rather than to the C_1; the -*e*'s of *mone* (OE *mōna*) and *chaunge* (inf.) are sounded in "& the mone chaunge" (408), which thus belongs to the BC type rather than to the C_1, and so on.[22]

This system worked satisfactorily for a large majority of the second half-lines of *Destruction of Troy*. But Luick was forced finally to admit the presence of a number of lines which could not be called corrupt on grounds of meaning or alliteration, yet which fell short of the number of syllables "required" according to the schematization of the seven types. Examples are 1505 "als other wemen" and 1602 "þat Xanthus hight." Luick took the position that since such lines were "irregular," they were therefore in general "avoided" by the poet (p. 417). He suggested that at least some of these apparently "shortened" types were due to faulty textual transmission, and that in others the inflectional -*e* of the adjective, normally silent in the verse, should count as a syllable (pp. 417–18).

Luick's analysis of the first half-lines (pp. 419 ff.) was similar in method and need not, therefore, be recapitulated in detail here. Almost all the types found in the second half-lines were found in the first half-lines as well, though with differing comparative frequencies. In addition, types with a third (secondary) accent were identified, of which some contained three alliterating syllables (pp. 421–26).

Luick proceeded to apply the metrical principles developed from the study of *Destruction of Troy* to other Middle English alliterative poems, including *Gawain* (pp. 572–83). An examination of the rhymes in the wheels of *Gawain* led to the opposite conclusion from mine, namely, that -*e* was always sounded when present in both words of a rhyming pair.[23] Surveying the rhymes from the point of view of this assumption, Luick concluded that in the dialect of the *Gawain*-poet -*e* had in general preserved its older value as a syllable, at least in poetic recitation (p. 574). The -*e*'s to be sounded in rhyme in the wheels, according to Luick's analysis, included the analogical *-e* in such adverbs as *tylle* (ON *til*) 1369 and the inflectional *-e* in the weak and plural forms of the adjective (pp. 575–76).

The kinds of *-e* thought to be sounded in rhyme were sounded also in the long lines of *Gawain* to produce the seven types, as in *Destruction of Troy*. Thus, in the second half-line "& his highe kynde" (5) the *-e* of the weak adjectival declension in *highe* and that of *kynde* (cf. OE *ʒecynde*, and *ʒecynd* f.) were sounded to produce the pattern x x ́ x ́ x (type BC, in our notation x x C x C x); in "as I tryst may" (380) the *-e* of the infinitive was sounded in *tryst[e]* to produce the pattern x x ́ x ́ (type B, in our notation x x C x C); and so on.[24] A list of seventeen "shortened" second half-lines is given, without detailed discussion, on p. 578; at the same time, the poet's tendency to avoid such lines is reaffirmed.[25]

Luick's system for the sounding of *-e* in the alliterative long line is open to objection on grounds both of phonology and metrical theory. It will have been observed that in the scansions both of *Destruction of Troy* and of *Gawain* the starting point is the assumption that *-e*, at least in certain classes of words, will normally be sounded. This assumption is not in fact valid for either poem; it does not accord with the chronology of the loss of *-e* as ultimately determined, among others, by Luick himself. If, on the other hand, *-e* is normally silent, then metrical reasons must be found to justify its sounding in certain lines. In his scansions of *Destruction of Troy* Luick often operates on the tacit assumption that a given line ought, where linguistically possible, to be made to conform to the pattern of maximum statistical frequency. He decrees, for example, the sounding of *-e* in "abidë now herë" (*Destruction of Troy* 1151) because two intermediate syllables necessarily come between chief syllables in an A verse (p. 411). But unless "als other wemen" (1505) and the other shortened lines in the poem are in fact corrupt, the pattern x C x C x must be admitted as a possibility. It should be counted among the poet's metrical resources; or to put the matter another way, there is nothing in the principles of the meter whereby the exact number of its occurrences can be predicted.

These principles apply with equal force to the seven "normal" types of the half-line. Seventeen clear cases of type C_1 (x x ́ ́, in our notation x x C C) were found by Luick in *Destruction of Troy* (p. 404) and five in *Gawain* (p. 578), e.g. "þer þe fox bade (OE *bād*)" (1699). There is thus no metrical reason to avoid C_1 by invoking an archaic mode of pronunciation in "as I tryst may." Nor is there any metrical necessity for sounding the *-e* of the weak adjectival declension in "& his highe kynde," whether or not we wish to sound the *-e* of *kynde* to produce the feminine ending; the pattern x x C C x is clearly exemplified in *Gawain*, according to Luick's own analysis, in such lines as 117 "þat þer-bi henged," 1242 "þat ȝe of speken," and others of the C type (see p. 579 for these examples). "& his highe kynde" is metrically similar to a number of second half-lines in which the sounding of *-e* in the adjective is not linguistically justified, e.g. 212 "with a brod (OE *brād*) egge" and 844 "& of hyghe (OE *hēah*) eldee." An inflectional *-e* in the dative singular of the adjective is not to be expected in late Middle English.

In his later writings Luick's views on the treatment of *-e* in the alliterative line became less conservative. He ultimately maintained that it was never to be sounded in intralinear position.[26] Speaking of the verse of *Destruction of Troy*, with which he considered *Gawain* to be closely linked, he posited a historical development whereby lines composed during the period when *-e* was sounded in the spoken language came to be recited without *-e* after the colloquial *-e* had been lost. Poets who had always heard the lines recited without *-e* would then compose variant lines substituting words in which *-e* had not originally been present.[27] A half-line like "watȝ on þat mon cast" in *Gawain* could therefore be viewed as resulting from the substitution of *mon* for alliterating synonyms like *freke* (OE *freca*) or *wyȝe* (OE *wīȝa*), words which had originally been dissyllabic in second half-lines of this type, but which the poet had been accustomed to hear read without the sounding of *-e*.

A survey of the long lines of *Gawain* reveals that second half-lines of comparatively few syllables in which it would be possible to sound one or more *-e*'s are regularly paralleled by lines in which the sounding of *-e* is not justified on linguistic grounds. In addition to x x C C (Luick's C_1), the tetrasyllabic pattern C x C x is clearly exemplified by "Felix Brutus" (13) and the pattern x C x C by "with hay & war" (1158). If C x C x is possible, then there is no

ALLITERATIVE LONG LINE: NORMAL   187

need to emend *best* to *best*[*e*] in "best ar holden" (259), where, moreover, such sounding would result in a hiatus. If we allow for the possibility of sounding *-e* in final position to provide a feminine ending, the half-lines "comlyche hade" (648) and "semlych ryche" (882) will be scanned according to the same pattern, so that there is no need to sound the *-e* of *-lyche* in these cases. In view of the poet's clearly exemplified use of the tetrasyllabic patterns C x C x and x C x C, the possibility of the variant pattern x C C x ought also to be conceded.[28] Such a pattern seems to be exemplified in "wolde wynne hidere" (1537), and, if the *-e* is sounded in the final word in the line, in "þat myȝt ride" (142). In an important group of second half-lines of this type the final word is a Romance stem-suffix derivative; the treatment of such derivatives elsewhere in the long line indicates that the accent was uniformly placed on the stem, and there is no metrical reason for adopting an artificial suffix-accent, as in the rhymes, to avoid the pattern (x) x C C x.[29] To this group belong, e.g., "watȝ clene verdure" (161), "þe proude cropure" (168), "as scharp rasores" (213), "wyth fayre pelures" (2029), and "þe self chapel" (2147). Here the sounding of *-e* in the adjectives is historically justified but not metrically necessary. The plurals *pelures* and *rasores* will be pronounced, like *schulderes* (156), as dissyllables in accordance with the strict avoidance of the final cadence C x x throughout the poem (compare the syncopation of the *-es* plural in certain of the short lines discussed above, p. 161).

To sum up: it is here maintained that *-e* does not count as a syllable within the long lines under any conditions. Since it was obsolete in the spoken language of the poet, its sounding must be justified in terms of metrical principles. But such principles cannot be clearly formulated or consistently applied, all attempts to do so being frustrated by the variety of the line itself. The sounding of *-e* cannot be argued by analogy with the wheels, for the metrics of the wheels and the long lines are entirely different. The same is true for analogies with the verse of Chaucer. And it must be said finally, although this is not intended as an argument and will not convince the sceptical, that the resultant reading is at least as satisfactory to the ear as a reading in which the *-e*'s are sporadically sounded. If, in the reading of second half-lines of comparatively few syllables, care is taken to give long vowels their due quantity and rhetorical emphasis is appropriately placed—always bearing in mind the fact that chief emphasis and alliteration need not coincide —it will be found that the movement of the verse can easily be sustained, with chief syllables falling naturally at rhythmically regular intervals. Read in this fashion, at least one line constitutes an argument in itself. The succession of three long syllables in 1141 "þre bare mote"—i.e. "just three long blasts on the horn"—shows a rhythmic parallel with the subject matter too striking to be due to coincidence. (*Mote* is here a collective noun, as in *BD* 375–76 "The mayster-hunte anoon, fot-hot, / With a gret horn blew thre mot"; there is thus no need to emend to *mote*[ȝ] as do GDS.)

It is impossible to be equally certain about -*e* in final position. Here we must take into account a phenomenon that has often been noted: the marked preference of the Middle English alliterative poets generally for the feminine ending.[30] So far as the *Gawain*-poet at least is concerned, this preference does not mean the *exclusive* use of the feminine ending. Luick observed that in *Gawain*, as in *Destruction of Troy*, the number of clearly masculine endings was comparatively large; that is, the authors of these two poems showed more of a tendency to place words lacking -*e* at the end of the line than earlier poets. He cited from *Gawain*, as examples of the masculine ending, the second half-lines 138 "so sware & so þik (sg.)," 816 "to fonge þe knyȝt," 1161 "wapped a flone (OE *flān*)," and others.[31] Such clearly masculine endings present no problem. Nor do the clearly feminine endings formed by the -*ed* of the preterite, the -*es* of the plural of nouns, and other suffixes that were normally pronounced as syllables in the spoken language.

In attempting to argue one way or the other about the lines in which the feminine ending would be constituted by the sounding of -*e*, one is all too likely to find oneself going in a circle. The poet sounded -*e* at the end of the long line because he preferred the feminine ending; the poet must have preferred the feminine ending, because he almost always uses words ending in -*e* at the end of the line.[32] The latter argument disregards an important point: the *Gawain*-poet composed in a traditional, highly stereotyped style in which certain words were associated with certain metrical positions. This style must have been evolving during the period when -*e* was still part of the spoken language, so that the presence of -*e* in certain words might originally have caused them to be favored in final

ALLITERATIVE LONG LINE: NORMAL

position over words lacking -e. But the question is whether the loss of the colloquial -e affected the recitation of words final in the alliterative line as well as those in intralinear position.

If the -e is silent in final position, the count of syllables in the second half-line will sometimes fall to three, e.g. in 142 "þat myȝt ride," 882 "semlych ryche," and 554 "big men boþe." But there is no essential metrical difference between "þat miȝt ride" and 94 "þat he myȝt trawe," where the suppression of -e results in the pattern x x C C, clearly exemplified elsewhere in the poem, or between "big men boþe" and "þre bare mote," the possible expressive value of which is discussed above.

It is possible, though by no means certain, that allowance should be made for a metrical tradition specifically affecting -e at the end of the line, comparable to that according to which -e's are sounded in intralinear position in rhymed verse.[33] Such a tradition would have operated to prevent the suppression of -e in such formulaic second half-lines as 4 "þe trewest on erthe," 49 "as leuest him þoȝt[e]," and others. If this class of -e's is sounded, a large majority of the lines of *Gawain* will have the feminine ending, with the masculine ending as a *bona fide* but infrequent variant.[34] I prefer to leave the question open; fortunately, it has little bearing on the most important metrical problem presented by the long line: its scansion in terms of the count of chief syllables.[35] We now turn to a final phase of this problem.

CHAPTER 8

The Alliterative Long Line: The Extended Form

ALTHOUGH the seven-stress theory, as we have seen, fails to produce an acceptable recitation of the long lines of *Gawain*, it has a certain neatness lacking in the four-stress theory in that it finds one metrical structure applicable to all the long lines alike. It is natural to feel that a form of verse which was, for the most part, stored in the human memory and conveyed to its audience by recitation must have had a perceptibly regular rhythm—regular in terms both of the recurrence of emphatic syllables in time and the grouping of such syllables into line units. The four-stress theory, while maintaining that the four-stress line is normal, also recognizes an "extended" form in which there are three stresses in the first half-line and thus five in the long line as a whole.[1]

We will return to the problem of the extended half-lines later. For the time being, let us consider those lines which can be adapted without difficulty to the four-stress reading according to the principles set forth above, lines such as:

```
             C        C   C      C
       Bi a mounte on þe morne meryly he rydes
             C         C      C      C
       Into a forest ful dep, þat ferly watȝ wylde,    [740-41]
                        . . .
                 C       C         C    C
       With mony bryddeȝ vnblyþe vpon bare twyges,
              C        C         C         C
       Þat pitosly þer piped for pyne of þe colde.[2]   [746-47]
```

Read aloud at a dramatically appropriate pace by one familiar with the language of the poem, these lines have a perceptibly regular rhythm. We can express this more precisely by saying that chief syllables are perceived as occurring at regular—i.e. at formally equivalent—intervals in a continuum of time. But it is also apparent to the attentive ear, without the necessity of mechanical measurement, that the time intervals between the chief syllables are not actually equal. In other words perceptible regularity in the rhythm of verse does not depend on isochrony, though isochrony, as we shall see, cannot be discounted altogether.

This statement is equally applicable to the rhythm of music. There are many musical compositions—in particular, works of a lyric or descriptive nature independent of repetitive physical movement such as marching or dancing—in which the measure bars are not taken by the performer to indicate literally equal intervals of time. These compositions may be provided by their editors with a recommended metronomic setting, so many beats per minute corresponding to so many notes of a certain value. But such a setting expresses an average, not a uniform, tempo, a norm about which the actual tempo fluctuates from measure to measure. The same holds, a fortiori, for meter, in which the free rhythms of speech resist isochrony more strongly than musical notes. It is possible to express the average pace of one's recitation, say, of a Shakespeare sonnet, metronomically—that is, in terms of a certain number of chief syllables per minute—but in attempting to recite it to a metronome one finds oneself constantly lagging behind or running ahead of the beat.[3]

Despite this omnipresent fluctuation of pace, the temporal aspect of meter is perceptible; the educated ear can distinguish metrical rhythm from that of prose. The possibility of making this distinction depends on the fact that metrical time, like metrical stress, is a relative rather than an absolute quantity. In a metrical recitation the temporal relationships among chief syllables are more nearly isochronous than the temporal relationships among these same syllables would be if the passage were read as prose. If metrical time is to be measured by scientific instruments, it must be measured in terms of this difference; it cannot be demonstrated from isolated lines or passages of verse. What we are dealing with, then, is a tendency toward isochrony, a modification of the temporal relationships among chief syllables in the direction of isochrony without its actually being attained. This tendency results in part from the natural correlation between increased emphasis and retardation of pace, on the one hand, and decreased emphasis and acceleration of pace, on the other. In metrical sequences of heavy syllables certain of them are subordinated—that is, read with slightly decreased emphasis—and in sequences of light syllables, certain are read as chief—that is, with slightly enhanced emphasis. If Shakespeare's line "To me, fair friend, you never can be old" were spoken as prose, emphasis might be placed on *me, fair, friend, nev-,* and *old,* with long pauses after *me* and *friend.* The resultant temporal pattern may be roughly indicated by transcribing the line "To mé— fáir fríend—you néver can be óld." But in a metrical recitation of the same line, *fair* is read with slightly less emphasis than *friend,* and *can* is read with slightly more emphasis than *-er* and *be;* the pauses, while still present, are not prolonged to the point where the continuity of the rhythm is broken. Hearing the line read in this way, the listener perceives the influence of the tendency toward isochrony and thus interprets the metrical structure correctly. From this analysis of what takes place in listening to meter, it follows that it should be difficult to recognize metrical patterns in a language one does not understand—and such, in fact, is the case.

The operation of the tendency toward isochrony can be demonstrated from the above-cited lines of *Gawain.* In these lines two pairs of chief syllables, *morne* and *mer-* and *bare* and *twyg-,* are juxtaposed, others being separated by one, two, three, and in one case four chief syllables ("rydes/ Into a for-"). In a metrical recitation the reader takes advantage of the syntactically decreed pause between *on þe morne* and *meryly,* the length of the vowel of *bare,* and the possibility of dwelling on *bare* with rhetorical emphasis, as when one says "It's a *cold* morning." In such sequences as "meryly he rydes/ Into a forest" and "þat pitosly þer piped" the series of intermediate syllables are allowed to run rapidly and without secondary emphasis.[4] Thus, though the temporal intervals among the chief syllables remain unequal—that between *bare* and *twyg-,* for example, being shorter than that between *pit-* and *pip-* —an effect of rhythmic regularity is produced.

The four lines quoted earlier were taken from a longer passage which may now be quoted in its entirety:

> Bi a mounte on þe morne meryly he rydes 740
> Into a forest ful dep, þat ferly watʒ wylde,
> Hiʒe hilleʒ on vche a halue, & holt-wodeʒ vnder
> Of hore okeʒ ful hoge a hundreth to-geder;
> Þe hasel & þe haʒ-þorne were harled al samen,
> With roʒe raged mosse rayled ay-where, 745
> With mony bryddeʒ vnblyþe vpon bare twyges
> Þat pitosly þer piped for pyne of þe colde.
> Þe gome vpon Gryngolet glydeʒ hem vnder
> Þurʒ mony misy & myre, mon al hym one.

In this, as in any passage of *Gawain*, there are certain first half-lines of the "extended" type, the clearest examples here perhaps being 742 and 743. Setting these aside for the time being, let us look at another first half-line, heavier than 740–41 or 746–47: "With roʒe raged mosse."

It is possible to read *roʒe*, *rag-*, and *mosse* in this half-line as chief syllables of equal rank, there being then three stresses or metrical units. But when a noun is preceded by two descriptive adjectives, it is natural to give the second of these slightly less emphasis than the first, as happens in fluent speech in such phrases as "a góod hòt dínner," "a shórt blàck dréss," "in pláin hònest wórds," and so on.[5] This tendency has been exploited in the traditional iambic pentameter line, as in Shakespeare's "Bare ruin'd choirs" and Tennyson's "The bare black cliff," where *bare* is a chief syllable, and *ru-* and *black*, respectively, are heavy intermediate syllables. It is one aspect of a more general tendency in English to reduce the stress on one of two juxtaposed heavy syllables.[6]

If instead of giving equal emphasis to *roʒe*, *rag-*, and *mosse*, we read the half-line so that *roʒe* and *mosse* predominate, subordinating *rag-* slightly while allowing it to retain strong secondary emphasis, then *raged* will be related to *roʒe* and *mosse* as *crooked* is related to *was* and *man* in "There was a crooked man." It will become a minor chief syllable, subordinate to *roʒe* and *mosse* but emphatic in relation to *-ed*, and it will fall at a temporal halfway point between the two major chief syllables. The result is a single compound metrical unit—*róʒe ràgéd*—in a line whose meter is otherwise simple. The alternative scansions of the line in its entirety may be expressed in metrical notation as follows:

                    C   C   C   C   C
(1) With roȝe raged mosse rayled ay-where
                    C   c   C   C   C
(2) With roȝe raged mosse rayled ay-where [7]

It will be observed that, read according to scansion (2), the first half-line becomes slightly more rapid than it is in scansion (1). The temporal interval between the two major chief syllables *roȝe* and *mosse* is thus altered in the direction of isochrony, though it remains greater than the intervals between *mosse* and *rayl-* and *rayl-* and *-where*. As a result, one who hears the line can interpret the four-part structure correctly, perceiving the four major chief syllables as occurring at rhythmically regular intervals.

If *raged* is subordinated to *roȝe* and *mosse*, as is here proposed, major emphasis and alliteration do not coincide. The alliterative pattern, expressed according to Oakden's formulation, is a a x / a x, the second alliterating syllable bearing minor emphasis. This may be thought of as an expanded variant of the pattern a x / a x, with supernumerary alliteration on a minor chief syllable; the first half-line is similar to certain first half-lines discussed above (p. 170) in which the second of two alliterating syllables is an unaccented prefix or preposition—e.g. 1798 "Now, dere, at þis de-partyng."

The interpretation proposed for "With roȝe raged mosse rayled ay-where" is equally applicable to a number of other lines scattered through the poem, e.g. 789 "Of harde hewen ston vp to þe tableȝ," 953 "Rugh ronkled chekeȝ þat oþer on rolled," and 1659 "Wyth stille stollen countenaunce, þat stalworth to plese." All these exemplify the alliterative pattern a a x / a x except 953, which has the pattern a a x / x a. In other metrically similar lines there is variation in the placement of the alliterating syllables—e.g. 610 "On brode sylkyn borde, & bryddeȝ on semeȝ," 2166 "& ruȝe knokled knarreȝ with knorned stoneȝ," 181 "Fayre fannand fax vmbe-foldes his schulderes," 419 "His longe louelych lokkeȝ he layd ouer his croun," and 786 "Of þe depe double dich þat drof to þe place." In the last three of these, all three important syllables in the first half-line alliterate.

In another first half-line in the same passage, "Of hore okeȝ ful hoge," one descriptive adjective precedes the noun and one (with adverbial qualifier) follows it. Here too it is possible to subordinate

ALLITERATIVE LONG LINE: EXTENDED 195

the second heavy syllable, in this case the noun. The subordination of a noun to a preceding descriptive adjective can be illustrated from the wheels, e.g. 1368 "Wyth blys & bryȝt fyr bette" and 2088 "Þe quyte snaw lay bisyde." (Similar subordination occurs in certain of the lines cited by Jespersen, p. 254, to illustrate the rhythmically caused weakening of the second of three strong syllables, e.g. "The course of true love never did run smooth.") If *okeȝ* is subordinated, a single compound metrical unit is formed as in line 745. The resultant scansion, together with the alliterative pattern, may be indicated as follows:

```
   C  c     C    C        C
Of hore okeȝ ful hoge a hundreth to-geder.
   a  a     a  / a        x
```

This interpretation throws into relief the two attributes signified by the adjectives, as happens also in speech in such phrases as "a shórt lífe and a mérry" and "góod mèn and trúe." Again we find that the proposed scansion is equally applicable to a number of other lines, e.g. 119 "Wylde werbles & wyȝt wakned lote," 152 "A strayt cote ful streȝt, þat stek on his sides," 583 "With gode cowters & gay, & glouez of plate," 889 "Wyth sere sewes & sete, sesounde of þe best," and 2165 "Bot hyȝe bonkkeȝ & brent vpon boþe halue." These lines show the same variation in the relationship between alliteration and emphasis as the previously analyzed group. In the last example there is double alliteration, the pattern being a b b / b a. In other similar lines the adjective-noun combination is followed by an infinitive or prepositional phrase, e.g. 209 "A spetos sparþe to expoun in spelle quo-so myȝt," 1731 "Whyle þe hende knyȝt at home holsumly slepeȝ," and 2369 "Þat oþer stif mon in study stod a gret whyle."

But the half-line "Of hore okeȝ ful hoge" may be read with two major emphases and one minor in a different way. If the attribute of hoariness is taken for granted and rhetorical emphasis placed on the oaks themselves and their huge size, then *hore* will be read as a minor chief syllable preceding the first major chief syllable of the line. Similar precedence of the first major chief syllable by a minor may be illustrated from the chorus "Could I Take Me to Some Cavern for Mine Hiding," from Gilbert Murray's translation of Euripides' *Hippolytus*:

        c   C c   C   c   C
To the strand of the daughters of the sunset
     C   c   C   c   C
The apple-tree, the singing and the gold.[8]

Here the meter is uniformly compound. Moreover, a descriptive adjective often receives slightly less emphasis than the noun following it in the spoken language (cf. the examples "ôld-mán," "rêd-bárn" cited by Bloch and Trager in *Outline of Linguistic Analysis*, p. 48, with "loud stress" on the nouns and "reduced loud" on the adjectives).

Similar alternatives involving the relative emphasis of a noun and a preceding descriptive adjective are presented by certain other lines in the poem. In 427 "Þe fayre hede fro þe halce hit to þe erþe" it is possible to read *fayre* as a major chief syllable, subordinating *hede*, but it seems preferable to give major emphasis to *hede*, the head itself and its action being presumably more important than its attribute of fairness (cf. 444 "For þe hede in his honde he halde3 vp euen"). In 578-79 "Queme quyssewes þen, þat coyntlych closed/ His thik þrawen þy3e3" *quyssewes* occurs as one of a series of nouns, all technical terms referring to parts of Gawain's elaborate armor, following *dublet* (571), *capados* (572), *sabatoun3* (574), *greue3* (575), and *polayne3* (576), all of which receive chief emphasis. Subordination of *queme* is clearly indicated.

We thus envisage three ways of reading the line "Of hore oke3 ful hoge a hundreth to-geder": (1) equal emphasis may be given to *hore*, *oke3*, and *hoge*, the first half-line then having three metrical units; (2) *oke3* may be subordinated to *hore* and *hoge* as a minor chief syllable; or (3) *hore* may be subordinated to *oke3* as a minor chief syllable. The resultant scansions are given below: [9]

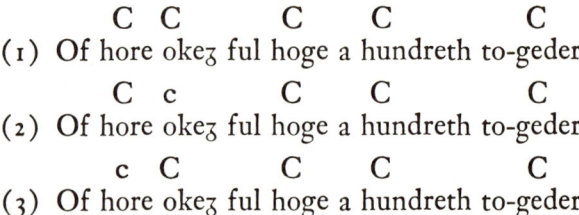

With the differing metrical interpretations of *hore oke3* in scansions (2) and (3) we may compare the differing interpretations of

ALLITERATIVE LONG LINE: EXTENDED

true plus noun in the lines "The course of true love never did run smooth" and "Let me not to the marriage of true minds."

The first half-line "Þurȝ mony misy & myre" in the same passage presents a similar set of three alternatives. *Mony* is a descriptive adjective of low alliterative rank.[10] It can in certain cases be unemphatic, as it is, for example, in the line:

        C   C   C C
With mony bryddeȝ vnblyþe vpon bare twyges

cited earlier as a clear example of the four-stress structure. The same unemphatic role is called for in two of its occurrences in the wheels:

        C   C   C
    Mony wylsum way he rode   [689]
        C   C   C
    Mony auntereȝ here-bi-forne   [2527]

But it is also possible to place rhetorical emphasis on *mony*, bringing out the idea it expresses, as in another line from the wheels,

        C   C   C
    In mony a bonk vnbene   [710]

In the first half-line "Þurȝ mony misy & myre," then, we may give equal emphasis to *mony*, *misy*, and *myre*, or we may subordinate *mony*, or we may allow *mony* to predominate over *misy*. (With the latter interpretation, compare such phrases in fluent speech as "mány a tìme and óft.")

Two other first half-lines in the passage—"Þe hasel & þe haȝ-þorne" and "Þe gome vpon Gryngolet"—lend themselves naturally to a reading with two metrical units. We are thus left with one unusually heavy first half-line: 742 "Hiȝe hilleȝ on vche a halue." But for this half-line, as for the others, possibilities of subordination suggest themselves. *Vche* appears as an intermediate syllable in the wheels in 2021:

        C   C   C
    He hade vpon vche pece

Like *mony*, it is a word that may or may not receive rhetorical emphasis. It can be read as a minor chief syllable or even reduced to an intermediate syllable, without secondary emphasis, in such lines as 1491 "Þat bicumes vche a knyȝt þat cortaysy vses" and 1984 "Vche mon þat he met, he made hem a þonke." *Hiȝe*, like *mony*, is a descriptive adjective of low alliterative rank. It does not, so far as I have observed, appear as an intermediate syllable in the wheels, but it is similar in range of meanings and stylistic values to *gret*, which does appear in this use in, for example:

        C   C   C
Scho made hym so gret chere   [1259]
  C   C   C
Gret rurd in þat forest.   [1149]

It is possible, therefore, to read "Hiȝe hilleȝ on vche a halue" with secondary emphasis on *hiȝe* and secondary emphasis—or perhaps not even that—on *vche*. It is also possible to read it with equal emphasis on *hilleȝ, vche*, and *halue*, as a first half-line of three metrical units.

The foregoing discussion leads to certain conclusions which are applicable to the long lines generally: (1) In any passage of the poem there are first half-lines which can be adapted naturally to a reading with two chief syllables, and in which secondary emphasis is not required. (2) Aside from these, there are certain first half-lines with three heavy syllables for which a reading with three formally equivalent chief syllables is possible, but which can also be adapted naturally to a reading with one compound unit—i.e. with two major chief syllables and one minor. (3) Once the possibility of such compounding, as an alternative to the "extended" form with three stresses, is admitted, it is difficult, if not impossible, to establish a clear boundary between those first half-lines which should be read as compound and those which should not. It is my belief that there are in fact no extended lines in *Gawain*, if by an extended line is meant one containing five chief syllables of equal rank. In all the first half-lines, however heavy, it is possible to subordinate one out of three stressed syllables—or in certain cases two out of four—so that two syllables will receive major emphasis. The four-part structure in this sense is applicable to all the long lines uniformly. There is, of course, no way of proving that where subordination is possible, it is also mandatory. Therefore, in the following scansion of 740–49 and in all other

ALLITERATIVE LONG LINE: EXTENDED 199

scansions presented below, the reader is at liberty to accord major rank (C) to as many syllables designated as minor chief (c) as he sees fit.

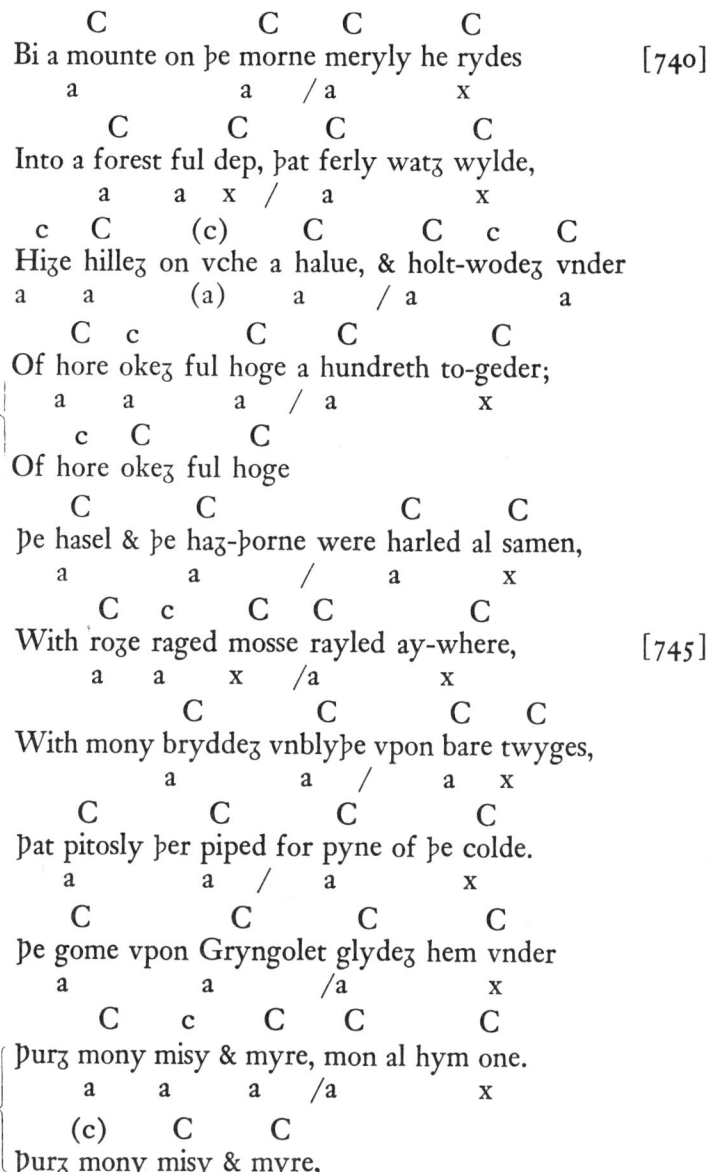

    C   C C C
  Bi a mounte on þe morne meryly he rydes   [740]
   a   a / a x

   C C C   C
  Into a forest ful dep, þat ferly watȝ wylde,
   a   a x / a   x

 c C (c) C C c C
 Hiȝe hilleȝ on vche a halue, & holt-wodeȝ vnder
 a a (a) a / a   a

   C c C C C
  Of hore okeȝ ful hoge a hundreth to-geder;
   a a a / a x

  c C   C
  Of hore okeȝ ful hoge

   C C   C C
  Þe hasel & þe haȝ-þorne were harled al samen,
   a a / a   x

   C c C C   C
  With roȝe raged mosse rayled ay-where,   [745]
   a a x /a   x

    C   C C C
  With mony bryddeȝ vnblyþe vpon bare twyges,
    a   a / a x

   C C   C   C
  Þat pitosly þer piped for pyne of þe colde.
   a   a / a   x

   C   C C   C
  Þe gome vpon Gryngolet glydeȝ hem vnder
   a   a /a   x

   C c C C   C
  Þurȝ mony misy & myre, mon al hym one.
   a a a /a   x

   (c) C C
  Þurȝ mony misy & myre,

Alternative modes of subordination are given for certain heavy first half-lines. Where a syllable may be read either with secondary emphasis, as minor chief, or without emphasis, as intermediate, it is labeled (c).

Whether the extended first half-line is interpreted as a subclass of, or a real departure from, the normal two-part form, it is obvious that the *Gawain*-poet was more inclined than other poets of the alliterative tradition to load the long line with heavy syllables, both alliterating and nonalliterating.[11] The metrical structure of 2338 "Bolde burne, on þis bent be not so gryndel," however one may wish to describe it, is certainly extended as compared to the type exemplified by *Destruction of Troy* 12603 "To a buerne on þe bent, in batell was slayne." But from this it follows also that the heavy first half-lines were recited and heard against the background of the type with two stresses, which must have served as the implicit norm against which the extension was defined.[12] Even if they are read with three equal chief syllables, then, they ought not to be equated with the triply stressed lines of the wheels, which derive from a wholly distinct metrical tradition. In context the extended first half-line must inevitably appear as a departure, whether in degree or in kind, from a rhythm strongly established by a large majority of half-lines of the "normal" type. The cumulative effect of the movement of the verse, in a continuous and animated recitation, may well be thought sufficient to cause the assimilation of all these half-lines to the two-part structure, in the manner here proposed.

It so happens that the possibilities of subordination considered in the foregoing discussion have involved only nouns and adjectives. But the same principles can be applied to heavy first half-lines containing verbs and adverbs. In lines of the type exemplified by 375 "Gawan gotȝ to þe gome, with giserne in honde" it is natural to emphasize the two persons opposing or confronting each other, rather than the action linking them. Such emphasis would make *Gaw-* and *gome* major chief syllables and *gotȝ* a minor chief syllable; cf. the metrical role of *went* in the uniformly compound meter of the nursery rhyme:

C   c   C   c   C   c   C
Taffy went to my house and stole a piece of beef.

The same structure, with varying relationship between alliteration and emphasis, applies to a number of other lines, 842 "Gawayn glyȝt on þe gome þat godly hym gret" and 970 "When Gawayn glyȝt on þat gay þat graciously loked" being especially close parallels. In 421 "Gauan gripped to his ax & gederes hit on hyȝt" the verb may similarly be subordinated, with emphasis falling on the agent and his implement.[13] In 221 "Þis haþel heldeȝ hym in, & þe halle entres" the adverb may be allowed to predominate over the verb, as it does also in modern English in "May I come in?" and "Fools rush in where angels fear to tread." But in 136 "Þer hales in at þe halle dor an aghlich mayster" and 458 "Halled out at þe hal-dor, his hed in his hande" major emphasis seems demanded by the verb and the first syllable of the compound noun *halle dor*, as in "He rúshed in with the news."

In certain cases a possible mode of subordination is indicated by the metrical treatment of the same or similar words in the wheels. Thus in 2012 "& bede hym bryng hym his bruny & his blonk sadel" *bede* may receive minor emphasis as it does in a similar line in the wheel that follows:

        C   C   C
    Þe burne bede bryng his blonk   [2024]

In others subordination of a particular word is indicated by a consideration of the whole passage in which it appears. In the first half of line 850 "Þe lorde hym charred to a chambre" *lorde* does not alliterate. The reference is to the lord of the castle, whom Gawain has just met and who is described in the lines immediately preceding, the narrator's final comment being:

    & wel hym semed forsoþe, as þe segge þuȝt,
    To lede a lortschyp in lee of leudeȝ ful gode.   [848–49]

After this, emphasis on *lorde* in 850 would be redundant. But in 981 "Þe lorde luflych aloft lepeȝ ful ofte" the reader's attention is being redirected to the lord after an account of how the ladies took Gawain aside. *Luflych* often, as here, seems to scan naturally as a minor chief syllable—e.g. in 1583 "He lyȝtes lu[f]lych adoun, leueȝ his corsour" and 254 "Liȝt luflych adoun, & lenge, I þe praye."

Finally, 742 "Hiȝe hilleȝ on vche a halue, & holt-wodeȝ vnder" shows that a compound metrical unit may occur in the second half-line as well as the first. The possibility of such compounding has been tacitly admitted by the adherents of the four-stress theory, since an extended second half-line of three chief syllables has never been proposed. Typical examples in which a third heavy syllable must be read as a minor chief in the second half-line are:

$$\overset{C}{\text{\& syþen}} \overset{C}{\text{þe brawden}} \overset{C}{\underset{a\ \ \ \ \ /\ \ a\ \ \ \ x\ \ \ \ x}{\text{bryne of bryȝt stel ryngeȝ}}} \overset{c}{\text{C}} \quad [580]$$

$$\overset{C}{\underset{a\ \ \ \ \ a}{[Þ]\text{ise}}} \overset{c}{\text{oþer}} \overset{C}{\underset{a}{\text{halowed}}} \overset{c}{\underset{/\ \ a}{\text{hyghe! ful hyȝe, \& hay! hay! cryed}}} \overset{C}{\underset{x}{}} \quad [1445]$$

The preceding is an unusual example of the maintenance of compound meter throughout the line.

$$\overset{C}{\underset{a}{\text{For suche a}}} \overset{C}{\underset{a\ \ \ /\ \ a}{\text{brawne of a best, þe}}} \overset{C}{\underset{a}{\text{bolde burne}}} \overset{c}{\underset{x}{\text{sayde}}} \overset{C}{} \quad [1631]$$

Second half-lines in which emphasis of a nonalliterating over an alliterating syllable is necessary in a dramatically expressive reading were cited above (p. 171) in another connection. A few examples are:

$$\overset{C}{\underset{(a)\ (a)\ \ a}{\text{Wyth what weppen}}} \overset{C}{\underset{a\ \ \ /\ (a)}{\text{[s]o þou wylt, \& wyth no}}} \overset{C}{\underset{x\ \ a}{\text{wyȝ}}} \overset{c}{\underset{x}{\text{elleȝ}}} \overset{C}{} \quad [384]$$

$$\overset{C}{\underset{a}{\text{For þe costes}}} \overset{C}{\underset{a\ \ /\ \ x}{\text{þat I haf knowen vpon þe,}}} \overset{C}{\underset{a}{\text{knyȝt,}}} \overset{c}{\underset{x}{\text{here}}} \overset{C}{} \quad [1272]$$

$$\overset{C}{\underset{a}{\text{Is ryched}}} \overset{C}{\underset{a}{\text{at þe}}} \overset{C}{\underset{/b\ \ a}{\text{reuerence}}} \overset{c}{\underset{b}{\text{me, renk, to}}} \overset{C}{\text{mete}} \quad [2206]$$

The alliterative long line of *Gawain* is remarkably diverse in structure. The metrical unit may consist of one, two, three, or more syllables. In addition to the normal count of four primary stresses or (major) chief syllables, there may be one or more strong secondary stresses or minor chief syllables in the line as a whole— i.e. the line may have one or more compound units. Or it may lack secondary stress entirely, so that its meter is simple throughout. It is possible that some of the heavy first half-lines should be read

ALLITERATIVE LONG LINE: EXTENDED

with a third primary stress—i.e. as having three metrical units—
though compounding is here held to be preferable in all cases.

Some of the heavier multisyllabled types are illustrated below,
with a compound interpretation suggested for each:

```
        c    C                  C     c         C   C
      'Nay, as help me,' quoþ þe haþel, 'he þat on hyȝe syttes,
       x    a             a    / a        a    x
        C         c          C      C              C
      To wone any quyle in þis won, hit watȝ not myn ernde.'
        a         a          a    / a              x    [256-57]
        C          C      c         C                 C
      Þis ax, þat is heue in-nogh, to hondele as hym lykes  [289]
        a          a      x    /    a                 x

        C      c                 C   C             C
      I hyȝt þe a strok & þou hit hatȝ, halde þe wel payed  [2341]
        a      x                 a  /a             x

        C·         c       C        C  c      C
      For boþe two here I þe bede bot two bare myntes  [2352]
        a         x       a    /(a) x    a      x
```

Among the heavier first half-lines special mention should be made of a variant in which, if the second important word is subordinated, the minor chief syllable falls not midway, but two-thirds of the way, between the two major chief syllables. A unit having three temporal subdivisions, comparable to a measure of 3/4 time in music, is thus implied, but only the first and third beats of this unit are expressed by metrical emphasis. Compound units of this type may be indicated in notation as follows:

```
            ┌──────── 3 ────────┐
            C         c    C           C   C
          & neuenes hit his aune nome, as hit now hat       [10]
            a       (?b)  ?b     a   /(?b)  a   ?b

            ┌──── 3 ────┐
            C             c    C   C         C
          Driuande to þe heȝe dece, dut he no woþe          [222]
            a                  a  /a         x
```

In these lines the alliterative pattern seems to imply subordination of the adjective. An interpretation giving chief emphasis to the adjective is also conceivable, however; compare the following:

>   C   (c)   C   c   C   C
>   Þenn Arþour bifore þe hiȝ dece þat auenture byholdeȝ   [250]
>   a   x   a   x / a   a

But a scansion according with the alliteration seems particularly appropriate in each case. In 222, the first half-line will then contain a five-syllabled compound unit followed by a unit consisting of a heavy monosyllable and a pause. In 250 there will be a more even division of the first half-line and hence a comparative steadiness of pace. In accordance with the tendency toward isochrony discussed above, the syllables preceding *dece* will be read more rapidly in 222 than in 250.

Multisyllabled types without secondary accent also occur:

>   C   C   C   C
>   Þe wyȝtest & þe worþyest of þe worldes kynde   [261]
>   a   a   /   a   x

>   C   C   C   C
>   Þat cortaysly hade hym kydde & his cry herkened   [775]
>   a   a   /   a   x

>   C   C   C   C
>   & radly þus re-hayted hym with hir riche wordeȝ   [1744]
>   a   a   /   a   x

Certain multisyllabled units may be read as either simple or compound, depending on whether one wishes to give rhetorical emphasis to a word falling between major chief syllables. The two possibilities are exemplified by 895:

>   C   C   ⎫
>   Ful hendely, quen alle þe haþeles ⎪   C   C
>   a   (a)   a   ⎬   re-hayted hym at oneȝ
>   C   c   C   ⎪   a   a
>   Ful hendely, quen alle þe haþeles ⎭
>   a   a   a

ALLITERATIVE LONG LINE: EXTENDED   205

It is possible that in the longer sequences of intermediate syllables syncopation, contraction, or other modes of reduction should be imposed where the language permits. In the lines quoted above we should perhaps syncopate inflectional *-es* and *-ed* in *costes* (1272) and *riched* (2206) in accordance with the treatment of such syllables in certain lines of the wheels (see above, p. 161). Similarly, trisyllabic words admitting of contraction, such as *myriest* (142), *worþyest* (261), and *reuerence* (2206), should perhaps be read as dissyllables. In 2341a "I hyȝt þe a strok & þou hit hatȝ" the vowel of the pronoun *þe* should perhaps be elided, and *hit* reduced to *t* and joined as an enclitic to *þou*. But the metrical structure of the long line is not tied to syllable count like that of the wheels. Such syllables as *-es*, *-ed*, *a*, and *hit* are in any case pronounced without emphasis and have very short duration, so that the rhythmic differences between readings in which they are sounded and readings in which they are suppressed are slight. The treatment of these and other intermediate syllables will depend to a large extent on the pace at which a given passage is recited; and here, as in music, some latitude in interpretation should be allowed to the individual performer.

The variety of the meter of *Gawain* far exceeds what can be indicated by syllable count and the identification of major and minor chief syllables. Intermediate syllables may differ among themselves in degree of emphasis and in pace; such differences are important in the actual effect of any given line, but cannot be expressed by notation. For example, in the following lines,

      C   C   C   C
Watȝ tried for his tricherie, þe trewest on erthe   [4]
  a   a   /   a   x

         C   C   C   C
With-inne þe comly cortynes, on þe colde morne,   [1732]
     a   a   /   a   x

the units *tricherie, þe* and *cortynes, on þe* have the same pattern (if we assume that *tricherie* is read as trisyllabic). But the two sequences of intermediate syllables differ in their temporal relationships, partly as a result of the differing position of the pause between half-lines. These lines provide an apt illustration of the comparative effects of the four- and seven-stress readings. According to the latter, they would be given some such scansions as the following:

$$\text{C c C c C c C}$$
Watȝ triëd for his tricherie, þe trewest on erthe

$$\text{C c C c C c C}$$
With-inne þe comly cortynes, on þe colde morne,

patterns comparable in metrical interest to that of "A pretty little buttercup, alone in a glade." It is important to note that in these uniformly compound interpretations the pattern is maintained partly by the heightening of emphasis on light syllables, as, in the line "Taffy was a Welshman, Taffy was a thief," *was* receives more than its natural emphasis. The compounding we have described in the meter of *Gawain* involves subordination rather than heightening; it occurs in half-lines that are heavier than normal and results from the natural tendency, in a continuous reading, to assimilate these to the metrical structure of other half-lines.

The various metrical units described above are not distributed equally between the two halves of the line. A survey of the verse of the poem reveals a tendency whereby the number of syllables to the unit diminishes in the course of the line—i.e. multisyllabled units are favored in the first half-line and monosyllabic or dissylabic units in the second. This means that the line tends to slow down progressively, since multisyllabled measures are read rapidly and measures of few syllables slowly, in accordance with the tendency toward isochrony discussed earlier. The second half of the line thus acts as a kind of brake on the meter, a conservative influence whereby the expansive tendencies of the first half-line are counterbalanced and so kept within bounds. The four short lines of the wheels—comparatively even in pace, usually end-stopped, and always culminating in a full stop at the end of the last line—have a similar stabilizing function on a larger scale; in content they serve to knit up the matter of each long-line paragraph, while often at the same time anticipating that of the next.

ALLITERATIVE LONG LINE: EXTENDED

The aim of this discussion has been descriptive: it has been concerned with the normal metrical structure of the long lines and with the patterns which are variants of, or departures from, that structure. Much remains to be said of the artistry with which these patterns are turned to stylistic account by the poet. Space allows for only a cursory discussion here, but a few passages at least may be cited to show how the resources of the meter are exploited to produce a range of effects.

In the description of the lord of the castle (842–50) seven out of eight first half-lines, and perhaps all eight, are of the heavy type, and multisyllabled units are frequent. In three instances the two major chief syllables of the second half-line are juxtaposed (843, 844, 849). The whole passage is thus unusually emphatic, and the emphatic syllables, both major chief and minor, are in a number of cases made still more conspicuous by being juxtaposed. Metrical emphasis is appropriately related to content, since the passage concerns the initial impact of a powerful and vital presence:

```
     C    c        C       C        C
   Gawayn glyȝt on þe gome þat godly hym gret,
     a    a        a  /   a        a
       C     C  c          C   C
   & þuȝt hit a bolde burne þat þe burȝ aȝte,
       x     a  a       /    a    x
     C  c         C           C    C
   A hoge haþel for þe noneȝ, & of hyghe eldee;
     a  a         x    /      a    a
     c   C         C         C    C
   Brode, bryȝt watȝ his berde, & al beuer-hwed,
     a    a        a    /     a    x
     C   c      C          C         C
   Sturne, stif on þe stryþþe on stal-worth schonkeȝ,
     a    a      a    /      a          x
     c   C        C      C    C
   Felle face as þe fyre, & fre of hys speche;
     a    a      a  /  a    x
      (c)      C         C            C   C
   & wel hym semed forsoþe, as þe segge þuȝt,
      (x)      a         a    /    a    x
```

<pre>
       c   C   C   C   C
  To lede a lortschyp in lee of leudeȝ ful gode.
       a   a   a / a   x
</pre>

As a contrast, we may cite the speech of the lady of the castle in lines 1508–15. Here there are only two heavy first half-lines in an eight-line passage. The frequent light multisyllabled measures run rapidly and, in combination with run-on lines and rambling syntax, produce an effect whose dramatic suitability is obvious:

<pre>
           C   C   C   C
  'I woled wyt at yow, wyȝe,' þat worþy þer sayde,
    (a)   a   a   /   a   x
           C   C   C   C
  '& yow wrathed not þer-wyth, what were þe skylle
    a   a   /a   (a)   x
      C   C   C   C
  Þat so ȝong & so ȝepe as ȝe at þis tyme,
      a   a   /   a   x
      C   C   C   C
  So cortayse, so knyȝtyly, as ȝe ar knowen oute,
      a   a   /   a   x
    c   C   C   C c   C
  & of alle cheualry to chose, þe chef þyng a-losed
    x   a   a   /   a   x
    C c   C   C   C
  Is þe lel layk of luf, þe lettrure of armes;
    a a   a   /   a   x
         C   C   C   C
  F[or] to telle of þis teuelyng of þis trwe knyȝteȝ,
         a   a   /   a   x
      C   C   C   C
  Hit is þe tytelet token & tyxt of her werkkeȝ.'
      a   a   /   a   x
</pre>

Metrical patterns contrast similarly in the opening interchange between the Green Knight and King Arthur. Here one must take into account the effect on metrical patterns of a dramatically expressive recitation. In both passages, I have scanned *þis* (lines 225, 252–53) as either a minor chief or an intermediate syllable. Actually, it would seem appropriate to give it minor emphasis in the blustering and vigorous speech of the Green Knight, but to read it without emphasis in Arthur's quiet reply.

```
      C    c        C      C       C
     Þe fyrst word þat he warp, 'wher is,' he sayd,
      x    a        a   / a        x
              3
           ┌─────────┐
           │C      (c)│ C      C      C
          'Þe gouernour of þis gyng? gladly I wolde
           a       (x) a    /a       x
      C    c     C              C    C
     Se þat segg in syȝt, & with hym-self speke
      a    a     a    /         a    x
                      C
                  raysoun.'                    [224-27]
                  C    C         C  (c)  C
           & [Arthur] sayde, 'wyȝe, welcum iwys to þis place,
                  a    a    /a       (x)  x
      C     (c)C   C             C
     Þe hede of þis ostel Arthour I hat;
      a     (x) a  /a            a
      C   c     C       C         C
     Liȝt luflych adoun, & lenge, I þe praye,
      a   a     x   /   a         x
         C        C        C C
     & quat-so þy wylle is, we schal wyt after.'  [252-55]
         a        a   /(a)  a  x
```

Finally, in the description of the death of the boar, metrical emphasis is maintained until the sword pierces the boar's heart. As he yields and drifts down the stream, the meter goes slack:

```
         C    c          C         C    C
     For þe mon merkkeȝ hym wel, as þay mette fyrst,
         a    a          x   /     a    x
      c  C      C         C C
     Set sadly þe scharp in þe slot euen,
      a  a     ?x   /    a   x
      C   (c)      C         C     C
     Hit hym vp to þe hult, þat þe hert schyndered,
      a    (a)     a   /    a     x
```

```
         C        C    C        C
& he ȝarrande hym ȝelde, & ȝedoun þe water
    a         a  /  a        x
             C
          ful tyt.                           [1592-96]
```

In these, as in other passages, meter is stylistically effective—effective not in itself but in relation to the content and detail of the narrative, the meanings expressed, and the kinds of words used to express them. Most of those who first knew the poem must have heard it in recitation, so that metrical patterns were perceived simultaneously with the other aspects of language. The modern student, regrettably, first comes to know the poem as a printed text, and can read it with little or no knowledge of how its language must originally have sounded. For him the metrical patterns are a separate object of study. But they must be included. The sounds and rhythms of words are essential to the style of *Sir Gawain and the Green Knight*.

NOTES

PART ONE. STYLE

1. Style and Meaning

1. This position has been argued with relation to the language of poetry by W. K. Wimsatt, Jr. See especially "Introduction: Style as Meaning" and chap. 3, "Diction," in *The Prose Style of Samuel Johnson* (New Haven, 1941), pp. 1–14, 50–62, and "The Substantive Level" and "Verbal Style: Logical and Counterlogical," in *The Verbal Icon* (with Monroe K. Beardsley, Lexington, Kentucky, 1954), pp. 133–51, 201–17. According to Wimsatt, "It is surely true that in a certain sense no two different words or different phrases ever mean fully the same. That is the literary sense. But there are other senses, the abstractive senses of science, philosophy, practical affairs, and religious dogma, in which different formulations can and do mean the same" (*The Verbal Icon*, pp. xii–xiii). It seems preferable to say that no two words or phrases have fully the same expressive value, defining meaning as one part of expressive value and style as another. But meaning and style are related in the same way in all language as it is used, whether its purpose be philosophical, scientific, and so on, or "literary" in the narrower sense. Wimsatt's syllogism in which the wording is varied throughout but the logic remains the same (*The Verbal Icon*, p. 204) is an artificial construction, lacking a true context; it does not show that stylistic variations are irrelevant to the use of syllogisms in discourse. If a syllogism is presented as an example in a book on logic or in a class lecture, its verbal formulation will determine its clarity and interest.

2. All citations are from the text as edited by Sir Israel Gollancz, Mabel Day, and Mary S. Serjeantson, EETS, 210 (London, 1940). Emendations, in square brackets, are theirs unless otherwise noted. I have not followed them in indicating expansions of abbreviations in the MS.

3. *Conclusion* is also found in Middle English. It is not a rare word, though it does not appear in *Gawain*; Chaucer uses it frequently. A comparison of the entries in *MED* for *fynisment* (s.v. *finishment* n.) and *conclusion* (s.v. *conclusioun* n.) shows that the former word is cited only from *Gawain* and two other texts, while there are over sixty citations for the latter in all its meanings. (The diacritical marks in *MED* entries have been omitted throughout.)

4. Neither the historical nor the critical definition of style presented here is to be identified with prescriptive definitions of style as excellence, or a kind of excellence, in the use of language. For such a definition see, e.g.,

F. L. Lucas, *Style* (London, 1955); the central question of the book is stated in the preface as follows: "What are the qualities that endow language, spoken or written, with persuasiveness or power?" (p. 8). Cf. p. 16: "Our subject, then, is simply the effective use of language . . . whether to make statements or to rouse emotions." Sir Herbert Read in *English Prose Style* is not so explicit as this, but a similar concept is implied by his treatment of the subject. Thus, in the chapter "Words," he remarks that "if style is reduced in the last analysis to a selective instinct, this instinct manifests itself most obviously in the use of words" (new ed. New York, 1952, p. 3). Effectiveness in the use of language is discussed by Sir Herbert not generally but in relation to each genre of writing. He speaks, for instance, of "the characteristics of a true narrative style—concreteness, economy and speed" (pp. 103–04).

5. The implications of language considered as a mode of action are to be distinguished from the logical implications of language, as when the major and minor premises of a syllogism imply the conclusion. The terms *meaning* and *implication* are analyzed in relation to language by Elder Olson in "William Empson, Contemporary Criticism, and Poetic Diction" (*Critics and Criticism*, ed. R. S. Crane, Chicago, 1952, pp. 45–82). Olson distinguishes "four conditions of meaning and inference" (p. 53), the third being the drawing of inferences from stated meanings. He goes on to discuss meaning in relation to poetry: "What the poetic character says in the mimetic poem is speech and has meaning; his *saying it* is action, an act of persuading, confessing, commanding, informing, torturing, or what not" (p. 54). In the present discussion a further distinction is drawn between the act of expressing certain meanings and the act of using certain words to express them. The latter is the determinant of purely verbal style.

6. Since I am concerned primarily with the language of literary works, I see no need to differentiate "meaning" as defined here from the "meaning" of a word to an animal that has learned it. For this distinction see Susanne K. Langer, *Philosophy in a New Key* (Harvard University Press, 1942), esp. chap. 3, "The Logic of Signs and Symbols." What I here call "meaning" is called "symbolistic meaning" by Mrs. Langer: "In talking *about* things we have conceptions of them, not the things themselves; and *it is the conceptions, not the things, that symbols directly 'mean'*" (p. 61). One can carry this further and distinguish between the concept of a subject of reference and the concept directly signified by a word used for reference; hearing, in *Othello*, a reference to "the Moor," we think of Othello himself, but only because we apply to him the idea directly signified by *Moor*. Both ideas can be entertained without responding to *Moor* as a sign. Subjects and modes of reference are discussed on pp. 12, 15–17.

Mrs. Langer's analysis of language as a uniquely human phenomenon is more adequate to the complexities of the subject than those in which "meaning" on the human plane and on the animal plane are confounded. Cf. I. A. Richards' references to "the kind of meaning that the least developed animals live by" and the "abstractive" act of a polyp or amoeba in responding to a stimulus (*The Philosophy of Rhetoric*, New York, 1936, p. 30).

7. During the past thirty years the American school of structural linguistics has applied the method of the natural sciences in the field of language, with brilliant results in the transcription of hitherto unrecorded languages and in foreign-language teaching. This method, as explained in Leonard Bloomfield's seminal book *Language* (New York, 1933) and later works, entails the consideration of language in terms of observable phenomena, primarily of speech, secondarily of written records, and the repudiation of "mentalism," i.e. the study of concepts. The phenomena susceptible of observation in the scientific sense include not only sounds and written letters but, more broadly, the environment in which they are produced and the behavior they elicit. Thus Bloomfield (pp. 74, 139) defines "the speech-sound" as "merely a means which enables us to respond to situations that would otherwise leave us unaffected, or to respond more accurately to situations that otherwise might prompt less useful responses. . . . In actual use, speech-sounds are uttered as signals. We have defined the *meaning* of a linguistic form as the situation in which the speaker utters it and the response which it calls forth in the hearer." See also his critique of mentalism, pp. 142–44. Such an approach is invaluable in erasing the preconceptions that have often impeded the understanding of languages totally different from our own, but it is of little use for the literary critic, who is concerned with what happens in the mind of the educated and discerning reader sitting in an armchair. Events of this sort cannot be measured or classified in the scientific sense, and even if they could be, the problem of evaluating them—of distinguishing between the discerning and the undiscerning response—would remain to be solved.

8. I. A. Richards conceives of a range between the extremes of "rigid" discourse, in which the meanings of words are set and stable (as in geometrical axioms), and poetry, in which the "virtue [of words] is to have no fixed and settled meaning separable from those of the other words they occur with," and in which "often the whole utterance . . . is not itself stable in meaning" (*Philosophy of Rhetoric*, p. 48). Considering the lines, from *Antony and Cleopatra*, "She looks like sleep, / As she would catch another Antony / In her strong toil of grace," he asks "Where, in terms of what entries in what possible dictionary, do the meanings here of *toil* and *grace* come to rest?" (ibid., p. 49). The metaphorical reference to an infinity of motion (in time? in space?) beclouds the issue. Presumably, an account of the expressive value of these words which would be fully satisfactory to everyone would be exceedingly difficult, if not impossible, to attain, but perceptive critics will agree within a general area of interpretation which is not infinite. So far as *grace* is concerned, this area will exclude the meanings "period . . . allowed by law for the payment of a bill of exchange" (*OED* s.v. *grace* sb. sense II, 7b), "short prayer . . . asking a blessing before . . . a meal" (sense III, 2), and others.

9. Cf. the anecdote quoted by I. A. Richards and C. K. Ogden in *The Meaning of Meaning* (8th ed. New York, 1956). Five African boys, when a table was tapped with the interlocutor's finger and the question "What is this?" was asked, gave in response five different words. "One lad had thought we wanted the word for tapping; another understood we were seeking the word for the material of which the table was made; another had the idea that we required the word for hardness; another thought we wished for a name for that which covered the table; and the last, not being able, perhaps, to think of anything else, gave us the word *meza*, table—the very word we were seeking" (J. H. Weeks, as quoted in *The Meaning of Meaning*, p. 78).

Roman Jakobson, in his essay "On Linguistic Aspects of Translation," published in the anthology *On Translation*, Harvard Studies in Comparative Literature, 23 (1959), 232–39, quotes Bertrand Russell's statement, "No one can understand the word *cheese* unless he has a nonlinguistic acquaintance with cheese" (p. 232). He continues, "If, however, we follow Russell's fundamental precept and place our 'emphasis upon the linguistic aspects of traditional philosophical problems,' then we are obliged to state that no one can understand the word *cheese* unless he has an acquaintance with the meaning assigned to this word in the lexical code of English . . . The meaning of the word *cheese* cannot be inferred from a nonlinguistic acquaintance with cheddar or with camembert without the assistance of the verbal code . . . Mere pointing will not teach us whether *cheese* is the name of the given specimen, or of any box of camembert, or of camembert in general or of any cheese, any milk product, any food, any refreshment, or perhaps any box irrespective of contents. Finally, does a word simply name the thing in question, or does it imply a meaning such as offering, sale, prohibition, or malediction?"

10. Multiple meaning as defined here differs from ambiguity—i.e. uncertainty as to which of two or more meanings is intended. The latter term is used by William Empson in *Seven Types of Ambiguity* to signify uncertainties of stylistic identification as well as uncertainties of definition. Speaking of the sentence "The brown cat sat on the red mat," Empson says "I should . . . isolate two of its 'meanings,' to form an ambiguity worth notice; . . . it might come out of a fairy story and might come out of *Reading without Tears*" (3rd ed. New Directions, 1953, p. 2). Empson defines ambiguity as "any verbal nuance, however slight, which gives room for alternative reactions to the same piece of language" (ibid., p. 1). Answering the imagined question "Is all good poetry supposed to be ambiguous?" he replies that he believes so (p. xv). Hesitation among alternative reactions to a "piece of language" and simultaneous reactions to many aspects of the language of a poetic passage in context are, however, two quite different responses.

11. An illuminating analysis of the process, with particular reference to the language of poetry, is presented by A. P. Ushenko in "Metaphor" (*Thought*, 30, 1955, 421–39). Ushenko distinguishes between the directly and indirectly signified meanings of a figuratively used word as the "explicit" and "implicit

components" of metaphor. "As a rule, only the vehicle of a metaphor is an explicit component because usually it alone contributes to the complex a literal meaning. The tenor is typically an implicit thought . . . The resultant [i.e. in Ushenko's terms, 'the metaphor itself, taken as a complex but integral whole'] is implicit in the sense in which metaphor is said to be elusive or unamenable to explicit or literal meaning by paraphrase" (p. 426).

Ushenko's article is designed as a critique of I. A. Richards' overly broad definition of metaphor as an aspect of all language and thought. (Cf. Richards, *Philosophy of Rhetoric*, p. 92: "That metaphor is the omnipresent principle of language can be shown by mere observation," and p. 94: "*Thought* is metaphoric, and proceeds by comparison, and the metaphors of language derive therefrom.") Ushenko emphasizes the necessity for analyzing poetic metaphor in context, and shows that its elusive character "does not put metaphor at the mercy of interpretations that vary uncontrollably from reader to reader" (pp. 426-27). See his analysis of the metaphorical description of old age as "life's setting sun," with particular reference to Shakespeare's sonnet "That Time of Year Thou May'st in Me Behold," pp. 426-28.

Cf. also the definition of metaphor in the "narrow sense" in Ernst Cassirer, *Language and Myth* (trans. Susanne K. Langer, Dover Publications, 1946), as "the *conscious* denotation of one thought content by the name of another which resembles the former in some respect, or is somehow analogous to it" (p. 86). One of these two concepts or items of thought content, according to Cassirer's formulation, "is semantically made to stand proxy for the other" (p. 87).

12. TG suggest this interpretation in their note to the line, citing *The Owl and the Nightingale* 658. See J. W. H. Atkins' note to this latter line in his edition of the poem (Cambridge, 1922), p. 57, and *OED* s.v. *hatchet* sb. sense 2.

13. Cf. the discussion of the difference between *spade* and *implement* in Wimsatt, "The Substantive Level" (*The Verbal Icon*, pp. 138-40), and the scheme of three levels of style, the "abstract or less than specific-substantive," corresponding to *implement*, the "minimum concrete or specific-substantive," corresponding to *spade*, and the "extra-concrete, the detailed, or more than specific," corresponding to *rusty garden spade*. The addition of *rusty*, however, results in a change other than that of mode of reference as here defined.

14. Kenneth Burke uses a chair to illustrate the difference between "semantic" and "poetic" meaning. "Semantic meaning would be a way of pointing to a chair. It would say, 'That thing is a chair.' . . . Poetic pointing, on the other hand, might take many courses, roughly summed up in these three sentences:

> 'Faugh! a chair!'
> 'Ho, ho! a chair!'
> 'Might I call your attention to yon chair?'

Of these, the third style of pointing obviously comes nearest to the semantic ideal. The first two, most strongly weighted with emotional values, with *attitudes*, would be farther off" ("Semantic and Poetic Meaning," *The Philosophy of Literary Form*, Vintage Books, 1957, p. 125). One might add that the choice of a meaning for purposes of reference can also have implications of attitude toward the object. Thus to call a chair "that thing" would usually imply disparagement.

15. Most of these meanings are cited in *OED* for the late sixteenth century or earlier; see *barren* senses 1, 3, and 4; *lofty* a. senses 1 and 2b; *canopy* sb. sense 1; *herd* sb.[1] senses 1 and 3. See also *canopy* sb. sense 2, *canopy* v., and *herd* sb.[1] sense 3b, all first cited from Shakespeare.

16. The distinction between *meaning* and *implication* is not to be equated with that between *referential* and *emotive language,* propounded in greatest detail by C. K. Ogden and I. A. Richards in *The Meaning of Meaning* (pp. 149 ff.), or with that between *denotation* and *connotation* as these words are used in literary criticism.

It is a dangerous oversimplification for the critic of poetic language to conceive of words as referring directly to things or entities. Rather, words evoke—cause the envisaging of—ideas which are used for purposes of reference. Reference is possible without meaning (i.e. without words); it can be accomplished by pointing a finger. When a word is discussed in the abstract, we assume not only a meaning but a subject of reference to which the meaning literally applies. For example, discussing the word *table* in its most common meaning, we assume reference to one of a certain class of objects within the larger class *furniture*. But in practice the same meaning may be used to refer to a different object altogether or to an abstract concept; to a flat rock on which food is set at a picnic or to the proffering of intellectual nourishment by a university curriculum.

Further, although implications, as here defined, *may* be emotive, they need not be. The sequence of words "Tomorrow, fair, with high temperature in the mid-seventies; winds southwest, ten to fifteen miles an hour" communicates certain opinions. It lacks emotional tone, but it nonetheless has implications; its verbal form implies the official weather report. Similar opinions could be communicated in different form ("I think it's going to be a nice day tomorrow," and so on). But here, as is usually true, the content of statement has the same implications as its form. One would not expect all these opinions about tomorrow's weather to be rattled off in a single statement in conversation.

The language of poetry is, strictly speaking, neither emotive nor referential as these terms are used by Ogden and Richards. ("The symbolic [here equivalent to 'referential'] use of words is *statement;* the recording, the support, the organization and the communication of references. The emotive use of words is a more simple matter, it is the use of words to express or excite feelings and attitudes"; *The Meaning of Meaning,* p. 149.) For the purposes of critical analysis, the poem is not an expression of the poet's feelings, nor is it a series of emotionally charged statements. It is a fiction, a representation by means of words of an experience of thought or speech. Like experiences in life, the fictional experience involves emotion, and if the poem is successful the reader will respond to that emotion. His response, however, is not caused by the expression of emotion in the poem; rather, it results from his grasp of the implications of the language of the poem on every level: the implications of what is expressed in the broad sense, and of the verbal form of its expression, including particular meanings, words as diction, and words as phonetic and metrical entities. Unless all these implications reinforce one another, the language of a poem fails to call forth a response.

If implications are included in the expressive value of language, then language can have other functions than the five analyzed by Ogden and Richards in *The Meaning of Meaning* (pp. 226–27). In addition to "the attitude [of speaker] to listener," for instance, it can imply the social relationship between speaker and listener, which is not the same thing. A man may love his king, his wife, and his small child, but he will express himself differently in talking to each.

Denotation and *connotation*, as applied to the language of poetry, express a division among the aspects of meaning. The idea evoked by a word may involve an element of emotion or attitude in addition to one of logic or fact, and the former is sometimes thought of as the word's *connotation*. For instance, *slender*, as compared with *thin*, might be said to connote prettiness or gracefulness—i.e. the speaker's favorable response to the person described. Connotation in this sense might be thought of as a form of implication, since it expresses something about the speaker. But connotation may be posited of a word in abstraction from context, implication only as it is used. A word may, in fact, imply the opposite of what it connotes. *Slender*, used ironically, not only takes on the indirect factual meaning "heavy" but implies an unfavorable response, a judgment of ungainliness. This implication depends on the word's connotations, but here they work in reverse.

M. H. Abrams, in his revision of *A Glossary of Literary Terms* by Norton and Rushton (New York, 1957), defines connotation as "the associated meanings [a word] implies or suggests." As an example he cites *horse* and *steed:* "Steed has a different connotation, deriving from the romantic literary contexts in which we commonly find that word used" (see s.v. "Connotation and Denotation"). The emotional element in the idea evoked by the word is here due to specifically literary associations; such connotations, like those of *slender*, can be made to work in reverse. Irony of this sort—what might be called an irony of diction—is important in the style of *Sir Gawain and the Green Knight*. Examples of it are discussed on p. 65 and pp. 104–05.

17. On the practical level, the analysis of style cannot be "complete" in the sense of dealing exhaustively with every aspect of the language of a literary work, nor is such completeness desirable. Each critic will have his special interests; each text will call for emphasis on certain problems. And the analysis of style need not include a consideration of level of diction and other

aspects of words as words to yield illuminating results. The names of two important scholar-critics, Erich Auerbach and Leo Spitzer, will occur to the reader in this connection. Both have carried out detailed stylistic studies of medieval literary texts; neither has concerned himself with problems of style in the strictly verbal sense.

Auerbach's *Mimesis* (trans. Willard Trask, Princeton, Princeton University Press, 1953) needs no introduction here. Among the works discussed in its chronologically arranged essays on style as "the representation of reality in western literature," none, unfortunately, is drawn from Middle English. Auerbach's method permits him to make direct comparisons between works in different languages; cf. his opening study of the *Odyssey* and the Old Testament. Only occasionally does he comment on qualities of diction, as in his discussion of the colloquial Latin of Petronius' *Banquet:* "The guests gathered at Trimalchio's party are southern Italian freedmen-parvenus of the first century; they hold the views of such people and speak their language almost without literary stylization" (p. 30).

Spitzer has recently extended his interests to the field of the Middle English lyric; see his "Three Great Middle English Poems," *Archivum Linguisticum, 3* (1951), 1–22, 137–65. In these interpretations many different devices of style are identified and related to a principle held to govern the form of each poem; none of the devices depends on the choice of a particular kind of word for the expression of meaning. Spitzer explains his methodology and discusses the relation of linguistic to literary analysis in chap. 1, "Linguistics and Literary History," of his book of the same title (Princeton, Princeton University Press, 1948). The process of stylistic analysis is described as one of "first observing details about the superficial appearance of the particular work . . . then, grouping these details and seeking to integrate them into a creative principle which may have been present in the soul of the artist; and, finally, making the return trip to all the other groups of observations in order to find whether the 'inward form' one has tentatively constructed gives an account of the whole" (p. 19).

2. The Historical Study of Style

1. The date of MS Cotton Nero A.x., in which are found the sole surviving copies of *Gawain, Purity, Patience,* and *Pearl,* is given by *MED* as c1400, and that of the composition of *Gawain* as ?c1390. *Gawain* is classified by *MED* as a West Midland text.

Mary S. Serjeantson, in "The Dialects of the West Midlands in Middle English," *Review of English Studies, 3* (1927), 54–67, 186–203, 319–31, identifies the dialect of Cotton Nero A.x. as Northwest Midland (p. 327), and concludes that "on the whole, Derbyshire seems the least improbable area to which the Nero MS. may be assigned, whatever the original dialects of the poems may have been" (pp. 327–28). In "The Dialect of MS. Cotton

PAGE 27

Nero A.x.," introduction to the GDS edition of *Gawain*, pp. xli–lxvi, she presents a detailed analysis of phonology, accidence, and rhymes. In her view the rhymes "do not indicate a dialect differing markedly, if at all, from that of the scribe, or perhaps it is safer to say that the evidence they afford is insufficient to determine this" (pp. lv–lvi).

J. P. Oakden, in *Alliterative Poetry in Middle English*, 1 (Manchester, 1930), chap. 1, and chap. 3, 72 ff., takes issue with Miss Serjeantson on certain points of dialect analysis, notably the value of place names (see especially s.v. Point 17, pp. 26–28). From a study of the rhymes in *Pearl* and *Gawain* and the alliteration in *Gawain*, *Patience*, and *Purity*, he concludes that the dialect of the poet belongs, within the Northwest Midland region, to "the area comprising S. Lancs. and N. W. Derby," with somewhat stronger evidence for the former (p. 85). Oakden finds, further, that "an area comprising S. Lancs., S. W. Yorks., N. W. Derby and Chs." is indicated by the regional distribution of the vocabulary of the poem in modern dialect use (pp. 85–86). For additional evidence of the same sort pointing to Lancs., Chs., and W. Yks., especially the first, see R. J. Menner, "*Sir Gawain and the Green Knight* and the West Midland," *PMLA*, 37 (1922), 518 and n. 1.

A further connection between *Gawain* and Lancs. has recently been pointed out by H. L. Savage. In Sir James P. Kay-Shuttleworth's novel *Scarsdale*, published in 1860, an emissary from the workers at a Lancashire cotton mill goes to the proprietors carrying, as a sign of peaceful intent, a branch of holly (see H. L. Savage, *The Gawain-Poet: Studies in His Personality and Background*, Chapel Hill, North Carolina, 1956, pp. 15–16). A continuity of tradition between this gesture and the *holyn bobbe* of the Green Knight, who tells Arthur's court, "ȝe may be seker bi þis braunch þat I bere here / Þat I passe as in pes, & no plyȝt seche" (265–66), is clearly indicated, though we do not know how widespread the custom may have been in the Northwest Midland area in the late 14th century. See also Savage's discussions of the scenic descriptions in *Gawain* and *Pearl* and the *euerferne* or polypody of *Patience* 438 (pp. 14–15), and his appendix B, "Linguistic Evidence as to Place of Origin of the Author of *Sir Gawain and the Green Knight*" (pp. 128–33). Here Savage reviews the material presented by Oakden and Miss Serjeantson, and, emphasizing the importance of the "unusually high proportion of ON words" pointed out by Oakden, concludes that "the poet . . . may have been reared either in Lancashire, or in the Yorkshire West Riding that adjoins Lancashire; possibly near the Ribble-Aire valleys, possibly not; but probably not very far north of that line, and certainly within an area of former Scandinavian settlement where ON words and locutions were thick" (p. 132). Within this area Savage seeks to connect the poet with one of the Lancashire manors held in the latter half of the 14th century by the French Count Enguerrand de Coucy, who lived in England for a number of years as a son-in-law of Edward III (pp. 133–38). This further step depends on a hypothesis to which a considerable portion of the book is devoted, namely, that the characterization of Gawain is modeled on Coucy. But this hypothesis has yet to win general acceptance.

Ralph W. V. Elliott has recently proposed to identify the Green Chapel with Ludchurch or Lud's Church, a fissure in the Castle Cliff rocks near Leek in northern Staffordshire ("Sir Gawain in Staffordshire: A Detective Essay in Literary Geography," *The London Times*, May 21, 1958, p. 12). The exact connections Elliott is able to draw between features of the terrain of this locale and the descriptions of the boar hunt and Gawain's journey from the castle to his rendezvous make his hypothesis more attractive than any of those previously proposed, at least to one who has not visited the actual scenes. (Oakden, *1*, 257–61, identified the castle with that at Clitheroe in Lancs.; Miss Day, introduction to the GDS edition of *Gawain*, pp. xix–xx, proposed Thursehouse or Thursehole, near Wetton Mill, Staffs., as the site of Gawain's second encounter with the Green Knight. For the less plausible suggestion of a locale in Cumberland, see TG, note to lines 709 ff.)

Regarding the poem's date of composition, Laura Hibbard Loomis, in *Arthurian Literature in the Middle Ages* (London, 1959), pp. 528–40, asserts that "the architecture, the costume, the armour, so accurately described, are appropriate to a date between 1360 and 1400 . . ." (p. 529). Menner, in his introduction to *Purity* (New Haven, 1920), pp. xxx–xxxviii, presents convincing evidence that *Gawain* was composed later than *Patience* and *Purity*.

Changes in wording, numerous scribal errors of various sorts, and the admixture of forms alien to the dialect of the poet as evidenced by alliteration and rhyme, suggest that one or more intermediary copies may well have separated the author's original from MS Cotton Nero A.x. The problem is difficult, and its solution awaits more precise knowledge of scribal practices and tradition in Middle English. An elaborate hypothesis involving seven scribes, each prone to certain types of scribal error, is presented by Oakden, *1*, 261–63. This hypothesis was adversely criticized by W. W. Greg in "A Bibliographical Paradox," *The Library*, 4th ser. *13* (1933), 188–91; a reply by Oakden appeared in the following volume (1934), pp. 353–58.

Metrical considerations, such as the treatment of final -*e*, do not provide reliable criteria for the dating of the poem. The problem of final -*e* is discussed in detail on pp. 140 ff.

2. A recent expression of the traditional judgment is that of Laura Hibbard Loomis: "The hero of *Gawain and the Green Knight* is likened to a pearl beside a pea (l. 2364), and so might the poem itself be reckoned among its contemporaries" (p. 528).

In praising the style of the poem, critics have frequently called attention to the poet's mastery of detail. According to Wells, "he was a lover of details, but he handled the details with a constructive power and a picturesqueness that create vivid impressions" (p. 56). Oakden, after asserting that "among the English romances [*Gawain*] must be accorded the highest place," goes on to say that "the poet discloses the details effectively and with a natural feeling for literary grace and form" (*Alliterative Poetry*, 2, 1935, 46–47). Dorothy Everett, too, speaks of the poet's use of detail: "[The *Gawain*-poet] had a mind stored with unusually vivid memories of sight and sound; and he knew how to select the telling details and phrases that would convey them" (*Essays on Middle English Literature*, Oxford, 1955, p. 80). According to Francis Berry, "The experience [specifically, that presented in ll. 720-32] is actualized in the muscular images and rhythms, in the firm grasp of concrete particulars" ("Sir Gawayne and the Grene Knight," in *The Age of Chaucer*, ed. Boris Ford, Pelican Books A290, 1954, p. 149).

John Speirs, in the essay on *Gawain* in his *Medieval English Poetry: The Non-Chaucerian Tradition* (London, 1957), finds in the poem a "delightful acceptance and vivid consciousness of what takes the senses in rich colour and decorative pattern, in costly magnificence of costume and tapestry, jewellery and embroidery, in elaborate and subtle craftsmanship in metal, wood and stone" (p. 222), and speaks further of "masses of bright colours and concatenations of differentiated sounds" (p. 222). But actually the depiction of material luxury and splendor in *Gawain* is restrained and economical as compared with other poems of the tradition (see pp. 103-04, 123-24). There is surprisingly little sensory detail in the poem, the poet's descriptive technique being utterly unlike that of a Keats or a Hopkins. There certainly is vividness, but this effect is achieved by different means (see pp. 128-29).

The metrical skill of the *Gawain*-poet has recently been singled out for praise by H. L. Savage, who speaks of his "knowledge of vowel and consonantal quality, his awareness of that elusive, but very real, nexus between sound and sense." Savage continues, "He seldom wrote a line lacking in zest, or imagination, or rhythm. . . . To say so much is simply to say that he was past master of his medium" (pp. 23-24).

3. Such a range of stylistic qualities can be envisaged also for syntactic constructions, word order, and so on. In modern English, for example, "I thought him to be honest" is more distinctively formal than "I thought he was honest," and "Blue are her eyes" is more distinctively formal than "Her eyes are blue." The principles of the historical study of style discussed here are therefore applicable to other aspects of language, although the illustrations given will consist almost entirely of single words.

4. *OED* labels *smitch* (s.v. sb.²) "Sc. and U.S." See also *EDD* s.v. *smitch* sb.¹ The variant *smidgen* is apparently restricted to the U.S.; see *A Dictionary of Americanisms* (2 vols., Chicago, 1951) and *A Dictionary of American English* (4 vols., Chicago, 1938-44), s.v. *smidgen, smidgeon*.

5. A count of citations in *OED* is often indicative of the comparative frequency of use of literary words. *Scintilla* has 4 citations in all, the earliest dated 1692; the earliest citation for *particle* is dated 1380, and there are 23 citations postdating 1692. (Counts include all meanings for both words.)

6. The sense of the origin of this word has been lost, even among educated speakers who are aware of its local dialect status. (One such speaker suggested to me a connection with Fr. *doigt* in the sense "fingertip.") The etymology I have given, however, seems clearly the correct one. *Doit*, in both the original and the extended meanings, is listed by Merriam-Webster's *Unabridged Dictionary*, published in America, as well as by *OED;* neither refers to a

variant pronunciation with [aɪ]. The word is not included in Hans Kurath's *A Word Geography of the Eastern United States* (Ann Arbor, Michigan, 1949), since the meanings "small bit, small piece" were not among those investigated in the studies on which the volume is based. The pronunciation [daɪt] goes back to the phonetic identity in early modern English of *oi* and long *i*, as when Pope rhymes *join/line*. See Helge Kökeritz, *Shakespeare's Pronunciation* (New Haven, 1953), "*i* in *line*, *oi* in *loin*," pp. 216 ff. For the equation of Dutch *ui* with English *oi*, see A. J. Barnouw, "Echoes of the Pilgrim Fathers' Speech" (Amsterdam, 1923), No. 32.

7. The subject has been comprehensively treated by R. M. Wilson in *The Lost Literature of Medieval England*, London, 1952. Wilson devotes an entire chapter to evidence for lost works in each literary form, including religious and didactic literature and historical narrative, as well as romance and lyric poetry. We owe *Gawain* itself, it will be recalled, to the preservation of a single manuscript. G. L. Brook, in his introduction to *The Harley Lyrics* (Manchester, 1948), p. 1, remarks that "one of the chief obstacles in the way of the study of medieval literature is the disappearance of valuable material. The total bulk of Middle English writings that have been preserved is considerable, but among those writings religious and didactic works preponderate enormously. Such a lack of balance is the natural result of the part played by the monasteries in the preservation of manuscripts. . . . More than half of the secular lyrics that have come down from before the end of the fourteenth century are preserved in a single manuscript, MS. Harley 2253, in the British Museum."

8. Kenneth Sisam, in his introduction to *Fourteenth-Century Verse and Prose* (Oxford, 1955), p. xviii, says of the West Midland poets of the late 14th century, "They preferred the unrimed alliterative verse, which from pre-Conquest days must have lived on in the remote Western counties without a written record." See Chap. 3, esp. pp. 57–58.

9. "Das Ziel ist also die Aufstellung einer Liste von Wörtern, durch deren Vorkommen die Lokalisierung eines Textes—neben den Mitteln der anderen, im engeren Sinn grammatischen Kriterien—ermöglicht wird" (p. 1).

10. Ed. by Richard Morris, EETS, 57, 59, 62, 66, 68, 99, 101 (1874–93). Four MSS containing relatively complete texts are printed by Morris in parallel columns. Sections of the poem found in other MSS are included in a group of appendices.

11. *MED* gives the date of composition of the poem as a1325—i.e. between 1300 and 1325. See also Wells, p. 340, and the introduction to the selection from *Cursor* in *Early Middle English Texts*, ed. Bruce Dickins and R. M. Wilson (London, 1951), pp. 114–15.

The most complete study of the phonology of the original poem is Otto Strandberg's *The Rime-Vowels of Cursor Mundi* (Uppsala, 1919). Strandberg considered that the evidence of the rhymes pointed to a Scottish original, but because of the author's statement that he had translated the book into "English tongue" for the love of "English people of England" (*Cursor*, 232–35), he preferred to assign it to the extreme north of England (pp. xiv–xv). Kaiser concludes from his study of the vocabulary that *Cursor* is of Scottish origin. He presents evidence that the Scots dialect spoken south of the Firth of Forth, as opposed to Gaelic, was thought of as "English," and that a Scot of that region would have considered himself an Englishman (pp. 8–13). Jordan (p. 14) assigns the poem to Northumberland or Durham; *MED* classifies it as a Northern text (*Plan and Bibliography*, p. 12).

12. EETS, 99, 101 (one vol.), pp. 109–261. For the assignment of T to Hereford, see pp. 134–35. C was assigned by Hupe to north Lancashire (p. 127). In another article, "On the Filiation and the Text of the Middle English Poem *Cursor Mundi*" (EETS, 99, 101, pp. 57–103), however, he described it as "written in the dialect of the neighbourhood of Durham" (p. 103). According to Dickins and Wilson, C "probably best represents the dialect of the original" (p. 115). Another MS, important because of its apparently close relationship to the original (see Hupe, "On the Filiation," p. 103) but unfortunately containing only about five thousand lines, is that belonging to the Library of the College of Physicians, Edinburgh. According to Hupe, this MS (E) is "a Northumbrian (or Scotch) copy" ("*Cursor* Studies," p. 130). E is assigned to Northumberland and called "the oldest manuscript" of *Cursor* by Jordan (p. 14), but *MED* considers it contemporary with C and T, dating all three a1400.

13. The lines:

> In sotherin englis was it draun,
> And turnd it haue i till our aun
> Language o [þe] northrin lede,
> Þat can nan oiþer englis rede. [C, 20061–64]

precede the story of *The Assumption of Our Lady;* they are omitted in T. Kaiser (p. 1) also quotes in Latin Trevisa's well-known description of the dialects of fourteenth-century England, which runs, in Higden's version, as follows: "Al þe longage of þe Norþhumbres, and specialliche at ȝork, is so scharp, slitting, and frotynge and vnschape, þat we souþerne men may þat longage vnneþe vnderstonde" (*Polychronicon Ranulphi Higden*, 2, ed. Churchill Babington, London, 1869, p. 163). According to Higden, the Midlands constituted a linguistic buffer zone: "Þerfore it is þat Mercii, þat beeþ men of myddel Engelond, as it were parteners of þe endes, vnderstondeþ bettre þe side langages, norþerne and souþerne, þan norþerne and souþerne vnderstondeþ eiþer oþer" (ibid.).

14. P. 17. Kaiser gives as an example the word *drightin*, for which a different word is used 221 times in T, but which he excludes from the list because it is found in such Southern writers as William of Shoreham.

15. "Die Sprache des Nordens ist . . . lebenskräftiger. Sie hat die Möglichkeiten, die vor allem durch Erhaltung des alten Sprachgutes, durch Ablei-

tung und Neubildung und nicht zuletzt durch Aufnahme skandinavischer Lehnwörter gegeben waren, zu ihrer Formung voll genutzt. Der Umfang des nördlichen Wortschatzes bleibt dem des Südens bei weitem überlegen" (pp. 114–15).

16. "Die gegebenen Belege lassen zunächst einmal deutlich erkennen, dass der Wortschatz des Dichters . . . zu dem der nördlichen Hälfte des Landes gehört. Für die Entscheidung der Frage 'Osten oder Westen' bietet sich leider keine direkte Vergleichsmöglichkeit, da für den Nordwesten kein grösseres Sprachdenkmal der ungefähr gleichen Zeit lokalisiert ist" (p. 163). Kaiser goes on to argue for a Northwestern, rather than Northeastern, localization of *Gawain* on the basis of the large number of words found only in *Gawain*, or found only in other alliterative poems in the same manuscript, *Gawain*, and *St. Erkenwald*. The findings of Max Kullnick, which he cites in this connection, are in many respects unreliable and are criticized in detail on pp. 48–51.

17. The line is discussed by J. R. R. Tolkien, "Chaucer as a Philologist: The Reeve's Tale," *Transactions of the Philological Society* (1934), p. 45.

18. The complete text of both versions, printed in parallel columns, was edited by Sir Frederic Madden, 3 vols., London, 1847. Madden's glossary is an invaluable tool for detailed study; a simple system of signs makes it possible to see at once whether any word or form occurs in both texts or only in one, and numerous citations are given. An edition by G. L. Brook is in prospect but, as this is written, has not yet appeared.

19. N. Bøgholm, *The Layamon Texts: A Linguistical Investigation*, Travaux du cercle linguistique de Copenhague, 3, Copenhagen, 1944; H. C. Wyld, "Studies in the Diction of Layamon's Brut," *Language*, *6* (1930), 1–24; *9* (1933), 47–71, 171–91; *10* (1934), 149–201; *13* (1937), 29–59, 194–237. There is a brief discussion of the vocabulary of the *Brut* in Oakden, *2*, 172–74. Since this is largely based on Wyld, and contains no material not to be found in Wyld or Bøgholm, it need not be given special consideration here.

20. Since the *Brut* of Wace was completed in 1155, Lawman's work, which was largely founded on it, cannot have been undertaken prior to the second half of the twelfth century. Toward the end of the poem (lines 31,949 ff., Madden, *3*, 285), there is an account of "Peter's Pence," a tribute paid by England to the Pope, concerning which the narrator remarks: "drihten wat hu longe / þeo laȝen scullen ilæste" (A 31,979–80). Since payment of the tribute was put to an end by King John in 1205 or 1206, completion of the poem prior to the latter date is indicated. See Madden, *1*, xvii–xxi, and notes on the passage; Joseph Hall, *Selections from Layamon's Brut* (Oxford, 1924), pp. vi–vii, and notes to lines 1739, 1754. *MED* dates the poem ?a1200, the A manuscript a1225, and the B manuscript c1300.

21. The A version is generally assigned to Worcester, where Lawman (lines 5–10) says he lived. The most comprehensive discussion of the phonology of the poem is that of Adolf Luhmann, *Die Überlieferung von*

Laȝamons Brut, Halle, 1906; see especially pp. 194–95. The B version is assigned by Jordan to Somerset; see p. 5. For the phonology of the B version see Otto Kühl, *Der Vokalismus der Laȝamon-Handschrift B*, Halle, 1913. The language of B is described by Kühl as Southern with an admixture of forms of West Saxon ancestry alien to the A text (p. 10).

22. For the relation of A and B to X, see the detailed discussion of errors common to both MSS in Rudolf Seyger, *Beiträge zu Laȝamons Brut* (Halle, 1912), pp. 55–59. For the relation of B to the original, see Madden, *1*, xxxiii–xxxiv, xxxvi–xxxviii, and Seyger, pp. 3–42.

23. Ibid., p. 18. After *The Owl and the Nightingale*, the adjective is cited by *OED* (s.v. *athel*) only from alliterative poems, the latest being Holland's *Houlate*, c1450. See also *MED*, s.v. *athel*, adj.

24. Ibid. See *OED* s.v. *bache* and *slade* sb.[1], *MED* s.v. *bach* n. (1). But the implication in Bøgholm's entry that *slade* is replacing an obsolescent word is misleading. *Bach(e)* survives in modern dialect English. *EDD*, s.v. *bach(e)*, gives several definitions, including "a river or stream" (sense 1). According to *English Place-Name Elements*, ed. A. H. Smith (Cambridge, 1956), s.v. *bece*[1], *bæce*, both "valley" and "stream" are current meanings for West Midland dialect *bache*, *batch*. The two meanings cannot always be clearly distinguished; thus in *MED* the definition "a stream or its valley" is illustrated by citations from the *Brut*.

25. Ibid. Since Old English literature is represented even less adequately than Middle English by the surviving texts, conclusions as to the status of Old English words must always be tentative. Status can most reliably be determined by a comparative check of the citations in BT and Supplement with those in Grein. The references for a given word in Grein are not necessarily exhaustive. Thus Robert P. Creed, in "The *Andswarode*-System in Old English Poetry," *Speculum*, 32 (1957), 523–28, points out that "roughly a third of the appearances of *andswarode* discussed in this article are not listed in Grein" (p. 523, n. 3).

Of the citations for *blanca* in BT and Supplement, only one is from prose. See *An Old English Martyrology*, ed. George Herzfeld, EETS, 116 (1900), p. 20, line 1; BT cite the text as ed. by Thomas Oswald Cockayne in *The Shrine* (London, 1864). For *hors*, a number of prose citations are given from sources including laws, a medical treatise, and the Bible. See, e.g., the account of the treatment for a horse's leprosy in *Leechdoms, Wortcunning, and Starcraft*, ed. Cockayne ("Rolls Series" 420, 1864–66), *2*, 156, lines 10 ff., where *hors* is used throughout; the prose section of the Paris Psalter (*The West-Saxon Psalms*, ed. James Wilson Bright and Robert Lee Ramsay, Boston, 1907), 31:10, 32:15; *King Alfred's Orosius*, ed. Henry Sweet, Pt. I, EETS, 79 (1883), p. 18, line 15; p. 21, lines 1, 5.

Fr. Klaeber's glossary to *Beowulf* (3rd ed. New York, 1950) is a convenient source of information on the status of words in the vocabulary of that poem, since symbols indicating distribution among the extant texts are used preceding words or meanings; similar indications are provided by R. J. Menner, glossary to *The Poetical Dialogues of Solomon and Saturn*, New York, 1941. I have occasionally availed myself of Klaeber's and Menner's designations, checking them in each case against the material in BT, Supplement, and Grein.

26. *Language, 9,* 47–48. But Wyld's opinion that the *Brut* was superior in style to later alliterative poetry "with the possible exception of the Morte d'Arthur in the Thornton MS." (p. 48) is shared by few, if any, students of the literature.

27. See the scheme presented in *Language, 9,* 49. The last two categories, "External Nature" and "Supernatural Beings," were not treated in the published series of articles.

28. For the contrasting roles played by *kniʒt* and poetical terms such as *rink* in the traditional style of Middle English alliterative verse, see pp. 53–62.

29. Material on the traditional character of the phraseology of the *Brut* may be found in Karl Regel, "Die Alliteration im Laȝamon," in Germanistische Studien, 1 (Vienna, 1872), 171–246, and John S. P. Tatlock, "Epic Formulas, Especially in Laȝamon," *PMLA, 38* (1923), 494–529. Regel's material, as his title indicates, consists almost entirely of traditional alliterating combinations. It is divided into groups, with alphabetical listing within each group; thus "fisc and fujel" comes under the heading of linked concrete words (p. 187) and "hunger and haete" under that of linked abstractions (p. 199). Since there is no general index, this system makes for delay in the location of particular phrases. Tatlock's list, in a single alphabetical series, includes over 125 "epic formulas," with parallels from Old and Middle English poetry (pp. 495–510). Some of these involve an alliterative linking, some a traditional rhyme, some neither. Both Regel and Tatlock draw their material from the A version; neither is concerned with the alterations of A's phraseology in B.

30. *Bord* corresponds to Latin *mensa* in a prose translation of Psalm 68:23, where "Fiat mensa eorum coram ipsis in laqueum" is translated "Beo bord oþþe mese hieræ beforan him on grine." See *Eadwine's Canterbury Psalter*, ed. Fred Harsley, EETS, 92, Pt. II (1889), p. 117. The word is also cited in this sense from a gloss by Grein. *Bord* "shield" is designated as poetic by Klaeber, glossary to *Beowulf;* the meanings "plank" and "table" apparently do not occur in the poem. Grein gives 30 citations from poetry for *bord* "shield" (s.v. sense 1).

31. *Bord* also has in Lawman, as it had in Old English, the meaning "side of a ship" (cf. modern *aboard*). The OE word is apparently derived in this sense from a Gmc. **bord-oz*, m., "border, rim," the product of which had become largely identified with that of Gmc. **bord-o(m)*, n., "board." *Bord* "shield," like *bord* "table," is generally taken to be a metaphorical use of the meaning "made of board, wooden," rather than of "border, rim." See the discussion in *OED*, s.v. *board* sb., and BT, s.v. *bord*, sense II.

32. Lines 14214, 18523; see Madden, 2, 170, 353. In the latter passage, the sense "plank" merges into the sense "table": "bordes heo brædden / al þat folc æt & dronc" (A version, 18523-24).

33. *The Buik of the Croniclis of Scotland*, ed. William B. Turnbull (3 vols. London, 1858), *3*, 457, lines 57806-07.

34. Thus OE *beonet-lēah*, later *Bentley*, "bent-lea, lea on which bent grass grows." For the phonology of *beonet* and a list of cognates in other Germanic languages, see *OED* s.v. *bent* sb.[1] See also *English Place-Name Elements* s.v. *beonet*.

35. See Short Title list, p. x. The two volumes are subtitled, respectively, *The Dialectical and Metrical Survey* and *A Survey of the Traditions*.

For the student of Middle English alliterative poetry this work is indispensable, and one cannot be too grateful for its existence. It is an authoritative source of clear and detailed information on the presumed dialect and dates, MSS, metrical patterns, content, and the traditional vocabulary and phraseology of the poems from the earliest Middle English fragments through the late fifteenth- and early sixteenth-century Scottish works, as well as material relating to Old English prose and the Middle English rhymed romances.

36. Pp. 190-91. In *1*, 86, the percentages of ON words are given for *Gawain, Pearl, Purity,* and *Patience* as part of the discussion of the dialect provenience of these poems. The percentage for *Gawain* is 10.3; one assumes that this figure is based on counts of distinct words rather than of occurrences. For study of dialect such counts are useful; for the study of style a *seriatim* count would be more valuable, since the impression of style derives from the reading of the successive words of a poem rather than its vocabulary in abstraction from particular passages.

37. In discussing descriptive adjectives as a subclass of "Poetic Words," Oakden says, "Under this heading it is only necessary to record the most important examples, for almost all the Middle English poetic adjectives make their appearance in alliterative verse" (2, 185). Under "Archaic Words" it is said that "a complete list of these archaisms cannot be given here, but representative selections will serve to illustrate the range and nature of the forms collected" (p. 187). See also "Examples of Poetical Nouns," pp. 185-86, and "Verbs Chiefly Confined to Poetry," p. 186.

38. Thus Oakden excludes from the list of "chiefly alliterative" words in the group including *Gawain* those words "which occur solely in one or more of these poems" (2, 180). Of the words retained in the list, he says, "These words circulated among the various alliterative writers, partly through a common tradition and partly through imitation" (p. 181).

39. However, Heinz Kittner's dissertation, *Studien zum Wortschatz William Langlands* (Halle, 1937) may be recommended to the student of *Gawain* both as a more recent source of information on particular words and for its general discussion of the relationship of the vocabulary of *Piers Plowman* to

that of the other alliterative poems, notably the works of the *Gawain*-poet, and that of Chaucer. In connection with this latter point, see below, p. 232, n. 16. The major part of Kittner's study (pp. 6–106 out of a total of 131 pages) consists of a dictionary of the non-Chaucerian vocabulary of *Piers Plowman*, with information on meaning, modern standard and dialect descent, and range of occurrence in Middle English texts, frequently including line citations. The words are divided into groups according to the languages from which they are derived, and further subdivided according to the different parts of speech. This method of presentation, though helpful to one wishing to survey and classify Langland's vocabulary, makes for delays in the location of particular words. It is unfortunate that a general word-index could not have been provided.

40. E.g. *bredeȝ* 2071, glossed as "limits" and derived from OE *brerd* "margin" (TG gloss as "planks," GDS as "boards"; both derive from OE *bred* "board"); *cemmed* 188, glossed as "folded, plaited," with a suggestion of relationship to OE *sēam* "seam" (TG and GDS gloss as "combed"; both derive from OE *cemban*); and *swete* 2518, glossed as "friendship," with a suggestion of relationship to OE *swēte* "sweet" (TG gloss as "following suit," GDS as "to match"; both derive from OF *suite*).

41. As a result, *delful*, which occurs only in B (Madden, glossary, s.v. *deolful*), *blonke*, which occurs only in A (s.v. *blancke*), and *derne*, which occurs in both texts (s.v. *deorne*), are alike cited from "Lawman."

42. "Es ist zu vermuten, dass eine Reihe dieser Wörter bereits zur Zeit des SG. altertümlich klangen und gerade deshalb von den alliterierenden Dichtern als ungewöhnlich empfunden und gern verwertet wurden" (p. 51).

43. Of the first subclass Kullnick says, "Viele von diesen Wörtern werden als nördliche zu bezeichnen sein" (p. 51); of the second, "Diese Wörter gehören gleichzeitig dem Wortschatz der geistlichen Dichtungen des Nordens an" (p. 52). But scarcely any of the words in either subclass have meanings associated with religious subject matter.

44. "Der Wortschatz Chaucers scheint mit dem der alliterierenden Dichtungen am ehesten in hocharistokratischen Dingen übereinzustimmen, was in der Gemeinsamkeit der behandelten Stoffe begründet ist" (p. 52).

45. "Dies dürften z.T. Wörter vulgärer Herkunft sein, die man sonst in pathetischen Versen nicht gern verwendete" (p. 52).

46. Statements on usage in Chaucer are based on citations in the Chaucer *Concordance*, ed. John S. P. Tatlock and Arthur G. Kennedy, Washington, D. C., 1927.

47. "Bei einigen mag es Zufall sein, dass sie nur in den alliterierenden Dichtungen belegt sind, andere aber müssen in besonderem Grade dazu beigetragen haben, das Wortbild dieser alliterierenden Dichtungen seltsam zu gestalten" (p. 52).

48. There is nothing to be gained by an exhaustive critique of the hundred odd words of Kullnick's group 5a. Its shortcomings as a list of unique occurrences are revealed by additional citations from Middle English texts

available in *OED* and *MED* for the first ten words: *asay, asswyþe, aumayl, avanters, awherfe, baleȝ, barbe, bastel-roueȝ, bay* adj., and *baye* v. *Asay* 1328 (*OED* s.v. *assay* sb. sense 9; *MED assai* n. sense 5a) represents a special application to hunting of the general sense "trial" (it is in fact cited from *Gawain* by *MED* under that sense). It thus seems unlikely that it means "the place where the trial was made," an alternative reading suggested by GDS. *Asswyþe* (*OED* s.v. *aswithe* adv. phr.) is a contracted form of the phrase *as swithe* (*MED* refers the reader to *swithe*); *swithe* adv. is common in Middle English. *Avanters* (*OED* s.v. *avanters*, *MED avanters* n.pl.) is cited by *OED* from the fifteenth century *Boke of St. Albans*, a hunting treatise. *Aumayl* (*OED* s.v. *amel* sb., MED *amal* n.) is found in *Libeaus Desconus, Sir Launfal*, and *Sir Orfeo*. The occurrence in *Sir Orfeo* is not cited by *OED*, or by *MED* s.v. *amal*; see line 364 of the poem in *Fourteenth Century Verse and Prose*, ed. Kenneth Sisam, and the note to that line. *Amell* n. and *ameled* a. are cited by *MED*, s.v. *ameled* ppl., from the Ashmole MS of *Sir Orfeo*. *Awherfe* (*OED* s.v. *awherf* v., *MED* s.v. *awherven* v.) is a rare derivative of the more common simplex derived from OE *hweorfan* (*OED* s.v. *wharve* v.); it is cited by *OED* and *MED*, aside from *Gawain* 2220, only from two late Old English texts. *Baleȝ* 1333 is emended by GDS to *b[oue]leȝ*, by TG to *ba[u]leȝ*. The MS form is undoubtedly corrupt, the scribe having caught the first four letters from *bale* "belly" in the first half of the line. There is thus no need to posit a development of an original *ou* in the English word (from OF *bouel, boel*) to *au*. *Barbe* had been cited earlier by Kullnick from Chaucer (see his p. 30). In *Gawain* 1457, where it is used with reference to arrows shot at the boar, it means "sharp process curving back from the point of a weapon" (see *OED* s.v. *barb* sb.[1] sense 8, *MED barb* n. sense 3a). In line 2310, the reference is to the blade of the Green Knight's ax. Here *barbe* is usually defined as "edge" (see TG and GDS glossaries and *MED* s.v. sense 3b). A. C. Luttrell has recently presented convincing arguments for interpreting "þe barbe of þe bitte" rather as a hook-shaped projection of the edge. See the second section of his two-part article "The *Gawain* Group: Cruxes, Etymologies, Interpretations," *Neophilologus*, *40* (1956), 292. Luttrell cites words from ON and OHG which, like *barbe*, mean "beard," and which are also used to refer to axes having a prominent projection of the blade. This definition results in a clearer understanding of lines 2310-12 than that afforded by the interpretation of *barbe* as "edge." Luttrell contends that the Green Knight in striking his third blow brought the ax all the way down ("homered heterly") on one side or the other of Gawain's throat, which was thus grazed by one of the sharp, hook-shaped ends of the blade ("snyrt hym on þat on syde"). It also makes better sense of "þe barbe of þe bitte"— i.e. the barb *of* the blade. The passage, as interpreted by Luttrell, exemplifies the poet's characteristic treatment of space, for which see below, pp. 123-24. *Barbe* in Chaucer (*TC* 2:110) has the quite different meaning "piece of . . . linen, worn over or under the chin" (*OED* s.v. sense 3, *MED* s.v. sense 2). *Barbe* is thus not a rare word in the totality of its meanings. In the sense "hook" it is cited by *MED* only from *Gawain* and a medical treatise dated

?a1425. *Bastel-roueȝ* is made up of two words, neither rare: *bastel* "bastion, turret" (*OED* s.v. *bastille* sb., *MED bastel* n. sense 1a) and *roof*. Neither TG nor GDS treat the two words as a compound. *Bay* 967 has yet to be explained satisfactorily; TG emend to *ba[lȝ]*. So far as I have been able to discover, neither *OED* nor *MED* cites the MS reading *bay* of this line. Both *bay* "an indentation of the sea into the land" (ultimately from late L *baia;* *OED bay* sb.², *MED bai* n.³), and *bay* "an opening in a wall" (ultimately from L *badāta;* *OED bay* sb.³, *MED bai n.²*), occur in English as early as the 14th century. From the latter word is derived *bay window*, of which the modern slang meaning "large protruding belly" may be relevant to the interpretation of *bay* in *Gawain* 967 "Hir buttokeȝ bay & brode." See the note in GDS, with a reference to an *OED* citation of 1428 for *bay window*. This is now antedated by a citation of 1405 in *MED* (s.v. *bai-window* n.). It seems significant that the word *bay* which is the first element of *bay window* is used in combination with *brode* in *Purity* 1392 "So brod bilde in a bay þat blonkkes myȝt renne." *Baye* v. "bark, bark at" is cited by *OED* (s.v. *bay* v.¹ senses 1 and 3) from *Boke of St. Albans* and *The Avowing of Arthur*, by *MED* (s.v. *baien* v. sense 1a) from *Sir Eglamour* and *Wars of Alexander*.

3. Style and the Alliterative Tradition

1. "Bald zeigte sich jedoch, dass der Wortschatz dieser eigenartigen Nachblüte alter Stabreimkunst im Mittelenglischen weit weniger vom Dialekt als von der archaisierender und typisierenden Stilkunst der Dichter beeinflusst ist" (p. 1). The abstractive, "typifying" tendency of the traditional style is discussed on pp. 81–83; see also the note that follows.

2. See introduction, pp. 1–5. "Der einzelne wird durch diese Ausdrücke [archaic words for "man, warrior"] zum Typus aller Helden erhoben. Dadurch wird die Dichtung idealisierend, typisierend. Ihr steht die charakterisierende, realistische Dichtung Chaucers . . . gegenüber, die diese hohen, stolz gewichtigen Bezeichnungen durch die individuellen, lebensvollen des täglichen Lebens ersetzen" (p. 5).

3. Brink expresses the figures for *lede* "38 mal a" (p. 14) and for *kniȝt* "41 mal a, 27 mal na" (p. 16). I prefer to express them as proportions, since it is the relationship between alliterating and nonalliterating uses that establishes the rank of a word, rather than the number of times used in either position.

4. *Lede* is classed under the general heading "Starkstabende Wörter" (p. 14), *kniȝt* under "Schwachstabende Wörter" (p. 16).

5. The enforced abridgment of Brink's published study, owing to high printing costs, is regrettable (see "Vorbemerkung"). It resulted, among other things, in the omission of a short study of the verbs. It also prevented Brink from discussing at any length the subject of the connections between the style of *Gawain* and that of Old English and Old Saxon poetry.

6. The *OED* head-words are *berne*, *freke*, *gome*[1], *athel* a. and sb.[2], *lede*, *rink* sb.[1], *shalk*, *segge*[1], *tulk* sb., and *wye*[1]. The last citations for all these words are poetic, with the exception of the dialect meanings of *freke* and *shalk*. *Rink* and *segge* are cited from Tottel's *Miscellany;* the other 16th-century citations are from Scots poetry. For *freke* and *shalk*, see also *EDD* s.vv. *freak* sb.[1], *shalk*. Both words are discussed in detail below. Information in *MED* is at present available for *burne* (s.v. *bern*, n.[1]), *freke* (s.v. *freke* n.), and *haþel* (s.v. *athel* n.).

According to both *OED* and *MED*, *bern* "warrior" (OE *beorn*) became confused in Middle English in form and meaning with *baroun* "baron," which had a variant *beron*, and *barn* "child" (OE *b(e)arn*). Under sense 4, "?as personal name," *MED* gives citations from the Pipe Rolls, the Subsidy Rolls, and the like, the latest of these being dated 1310. Reaney, in the entry for *Barne* in *A Dictionary of British Surnames*, gives two groups of forms. The first, including *Barn, Bearn*, and *le Barn(e)*, he derives from ON *barn* "child." The second includes *Beornus, Bern*, and *Beorn*; of this group Reaney says, "In Yorks., Lincs., Staffs. and Suffolk we have the Scandinavian personal-name *Biǫrn*, anglicized as *Beorn*. In Dorset and Worcs. we may have OE *Beorn*. The source may occ. be OE *beorn* 'warrior.' " Whether or not OE *beorn* gave rise to a name of the occupational type, the citations under all meanings of the word as a common noun are taken exclusively from poetry, and the evidence thus indicates that it was elevated and poetic at the time of the composition of *Gawain*. (Cf. the discussion of the name [*le*] *Freke*, on p. 55.)

7. See *Ordbog* s.v. *tulkr*. *Tulk* is discussed in detail below.

8. Pp. 13–15. The nonalliterating occurrence in *Gawain* belongs to *freke* (see p. 65); the "questionable" occurrence belongs to *wyȝe* (see p. 57).

9. P. 16. Brink erred, however, in saying that *syr(e)* occurs in independent use only in line 1083; see also 685 and 751, although in the latter it refers to Christ rather than to a man. In 1372 "Thenne comaunded þe lorde in þat sale to samen alle þe meny" *lorde* is emended to *syre* by GDS; one would expect the first of two nouns in such a combination to alliterate.

10. Ibid. The figures for each word in *Gawain* are: *kniȝt*, 41a:27na; *lorde*, 35a: 12na; *mon*, 41a: 33na.

11. *Prince*, a word related in meaning to *kniȝt, lorde*, and *mon*, was considered by Brink, together with *God* and *Kryst*, as indeterminate (*schwankend*) in status, since it had different alliterative rank in different poems. See "Anhang," p. 16. The treatment of *prince* in *Gawain* is similar to that of *world, court*, and *sesoun*, for which see pp. 74–75.

12. *Northumberland Words*, ed. R. O. Heslop (English Dialect Society, 1892–94), s.v. *freak*.

13. *Popular Ballads, 1*, ed. Robert Jamieson (Edinburgh, 1806), 343, "Song II."

14. *Scalc* is listed by Bøgholm, *The Layamon Texts*, p. 20, as an OE poetic word always altered by the B reviser.

15. "Bei diesen stilistischen Untersuchungen ergab sich nun ein formelles Kriterium, nämlich das mehr oder weniger häufige Vorkommen des einzelnen Wortes in stabender Stellung" (p. 1).

16. The technical motive for the use of poetic-archaic words is emphasized by Heinz Kittner in his discussion of the vocabulary of *Piers Plowman* (see above, p. 227, n. 39). Kittner does not dispute Brink's conclusions as to the artistic motives of the *Gawain*-poet. He points out, however, that words of the type exemplified by *rink*, as used by Langland, tend to mean not "man, warrior, hero" but simply "man, human being," citing in illustration such lines as "Bestes ruwelen hem al by reson and renkes ful fewe" (C text, xiv, 192; Kittner, p. 115) and maintaining that in this meaning they do not idealize their subject matter. He concludes that "wir werden unserem Dichter und seinem Werk gewiss gerecht, wenn wir die Anwendung der Alliteration bei ihm weniger künstlerisch als beinahe etwas handwerksmässig finden (gemessen an einer für den Stabreimdichter im allgemeinen von Brink betonten künstlerischen Tendenz)" (p. 117).

17. For the meanings of *tulkr* in Old Norse, see *Ordbog*. I am indebted to Professor Konstantin Reichardt for valuable aid in the study of the history of *tulkr* and other words of Old Norse derivation. As with OE words, the statement that a word "does not occur in poetry" in Old Norse must be based on citations from the extant literature in the most authoritative dictionaries. I have in each case compared the material in *Ordbog* with that in *LP*. *Tulkr* does not appear in *LP*; it is cited from several prose texts in *Ordbog*. References to the sagas have been checked to ensure that the passage cited is prose.

18. Whether Antenor or Aeneas is intended by "þe tulk þat þe trammes of tresoun þer wroȝt" (3), negotiations resembling those of a spokesman or intermediary would presumably be involved. But cf. *Wars Alex.* 3438–39 "For sen I wan in-to þe werld my witt has bene aye / Quen treid was a trechory, þe tulkis to be hedid ('beheaded')," where *tulkis* simply means "people, men." In *Gawain* 2133 "& talk wyth þat ilk tulk þe tale þat me lyste" the addition of *ilk*, which is not necessary for the metrical constitution of the line, indicates that the poet is deliberately creating a repetitive sound-pattern and thus that the linking of *tulk* with *talk* may be based on consonance rather than on the association of *tulk* with speech.

19. On the *Gawain*-poet as the author of *St. Erkenwald*, see the introduction to H. L. Savage's edition of the latter poem (New Haven, 1926), pp. liii–lxv. N. 15, p. liii, contains a list of the authorities who had agreed in this opinion. TG, in the introduction to their edition of *Gawain*, call the ascription "dubious" but do not clarify the grounds of their scepticism in detail, saying only that the similarity of "workmanship" between *St. Erkenwald* and the poems in MS Cotton Nero A.x. is not as close as that among the latter poems (p. xviii). Oakden includes *St. Erkenwald* among the works of the *Gawain*-poet (*Alliterative Poetry*, 1, 87–89, 253–55), as do GDS (p. x).

The alliteration in *Destr. Troy* and *Wars Alex.* shows certain dialect differences from that in *Gawain* (for the dialect of *Gawain*, see Oakden, *1*, pp. 73 ff.; for *Destr. Troy*, pp. 67 ff.; for *Wars Alex.*, pp. 95 ff.; note particularly point 19, alliteration or lack of alliteration between OE *cw* and *hw*). Oakden distinguishes between *Destr. Troy* and *Wars Alex.* on metrical grounds (*1*, pp. 255–56). The metrical and dialect differences confirm one's impression of three quite distinct styles in the three poems.

20. See the introduction to his edition of *Purity*, pp. xxiii–xxvi. But Miss Day, in her introduction to *Gawain*, Pt. III, xiii–xviii, presents some parallels which she feels may indicate the influence of *Wars Alex.* on the *Gawain*-poet, rather than the reverse.

21. According to Miss Day, "there is . . . no reason why *Alexander* should not belong to the late fourteenth century" (p. xiii).

22. *William of Palerne* is dated by *MED* a1375; *Winner and Waster*, c1353.

23. Using Oakden's method of schematization (see *1*, 132, No. 3 for the OE types; *1*, 167–68, No. 5 for the ME types), we may express the "normal" or predominant alliterative pattern of the long lines of *Gawain* as a a (a) / a x; this has the variants a x / a x and x a / a x, with only one alliterating syllable in the first half-line. In none of these types does the last important word of the line participate in the alliterative pattern. According to Oakden's figures on alliteration in *Gawain* (*1*, 190–91), a a / a x occurs 1532x, a a a / a x 239x, a x / a x 40x, x a / a x 59x, giving a total of 1870 out of 2025 long lines, with 155 lines unaccounted for. Alliteration may fall on the last important word in the line by virtue of transference of position, as in the patterns a a / x a (23x) and a a a / x a (4x), or there may be a supernumerary ("ornamental") alliterating syllable, as in the patterns a a / a a (70x), a a a / a a (14x), a x / a a (6x), x a / a a (4x), or there may be double alliteration, as in the patterns a b / a b (10x), a b / b a (5x), a a / b b (2x), and others. Each of the roughly 7% of long lines in which the alliteration falls on the last word must be treated as a separate case, and the discussion will in general deal with the "normal" lines without explicit reference to the exceptions. It is possible also for the final important word to show "anticipatory alliteration" with the line that follows; this occurs, according to Oakden, 112x in all (*1*, 155). Such alliteration will be discussed in particular cases where relevant.

24. For a detailed discussion of feminine endings in Middle English alliterative poetry, see pp. 188–89 and p. 270, n. 34.

25. See especially Magoun's article "Oral-Formulaic Character of Anglo-Saxon Narrative Poetry," *Speculum*, *28* (1953), 446–63, where references to the work of Parry and to the subsequent work of Albert B. Lord are given. Magoun quotes Parry's definition of the formula as "a group of words which is regularly employed under the same metrical conditions to express a given essential idea" (p. 449), as well as his definition of the formulaic system as "a group of phrases which have the same metrical value and which are enough

alike in thought and words to leave no doubt that the poet who used them knew them not only as a single formula, but also as formulas of a certain type" (p. 450). Magoun demonstrates the formulaic character of Old English poetry through sample analyses of lines 1-25 of *Beowulf* and lines 512-35 of *Christ and Satan*, showing that in each passage a large proportion of the half-lines are duplicated or paralleled elsewhere. Like Parry, he associates the formulaic style with the technique of oral improvisation as learned by the unlettered poet or "singer," one who improvises or performs traditional stories in verse rather than memorizing and reciting them in fixed form. See also Magoun, "Bede's Story of Cædman: The Case History of an Anglo-Saxon Oral Singer," *Speculum, 30* (1955), 49–63. The application of Parry's principles to Old English poetry has been furthered by Stanley B. Greenfield and Robert P. Creed, both of whom explicitly associate themselves with Magoun. See especially Greenfield, "The Formulaic Expression of the Theme of 'Exile' in Anglo-Saxon Poetry," *Speculum, 30*, 200–06, and Creed, "The *Andswarode*-System in Old English Poetry," *Speculum, 32* (1957), 523–28. Ronald A. Waldron has extended the field of investigation into Middle English in his "Oral-Formulaic Technique and Middle English Alliterative Poetry," *Speculum, 32*, 792–801. Using Magoun's methods, Waldron identifies a number of formulas and formulaic systems common to *Gawain* and 15 other alliterative poems, and presents an analysis of lines 1-25 of *Morte Arthure*, with results similar to those obtained by Magoun for *Beowulf* and *Christ and Satan*. Waldron concludes, "It would be rash to . . . say that [Middle English alliterative poetry] must therefore be of oral origin. The most we can say is that it was written by poets who were familiar with a body of formulas which probably originated in a tradition of oral composition" (p. 800). This opinion seems wholly reasonable. It follows, therefore, that the verse of *Gawain* is unlikely to be "totally formulaic" in character (cf. Magoun, *Speculum, 28*, 446: "Parry, aided by Lord, demonstrated that the characteristic feature of all orally composed poetry is its totally formulaic character"). For this reason, and since the subject of this study is the diction and phraseology of *Gawain* as elements of style rather than as exemplars of a formulaic method of composition, I shall not attempt a classification of formulas or an analysis of the permutations of a given formula or formulaic system. Space forbids also an exploration of the highly interesting subject of traditional grammatical patterns in *Gawain*. Such patterns are described by Waldron as " 'empty' rhythmical-syntactical 'moulds' ready to be filled with meaning" (p. 798, n. 14). He presents schematizations for a number of them, e.g. "There is no (NOUN + PREP PHR)," for which see *Gawain* 1853 "þer is no haþel vnder heuen to-hewe hym þat myȝt." Matters of traditional syntax will of course be relevant at certain points; cf. the discussion of pleonastic phrases of place, p. 72.

26. Cf. also *Alex. Maced.* 343, "preeued knightes," 483 "seemelich knightes," and 491 "armed knightes"; *Jos. Arim.* 537 "he and fourti knihtes" and 675 "fro þe seue knihtes"; *Parl. 3 Ages* 525 (W text only) "two ful tried

knyghtes"; *Siege Jerus.* 342 "xii siker kny3tes" and 433 "with a þryuande kny3t"; *WPal.* 3676 "þe kene 3onge kni3t" and 4501 "to a worþi kni3t."

27. The traditional alliterating adjectives are discussed separately on pp. 77–90.

28. For studies of traditional phraseology in Lawman's *Brut,* see pp. 40–42 and p. 224 n. 19.

The alliterative phrases in the works of the *Gawain*-poet were studied in detail by Johannes Fuhrmann, whose *Die alliterierenden Sprachformeln in Morris' Early English Alliterative Poems und im Sir Gawayne and the Green Knight* (Hamburg, 1886) is outstanding in range and number of parallels cited. Fuhrmann divides the phrases into groups according to etymological derivation, and subdivides them according to subject matter and the logical relationships between the constituent words; this elaborate system of classification, in the absence of a general index, makes for delay in the location of a given phrase.

The collection of duplicate or similar phrases in alliterative poetry was originally undertaken with a view to determining which poems were of common authorship; cf. Moritz Trautmann, *Über Verfasser und Entstehungszeit einiger alliterierender Gedichte des Altenglischen* (Halle, 1876); Curt Reicke, *Untersuchungen über den Stil der mittelenglischen alliterierenden Gedichte Morte Arthure, The Destruction of Troy, The Wars of Alexander, The Siege of Jerusalem, Sir Gawayn and the Green Knight* (Königsberg, 1906). Thus Trautmann (p. 20) cites as one piece of evidence of common authorship for *Alexander A* and *B* the second half-lines "as hym leefe thought" (*A*, 60) and "as him dere thoute" (*B*, 1133). Reicke, in differentiating between the styles of *Morte Arth.* and *Destr. Troy,* cites a large number of second half-lines from both poems in which the poet concludes a description of a group of retainers with some such phrase as "and oþer grette lordes" (pp. 75–79). Differences between the two poems are shown in the wording and frequency of the use of such phrases. His collection includes dozens of examples of the adjective-plus-*kni3t(es)* formula. For the history of these studies of authorship, with bibliographical references, see Savage, introduction to *St. Erkenwald,* pp. xlviii–lxv.

The attempt to identify common authorship through parallels, without discriminating between traditional and original phraseology, was early discredited. Later critics were more conservative, arguing for influence or common authorship only on the basis of words and phrases whose occurrence was limited to one or two poems; cf. Robert J. Menner, introduction to *Purity,* pp. xxiv–xxvi, xxxiii–xxxvii; Savage, pp. lvi–lx; Magoun, introduction to *The Gests of King Alexander of Macedon* (*Alexander A and B*) (Cambridge, 1929), pp. 102–04, 108–12.

The phraseology of the rhymed romances has been discussed most recently by Albert C. Baugh, "Improvisation in the Middle English Romance," *Proceedings of the American Philosophical Society, 103* (June, 1959), 418–54.

Baugh refers to the work of Parry and its application to Old English poetry by Magoun, although he does not wholly adopt Magoun's terminology or methods of analysis of formulaic systems. The material cited by Baugh is extensive and includes parallel details and themes as well as phrases; it is largely confined to descriptions of battle in the romances treating the "Matter of England" (p. 420, n. 13a). A bibliography of studies of the phraseology of the romances is given on p. 420 in n. 14. A study of the traditional vocabulary of the romances was carried out by A. R. Dunlap; see "The Vocabulary of the Middle English Romances in Tail-Rhyme Stanza," *Delaware Notes*, 36, new ser. 3 (1941), 1–43.

Overlapping of the poetic vocabulary of alliterative poetry with that of the rhymed romances is shown by the fact that among the elevated synonyms for "man, warrior," *burne, freke,* and *gome* occur in the romances as well; these three words are called "non-alliterative but poetic" by Oakden (2, 183). Of the alliterative phrases from the rhymed romances listed by Oakden (2, 315–43), many occur also in alliterative poetry; the label A. in bold-faced type makes it easy to identify a number of these on any page.

29. *Alliterative Poetry*, 2, Pt. III, "The Alliterative Phrases," 195–379. See especially "The Non-Rhyming Alliterative Poems of the Fourteenth Century," 263–312.

30. Notably by Waldron. See his n. 13, p. 797: "I have noticed a marked tendency in these poems for the second half-line to end on one of a limited number of favourite words . . . Lists of second half-lines made on this principle reveal a number of different formulas and formulaic systems for each of these frequent end-words."

31. "No legitimate [excuse] can be adduced to explain the use of tags within the alliterative long line itself. . . . The second half-line is frequently devoid of any real significance, and the majority of the poets seem to have resorted to these tags 'to fill out their verses' " (2, 381). Formulaic repetition and inept repetition are thus confounded.

32. For "as him likez" and its variants, see *Morte Arth.* 32, 55, 63, 69, 84, 97, 107, 140, 162, 186, 205, etc.; for "witow for soþe," see Oakden, 2, 386; for "as the (boke, etc.) telles," ibid., pp. 387–88.

33. According to Gollancz, the name *Gringolet* occurs in English only in *Gawain*. In *The Anturs of Arther at the Tarnewathelan* the horse is named *Grizel (Greselle),* and this name occurs in alliterative combination with *gode* and *gone* but not with *graype* or *gorde* (see the text in *Three Early English Metrical Romances,* ed. John Robson, London, 1842, p. 20). For Gollancz's statement see "Gringolet, Gawain's Horse," *Saga Book of the Viking Club,* 5, Pt. I (1907), 105.

34. Some of the combinations apparently invented and used repetitively by the *Gawain*-poet were first brought to my attention by Miss Leah J. Zahler.

J. D. Ebbs, "Stylistic Mannerisms of the *Gawain*-Poet" (*JEGP*, 57, 1958,

522–25) lists the parallel between lines 1 and 2525, together with a few others. He does not deal with the problem of formulaic style in *Gawain*, however.

35. For the stylistic value of *fole* and other words discussed by Brink under "Designations for Warhorse," see p. 76 and p. 239, n. 50.

36. Waldron, p. 794, points out that a pair of alliterating words must be distinguished from a true formula, which is always completely phrased and must be described partly in terms of its position in the line. The category "traditional alliterative combinations" is therefore broader than that of formulas, and each alliterative combination may involve one or more complete formulaic patterns. But for the *Gawain*-poet, at least, the traditional combinations themselves seem to have provided the idea for the line, whether or not a traditional formulation was used. For example, he combines *haþel* and *hors* in ways analogous to the traditional combination "burne on blonk" (Fuhrmann, p. 18; cf. *Beowulf* 856a "beornas on blancum"). Thus he writes "His haþel on hors watz þenne" (2065). But he also combines the two words in other ways: "Þat a haþel & a horse myȝt such a hwe lach" (234); "He with his haþeles on hyȝe horsses weren" (1138). Similarly with *burne* and *blonk*, he writes "Þe burne bode on bonk, þat on blonk houed" (785), and "Þe burne bede bryng his blonk" (2024). Nothing would be gained, for the purposes of this study, by trying to identify each of these modes of combination as a particular formula and the whole group of combinations as a system.

None of the alliterating combinations of "man, warrior" and "warhorse" is listed by Oakden. For *freke-fole* cf. *Gawain* 196 "Such a fole vpon folde, ne freke þat hym rydes" as well as 803, cited previously. For *burne-blonk* see above. For *wyȝe-world* see Oakden, 2, 310; cf. *Gawain* 938 "& sayde he watz þe welcomest wyȝe of þe worlde," 1781 "Bifore alle þe wyȝez in þe worlde wounded in hert," etc. For *king-crown* see Oakden, 2, 276, 321; cf. *Gawain* 364 "To ryd þe kyng wyth croun."

37. For "now or never" see Oakden, 2, 296 (*Gawain* only) and 375 (Chaucer). The phrase is first cited by *OED* (s.v. *now*, sense 8) from 1560. For "hold in (one's) hand," see Oakden, 2, 287, 328.

38. See *Sixteenth-Century English Poetry*, ed. Norman E. McClure (New York, 1954), p. 81.

39. This analysis could be interpreted as implying that there are three degrees of stress: a strong stress falling on chief syllables, a strong secondary stress falling on important intermediate syllables, and a weak stress falling on unimportant intermediate syllables. I do not, however, wish to suggest any such view. Between the strongest of chief syllables and the weakest of intermediate syllables there would seem, rather, to be an indefinite number of degrees of stress. *Boþe* (17) and *most* (638) are alike in being important intermediate syllables, but *most* will tend to receive the greater stress because the idea it expresses is itself emphatic in the line and that expressed by *boþe* is not. Otto Jespersen's system of metrical analysis, in which four grades of stress are distinguished ("Notes on Metre" in *Linguistica*, Copenhagen,

1933, pp. 249–74), is certainly a more adequate means of describing the varying patterns of emphasis possible within a uniform metrical structure than systems in which syllables are said to be either "strong" or "weak," but it too is abstractive. And Jespersen's view that in iambic verse a naturally strong intermediate syllable is reduced from 4 ("strong") to 3 ("half-strong") or even 2 ("half-weak") seems too categorical. When the intermediate syllable is extremely emphatic, the reduction may be a matter of "3.75" or even "3.9" as compared to a natural "4." The essential point is that the stress given the intermediate syllable is to some degree restrained or controlled by the metrical form. For further reference to Jespersen's essay, see below, p. 271, n. 6.

40. *Mon* "one" does of course occur in *Gawain* and, as is to be expected, occupies intermediate position almost exclusively. Cf. 565 "What may mon do bot fonde?" and 2355 "þenne þar mon drede no waþe." In both these lines the first chief stress falls on either the first or second word, and the second falls on the word following *mon*. An exception to the rule may be 2238 "Of steuen mon may þe trowe," where *mon* should perhaps be read as the second chief syllable, subordinating *may þe*. It also seems possible, however, to subordinate *mon* and place chief stress on *may*.

41. See Brink, pp. 18–19. The last citations in *OED*, s.v. *erd*, are from *Cursor* and *Gawain*. *MED*, s.v. *erd* n.¹, point out that in the North and parts of the EML area, *erd* became confused with *erþe* and assumed the meanings of the latter. This explains its descent into modern dialects; it is listed by *EDD* as a variant form of *earth* sb.¹ But *erd* "region," as a poetic word, and *erþe* "the earth," as a colloquial word, were apparently quite distinct for the *Gawain*-poet (see discussion on pp. 72–73), and the distinction was retained in the MS of the poem.

42. In *Morte Arth.* 2241, *erþe* is used within the line in the same way; it receives chief stress but does not alliterate: "And he rusches to þe erthe, rewthe es the more." Parallels occur in Lawman and in Old English poetry, e.g. *Brut* 799–800 "leteð ða Grickisca / gliden to grunde" (A version, Madden *1*, 34); 20076–77 "feollen þa uæie / uolden to grunde" (*2*, 419); *The Battle of Maldon* 285b–87 "Þa æt guðe sloh / Offa þone sælidan, þæt he on eorðan feoll / And þær Gaddes mæg grund gesohte."

43. See p. 70 and n. 41. *MED* cites, s.v. *erd* n.¹ sense 3b, "þe grettest on erde," *Wars Alex.* 271b; *Morte Arth.* has "all, that regnede in erthe" (2035), etc.

44. The history of *frith* in the meanings "wood," "sparsely wooded area," and "open space between woods" (apparently derived, with metathesis, from OE *fyrhþ*, f., and *gefyrhþe*, n., "wood"; see *OED* and Supplement) is complicated by the existence of a homonym *frith* "peace" (from OE *friþ*, "peace") and by a meaning "royal forest, game preserve" which is assigned by *MED* to the former word (s.v. *frith* n.²) and by *OED* to the latter (s.v. *frith* sb.¹). The association of the meanings "game preserve" and "wood"

seems more probable than the association of "game preserve" with "peace." *MED* does not give an etymology for *frith* "wood," but says that it is "originally probably distinct from" *frith* 1 "peace." The meaning "game preserve," which one would not expect to be poetic, is cited by *MED* (s.v. sense 1a) from the Rolls of Parliament 1464.

45. The words listed in supplementary paragraphs (*Anhänge*) are omitted, since they are not discussed fully by Brink and space forbids full discussion of them here.

46. However, neither *OED* (s.v. *folk* sense 2b "retainers, followers; servants, workpeople") nor *MED* (s.v. *folk* n. sense 4 "a body of retainers, followers, servants or attendants; subjects [of a king]; household") distinguishes between "retainers" and "servants" as separate meanings. Nor does *folk* clearly mean "retainers," as distinct from "people" generally, in any of its occurrences in *Gawain*. *Folk* seems, therefore, to be similar to *world* and *court*, in that it is of high alliterative rank, while not distinctively elevated or poetic in the meanings in question.

47. Not counting two occurrences, one in the bob (561) and one in the wheel (588) without ornamental alliteration.

48. See *OED* s.v. *shaft* sb.² sense 1b. Apparently *schafte* has the poetic sense "spear" only in line 205; see TG and GDS glossaries. Brink points out that *shaftes* "spears" occurs in *The Knight's Tale* (A2605) in alliterating combination with *sheeldes:* "Ther shyveren shaftes upon sheeldes thikke."

49. *Sword* occurs in *Gawain* only once, in 2319 "Braydeȝ out a bryȝt sworde, & bremely he spekeȝ." Since this line is paralleled by 1584 "Braydeȝ out a bryȝt bront" and since the poet is prone to repetitive phrasing, one suspects that the more colloquial word *sword* in 2319 may be a scribal substitution.

50. See *MED* s.v. *fole* n. senses 1a and 2a; *OED* s.v. *foal* sb. senses 1 and 2. Sense 2 "a horse" is last cited from Douglas's *Aeneis* (1513).

51. The *Gawain*-poet's use of adjectives is discussed in detail by Karl Schmittbetz in "Das Adjektiv in 'Syr Gawayn and the Grene Knyȝt'," *Anglia*, 32 (1909), 1–60, 163–89, 359–83, and *Das Adjektiv im Verse von "Syr Gawayn and þe Grene Knyȝt*," Bonn, 1908. In the latter the participation of descriptive adjectives in general in the various alliterative patterns of the long line is discussed, and a group of examples given for each pattern, but no one adjective is treated exhaustively, nor are adjectives compared in terms of frequency of occurrence or proportion of alliterating to nonalliterating uses.

52. See esp. pp. 28–29. Speaking of the adjectives of group III, Brink says "Ich werde zu zeigen versuchen, dass bei diesen wie bei jenen anderen [those of groups I and II] ihr poetischer Charakter der Beweggrund ihrer Anwendung und ihrer starken Stabung ist."

53. I have transferred from group I to group III *mensk(ful, -ly)*, *rad* "cowardly," and *ronk*. See *EDD* s.v. *mense, menseful; rad* adj.¹; *rank* adj.

Brink glosses the single occurrence of *ronk* in *Gawain* 513 as "proud, beautiful" (p. 32), but the reference is to blossoms blooming in rows, and *EDD* sense 4 "close together . . . numerous" (applied, for example, to corn) seems exactly right.

I have omitted from group I *mere* "glorious," which, according to Brink's figures, occurs 4a:0na. In its three occurrences in the long lines, however, the spelling *mere* must stand for *mery*. Final *-e* is substituted for *-y* elsewhere in the text, as in *fole* "folly" 1545 and *Mare* "Mary" 1769 (GDS' emendation to *Mar[y]e* is unnecessary). TG add an acute accent to the *-e* of such words; see their note on the text, facing p. 1. The spelling *mere* occurs twice (153, 878) in the phrase "a mere mantile," which is exactly paralleled by "a mery mantyle" in 1736 and in *Wars of Alexander* 2864. In the third occurrence of *mere*, the first half-line "'Ma fay,' quoþ þe mere wyf" (1495) is paralleled by "'Madame,' quoþ þe myry mon" in 1263. In "a mery mantyle," *mery* means "handsome"; in "þe myry mon," "þe mere wyf," it means not "merry" but "pleasant, agreeable"; see the discussion of the history of its meanings, on pp. 86–88. A further argument for interpreting *mere* in 1495 as a form of *merry* is the emphasis throughout the bedroom scenes on both good cheer and "merriment" in the modern sense, as in the lady's "lyppeʒ smal laʒande" (1207) and the ironic "Gawayn þe blyþe" (1213). I have therefore added these three occurrences of *mere* to Brink's count of alliterating uses for *mery*, group II. The fourth occurrence of *mere*, and the only one in which it undoubtedly stands for the Middle English derivative of OE *mǣre* "glorious," is in the wheels, line 924, where it rhymes with *here* "hear" (and alliterates with *manereʒ*).

54. I have substituted "na" here for Brink's "questionable," which can only refer to 1194 "& lenged þere selly longe, to loke quen he wakened."

55. MS illegible; both TG and GDS supply *w*, TG stating that it is derived from the offset.

56. Certain of the words in group II, e.g. *felle*, seem to belong rather to group III, and certain words in group III, e.g. *styf*, to group II. But the distinction between the two groups is not of crucial importance, the essential point being descent into the modern period.

57. *Dere* has 2 nonalliterating occurrences according to Brink's figures, but I have disregarded line 1842 in the wheels: "I am derely to yow biholde." Here *derely* neither alliterates nor rhymes.

58. The line in question is 1885 "& syþen he mace hym as mery among þe fre ladyes."

59. Brink's figures for *mery* are 20a:3na. For the additional alliterating occurrences, see above, n. 53. In the count of nonalliterating occurrences I have disregarded line 1891 in the wheels: "þus myry he watʒ neuer are." Here *myry* neither alliterates nor rhymes.

60. The line in question is 2166 "& ruʒe knokled knarreʒ with knorned stoneʒ."

61. Brink apparently counts as na line 632 "For ay faythful in fyue & sere fyue syþeȝ," where, however, there is double alliteration. Cf. the alliterating combination of *sere* and *sypes* in the wheels: "He sayned hym in syþes sere" (761).

62. Brink's count is 7a; he designates as "questionable" line 1751, with double alliteration: "As mon þat watȝ in mornyng of mony þro þoȝtes." For the linking of *þro* and *þoȝt* see 645, 1867.

63. With the main list under this heading (pp. 49-52) I have combined two smaller groups discussed separately for historical reasons by Brink (pp. 52-53) into a single alphabetical series.

64. See Brink's preliminary discussions of adjectives of group II, pp. 33-35, and group III, pp. 40-42.

65. The phrase is listed in *OED* s.v. *stiff* a. sense 12. See also Oakden, *2*, 304 (s.v. "sa stiffe and sa strang"), 338, 348; Fuhrmann, p. 57. For the parallel phrases "bold in battle" and "fell in fight," see p. 104 and p. 248, n. 33.

66. *Stel-gere* appears in combination with *stedes* in *Alexander A* 416 "Strained in stel-ger on steedes of might." For "heard under helme" see *Beowulf* 342, 404, 2539; for "worthy under weed" see Oakden *2*, 343; cf. ibid., pp. 350, 361, and *CT. Th.* B 2107. See also the parallels to "lufsum vnder lyne," *Gawain* 1814, cited by TG in their note.

67. "Stiff in stour" is listed in *OED* s.v. *stiff* a. sense 12. See also Oakden *2*, 304, 338.

68. For a possible indecent play on words in the line, with a consequent play on the material reference of *stif*, see Paull F. Baum, "Chaucer's Puns," *PMLA*, 71 (1956), 232, s.v. *burdoun*, and D. Biggins, "Chaucer's General Prologue A 163," *Notes and Queries*, Dec. 1959, pp. 435-36.

69. A great deal of information on the meanings expressed by adjectives in *Gawain* is to be found in the lists given under subject-matter categories by Schmittbetz in *Anglia*, 32, 32-56. Under the heading "Words for the Expression of Esthetic Feelings" (pp. 40-41), for example, 48 different adjectives are listed; of these, the overwhelming majority imply favorable response (*fayre*, *comlych*, *bene*, *louely*, *daynte*, etc., vs. *ugly*, *unbene*, and *unmete*). But the usefulness of these lists is diminished by the fact that Schmittbetz gives scarcely any indications of frequency of occurrence, and no statistics. Thus *fayre*, according to Brink's figures (p. 52), occurs 25a:7na in *Gawain*, or a total of 32 times, but *bene* occurs only twice, once as an adjective (2475) and once as an adverb (2402).

70. Cf. Arthur Gilchrist Brodeur, *The Art of Beowulf* (Berkeley, California, 1959), p. 17: "[Germanic heroic] poetry exemplified and maintained the warrior's code, and expressed an ideal of conduct conditioned by the nature of the Germanic social order. Accordingly, the concepts with which poets dealt found expression, for the most part, in terms which named or described them typically, and which, directly or by connotation and sug-

gestion, stressed those qualities of person or thing which seemed right, good, pleasant or characteristic to that society for which the poetry was composed."

71. Certain effects of this kind are discussed at some length in Chap. 4; see pp. 104–05, 118.

72. See *The Later Genesis*, ed. B. J. Timmer (Oxford, 1948), line 384a "grindlas greate."

73. See esp. ch. 8, pp. 194 ff. Scansions of lines 222 and 250 are given on pp. 203–04.

4. The Criticism of Style

1. See above, pp. 7–9.

2. For a summary of the important theories as to the relation of the two stories, see GDS, pp. xxvi ff., where references are given.

3. So TG; GDS retain the MS reading *glaumande*. See discussion on pp. 99–100.

4. The material presented in this note is selective. It should be pointed out that any collection of parallels, however large, must perforce be based on only a part of the tradition, namely, those alliterative poems which have survived by chance. Nor can an exhaustive collection of parallels between a passage in *Gawain* and the extant poems be made within practicable limits of time until concordances are available, including one to the 14,000 odd lines of *Destruction of Troy*. All that is to be demonstrated here is that the poet tends to use language at set positions in the line and in set patterns, many or most of which he derived from the tradition, some of which he may have devised himself and used again where appropriate. It seems certain that more of the phraseology of any passage of the poem is traditional than parallels in the extant literature would indicate. See above, the discussion of alliterating formulas presumably original with the *Gawain*-poet, pp. 63–64.

The following parallels, some of which are cited in Oakden's lists, occur elsewhere in *Gawain* and other alliterative poems:

37: *vpon kryst-masse* as second half-line, *Gawain* 471.

38: *lord-ludes*, *WPal.* 1439; Oakden, p. 291; *of þe best* in final position, *Gawain* 863, 880, 889, 1000; *Parl. 3 Ages* 458 (W text only); *Winner & W.* 315; cf. *Brut* (B version) 7425 *cniht mid þe beste*, cited above, p. 43.

39: *breþer* in final position, *Wars Alex.* 2512; *broþer* in final position, *Siege Jerus.* 937, 990; *WPal.* 4938.

40: *oryȝt* (*aryȝt*) as second unit of first half-line, *Gawain* 1911; cf. *ryȝt* 373; *merþe* in final position, *Gawain* 541, 860, 1763.

41: *ful mony* in final position, *Gawain* 188; *Alex. Maced.* 388; *Parl. 3 Ages* 126, 129; *Siege Jerus.* 619; *mony* in final position, *Gawain* 310, 454, 529, etc.;

Jos. Arim. 8; *Morte Arth.* 22, 27; *Siege Jerus.* 43, 285; *Wars Alex.* 113, 1394; *Winner & W.* 141. Cf. also *ful clene, Gawain* 792; *ful hyʒe* 794; *ful þik* 795, etc.

42: *þise gentyle kniʒtes* as second half-line, *Morte Arth.* 4109; *gentyle kniʒtes* in final position, *Morte Arth.* 115; for *gentle knight* as a stock phrase see *OED* s.v. *gentle* a. sense 3.

43: *kayred to þe court*, cf. *Morte Arth.* 6, *Parl. 3 Ages* 246; Oakden, p. 272; *kayre-court, Gawain* 2489; *to þe court* as second unit of first half-line, *Gawain* 1048; cf. *whan he kom first to þis kourt, WPal.* 507; *sacrifice to make, Siege Jerus.* 315; *festis to make, Parl. 3 Ages* 385.

45: *Mete-mirþe, Gawain* 1007, 1952; see p. 101 and below, n. 27; *a-vyse(d)* in final position, *Gawain* 771, 1389; for a parallel to the line as a whole, cf. *Destr. Troy* 3464 "With all þe reuell & riolté þat Renkes couthe deuise."

46: *glaum ande gle*, pp. 99–100 and below, notes 21–25; *to here* in final position, *Gawain* 492, 1022; *Jos. Arim.* 109; *Siege Jerus.* 129; see also Oakden, p. 382, where the adjective-infinitive construction as a common second half-line is discussed.

47: *on nyʒtes* in final position, *WPal.* 739; cf. also *boþe dayes & niʒtes* as second half-line, *WPal.* 578.

48: *halleʒ and chambreʒ*, see below, n. 10; *chambre(s)* in final position, *Destr. Troy* 487, 503, 5305; *Morte Arth.* 158; *Wars Alex.* 53, 111, 151, 358.

49: *lordeʒ & ladies*, cited over 25x by Oakden, p. 291; *so lef hit hym þoʒt* as second half-line, *Gawain* 909; *lef hit me þynkes, Gawain* 1111; *as hir lefe thought, Destr. Troy* 407; *whethire me leue thynkys, Morte Arth.* 350; cf. also *þei þem lothe thought, Alex Maced.* 369; *as hym goode thought, Alex. Maced.* 328; *as þem faire thoghte, Morte Arth.* 495; *þou hym bale þouʒte, Siege Jerus.* 592 (all second half-lines).

50: *All þe wele of þe worlde, Gawain* 1270; *þe wele of this werlde, Parl. 3 Ages* 637; *There es no wele in this werlde, Winner & W.* 268; for *weal and world* in stock combinations, see *OED* s.v. *weal* sb.¹ sense 1.; *wone-worlde,ˆ Alex. & D.*, 551, 557; *PPl.* A viii, 111; Oakden, pp. 210, 228, 311; *samen* in final position, *Gawain* 744, 1345; *Wars Alex.* 175; *samme, Alex. Maced.* 342; *Siege Jerus.* 552.

51: *kyd knyʒteʒ, Morte Arth.* 1272; *Parl. 3 Ages* 529 (W text only); *Wars Alex.* 52; *þe kuddest kniʒt, WPal.* 3047; *kid(dest)-kniʒt, Gawain* 1520; *Destr. Troy* 1741, 2124; *knyʒt vnder Kryst, WPal.* 3671; Oakden, pp. 252, 274; *knyʒt-Kryst, Gawain* 1279; *Morte Arth.* 346; *seluen*, noted by Waldron, *Speculum*, 32, p. 797, as occurring 364x in final position in 16 alliterative poems (see above, p. 233, n. 25); *Gawain* 113, 285, 1046, etc.; cf. *vnder Criste euyn* as second half-line, *Destr. Troy* 309; *þat undyr Criste lyffes, Morte Arth.* 405; *to drighten hym selvyn, Parl. 3 Ages* 448.

52: *Louely-lady, Parl. 3 Ages* 247; *PPl.* B vi, 10; *WPal.* 671, 699, 965; *while hee lyfe hadde* as second half-line, *Alex. Maced.* 29; *while he lif hadde, Siege Jerus.* 98; *or we þe lif haue, Siege Jerus.* 512; cf. also *þat þu grace hade, Destr. Troy* 224; *lat me a place haue, Wars Alex.* 355 (all second half-lines).

53: *comelyche kyng, Morte Arth.* 2058; *Siege Jerus.* 764, 957; *Winner &*

W. 86, 199, 319; *comly quene, Wars Alex.* 354; *haldes* in final position, *Gawain* 436, 698, 1256, 2348; *Morte Arth.* 64.

5. See above, the discussion of the elevated synonyms for "man, warrior," pp. 53–60, and of the adjective-*knights* combination, pp. 62–63.

6. Cited by Oakden, *2,* 183, as "definitely poetic." See also *OED* s.v. *cair* v. sense 1 (intr.) "a poetic word for 'to go'." *Cair* survives in modern dialect use in such transitive senses as "to stir . . . to rake" (*EDD*).

7. *Kyd* ppl. a. (*OED* s.v. *kid*) represents a special development of the pa. pple. of *kithe,* from OE *cȳðan* (the forms (ʒe)*cȳðed,* (ʒe)*cȳðe* of the pa. pple. of *cȳðan* had the variants (ʒe)*cȳ̆d*(*d*), (ʒe)*cȳ̆dde* already in Late Old English; see Sievers-Brunner, No. 406 and n. 3). *Kithe* v. "to make known" has descended into Scots and Northern dialect English. *Kid* ppl. a. is cited by *OED,* after the thirteenth century, only from poetry. *Kid,* as pa. pple. of *kithe,* is also cited only from poetry after the thirteenth century by *OED* (s.v. *kithe* sense 5) in the meanings "made known, declared; hence, known, well-known, famed." The two words are thus not wholly distinct. Apparently, an elevated poetic meaning "renowned, glorious" developed as a result of the frequent use of the participle "known," for purposes of alliteration, with reference to renowned and glorious *kynges, kniʒtes,* and *conquerours,* while the possibility of use in the more everyday meaning remained. (Cf. the development in poetry of *bent* "field" into *bent* "battlefield," discussed above, pp. 45–46.) Whether the elevated or colloquial meaning of *kid* is intended in any given occurrence must therefore be determined from the context. In the lines cited by *OED* s.v. *kid* ppl. a. from Wyntoun's verse *Chronicle,* "Threpyt [contended that] thai ware spyis / Or to the Kyng kyd innymys," the meaning is clearly "known" and the occurrence belongs rather with the citations for the pa. pple. of *kithe.* In the phrase *kyd conquerour* as used in, e.g., *Morte Arth.* 65, *kyd* has its distinctively poetic meaning "renowned." In line 51 of the passage from *Gawain* under discussion, the word has its elevated meaning and value. But in *Gawain* 1520 "& ʒe ar knyʒt com-lokest kyd of your elde" it has its participial meaning and is less elevated in quality; emphasis is primarily on Gawain's "comeliness," though there is also a suggestion of his "renown."

8. See above, the discussion of chief and intermediate position in the wheels and the relation of metrical structure to emphasis, pp. 65–69.

9. In the chapter entitled "The Use of Tags in Middle English Alliterative Poetry" Oakden discusses a number of these phrases, including *on bent, on felde, upon folde;* also *under Criste, under God, under heuen; Alliterative Poetry, 2,* 389–91. He does not, however, include the "in hall" type, for which see below, n. 10. For a discussion of the relation between pleonastic use and the alliterative rank of nouns, see above, pp. 72–73.

10. OE *flet*(*t*) meant both "floor" and "hall"; cf. *Beowulf* 1568b "heo on flet gecrong," where the reference is to the "floor" of the underwater cave, and 2016–17 "mæru cwen . . . flet eall geondhwearf," i.e. moved all about the hall. To judge from such cognates cited by Holthausen, s.v. *flett,* as

ON *flatr* (from which is derived modern English *flat* a.) and Lithuanian *pladina* "flat or shallow boat," the original meaning was "flat area, floor" and the meaning "building (covering a floor)" was a figurative development. The phrase *on flet(t)* occurs in Old English poetry, but may mean either "in hall" or "on floor." In Middle English poetry *on flet(t)* "on floor" is frequently used to mean "in hall"; thus in *William of Palerne* 5368, "I fostered ʒou on mi flet" means "I fostered you in my dwelling." In *Gawain, on (þe) flet* is often used literally, e.g. "& vnder fete, on þe flet" (859); but it can also mean "in hall," e.g. "Bi-fore alle þe folk on þe flette" (1374). *In (þe) flet* also occurs in Middle English; see *MED* s.v. sense 1(b).

"Semely appon sille" is not listed among Oakden's alliterating phrases, but "semely in sale" is cited from *Golagrus and Gawain* and "semliest in sale" from *Amis and Amiloun*, Oakden, 2, 358, 335. "Semely in sale" is similar to "hende in halle," cited by Oakden from the alliterative and rhymed romances, 2, 286, 328, 355; cf. "as hende as hawk in halle," *Pearl* 184. The corresponding phrase for reference to women is of course *in bour;* see Oakden, 2, 319, where numerous citations for "bryghte in bour" are given. In the passage under discussion "in halleʒ & chambreʒ" (48) appears to be a periphrastic expression for "castle," equivalent to "in public and private rooms." Cf. *Gawain* 1664–66:

> Quen þay hade played in halle
> As longe as hor wylle hom last,
> To chambre he con hym calle . . .

11. *MED* gives 9 meanings in all for *a-vyse* (s.v. *avisen* v.). The meaning "to think up (sth.), contrive, devise" (sense 6) is cited only 6x as compared with 12 citations for sense 1a "to look at (sth.), examine, scrutinize" and 17 for sense 4a "to bethink oneself, consider, take thought." In *OED* the only Middle English citation for the meaning "to devise" (s.v. *advise* v. sense 4) is *Gawain* 45. OF *aviser*, from which *ME avisen* is derived, had the meanings "to look at, recognize; (refl.) to look at, take example from," but not "to devise" (see Godefroy). The latter meaning is, however, suggested by the definition of the pa. ptc. *avisé* in Godefroy as "endowed, adorned, furnished." Cf. *RRose* 475–76 and 478 "Alle these thingis, well avised, / As I have you er this devysed, / . . . Depeynted were upon the wall," cited by *MED* s.v. sense 6 as corresponding to *bien avisé* in the original.

There was also in Middle English a verb *vise(n)*, which is explained by *OED* (s.v. *vise* v.) as partly an aphetic form of *avise* or *devise*, partly from OF *viser* "to see, search, examine, consider" (Godefroy). ME *vise(n)* had the meaning "to devise," among others. This meaning is cited by *OED* (s.v. sense 1) from a poem dated c1325 in a line which closely resembles *Gawain* 45: "With alle þe murþes þat men may vise." It is also cited from *Wars of Alexander*.

It is probable that the use of *avise* to mean "devise" in *Gawain* 45 and elsewhere in Middle English should be ascribed to the general tendency to confuse related derivatives having the prefixes *a-, en-,* and *de-.* See the discussion of this tendency in Pt. II, p. 136.

12. *Weal* is also used in modern English, mainly in contexts of formal discourse, in such phrases as "the public weal." Modern *commonweal* reflects the development of a similar phrase into a compound.

13. For examples of i-mutation of *a* to *æ(e)* in Old Norse, see Adolf Noreen, *Altnordische Grammatik*, *1* (Halle, 1923), No. 63, 1. TG explain *happen* as a blend of *hap* and *heppin;* GDS, as a blend of *heppinn* and OE *gehæp* (see their glossaries); *OED* (s.v. *happen* a.) labels the *-en* suffix "uncertain."

14. Statements about usage in Old Norse are based on checks of the citations given in *LP* and *Ordbog*. *Heppinn* is cited only 3x from poetry in *LP*; in *Ordbog* it is cited from *Flateyjarbók* and *Grettissaga,* in both of which the context is prose.

15. The data for English *hap, happen* and ON *happ, heppinn* show an illuminating contrast with the data for English *mote* "hill" and *mote* "castle," OF *mote* "hill" and *mote* "castle." *Mote* "castle" as a poetic word in English may be due to the influence of French poetry.

16. The last reference in *OED* for *neven* v. is to Skelton; under *nemn,* citations from sixteenth-century prose and poetry (including Spenser) and one seventeenth-century citation are given.

17. *Neuyn,* 318; *neues,* MS Dublin only, 2119. In the latter the context demands the meaning "name"; a macron has evidently been omitted by the scribe.

18. See BT and Supplement. A problematic use is cited in BT (s.v. sense 3) from the metrical part of the Paris Psalter, Ps. 105:18, where the Vulgate text, "[Deus] qui fecit magnalia in Ægypto, mirabilia in Terra Cham, terribilia in mari rubro" is rendered "[God] þe on Egypton æðele wundur / and on Chananea cymu worhte / and recene wundur on þam readan sæ" (ed. Krapp, p. 84). BT gloss "coming swiftly and so causing terror (?cf. *fær*)." But despite the parallelism, it is possible that the poet did not intend *recene* to be equivalent to *terribilia*. In the first part of the verse, "Obliti sunt Deum qui salvavit eos" has been expanded into "Godes hi forgeaton, þe hi of gramra ær / feonda folmum frecne generede"; the idea of *terribilia* in the latter part of the verse has thus been anticipated by *frecne*. In its application to speech (see the citation in Supplement), *recen* is opposed to "lisping"; it may mean either "fluent" or "proper, correct."

19. In the *Lindisfarne Gospels, reconlice* corresponds to *protinus* in Mark 6:25; *hreconlice* to *protinus* and *cito* in Mark 1:18 and Matthew 28:8 respectively. In Rushworth[2], *ricenlice* corresponds to *protinus* and *continuo* in Mark 1:18 and 1:31 respectively. See BT; for full texts see *The Gospel according to Saint Mark,* ed. W. W. Skeat, Cambridge, 1871 and *The Gospel according to Saint Matthew,* ed. Skeat, Cambridge, 1887.

20. See *OED* under Forms. For development of a *d*-sound between *n* and *l,* as in *spindle* < OE *spinel,* see Jordan, No. 202.

21. Final -*e* in the ending of the present participle had ceased to be pronounced in the spoken language in early Middle English (cf. Jordan, No. 138; Luick, No. 456, 1. But all final -*e*'s had presumably ceased to be pronounced in the spoken language of the *Gawain*-poet, since the silencing of -*e* is thought to have taken place in the North Midlands in the second half of the 14th century (cf. Jordan, No. 141, Luick, No. 473). Any sounding of -*e* in the poem must therefore be based on metrical rules, and the nature of such rules for the alliterative long line remains to be determined. The problem is taken up in detail on pp. 182 ff.

22. Cited by E. S. Olszewska in a discussion of the phrase "game & glathe," pp. 59–61, in "Norse Alliterative Tradition in Middle English," Pt. I, Leeds Studies in English and Kindred Languages, 6 (1937), pp. 50–64.

23. Cf. Olszewska, p. 59; the phrase "gamen and gle" is cited by Oakden from the *Poema Morale*, p. 261, also from Middle English alliterative poetry, p. 283, and the rhymed romances, p. 326.

24. *Glaumr* does occur in poetry; it is cited a total of 16x by LP in the meanings "noise" and "gaiety." But it also occurs in prose and is cited by *Ordbog* from *Fornmanna Sögur*, *Stjórn* (a prose translation of the Bible), *Heilagra Manna Sögur*, and other prose texts.

25. Olszewska cites the phrase "glaumr ok gledi" from *Stjórn*. I am indebted to Professor Konstantin Reichardt for the information that in II Kings 11:20, "með glaum oc glaeði" is part of a loose translation of "Laetatusque est omnis populus" and that the same phrase occurs in *Fornmanna Sögur*.

26. Confusion between words so similar in form and meaning (and probably also in stylistic quality) seems inevitable. There is evidence for such confusion between *glam(m)* and *glaumr* in Old Norse; see the citation in *Ordbog* s.v. *glam(m)* from *Fornmanna Sögur* VI, where a variant reading *glaum* is referred to. But *glaumr* meant both "noise" and "gaiety," *glam* only "noise." The *Gawain*-poet uses words precisely, and one therefore imagines that *glam* in 1426, where the yelping of dogs is referred to, was the word originally used by the poet, although in 1652 *glam* may have been substituted scribally for an original *glaum*.

27. "Mete and mirþe" is not given by Oakden. Fuhrmann (p. 29) lists it with the following citations: *Gawain* 45, 71, 1007; *Anturs of Arther*, st. 14, line 12 (Ireland MS) "With alle the myrthes at thi mete"; *PPl.* A.xi.39 "Atte Mete in heor Murþe whon Munstrals beoþ stille." In the *PPl.* passage, *Murþe* and *Munstralsye* have been personified in degraded fashion as equivalent to "Lecherie and losengrie and loseles tales" (ibid., line 36); in the passage from *Gawain* the satisfaction of the appetite at table (*mete*) is associated with *mirþe*, which is in turn associated with the innocent pleasures of dancing and music (the *gle, dere dyn,* and *daunsyng* of lines 46–47).

For "mete and mele" see Oakden, 2, 244, 294; for "mirth and melody," ibid., pp. 295, 333; for "mirth and minstrelsy," ibid., p. 295 (cf. "myrthe of mynstrals," ibid., p. 333). "Mirth and minstrelsy" is listed by Fuhrmann, p. 69. The combination of "mete and minstrelsy" in *Gawain* 484 is also unusual in Middle English. It is not listed by Oakden; Fuhrmann cites for it, in addition to *Gawain* 484 and *Purity* 121, only the line from *PPl.* already quoted and a line from *Sir Beues of Hamtoun*. For the latter see the edition of Eugen Kölbing, EETS, ES, 46, 48, 65 (one vol.), p. 147, line 2844. Cf. also *Gawain* 1952-53 "With merþe & mynstralsye, wyth meteȝ at hor wylle, / Þay maden as mery as any men moȝten."

28. See *OED* s.v. *jolly* sense 5 "of cheerful courage, light-hearted, gallant."

29. *Rechless* (s.v. *reckless* a.), as defined by *OED*, seems always to imply "negligent carelessness" or "heedless rashness." *Careless* had a now obsolete sense "free from care" in Middle English; see *OED* s.v. sense 1. *Din* sb. is defined by *OED* as "a loud noise; particularly a . . . sound which stuns or distresses the ear." Its Old English ancestor *dyne* is defined by BT as "a din; noise," and is illustrated by the phrase *domdæges dyn*. *Din* in modern dialect use means "noise, loud talking" (*EDD* s.v. *din* sb.) and it seems to refer chiefly to noise made by human beings, as it does in the passage under consideration here. A loud noise is certainly not involved in line 1183, when Gawain hears the "littel dyn at his dor" made by the stealthy entrance of the lady.

30. It is characteristic of the style of *Gawain* that the only jewels mentioned by name are the diamond (617), which appears in the climactic detail of the description (566-618) of the arming of Gawain prior to his setting out in search of the Green Knight, and the pearl, which appears once as an adornment of the lady of the castle (954) and once in an analogy (2364).

31. Martha C. Thomas, in her study *Sir Gawayne and the Green Knight: A Comparison with the French Perceval* (Zürich, 1883) cites the line "Qu'il est enfes, le roi Artus," *Perceval le Gallois* 9439, as a parallel to *Gawain* 86 and 89 (p. 39). But the point is that this line does *not* occur in the passage in which Arthur's custom is described, lines 12,628 ff.

32. *La Queste del Saint Graal, roman du XIIIe siècle*, ed. Albert Pauphilet (Paris, 1923), pp. 4-5. "Et li rois comande que les napes soient mises, car il est tens de mengier, ce li est avis. 'Sire,' fet Kex li seneschaux, 'se vos asseez ja au disner, il m'est avis que vos enfraindroiz la costume de ceanz. Car nos avons veu toz jorz que vos a haute feste n'asseiez a table devant que aucune aventure fust en vostre cort avenue voiant toz les barons de vostre ostel.' 'Certes,' fet li rois, 'Kex, vos dites voir. Ceste costume ai je toz jors tenue et la tendrai tant come je porrai. Mes je avoie si grant joie de Lancelot et de ses cousins qui estoient venu a cort sain et haitié qu'il ne me sovenoit de la costume.' 'Or vos en soviegne,' fet Kex."

33. "Stiff in stour," Oakden, *2*, 304, 338; "stithe in stour," ibid.; "steryne in stour," ibid., p. 304; "bolde in batell," ibid., p. 270; "a feller in fight," ibid., p. 281 (cf. *Gawain* 874). See the discussion on pp. 79-80 and p. 241, notes 65-67.

34. "Stande still in a stede," etc., Oakden, 2, 338; cf. also "on stede er on stalle," ibid., p. 247.

35. I have noted the following parallels, some of which are cited by Oakden, in other alliterative poems:
    136: *mayster* in final position, *Siege Jerus.* 222, *Wars Alex.*, 310, 767*, 1545, 1920, 2251, 3400, in four cases preceded by an alliterating adjective.
    137: *most-molde*, *Morte Arth.* 3322, *PPl.* Prol. 64; *mesure-molde*, *Wars Alex.* 25; Oakden, 2, 293 s.v. *man apon molde*; cf. *mightiest on molde*, ibid.; *meryest on molde*, ibid., p. 332 s.v. *man of mold*, p. 357 s.v. *mold*; see also line 142 below; *high* in final position, *Morte Arth.* 39; *Siege Jerus.* 413.
    138: *so þik* in final position, *WPal.* 1795; *so mekil & so thike*, *Wars Alex.* 69; *so many and so thikke*, *Winner & W.* 190; cf. *Destr. Troy* 5531 "ffro þe hed to þe hele, herit full thicke"; *so þikke* in final position, *Gawain* 1770.
    139: *grete* in final position, see above, p. 84; *Destr. Troy* 1178; cf. *Destr. Troy* 3805 "He was long & large, with lemys full grete."
    140: *were* in final position, *Alex. Maced.* 138, *Morte Arth.* 150, *Wars Alex.* 305, 1427; cf. *Destr. Troy* 138 *lorde as he were*; *Siege Jerus.* 83 *le[ngede] þat y were*; *Wars Alex.* 239 *enquirid if he were*.
    142: *myriest-myȝt*, *Morte Arth.* 3239; cf. *meryest on molde*, line 137 above; *ride(s)* in final position, *Alex. Maced.* 411, 428; *Morte Arth.* 2166, 2849; *Wars Alex.* 999, 1731, 2062; *WPal.* 1600; for the line as a whole, cf., e.g., *Havelok the Dane* 9–10 "He was þe wihtest man at nede / Þat þurte riden on ani stede," paralleled in 25–26, 87–88, etc.
    143: *Bak-brest*, Oakden, 2, 267, 315; also *Destr. Troy* 3967, *Wars Alex.* 932; *brest-body*, Oakden, p. 270; *sturne* in final position, *Alex. Maced.* 110, 146, 337, 452, 680; *WPal.* 3780; otherwise strongly alliterating.
    144: Cf. *His wombe and hys wenges*, *Morte Arth.* 768. For a more general parallel cf. *Parl. 3 Ages* 112, 114 "He was balghe in the breste and brode in the scholdirs . . . And in the medill als a mayden menskfully schapen"; cf. also *RRose* A 825–26 "His shuldris of a large brede, / And smalish in the girdilstede."
    145: *fetures-forme*, Oakden, 2, 283; *þat he hade*, *Parl. 3 Ages* 346.

36. See GDS glossary s.v. *much*, TG s.v. *more*. *Most* "greatest" is probable if only because of the poet's tendency toward repetitive phraseology; it echoes line 137 and is echoed later by the servant's description of the Green Knight in 2100 "& more he is þen any mon vpon myddelerde." For the construction, cf. 1381 "here is wayth fayrest."

37. See p. 104 and above, n. 33, discussion of the alliterative phrase "steryn in stour"; other combinations in which it occurs are "stiffe and sturne," Oakden, 2, 304, "sterne and stoute," ibid., "stuerne . . . and stalworth," ibid. But *sterne* in *Alex. Maced.* is atypically of low alliterative rank; see above, parallels to line 143 in n. 4.

38. See above, p. 73. The exception is 1808 "& I am here [on] an erande in erdeʒ vncouþe."

39. *Minna* is cited 30x by *LP* in the meaning "remember" (s.v. sense 1); it also means "revenge" and "kiss" (senses 2 and 3). In the meanings "to refer to," "to remind someone," and "to remind oneself, remember," it is cited in *Ordbog* from, e.g., *Heilagra manna Sögur, Saga Ólafs Konungs Hins Helga,* and *Fornmanna Sögur.*

40. *The Harley Lyrics,* ed. G. L. Brook, pp. 48–50, line 27.

41. Ibid., p. 33, line 28.

42. See the introduction to *The Siege of Jerusalem,* ed. E. Kölbing and Mabel Day, EETS, 188 (1932), p. xv, "(d) Conclusion," and the description of the phonology of MSS C, D, and E, which have the variant readings, on pp. xiv–xv.

43. See I. Jackson, in *Notes and Queries,* Jan. 21, 1950, p. 24; G. V. Smithers, ibid., April 1, 1950, pp. 134–36, discussed in *The Year's Work in English Studies* for 1950, ed. Frederick S. Boas and Beatrice White (London, 1952), pp. 80–81.

44. A comparison between the number of parallels cited for lines 39–53 and those cited for lines 136–50 will show this clearly. Some of the key words of the latter passage, such as *sware, lyndes, etayn, muckel, ꞌsmale,* and *folʒande,* are of infrequent occurrence in the extant alliterative poems; *womb* usually refers to women in childbirth or the belly to be filled with food, rather than to part of the human body as a visible form.

45. To change *mayster* to *wyʒt* would presumably have involved recasting the line, since *wyʒt* seems always to occur within the line; cf. *Morte Arth.* 959, *Siege Jerus.* 348. In *Jos. Arim.* 196, 197, it occurs, with questionable meaning, within the line but does not alliterate.

46. *Hales* is cited 2x in the glossary of *Wars Alex.* in the meanings "to rush," "to draw quickly, come" (in both cases referring to a human being): lines 962 and 2817. The earliest meaning, according to *OED,* is "to draw or pull along . . . esp. with force or violence," which is cited from Lawman (s.v. *hale* v.[1] sense 1b). The intransitive senses developed later and the application to persons is apparently figurative and limited to poetry.

47. *Alder* "chief, ruler," derives from OE *ealdor,* Anglian *aldor; alder* "elder" from OE *ieldra,* Anglian *ældra* (*eldra*). TG give the former derivation. GDS the latter. See *OED alder* sb.[2] and *elder* a. and sb.[3]

48. *Bot,* which begins line 248 in the MS, would seem to be an erroneous repetition, the eye of the scribe having presumably been caught by initial *bot* in the line preceding. The repetition of unstressed words (though usually within a single line) is one of the types of scribal error most prevalent in the *Gawain*-MS; cf., in *Gawain,* lines 95, 182, 1137, etc.

49. The extent to which, allowing for differences in purpose and subject matter, these generalizations apply to *Patience, Purity,* and *St. Erkenwald*

(and perhaps also *Pearl*) cannot be determined here. Examples from the work of the *Gawain*-poet will accordingly be confined to *Gawain* itself.

50. The effectiveness and importance of the *Gawain*-poet's treatment of space is discussed in detail, though in somewhat different terms, by Alain Renoir in "Descriptive Technique in *Sir Gawain and the Green Knight*" (*Orbis Litterarum*, *13*, 1959, 126–32). Renoir makes an interesting and revealing analogy between the narrative technique of the *Gawain*-poet, with particular reference to the beheading of the Green Knight, and the use of the camera eye in motion pictures:

> The technique of [the Gawain-]poet is to draw a single detail out of a uniformly illuminated scene which is then allowed to fade out in obscurity and of which we may be given an occasional dim glimpse at psychologically appropriate moments. The twentieth century is thoroughly familiar with this device. In effect, it is that most commonly associated with the cinematograph, where the camera may at will focus either upon the whole scene or upon a single detail, while *illumination may be used so as to keep the audience aware of the background against which the action takes place* [italics mine]. We must note that the device is primarily concerned with the utilization of space (p. 127).

Renoir speaks, again, of "the effective use of both space and motion" throughout the poem, citing as an example Gawain's "first sight of Bercilak's castle, seen through the very same branches which we have so often found on either side of the cinematographic screen under similar circumstances" (p. 131).

PART TWO. METER

5. The Phonological Evidence

1. One thinks of poems forming shapes perceptible to the eye rather than the ear, like Herbert's "The Altar" and "Easter Wings"; of E. E. Cummings' visual effects in passages like:

> mOOn Over tOwns mOOn
> whisper
> less creature huge grO
> pingness

and of Richard Wilbur's conspicuous use of the letter *o* in his poem (entitled "o") on the circle. But such exceptions only prove the rule.

2. See Friedrich Knigge, *Die Sprache des Dichters von Sir Gawain and the Green Knight, der sogenannten Early English Alliterative Poems, und De Erkenwalde* (Marburg, 1885), p. 64 (OE *cw*), pp. 69-70 (OE *hw*). Oakden utilizes the spelling of OE *hw* as *wh* or *qu*, and the reversed spelling *wh* for OE *cw*, OF *qu*, as criteria of (scribal) dialect provenience; see *Alliterative Poetry, 1*, 28-29; for the alliteration of original *hw* with *cw* in *Morte Arthure* and *Destruction of Troy*, see pp. 64 and 67 respectively; for the application of the criteria to the *Gawain* MS and the distinction between scribal spellings and alliterative linkings see pp. 78-79.

3. "Romance," as applied to the vocabulary of *Gawain* in the discussion that follows, is equivalent to "of OF derivation."

4. What follows is a necessarily brief outline of the phonological problems relevant to metrical analysis. Detailed discussion of the accentual treatment of OF loan words in Middle English will be found in Luick, *Historische Grammatik, 1*, Nos. 419-22; see also the same author's "Über die Betonung der französischen Lehnwörter im Mittelenglischen," *Germanisch-Romanische Monatsschrift, 9* (1921), 14-19. For briefer accounts see Jordan, *Mittelenglische Grammatik*, Nos. 218, 245-47, and Henry Sweet, *A New English Grammar, Logical and Historical* (Oxford, 1892), Nos. 785-88. A particularly interesting presentation, although chiefly concerned with the modern period, is that of Jespersen in *A Modern English Grammar on Historical Principles, 1* (London, 1933), chap. 5. See especially the discussion of "the several principles which determine the place of stress either in a word ('word-stress') or in a group of words ('sentence-stress')" (No. 5.1). The accentual treatment of Romance words in English is discussed in detail in Nos. 5.51-5.68. The section on stress in Elizabethan English in Kökeritz, *Shakespeare's Pronunciation*, pp. 332-39, is helpful for an understanding of

the problem in Middle English. See also the section on unstressed vowels, ibid., pp. 255–94. For stress in Old English see Alistair Campbell, *Old English Grammar* (Oxford, 1959), chap. 2, especially Nos. 71–86, "Word Accent."

5. For a discussion of this vowel in Old French see M. K. Pope, *From Latin to Modern French with Especial Consideration of Anglo-Norman* (Manchester, 1952), No. 102.

6. The 1st pers. sg. pres. indic. of OF verbs will be cited in preference to the infinitive, which had an accented inflectional ending. This ending need not be considered, since it was regularly replaced in Middle English by unaccented -*e(n)*.

7. In Old French, in contrast to modern French, there was apparently a genuine differentiation among syllables in terms of intensity. The influence of Germanic modes of accent on primitive Old French and the gradual diminution of tonic accent in Old French after 1100 are discussed by Pope, No. 223. "The wholesale reduction and elimination of atonic syllables made of Old French a language in which all words were either *oxytone* or *paroxytone*, and, if paroxytone, then always ending in a syllable containing [the neutral unaccented vowel]" (ibid.).

8. For the treatment of OF *richesse* in Middle English as a plural in -*es* after shift of accent, see p. 138.

9. The loss of initial unstressed vowels or prefixes (aphaeresis) is discussed by Jespersen, *Grammar*, *1*, Nos. 9.95–9.97; cf. Luick, No. 465; Jordan, No. 249a. See also the discussion of aphaeresis in Elizabethan English in Kökeritz, *Shakespeare's Pronunciation*, pp. 280–81. For aphaeresis and interchange of prefixes in Anglo-French, see Pope, Nos. 1136–38.

10. *Ennurned* 2027 is emended by GDS to *enu[ire]ned* "set as a border," but is retained by TG. The line alliterates on *v*, but may be of the x a / a x type as defined by Oakden, *1*, 132. For the occurrence of the type in *Gawain* see ibid., p. 190, No. 5.

11. For this functional or phonemic use of stress with lists of examples, see Jespersen, Nos. 5.71–5.74, Sweet, No. 887.

12. For additional illustrations see Campbell, No. 73. Exceptions to the rule were due chiefly to the practice of forming verbs from nouns and nouns from verbs; the derivative was stressed in accordance with the original word in either case. Thus *ándswarian* v. "answer" was derived from *ándswaru* n., and *forgíefnes* from *forgíefan*. See Campbell, No. 77.

13. Anticipating the section on metrical evidence, we may point out that *rebel* n. and a. scans in Chaucer within the line both as *rébel* and *rebél*. For the latter mode of accentuation cf. *CT.Mk.* B 3415 "And art rebel to God, and art his foo."

14. For secondary (countertonic) accent in Late Latin and Old French see Pope, Nos. 216, 234; for the reduction of countertonic vowels, beginning in the later thirteenth century, see No. 236. Cf. Jespersen, No. 5.61.

15. Again we will anticipate by citing metrical evidence. *Despitous* seems to have both stem-accented and prefix-accented forms in Chaucerian verse. The former is exemplified by *CT.Kn.* A 1777 "As wel as to a proud despitous man." The latter seems to be exemplified in *BD* 624 "The dispitouse debonaire." If the line is headless, the meter would imply accent on the stem, but so far as I know, Chaucer does not write headless lines beginning with *the* (though he frequently begins them with *and*, *of*, and other unemphatic words). If the line is not headless, the final *-e* of the weak adjectival declension must be sounded. *TC* 2.435 "O cruel God, O dispitouse Marte" is certainly not a headless line. A syllable is lacking unless *dispitouse* is accented on the prefix and suffix, and the final *-e* (of the vocative) sounded.

16. *OED* characterizes *aunter* as a colloquial form (s.v. *adventure* sb.). It is found in modern dialect English, according to *EDD* (s.v. *aunter* sb.), in Cum. Wm. Yks. Lan. *Aunter* n. and the cognate verb and adjective occur in *Gawain* (for discussion see p. 167). In 2482 "& mony a venture in vale [he] venquyst ofte" TG read *aventure* (cf. 792 "mony luflych loupe," 2493 "mony syker knyʒt," etc.). According to *OED* (s.v. *venture* sb.), "The [aphaeretic] form is no doubt partly due to the initial *a-* of *aventure* having been taken as the indefinite article, especially after the stressing *avénture* had become usual. In 15th-century texts it is probable that occasional instances of *a venture* or *a venter* should be read as one word."

17. The lines in question (8089 ff.) state that the king threw *riches* into an altar fire; B has ʒiftes. There is no direct parallel in Wace.

18. For association of loss of *-e* with loss of accent, see pp. 138, 141. For early loss of *-e* in OF suffix-syllables see Luick, No. 461 and n.; Jordan, No. 244.

19. See Luick, No. 466, 4 and n.3; Jordan, No. 247 and notes. The cited MS of *Cursor* and that containing *Gawain* and *Pearl* date from the late 14th century and the end of that century respectively. For the former see p. 257, n. 1; for the latter p. 218, n. 1.

20. A mode of accentuation in which the suffix continued to be accented is assumed by Wyld; see his discussion of *fortune*, *value*, and similar words in *A History of Modern Colloquial English* (Oxford, 1953), p. 265. But I have been able to find no evidence in Middle English verse for colloquial suffix-accentuation; predominance of the stem is uniformly indicated.

Luick (in *Germanisch-Romanische Monatsschrift*, 9, 15–18) cites words like *pleasure* (OF *plaisir*) and *leisure* (OF *leisir*), where *-ure* is irregular, as evidence for a systematic alternation, after shift of accent back to the stem, between reduced and full pronunciations of the suffix in late Middle English. The modern forms of *pleasure* and *leisure* would, according to this argument, have originated, following the development of forms with the reduced suffix *-er*, as back-formations on the analogy of *measure* (OF *mesure*), *nature* (OF *nature*), and the like, which had both *-er* and *-ure* forms (pp. 17–18).

Kökeritz, in his discussion of *-ure* in *Shakespeare's Pronunciation* (p. 271), maintains that by Shakespeare's time "this ending was always pronounced [ɚɹ], unless syncopated to [r]; there is no trace of the modern spelling-pronunciation [tʃə]." Cf. the Elizabethan rhyme *creature: await her*, cited elsewhere by Kökeritz (p. 198, n. 4); the 17th-century homonyms *pastor: pasture* and *gesture: jester* cited by Jespersen (*A Modern English Grammar*, I, No. 9.333); and the 15th-century spellings *paster* "pasture" and *aventer* "adventure" cited by Wyld (p. 277).

21. *EDD* cites the line "From him I haue expresse commandement" (*I Henry VI* 1.3.20, First Folio) (cf. Kökeritz, *Shakespeare's Pronunciation*, p. 293), as well as *Cursor* 6481 "Þis er comandementis ten." The latter is taken from MS Göttingen (see below, p. 257, n. 1). In the other three MSS printed in the EETS edition, the noun is preceded by the definite article; Cotton reads "Þir er þe comamentes ten." *Commandment* is thus metrically ambiguous here as it is elsewhere in *Cursor*; see discussion on, pp. 153–54.

22. See the discussion of the suffixes *-al, -ail, -ol*, all pronounced in Elizabethan English with the reduced vowel or syllabic *l*, in Kökeritz, *Shakespeare's Pronunciation*, pp. 267–68, and the pun *traveller-travailer, As You Like It*, 2.4.18, cited on p. 151.

23. A succinct yet clear and comprehensive account of the sources of *-e* in the several parts of speech in Middle English may be found in Samuel Moore, *Historical Outline of English Sounds and Inflections*, rev. Albert H. Marckwardt (Ann Arbor, Michigan, 1951), Nos. 45–50.

24. For analogical loss and acquisition of *-e* in Middle English see Jordan, No. 141, n. 2; Luick, No. 473, n. 2; cf. Moore and Marckwardt, p. 61, n. 58 (loss of *-e* in the dat. sg. of originally masc. nouns) and No. 47, 1b (acquisition of *-e* in originally fem. nouns). A large amount of material, although restricted to monosyllabic nouns, may be found in Ruth B. McJimsey, *Chaucer's Irregular -E* (New York, 1942).

25. For loss of *-e* as a third syllable see Jordan, Nos. 138 (native words), 244 (Romance words); Luick, Nos. 456–58 (native words), 461 (Romance words). For loss of *-e* in words unstressed in phrase groups see Jordan, No. 152, Luick, No. 454.

26. According to Luick (No. 473 and n. 1, 5), *-e* was entirely lost in the North by the 13th century, in the Midlands in the course of the 14th century, and somewhat later in the South. According to Jordan (No. 141), *-e* was lost in the North during the 13th century and in the North Midlands in the first half of the 14th century; it was obsolescent in Chaucer's time in the South Midlands. See also Karl Brunner, *Die englische Sprache*, I (Halle, 1950), 289–90. According to Morsbach (*Mittelenglische Grammatik*, Halle, 1896, Nos. 75–79), the silencing of *-e* in the North was not completed until the middle of the 14th century, in the Midlands not until the middle of the 15th, and still later in the South. But the spellings alone of the MSS of *Cursor* and the MS of *Gawain*, even if the metrical usage and rhymes of these poems be discounted, suffice to show that Morsbach's chronology is overconservative (see pp. 141–42, 154–60).

Loss of -e in words of this final category must have preceded the unvoicing of originally intervocalic *v* to *f* in such words as *love* n. and v. (OE *lufu, lufian*), *above* (OE *abūfan*), and *give* v. (OE ʒiefan, ON *gefa*). This unvoicing is usually assigned to the thirteenth century in the North; it spread southward into Yks. and Lancs. and is reflected in such spellings in *Gawain* as *luf, abuf.* See Jordan, No. 217; for further examples in the *Gawain* MS, see Knigge, pp. 54–55. Cf. Chaucer's prayer (*TC* 5.1793 ff.) that his verse be not "mysmetre[d] for defaute of tonge," which seems to indicate that -e was disappearing as a syllable in the spoken language during the latter part of his lifetime. See Kökeritz, *A Guide to Chaucer's Pronunciation* (New York, 1962), pp. 10–11: "In the colloquial language of the period, final unstressed *e* . . . was dying fast; some speakers probably used it only in set expressions like *atte laste, to bedde, in towne,* etc. Chaucer, however, continued to use the obsolescent pronunciation . . . as an important metrical device." See also below, p. 260, n. 18.

27. A more detailed account than the above, but similar in outline, is that presented by E. Talbot Donaldson, "Chaucer's Final -E," *PMLA, 63* (1948), 1101–24; see especially pp. 1110 ff. Donaldson shows that the metrically implied sounding of -e in Chaucer, both within the line and in rhyme, is consistent with the developments in various classes of words posited by historical grammar.

28. Final -e's whose presence is not justified in terms of historical grammar are called "scribal -e's." See Moore and Marckwardt, No. 49.

29. The etymology of the name is discussed by TG in their note to line 109. They point out that "in Welsh the name is *Gwalchmai* . . . but [that] all other traditions (which represent earlier Welsh tradition) agree in following the type ending *-wain,* both Old French and Middle English and William of Malmesbury (who has *Walwen*). The Welsh form is evidently an altered one." Reaney (s.v. *Gavin*), cites the suggestion that "there was an alternative [Welsh] name *Gwalchgwyn.*"

30. See Map 2, "Endings of the Present Tense," *MED, Plan and Bibliography,* p. 8.

31. See Jordan, No. 135 and n.; Luick, No. 460, 2a and n. 1.

32. See Jordan, No. 291 and n.; Luick, No. 475 and n.; Brunner, *1,* 290. Orthographic evidence from MS Cotton of *Cursor* is presented on pp. 141–42. Contraction of -*ed* in Chaucerian verse is occasionally indicated by the meter, as in *CT*.Kt. A1197 "And he loved hym als tendrely agayn." Other examples from Chaucer are cited in connection with the possible contraction of -*ed* and -*es* in certain lines of the wheels of *Gawain;* see p. 161.

33. See Kökeritz, *Shakespeare's Pronunciation,* pp. 264–65, where these and other examples are given.

34. For trisyllabic words see Jordan, No. 139; Luick, Nos. 469–70. In certain cases, syncopation of the middle syllable could take place as an alterna-

tive to loss of *-e, -es, -ed;* thus Luick cites such variant forms as *chiknes* and *chikens, evere* (with syncopation of medial *e*) and *ever, hundred,* and *hunderd* (No. 470 and n. 4). For purposes of metrical analysis, these variants are equivalent. For unaccented words see Jordan, No. 153; Luick, No. 471. See also Brunner, *1,* 290.

6. The Metrical Evidence

1. For information on the EETS edition and the date of composition of the original poem, see p. 222, notes 10 and 11. The four MSS printed in parallel columns by EETS are, left to right, Cotton Vespas. A.iii. (C), Fairfax 14 (F), Theol. 107r. in the Library of Göttingen University (G), and R.3.8. in the Library of Trinity College, Cambridge (T). C, which is the best of the extant MSS of the whole poem, and T, which differs from it importantly in vocabulary, are discussed on pp. 36-37 and n. 12, p. 223. According to H. Hupe (EETS, 99, 101), F belongs to west Yks., with characteristics of Lancs. (p. 133); G belongs to west Lincs. (p. 132). *MED* dates all four MSS a1400—i.e. between 1375 and 1400. There is thus a gap of about 75 years between the original poem and the extant versions.

2. As seems inevitable in the realm of metrics, I have had in carrying out this study to find some of my own terms and to reformulate basic principles. Two special acknowledgements are appropriate here.

My indebtedness to William Thomson's *The Rhythm of Speech* (Glasgow, 1923) will be apparent from my borrowing of the concept of the metrical measure (which I call the "unit") and the term *compound*. Both the theoretical and interpretive sections of this book contain a great deal of material of value for the student interested in the perceptible differences among lines written in a single metrical form. It must be added that Thomson's almost perversely idiosyncratic terminology and his expression of metrical nuances through a system of notation using fractions of several different denominators present formidable obstacles to sustained reading and comprehension.

My indebtedness to Elder J. Olson began in the classroom; it includes the study of his unpublished doctoral dissertation, *General Prosody: Rhythmic, Metric, Harmonics,* Chicago, University of Chicago, 1938. Olson is concerned with the formulation of a theory of prosody under which the metrical system of any given language can be subsumed. Despite this theoretical emphasis, *General Prosody* includes a number of detailed and illuminating analyses of passages of English verse. A summary of Olson's views may be found in his article "Verse" in *The Encyclopaedia Britannica,* Chicago, London, and Toronto, 1957.

3. For the schematization of the five types and their subtypes, see Eduard Sievers, *Altgermanische Metrik* (Halle, 1893), Nos. 15-16, pp. 31-35. Ex-

amples of types C and D respectively, with juxtaposition of chief syllables, are the half-lines "ymb sund flite" (*Beowulf* 507b) and "feond mancynnes" (*Beowulf* 164b; cf. Sievers, No. 16, 4a, p. 34).

4. Ed. Madden (see p. 224, n. 18), *2*, 450.

5. Cf. the unequivocal statements of Adolf Tobler in *Vom französischen Versbau alter und neuer Zeit* (5th ed. Leipzig, 1910): "Der Vers ist (innerhalb der französischen Dichtung) ein in jedem einzelnen Falle an eine bestimmte Zahl von Silben gebundenes Glied poetischer Rede, das zu andern Gliedern derselben in einem bestimmte Verhältnisse der Silbenzahl (Gleichheit oder bestimmte Verschiedenheit) steht" (p. 1); "für den französischen Versbau [ist] zu keiner Zeit Regel gewesen . . . dass regelmässiger Wechsel zwischen betonten und tonlosen Silben stattfinde, dass zwischen zwei betonte Silben mindestens und höchstens eine tonlose trete" (p. 4); "dem französischen Verse genügt es aber auch nicht, eine bestimmte Zahl von Hebungen zu einem Ganzen zu vereinigen, zwischen denen Senkungen aus Silben von wechselnder Zahl stünden oder allenfalls auch fehlen könnten, wie dies etwa vom alten deutschen epischen Verse und zum Teil noch vom neudeutschen gilt" (p. 7).

6. Quantitative Latin verse continued, of course, to be written during the medieval period and later. An account of the relationship between the two prosodic systems in the Latin language from preclassical times on may be found in Fred Brittain, *The Medieval Latin and Romance Lyric to A. D. 1300* (2nd ed. Cambridge, 1951). See also F. J. E. Raby, *A History of Christian-Latin Poetry from the Beginnings to the Close of the Middle Ages* (2nd ed. Oxford, 1953), pp. 20–26. According to Brittain, "three main features of Medieval Latin versification" are "accentual rhythm, isosyllabism, and rhyme" (p. 6). Brittain quotes Dom Anselm Hughes' explanation of the adherence in accentual Latin verse to a consistent number of intermediate syllables between chief syllables as due to the practice of singing a great many stanzas (of a hymn) to a single melody; substitution of, e.g., a dactyl for a spondee would create difficulties for the singer (p. 8). Descriptions of scansion patterns, together with occasional schematizations, are provided by Stephen Gaselee in the notes to *The Oxford Book of Medieval Latin Verse* (1928), pp. 215, 220 ff.

7. Gaselee, p. 126. This poem exemplifies the "Goliardic" meter; see Gaselee, notes to poem 52, p. 222; Brittain, pp. 16–17. The Goliardic line is printed by Gaselee and Brittain without a typographical break, but in his schematization Gaselee indicates the pause after the seventh syllable with a double bar. In effect, there are two lines, one of four trochees, with the second syllable of the fourth omitted, followed by one of three complete trochees. The former is equivalent to a headless line of *Cursor*, or of Chaucerian tetrameter, with a masculine ending.

8. See EETS, 99, 101, p. 13 (Wace, "L'Établissement de la fête de la conception Notre-Dame").

9. H. Hupe discusses the meter of *Cursor* in "Notes on the Versification," pp. 253–61 of his *Cursor Studies* (EETS, 99, 101, pp. 111 ff.) and provides "Two Specimens of a Critical Text" with appended notes (ibid., pp. 201–52). In these specimen passages -*e*'s which are to remain silent are italicized, and an -*e* is occasionally added, where not present in the MSS, for the sake of the meter. Hupe's critical text is itself subjected to detailed criticism by Richard Morris ("Preface," EETS, 57, pp. xxii–xxviii). Hupe's study of the meter is nonetheless instructive, and I have availed myself of a few of his examples in the discussion below. Charles L. Crow's dissertation, *Zur Geschichte des kurzen Reimpaars im Mittelenglischen* (Göttingen, 1892) is concerned with the meter of *The Harrowing of Hell*, *Cursor*, and Chaucer's *House of Fame*. The study of *Cursor* (pp. 18–45) includes a system for the apocopation or sounding of -*e*, with occasional addition of -*e* for the sake of the meter. There is also a detailed discussion of the accentuation of native and Romance polysyllables. But Crow mistakenly assumes that the accentuation of a word in rhyme guarantees the same mode of accentuation within the line. As one of the characteristic "liberties" of the ME tetrameter couplet he identifies "schwebende Betonung, d.h. die Verschiebung des Versaccents auf eine Silbe, welche schwächeren Wortaccent hat als eine daran stossende Silbe in der Senkung. . . . Das Me. hat die Erscheinung aus dem Französischen mit übernommen. Für die Bestimmung ihres Umfanges haben wir eine Grundlage und Grenze an den Reimen: so weit für diese eine nebentonige Silbe ausreicht, wird sie für eine Hebung im Versinnern genügen" (p. 8). This mistaken principle leads him into a number of clearly erroneous scansions in which insufficient allowance is made for the possibility of reversed feet. *After*, for instance, is said to exemplify "schwebende Betonung" in 20831 "Efter þe upstei o þat drightin" (see the third group of examples, p. 36). It is important to distinguish, as Crow fails to do, between the accentuation of stem-suffix derivatives in rhyme and their accentuation within the line. See pp. 151–53.

10. A metrical "unit" is here defined as consisting of a chief syllable and the intermediate syllable or syllables (if any) between it and the next chief syllable. Where chief syllables are juxtaposed, the first one constitutes a monosyllabic metrical unit. "Metrical unit" is thus equivalent to "measure" as that term is applied to verse in Thomson's *The Rhythm of Speech*. Thomson defines a measure as "a portion of rhythm beginning with one strong accent and lasting up to, but not including, the next" (p. 6). I have preferred the term "unit" to "measure" because the latter is associated largely with music, and its use might seem to imply that metrical rhythm is held to be identical with musical rhythm. The two are differently constituted, though the tendency toward isochrony, discussed on pp. 190–92, applies to both.

11. I am arbitrarily assuming that the -*e* of *here* infin. is not sounded, even though it rhymes with an adjective in the plural (*sere*) in which the sounding of an inflectional -*e* would be historically justified. The rhymes of *Cursor* indicate the same treatment of -*e* as those of the wheels of *Gawain*; arguments

for the suppression of *-e* in all rhyme-words in the wheels are presented on pp. 156–58, and may be applied retroactively to *Cursor*.

12. Although this tendency is sufficiently marked to be formulated as a principle of the meter, there is evidence that the poet very infrequently composed a line in which a pause is substituted for an intermediate syllable and no reversed foot follows. Such a pattern seems indicated, for example, in 11299:

>   x   C x   C   C x   C
>   For maiden child eft als lang

where C and G agree in wording, and F and T show revision eliminating a rhyme with the Northern word *gang* "go." The instances are so rare as to be suspect. Their apparent occurrence may be due to errors in the original copy of the poem, though it would be unwise to state this categorically. Thus Crow cites 23938 "Baþe quik and ded, frend and fa" (E) as a line lacking a third intermediate syllable (p. 20), where C has *and* as a third intermediate syllable and *ded*[*e*], with plural inflection, is also possible. Cf. also such lines as 6743 "Qua stelis scep, or ox, or cu" and 6764 "Ox or ass, or cou or scepe," where the third intermediate syllable could have been omitted without detriment to the sense. (In line 7, "O brut þat bern bald of hand," *bern* is dissyllabic; cf. Jordan, No. 148, where *berin* is given as an example of the Northern development of a parasitic vowel in final *-rn*.)

13. Cited by Haenisch in "Inquiry into the Sources of the *Cursor Mundi*," EETS, 99, 101, p. 25.

14. Pp. 249–74. For the two modes of accentuation of *uphill*, see p. 254; cf. his *Modern English Grammar*, 5.42.

15. The *-es* of the plural is syncopated; cf. above, the discussion of early loss of *-es* and *-ed*, pp. 142–43.

16. These examples of adjectives in which a historically justified *-e* is to be sounded in *Cursor* are given, with many others, by Hupe on p. 180, "A Criticism of the Phonology," in *Cursor Studies* (pp. 135–89).

17. Cf. *Pearl* 486 "And quen mad on þe fyrst[*e*] day!" Here, as in certain other phrases, the implied treatment of *-e* in *Pearl* is strikingly reminiscent of *Cursor*. The metrical problems posed by *Pearl* cannot be solved here, but it may be noted in passing that most, if not all, juxtaposition of chief syllables, where a reversed foot does not follow by way of compensation, can be avoided by sounding a historically justified *-e*. In the first five stanzas such *-e*'s may be sounded in *hert*[*e*] 17, *stylle* 20, *hert*[*e*] 51, *fast*[*e*] 54, and perhaps also *fyrs*[*e*] 54 (MS *fyrte*; so emended in Gordon's edition). A list of rhymes in *Pearl* between words lacking and words entitled to a sounded *-e* is given by Gordon, p. 107.

18. According to Donaldson, statistics on a group of nouns and verbs frequently used by Chaucer, in cases where elision with a following vowel does

not occur, show approximately three sounded -*e*'s to one unsounded ("Chaucer's Final -*E*," pp. 1104-05).

19. To my knowledge, the tripartite structure of the short lines has not been questioned since the beginning of the century. See, e.g., the description in TG, "The Rhymed Lines," p. 120. Joseph Fischer, in *Die stabende Langzeile in den Werken des Gawaindichters*, Bonner Beiträge zur Anglistik, ed. Trautmann, 11 (Bonn, 1901), one of the studies advocating the seven-stress theory (see pp. 172 ff. and p. 264, n. 8), found in the wheels the (assumed) structure of the first half-lines, i.e. one of four stresses. His proposed emendations alone would indicate that four stresses are one too many. See the list on pp. 57-58, in which "Þis dint þat þou [me] schal dryue" (389) is typical.

20. See Moore and Marckwardt, No. 47, 1e, p. 61. "The 'petrified' dative . . . occurs in certain phrases consisting of a preposition immediately followed by a noun; e.g., *out of towne* [OE *tūn* m.]." *For sothe* rhymes with *bothe* in Chaucer; see McJimsey, No. IB1, p. 71, where the phrase is included in a list of petrified datives with sounded, originally inflectional, -*e*.

21. Cf. Donaldson, "Chaucer's Final -*E*," pp. 1121-24, where Chaucer's rhyme system is discussed and certain rhymes in *Sir Thopas* are cited as purposeful exceptions. Donaldson points out that although Chaucer uses both words ending in -*y* and words ending in -*ye* frequently in rhyme, he does not combine the two classes, with one rhyme in *Sir Thopas* as the exception that proves the rule (p. 1122).

22. For the etymology of the name *Gawain*, see above, p. 256, n. 29.

23. The name of the fox is exemplified in *Gawain* in variants of two form-groups, neither of which goes back to an original with -*e*. *Reynarde* 1920 and *Reniarde* 1728 are related to OF *renard* (*-nart*), *regnard* (*-nart*), ultimately from Gmc. *ragin-harduz. *Renaud* 1898 and *Renaude* 1916 are related to OF *renaud*, ultimately from Gmc. *ragin-waldaz. See Fernand Mossé, "Anthroponymie et histoire litteraire: Le *Roman de Renart* dans l'Angleterre du moyen age," *Les Langues Modernes*, 45 (1951), 22-36; the forms *Reniarde* and *Renaude* in *Gawain* are discussed on p. 27. Cf. also the entries in Reaney, *A Dictionary of British Surnames*, s.v. *Reynard* and *Reynold*.

24. Luick, in his studies of the alliterative long line in Middle English ("Die englische Stabreimzeile im XIV., XV., und XVI. Jahrhundert," *Anglia*, 11, 1889, pp. 392-443, 553-618), concluded that -*e* was to be sounded in the rhymes of the wheels when present in both rhyming words. He cited the two rhymes discussed above in which a final -*e* must be pronounced, together with the rhyme *quelle* (infin.): *melle: yelle* (3rd pers. pl. pres. indic.), 1449-1451-1453, deriving *melle* from OF *meslée* rather than ON *milli* or ODan. *melle* (see TG, GDS glossaries). For him the fact that, in two of these rhymes, the word with final -*e* comes first was evidence that the reader would normally expect to sound -*e*. If the first word was pronounced with -*e* silent, the pronunciation of the second would produce a false rhyme (pp.

572–74). But the assumption that rhymes are read inductively, part by part, is open to question. Even in modern verse there are rhymes in which the pronunciation of the first rhyme-word depends on the reader's knowledge of what the second will be. Thus in Gerard Manley Hopkins' "That Nature is a Heraclitean Fire and of the Comfort of the Resurrection" the phrase "I am, and" is pronounced, in a good reading, to rhyme with *diamond*, which follows. But this does not prove that "I am, and" would necessarily be so pronounced in speech. And similarly with metrical patterns; it is often impossible to know how to read the first two or three syllables of a line until the pattern of the line as a whole is comprehended.

25. Two of the three emendations presented here, that of *meʒel-mas* 532 to *meʒel-mas[se]* and that of *derk* 1177 to *derk[e]*, were proposed by Oliver F. Emerson in "Imperfect Lines in *Pearl* and the Rimed Parts of *Sir Gawain and the Green Knight*," *Modern Philology, 19* (1921), 131–41. Emerson proposed also the emendation of *lel* to *lel[e]*, with plural inflection, in 35 "With lel letteres loken" (p. 139). Such an emendation is not necessary, though the possibility that the poet read the line in this way cannot be ruled out. The ME derivative of OF *leël* (L *legalis*) must have had, besides the monosyllabic form implied by the spelling in *Gawain* 35, a dissyllabic form reflecting the stem-suffix composition of the word. Cf. the distinction made by educated speakers in modern English between *real* (OF *real, reël*, late L *reālis*) and *reel* n. (OE *hrēol*, with monophthongization of *ēo* at the end of the Old English period).

Emerson does not discuss the sounding or nonsounding of -*e* in cases where the letter appears in the text. In addition to the three emendations for words in intralinear position, he proposed emendation to -*e* in four rhyme-words— *ʒod* 1146, *stod* 1768 (assuming a subjunctive), *þonk* 1975, and *wlonk* 1977— on the principle, here held to be invalid, that -*e* is sounded when historically present in both words of a rhyming pair (pp. 139–40).

26. E.g. 206 "To be thy knight[e] lowde and stille"; 607 "Wille be thy knight[e] for his sake"; 2007 "The hardy knyght[e], syr gawayne"; 3510 "The knyght[e] kest A rewfull rowne." The emendations are mine. See the ed. of J. Douglas Bruce, EETS ES, 88 (1903). There could be no better evidence than such a spurious form for the loss of -*e* in the spoken language.

27. MS *for wonder*; emendation to *forwonder* is proposed above, p. 109.

7. The Alliterative Long Line: The Normal Form

1. Of the three detailed studies of the metrics of *Gawain* and the other works of the *Gawain*-poet cited below, p. 264, n. 10, that of Kuhnke does not discuss the accentual treatment of Romance derivatives, while in those of Fischer and Thomas metrical principles are used to determine accentuation to an extent which impairs the usefulness of their findings for the purposes of

the present study. The section on Romance words in Fischer (pp. 35–38) may be consulted for detailed information on the alliterative treatment of Romance derivatives in the works of the *Gawain*-poet. But Fischer's practice of assuming the modern mode of accentuation in words for which "the meter gives no certain indications" (p. 36) leads him, e.g., to accent the second syllable of *renon* in *Gawain* despite the *r*-alliteration and the evidence for a prefix-accented variant in Middle English; see pp. 166, 169. Thomas believed that the meter of *Gawain* was prevailingly anapestic or dactylic (see below, p. 267, n. 25). In his study words are often stressed in such a way as to maintain this pattern. Cf. his examples from French prose, p. 6, and the statement, p. 33, that "als Gegebenes ist . . . wohl in allererster Linie der Versrhythmus anzunehmen, und auf seine Kosten manche schlechte Alliteration, manche ungewöhnliche Betonung zu setzen."

2. See *MED* s.v. *commaunden* v. sense 6c. *Command* (OF *comander*) and *commend* (OF *comender*), both ultimately from Latin *commendare*, were not completely distinct in Middle English; cf. *MED* s.v. *commenden* v. sense 1c.

3. Cf. the discussion of the principle of "Contrast" in Jespersen, *A Modern English Grammar*, Nos. 5.1, 5.24. Jespersen suggests that the modern accentuation of *object* and *subject* and other pairs of words may be due to this principle (No. 5.55).

4. Kökeritz, in *Shakespeare's Pronunciation*, p. 335, refers to forms of *maintain* indicating accent on the first syllable. The word scans both C x and x C in Shakespeare's verse (ibid., p. 393).

5. A tendency to alliterate on unstressed syllables is discernible in Middle English alliterative verse as early as *The Proverbs of Alfred* and Lawman's *Brut*, and such alliteration is common in many of the poems of the 14th century. See the detailed discussion in Oakden, *1*, 177–79, where examples of alliteration on unstressed prefixes, unaccented prepositions, auxiliary verbs and pronouns from *Alexander of Macedon* (*Alexander A*) are given.

6. Most of the long lines in *Gawain* in which alliteration is entirely lacking lend themselves readily to emendation, and it seems certain that the remainder are corrupt as well. The two cited by Oakden in his breakdown (*1*, 190–91) of the alliterative types in *Gawain* are 971 "Wyth leue laȝt of þe lorde he went hem aȝaynes" and 1906 "Þe lorde lyȝteȝ bilyue & cacheȝ by sone." In the former, *went* is emended to *lent* by GDS (cf. 1319), left unchanged by TG. In the latter both GDS and TG emend *cacheȝ by* to *lacheȝ hym*. Fischer, in his study of the long line in the works of the *Gawain*-poet (see below, n. 10), lists these and a number of others (pp. 47–48); all of these are emended by GDS and all but two by TG. Thus in 958 "Chymbled ouer hir blake chyn with mylk-quyte vayles" *mylk* has obviously been substituted for *chalk* and the latter is restored by both editors (cf. 798). In other lines it is less easy to determine the original wording, but this does not affect the general principle that, for the *Gawain*-poet at least, the two halves of the long line invariably

had at least one alliterative link. A few other lines may be cited here. In 157 "Heme wel-haled hose of þat same grene" *of* technically fulfills the alliterating requirement, but *ilk* should probably be substituted for *same;* cf. 173 "Þe fole þat he ferkkes on, fyn of þat ilke [i.e., green]." In 2444 " 'Þat schal I tell þe trwly', quoþ þat oþer þenne" read "þe toþer" (see *OED* s.v. *tother* pron. sense 1, cited from *Cursor*); in 2467 "Þerfore I eþe þe, haþel, to com to þy naunt" read "þyn aunt," with alliteration on vowels and *h* in the a a / x a pattern (see Jordan, No. 171).

7. The contracted form *bos* of *bihoves*, identified by *MED* as Northern and North Midland, is found in *Purity* 687 "Me bos telle to þat tolk þe tene of my wylle" and *Pearl* 323 "Þurȝ drwry deth boȝ vch man dreue," in both of which the meter seems to require it. Cf. *Cursor* 6911, where C has "O þair mater be-houis me sese," while G has "Of þis mater ȝit bos me ses." The contracted form appears also in such alliterative poems as *Destruction of Troy* and *Wars of Alexander*. (These examples are taken from *MED* s.v. *bihoven* v. senses 1c and 2b.) But the meter of *Gawain* nowhere necessitates the contracted form, nor is it indicated by the spelling, though the verb occurs over 10x in the long lines.

8. The seven-stress theory grew out of an eight-stress theory, modeled on a similar analysis of Old English verse, in which four stresses were allowed to each half-line. The eight-stress theory was presented by F. Rosenthal in "Die alliterierende englische Langzeile im 14. Jahrhundert," *Anglia, 1* (1878), 414–59; it was modified by Moritz Trautmann ("Zur Kenntnis und Geschichte der mittelenglischen Stabzeile," *Anglia, 18*, 1896, pp. 83–100) to allow for the obvious difference in length between the two half-lines in Middle English, the second being consistently shorter than the first. See the account of the early history of the controversy given by Max Kaluza, himself an advocate of the seven-stress theory, in *Englische Metrik in historischer Entwicklung*, Normannia, 1 (Berlin, 1909), pp. 183-91.

9. *Studies by Members of the Department of English, 2,* University of Wisconsin Studies in Language and Literature, 11 (Madison, Wisconsin, 1920), 58–104.

10. See Luick, in *Anglia, 11*, 392–443, 553–618, and "Der mittelenglische Stabreimverse" in Hermann Paul, *Grundriss der Germanischen Philologie*, 2nd ed., *2*, Pt. II (Strassburg, 1905), 160–68; W. W. Skeat, "An Essay on Alliterative Poetry," in *Bishop Percy's Folio Manuscript*, ed. John W. Hales and Frederick J. Furnivall, *3* (London, 1868), xi–xxxix; Menner, introduction to *Purity*, pp. liv-lv and n. 4; Sisam, *Fourteenth Century Verse and Prose*, pp. 215–16; TG, pp. 118–19; Oakden, *1*, 174–76. Luick's analysis of the ME line, which was adapted from Sievers' analysis of the OE line, is discussed in some detail on pp. 183 ff. The system developed by Luick was accepted and applied in detail to the works of the *Gawain*-poet by Julius Thomas in *Die alliterierende Langzeile des Gawayn-Dichters* (Jena, 1908). It was utilized also by Max Deutschbein in an interesting and sta-

tistically detailed study of the relationship of Old English to Middle English alliterative verse, *Zur Entwicklung des englischen Alliterationsverses* (Halle, 1902).

Trautmann's seven-stress analysis of the long line was applied in detail to *Gawain* and the other poems of the *Gawain*-MS by Bruno Kuhnke and Joseph Fischer. See Kuhnke, *Die alliterierende Langzeile in der mittelenglischen Romanze Sir Gawayn and the Green Knight*, Studien zum germanischen Alliterationsvers, ed. Max Kaluza, 4 (Berlin, 1900) and Fischer, *Die stabende Langzeile in den Werken des Gawaindichters*. George R. Stewart, Jr., in "The Meter of *Piers Plowman*," *PMLA*, 42 (1927), 113-28, attempted to reconcile the seven- and four-stress theories, but in effect aligned himself with the former. See below, n. 13.

11. "Most of [Middle English alliterative verse] is indeed nearer to Modern English than to Anglo-Saxon—some of it is essentially Modern English" (p. 61). See also p. 67, where, after quoting lines 169-82 of *The Tale of Gamelyn*, he continues, "To put its scansion out of all doubt—for I want to reach the interested layman in ME . . . as well as the specialist —I have rendered it into Modern English. The movement is like this: 'Heark ye, and listen ye and hold ye your tongue. . . .'"

12. "A compound measure consists of two or more simple measures unified by an initial accent stronger than those of the other constituent measures" (p. 198). The varieties of compound meter are schematized by Thomson on p. 11. Olson calls this sort of structure "superimposed" or "mounted" rhythm ("Verse," p. 97).

13. See pp. 69-70. The analogy is actually drawn between the nursery rhyme and the rhymed meter of *The Tale of Gamelyn*, with which the present study is not concerned. But Leonard considered the meter of *Gamelyn* to be indistinguishable from that of the ME long alliterative line; cf. his challenge to the reader to sort out unidentified passages from *Gamelyn* and *Piers Plowman*, or *Gamelyn* and *William of Palerne*, pp. 77-81.

Leonard's formulation presents the seven-stress theory at its most intelligible and convincing from the standpoint of metrical recitation and the listening ear. The argument that the resultant reading is too slow and heavy, which is presented in detail below, applies a fortiori to scansions in which more than four of the seven stresses, or all seven, are counted as primary. Trautmann, for instance, makes no distinctions among the seven either in theoretical formulation or the marking of accent in scanned passages (cf. the discussion in "Zur Kenntnis und Geschichte," pp. 83-84, and the scansion of *Gawain* 37-54, ibid., pp. 85-86). Kuhnke and Fischer find two, three, or four primary stresses out of four in the first half-line (cf. the sample scansions in Kuhnke, pp. 14, 16, and the scansion of *Gawain* 1-59 in Fischer, pp. 27-29).

It should be borne in mind that secondary stress and secondary (i.e. minor) rank in meter are not the same thing. In Shakespeare's line "Ruin hath taught me thus to ruminate," -*nate* has secondary stress in grammatical terms, but primary rank in metrical terms—i.e. it is equivalent to *ru-* as an element of metrical structure. But in the opening line of Meredith's "Love in the Valley," which in our notation would be scanned as follows:

<pre>
C   c   C   c   C   c   C   c
Under yonder beech-tree single on the green-sward,
</pre>

-tree and *-sward* have both secondary grammatical stress and secondary rank as minor chief syllables in a uniformly compound metrical structure. (Text from *The Oxford Book of Victorian Verse*, ed. Arthur Quiller-Couch, Oxford, 1925, p. 449.) The scansions of Kuhnke and Fischer imply a structure of seven formally equivalent chief syllables, a syllable bearing secondary stress occasionally serving as one of these, as in Shakespearian verse. This structure is even less applicable to the long lines than the uniform compound structure posited by Leonard. Such sequences as one secondary stress plus three primaries, or two primaries, one secondary, and one primary, are impossible to recite or hear as metrical *forms*, though they may constitute description of nonessential variation *within* a form.

Stewart, in "The Meter of *Piers Plowman*," 113–28, attempts to show that for the long lines of *Piers Plowman*, and hence for Middle English alliterative verse generally, the seven- and four-stress interpretations "harmonize as dipodic verse" (cf. pp. 113–14)—i.e. as compound meter in which four primary and three secondary stresses occur in alternation. In effect, therefore, he scans the lines as Leonard does; where Leonard cites "Four and twenty blackbirds," Stewart cites "Taffy was a Welshman" as an analogue to the ME alliterative line (p. 114). The question remains, however, whether three secondary stresses as well as four primaries are in fact present uniformly in the long lines of *Gawain*.

14. A scansion of this passage according to the seven-stress system will be found in Fischer, pp. 27–28. Many stresses counted as secondary in the examples below are counted as primary by Fischer, e.g. *vp* in 12b "lyftes vp homes."

15. See TG, p. 118, No. 5, and, on p. 120, the statement that "each line of the wheel contains three stresses and is metrically equivalent to a three-lift half-line of the alliterative type." Oakden, speaking of the extended form of the half-line, says that "in many cases it is very difficult to decide whether the half-line ought to be read with three stresses or with two. On the other hand, there are examples of lines with two alliterating syllables only and three stressed syllables" (*1*, 172). Sisam remarks that "three stresses are not uncommonly found in the first half line" of *Gawain* (*Fourteenth Century Verse and Prose*, p. 216) but does not elaborate.

The extended form of the long line is treated as a separate problem below, Chap. 8.

16. Cf. Fischer, p. 21: "*e* ist zu lesen . . . zur erlangung der notwendigen taktanzahl." In Fischer's scansions one of the seven stresses often falls on *-e*, as in *Gawain* 71a "Álle þis mírþè þay máden" (ibid.). Frequent emendations

to provide more syllables are a characteristic feature of the seven-stress systems. Menner, introduction to *Purity*, p. liv, n. 4, remarks that "The great number of rash emendations that Fischer finds necessary in order to provide enough words for seven stresses to the line inclines one to extreme distrust of his work and of the soundness of his theory."

17. MED gives ?a1400 as the date of composition of *Destruction of Troy* and c1450 as the date of the MS. The poem is listed by *MED*, with *Sir Gawain and the Green Knight*, among West Midland texts (*Plan and Bibliography*, p. 12), without specification as to North or South. Oakden concludes from the alliteration that "the dialect was extreme N.W. Midl., farther north than that of *Sir Gawayn*" (*1*, 67).

18. Cf. Oakden, *1*, 131–51, where the transition from Old English to Middle English verse is discussed in detail, Siever's OE types being taken as a point of departure, and pp. 174 ff., where the "normal half-lines" of fourteenth-century alliterative poetry are analyzed. A table showing the comparative frequencies of the different types of the half-line is given on p. 176. A similar but briefer analysis may be found in TG, pp. 118–19. Max Deutschbein's study of the transition based on Luick's findings has been referred to above (p. 264, n. 10).

19. Specifically, from B and C with resolution of the second and first stress respectively; its development was attributed to the widespread lengthening of accented vowels, particularly *a*, *e*, and *o*, in open syllables in Early Middle English. An OE half-line such as "ðæt he faran wolde" would be schematized in Sievers' system as a C verse, x x ⏑ ⌣ x ⊥ x; its ME analogue, with lengthened *a* in *faren*, would have the pattern x x ⊥ x ⊥ x. See the discussion, in which this example is given, on pp. 403–04. For the lengthening of *a*, *e*, and *o* in open syllables, see Jordan, No. 25; Luick, No. 391.

20. P. 403. The theory, expressed here by Luick for the first time, that alliterative verses recited without sounding of *-e* gave rise to new patterns imitated by younger poets, has important implications for the scansion of late Middle English alliterative verse. See p. 186 and below, notes 26, 27.

21. Pp. 404–10. Luick identified the dialect of *Destruction of Troy* as Northwest Midland (pp. 405–06), but concluded from this only that *-e* in the spoken language of the poet had "undergone some diminution (einbusse erlitten)" (p. 406).

22. For the scansion of "Colchos by name" see p. 409; for "as hym grace felle," p. 412; for "& the mone chaunge," p. 415.

23. See pp. 156–58. Luick's argument from the order of the rhyme-words is disputed above, p. 261, n. 24.

24. For the scansion of "& his highe kynde," see p. 579; for "as I tryst[e] may" p. 578.

25. Thomas' study, as has been said, was founded on Luick's, and accorded with Luick's in general with respect to the treatment of final *-e*.

But Thomas differed from Luick in that he found in the long line, as written by the *Gawain*-poet and also by the author of *Piers Plowman*, a prevailingly anapestic or dactylic meter from which the poet occasionally departed for the sake of variation (pp. 5–7). In Thomas' system, therefore, the pattern of two intermediate syllables between chief syllables is maintained wherever possible through the sounding or nonsounding of -*e*. In the second half-line of *Gawain* 68 "De-bated busyly aboute þo giftes" the -*e* of *aboute* is sounded (see the first list of examples of the pattern x ´ x x ´ x, p. 44), while in 189 "Folden in wyth fildore aboute þe fayre grene" the same pattern is produced by allowing the -*e*'s of *aboute* and *fayre* to remain unsounded (see the examples of apocopated -*e* in prepositions, p. 29). This prevailing metrical pattern, it need hardly be said, derives from the very accentuations and soundings or nonsoundings of -*e* which it is supposed to validate.

Thomas adopts the same ambivalent attitude toward "shortened" lines as Luick, although he is somewhat less conservative. After discussing Luick's suggestions for the transformation of certain shortened lines into normal ones, he remarks that "einesteils blieben doch einige sichere Fälle des verkurzten Typus A, bei denen man nicht so leicht ein -*e* einfügen könnte, und die man schliesslich als wenige Ausnahmen oder schlecht überlieferte Verse ansehen müsste. Andernteils halte ich es für sehr gewagt, in einer Uniformierung der Verstypen zu weit zu gehen. Zum Effekt der Abwechslung kann der Dichter recht wohl weniger gebräuchliche Verstypen angewandt haben" (p. 46).

26. This view is clearly expressed in *Historische Grammatik*, No. 473, n. 1: "Durch den Reim wird der Abfall [of -*e*] für den Norden vom 14. Jahrhundert an als fest durchgeführt erwiesen, als schon vorhanden für RM, also für die Sprache des nordlichen Mittellands in der ersten Hälfte des 14. Jahrhunderts ... Andererseits [i.e. in contrast to Chaucer and his followers] haben die älteren nordenglischen Dichter im Vers vielleicht zum Teil noch -*e* gebraucht ... namentlich im Alliterationsvers in grossem Umfang zur Herstellung des klingenden Ausgangs, aber nicht mehr für eine Innensenkung."

27. "Auf dem Gebeit des *nordenglischen* Dialektes und in den angrenzenden Teilen des Mittellandes erlitt das Metrum eine weitere Umbildung. Hier war um jene Zeit das End-*e* verstummt oder im Verstummen begriffen; viele aus früheren Zeiten oder aus dem Mittellande übernommen Verse wurden daher im Munde der Nordländer verkürzt und dann in dieser Form nachgeahmt. Das Versinnere wurde durch diesen Vorgang weniger betroffen, aber sehr stark der Ausgang. Den klingend endigenden Typen A, C, BC treten Varianten mit stumpfen Ausgang zur Seite.... Freilich liegen Anzeichen vor, dass die Dichter mindestens im Versausgang das End-*e* noch gesprochen wissen wollen, obwohl es in gewöhnlicher Rede schon verstummt war, und dadurch so viel als möglich den klingenden Ausgang herstellen." (*Grundriss der germanischen Philologie*, 2, Pt. II, 164–65.)

28. Thomas admits the presence in the long lines of the *Gawain*-poet of the "shortened" types ´ x ´ x and x ´ ´ x, of which he gives examples on pp. 46 and 49 respectively. His belief that the long lines uniformly have the feminine ending rules out the pattern x ´ x ´.

29. Luick (in *Anglia*, 11, 580) rules out the native mode of accentuation in these cases on metrical grounds, even in such a half-line as "at hyndeʒ barayne" (1320), where accent on the first syllable of *barayne* results in the pattern x ´ x ´ x, a "shortened" type found elsewhere in *Gawain*. He allows, however, for the possibility of a balanced or "hovering" accent, the resultant pattern being a cross between the A and C types (p. 581).

30. Oakden (*1*, 157 ff.) discusses certain important "tendencies [in ME alliterative verse] which were already apparent in the alliterative poems written in the early ME period," among them certain changes in the metrical patterns of the OE half-line resulting in a proportionate increase in half-lines with "Rising-Falling-Rhythm"—i.e. half-lines both beginning and ending with unaccented syllables: "this [rhythm] is found in late OE verse, but in the early ME alliterative poems became . . . the most frequently used of all the types" (p. 175). Oakden goes on to summarize the comparative frequencies of the several metrical patterns in the first and second halves of the ME alliterative line. He remarks that "the *Rising-Rhythm* is not common in the 2nd. half-line, largely because the ending '/ x' [in our terms, C x] had become so popular" (p. 176). See also Oakden's analysis of the metrical patterns of Lawman's *Brut*, pp. 143-44, where it is shown that in the second half-line feminine endings preponderate markedly over masculine.

Deutschbein (*Zur Entwicklung des englischen Alliterationsverses*, No. 8) presents statistical tables showing the comparative frequencies of metrical patterns of the falling and rising types—with feminine and masculine endings, respectively—in the first and second half-lines of *Beowulf*, *Andreas*, *The Battle of Maldon*, and *Be Domes Dæge*. (This last is printed as *The Judgment Day II* in *The Anglo-Saxon Minor Poems*, ed. Elliott van Kirk Dobbie, *The Anglo-Saxon Poetic Records*, 6, New York, 1942, pp. 58-67.) According to Deutschbein's figures, the proportion of feminine endings to masculine in the second half-line is much higher in *Be Domes Dæge* than in *Beowulf*.

31. In *Anglia*, 11, 577. Thomas attempted to prove that the long line as written by the *Gawain*-poet invariably had the feminine ending; his findings for *Purity* were convincingly disputed by Menner in his introduction, p. lv, n. 1. He examined only the first 300 lines of *Gawain* (see pp. 10-12), thus ignoring most of the examples of the masculine ending cited by Luick.

32. This fallacy is exhibited by, e.g., Luick's argument that the poet of *Destruction of Troy* must have tried to avoid the masculine ending, since most of the nouns occurring in the nominative and accusative singular at

the end of the line were feminine in Old English (and would thus be expected to have -e in Middle English). See *Anglia, 11*, 406.

33. Donaldson (*PMLA, 63*, 1123) remarks that "the better Middle English scribes show a pronounced tendency—frequently remarked upon—as between forms with and without -e to place at the end of the verse the form with -e."

34. The *Gawain*-poet does apparently show his preference for the feminine ending in certain lines where a weak form of the preterite is used in final position, a strong form being used in intralinear position. The pattern seems too consistent to be due to scribal substitution. Thus he writes "De-liuerly he dressed vp er þe day sprenged" (2009) but "He sperred þe sted with þe spureȝ, & sprong on his way" (670), and "& made myry al day til þe mone rysed" (1313), but "Bot ros hir vp radly, rayked hir þeder" (1735).

35. Cf. the discussion of the sounding of -e in *Parl. 3 Ages* in the introduction to the recent edition by M. Y. Offord (EETS 246, Oxford, 1959). Reference is made there to an unpublished paper by Mabel Day on the meter of *Parl. 3 Ages* and *Winner & W.*, in which the conclusion is reached that "final -e within the line had lost its value" but that -e was probably pronounced in final position (p. xxix). But the further statement that -e "may have occasionally been sounded for metrical reasons [within the line]" (ibid.) implies a more conservative view than that expressed here with regard to the meter of *Gawain*.

8. The Alliterative Long Line: The Extended Form

1. For a detailed discussion of the extended first half-lines, with a classification into types, see Oakden, *1*, 170–74. A table of percentages, showing the comparative frequency of occurrence of these half-lines in the poems of the Alliterative Revival, is presented on p. 171. From this table it is clear that the author of *Gawain* used the extended first half-line much more frequently than the other poets. In *Gawain, Purity, Patience,* and *St. Erkenwald* the percentages, as determined by Oakden, are 15.3, 15.8, 13.7, and 17.5 respectively, while in the other poems 12% is the maximum. *Wars Alex.* has 9.66, *Morte Arth.* has 4.3, and *Destr. Troy* has none.

2. From this point on, only chief syllables will be indicated in metrical notation. It is assumed that final -e never constitutes a syllable within the line, but that final -ed and -es are normally syllabic. The possible syncopation of these syllables in certain cases will be discussed below. In words final in the line the decision whether or not to sound final -e is left to the reader (see above, pp. 188–89), but he is reminded that such sounding ought to be phonologically consistent and not dependent on the vagaries of the spelling. If -e is sounded in *Troye* (line 1), it ought to be sounded also in

wroȝt[e] (3), from OE *worhte, wrohte;* in *hat[te]* (10), from OE *hātte;* and so on.

3. It must be understood that there is no one "correct" tempo or pace, whether in musical performance or in metrical recitation. There are tempos which are clearly too fast, tempos which are clearly too slow, and a range of appropriate or effective tempos between these extremes, one of which may be recommended for a piece of music by an editor. My own recitation of the four lines quoted above from *Gawain* averages roughly about 100 chief syllables per minute; at an average pace of below 85, the lines seem to drag, and at an average pace of over 115, they seem hurried. While all readers may not agree with this definition of the limits, the general principle that it is possible to read the long lines of *Gawain* too slowly or too fast can hardly be disputed. Compare the discussion of tempo in Old English verse in John Collins Pope, *The Rhythm of Beowulf* (New Haven, 1942), pp. 26–29. The rhythms of normal verses are transcribed in musical notation by Pope with a time signature of 4/8; this time is said to represent "a range of tempos," there being, in general, "between 100 and 140 quarter-notes to the minute" (p. 29).

The average pace at which a metrical passage is read is thus an aspect of interpretation rather than of structure. Metrical structure shows itself in the influence of this average or norm on the pace of particular sequences of syllables.

4. Such sequences as "þat pitosly þer piped" and "Into a forest" are, needless to say, metrically ambiguous; cf. *pitously* in *BD* 711:

      C   C   C   C
Thus pitously, as I yow telle

and *in-to* in *Gawain* 2023 (from the wheels):

      C   C   C
Þe gayest in-to Grece.

5. It sometimes happens, of course, that two such adjectives are given equal stress, as in "I want to have a góod lóng tálk with you" or "She's a níce, kínd pérson." Such stressing is rhetorical; it reflects the speaker's wish to emphasize each adjectivally signified meaning independently. Note that "a góod lóng tálk," in the sentence quoted above, is slower in pace than the same sequence of syllables in the less emphatic sentence "We had a góod lòng tálk."

6. This phenomenon is discussed by Otto Jespersen in his "Notes on Metre," in *Linguistica*, pp. 249–74. "Verse rhythm is based on the same alternation between stronger and weaker syllables as that found in natural everyday speech. Even in the most prosaic speech, which is in no way dictated by artistic feeling, this alternation is not completely irregular: everywhere we observe a natural tendency towards making a weak syllable follow after a strong one and inversely. . . . Thus syllables which ought

seemingly to be strong are weakened if occurring between strong syllables" (p. 254). One of Jespersen's illustrations is the line "The still sad music of humanity" (ibid.), where the second of two descriptive adjectives preceding a noun is subordinated as in the examples quoted above. See also the section on "Rhythmic Stress" in Jespersen's *Grammar* (*1*, Nos. 5.41–5.46), especially Nos. 5.41 and 5.44.

7. It may be useful here to express the difference in terms of the numerical notation used by Jespersen in "Notes on Metre." While recognizing that "in reality there are infinite gradations of stress" (p. 253), Jespersen defined, as sufficient for purposes of metrical analysis, four degrees which he called "strong," "half-strong," "half-weak," and "weak," designated by the quantities 4, 3, 2, and 1 respectively. These correspond to the four phonemic grades of stress posited by contemporary structural linguists, for a succinct description of which see Bernard Bloch and George L. Trager, *Outline of Linguistic Analysis* (Baltimore, Maryland, 1942), No. 3.7, (2). Adopting Jespersen's notation, scansions (1) and (2) may be expressed as follows:

```
         2   4   4 1   4   4 1 2   4
(1) With roȝe raged mosse rayled ay-where
         2   4   3 1   4   4 1 2   4
(2) With roȝe raged mosse rayled ay-where
```

A complementary method of notation, emphasizing temporal rather than accentual relationships, may be borrowed from music. This method has been successfully utilized to express the rhythms of Old English poetry by Pope in *The Rhythm of Beowulf*. In terms of the values of musical notes my reading of the line according to the two scansions may be expressed as follows:

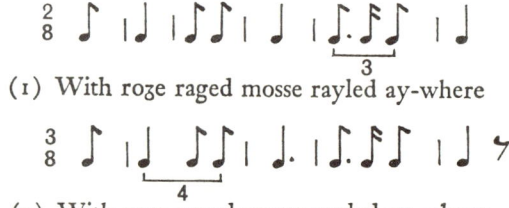

(1) With roȝe raged mosse rayled ay-where

(2) With roȝe raged mosse rayled ay-where

In general, I have been unable to arrive at musical transcriptions of the rhythms of passages of *Gawain* of the satisfactory and definitive character of Pope's notation of Old English verse. There seem to me to be two reasons for this. First, the ME long lines contain more words of the unemphatic parts of speech, such as the definite and indefinite articles, and more unaccented syllables generally, than the OE lines. The temporal relationships between such syllables and the more emphatic syllables are often difficult to define and tend to alter with alterations in the average pace of one's reading. Second, the metrical unit of the ME long lines is more varied in its modes of temporal subdivision than that of the OE lines. In musical terms this means

PAGES 194–201

that one must constantly change the time signature or substitute two-part measures for what seems to be the prevailing measure of triple time. The use of Jespersen's numerical system is also attended by certain practical difficulties; one hesitates, in certain cases, between grading unemphatic syllables 1 and 2, nor does one always feel certain that two syllables, say, of grade 2 in a given line, really have the same intensity. See further, above, p. 237, n. 39.

Rather than attempt a precise notation of either temporal or accentual values, I have preferred simply to indicate the chief syllables in each line, believing that if these are made emphatic relative to neighboring syllables in a continuous and fluent reading, the influence of the tendency toward isochrony will naturally assert itself.

8. *Euripides* (5th ed. New York, 1912), p. 39.

9. According to Jespersen's numerical method of metrical notation, *hore, okeʒ,* and *hoge* would be stressed 4 4 4 in scansion (1), 4 3 4 in scansion (2), and 3 4 4 in scansion (3). In musical terms the notation of scansion (1) would require measure bars before *hore, okeʒ* and *hoge,* that of scansion (2) before *hore* and *hoge,* and that of scansion (3) before *okeʒ* and *hoge.*

10. The significance of "low alliterative rank" is explained above, pp. 52–53; cf. the discussion of *gret* and *hyʒe,* pp. 83 ff.

11. See p. 270, n. 1, for comparative statistics.

12. Subordination of one out of three heavy syllables in the first half-line accords with the views of Luick, who scans heavy first half-lines in *Destruction of Troy* with two primary accents and one secondary (*Anglia, 11,* 421–23), and who remarks, concerning the heavy first half-lines in *Gawain,* that "an drei wirkliche hebungen ist kaum zu denken" (p. 582).

13. Luick, in *Anglia, 11,* 583, cites the first half-lines "His lif liked hym lyʒt" (87), "Þe lorde laches hym by þe lappe" (936), and "& bred baþed in blod" (1361), with the comment that "hier wird das verbum minder betont sein als die nomina."

Bibliography

See also Short Titles, pp. ix–x

OLD AND MIDDLE ENGLISH

EDITIONS

Alexander and Dindimus, see *The Gests*.
Alexander of Macedon, see *The Gests*.
The Anglo-Saxon Poetic Records: A Collective Edition, ed. George Philip Krapp and Elliott Van Kirk Dobbie, 6 vols. New York, Columbia University Press, 1931–53.
The Anturs of Arther at the Tarnewathelan: Three Early English Metrical Romances, ed. John Robson, Camden Society, 18; London, John Bowyer Nichols and Son, 1842.
Beowulf and the Fight at Finnsburg, ed. Friedrich Klaeber, 3d ed. Boston, Heath, 1950.
Beues of Hamtoun, see *The Romance*.
The Buik of the Croniclis of Scotland; or, A Metrical Version of the History of Hector Boece; by William Stewart, ed. William B. Turnbull, Rerum Britannicarum Medii Aevi Scriptores, or Chronicles and Memorials of Great Britain and Ireland during the Middle Ages ("Rolls Series"); 3 vols. London, Longman . . . Roberts, 1858.
Chaucer, Geoffrey, *The Complete Works*, ed. Fred N. Robinson, 2d ed. Boston, Houghton Mifflin, 1957.
The Cheuelere Assigne. Middle English Metrical Romances, ed. Walter H. French and Charles B. Hale, New York, Prentice-Hall, 1930.
Cursor Mundi, ed. Richard Morris, with essays by Hugo C. W. Haenisch and H. Hupe, EETS, 57, 59, 62, 66, 68, 99, 101; London, Kegan Paul, Trench, Trübner, 1874–93.
Destruction of Troy, see *The Gest*.
Dickins, Bruce, and Richard M. Wilson, eds., *Early Middle English Texts*, London, Bowes and Bowes, 1951.
Eadwine's Canterbury Psalter, ed. Fred Harsley, Pt. II, *Text and Notes*, EETS, 92; London, Trübner, 1889.
The Gest Hystoriale of the Destruction of Troy, ed. George A. Panton and David Donaldson, EETS, 39, 56; London, Trübner, 1869–74.
The Gests of King Alexander of Macedon: Two Middle-English Alliterative Fragments, Alexander A and Alexander B, ed. Francis P. Magoun, Jr., Harvard University Press, 1929.
A Good Short Debate between Winner and Waster: An Alliterative Poem on Social and Economic Problems in England in the Year 1352, ed. Sir Israel

Gollancz, Select Early English Poems, 3; London, Oxford University Press, 1920.
The Gospel According to St. Mark in Anglo-Saxon and Northumbrian Versions, Synoptically Arranged, with Collations Exhibiting All the Readings of All the MSS, ed. Walter W. Skeat, Cambridge University Press, 1871.
The Gospel According to St. Matthew in Anglo-Saxon, Northumbrian, and Old Mercian Versions, Synoptically Arranged, ed. Walter W. Skeat, Cambridge University Press, 1887.
The Gothic and Anglo-Saxon Gospels in Parallel Columns with the Versions of Wycliffe and Tyndale, ed. Joseph Bosworth and George Waring, London, John Russell Smith, 1865.
The Harley Lyrics: The Middle English Lyrics of MS. Harley 2253, ed. George L. Brook, Manchester University Press, 1948.
Higden, Ranulf, see Polychronicon Ranulphi Higden Monachi Cestrensis.
Joseph of Arimathie, ed. Walter W. Skeat, EETS, 44; London, Trübner, 1871.
King Alfred's Orosius, ed. Henry Sweet, Pt. I, Old-English Text and Latin Original, EETS, 79; London, Trübner, 1883.
Laʒamon's Brut, ed. Sir Frederic Madden, 3 vols. London, Society of Antiquaries, 1847.
―――― Selections, ed. Joseph Hall, London, Oxford University Press, 1924.
Langland, William, Piers Plowman: The A Version; Will's Visions of Piers Plowman and Do-well, Vol. 1, ed. George Kane, University of London, Athlone Press, 1960.
―――― The Vision of William Concerning Piers Plowman, together with Vita de Dowel, Dobet, and Dobest, ed. Walter W. Skeat, EETS, 28 (A Text), 38 (B Text), 54 (C Text), 67 and 81 (General Preface, Notes, and Indexes); London, Trübner, 1867-85.
The Later Genesis, ed. from MS. Junius 11 by B. J. Timmer, Oxford, The Scrivener Press, 1948.
Leechdoms, Wortcunning, and Starcraft of Early England: Being a Collection of Documents, for the Most Part Never before Printed, Illustrating the History of Science in This Country before the Norman Conquest, ed. Thomas Oswald Cockayne, Rerum Britannicarum Medii Aevi Scriptores, or Chronicles and Memorials of Great Britain and Ireland during the Middle Ages ("Rolls Series"); 3 vols. London, Longman . . . Roberts, 1864-66.
Liber Psalmorum. The West-Saxon Psalms: Being the Prose Portion, or the 'First Fifty,' of the So-Called Paris Psalter, ed. James W. Bright and Robert L. Ramsay, Boston, Heath, 1907.
Morte Arthure, ed. Erik Björkman, Alt- und mittelenglische Texte, 9, Heidelberg, 1915. (The alliterative poem, called Morte Arthure (1) in Plan and Bibliography.)
Le Morte Arthure, ed. J. Douglas Bruce, EETS, ES, 88; London, Kegan Paul, Trench, Trübner, 1903. (The rhymed poem, called Morte Arthure (2) in Plan and Bibliography.)
An Old English Martyrology, ed. George Herzfeld, EETS, 116; London, Kegan Paul, Trench, Trübner, 1900.

Paris Psalter: metrical portion, see *The Anglo-Saxon Poetic Records,* Vol. 5; prose portion, see *Liber Psalmorum.*
The Parlement of the Thre Ages, ed. M. Y. Offord, EETS, 246; London, Oxford University Press, 1959. (Citations, unless otherwise noted, are from the T text, i.e. Addit. MS 31042.)
Patience: An Alliterative Version of Jonah by the Poet of Pearl, ed. Sir Israel Gollancz, Select Early English Poems, 1; London, Oxford University Press, 1924.
Pearl, ed. Eric V. Gordon, London, Oxford University Press, 1953.
The Poetical Dialogues of Solomon and Saturn, ed. Robert J. Menner, New York, Modern Language Association of America, 1941.
Polychronicon Ranulphi Higden Monachi Cestrensis; together with the English Translations of John Trevisa and of an Unknown Writer of the Fifteenth Century, ed. Churchill Babington and Joseph Rawson Lumby, Rerum Britannicarum Medii Aevi Scriptores, or Chronicles and Memorials of Great Britain and Ireland during the Middle Ages ("Rolls Series"); 9 vols. London, Longman . . . Roberts, 1865–86.
Purity, ed. Robert J. Menner, Yale Studies in English, 61; New Haven, Yale University Press, 1920.
"Rolls Series," see *The Buik of the Croniclis of Scotland; Leechdoms, Wortcunning, and Starcraft of Early England; Polychronicon Ranulphi Higden Monachi Cestrensis.*
The Romance of Sir Beues of Hamtoun, ed. Eugen Kölbing, EETS, ES, 46, 48, 65; London, Kegan Paul, Trench, Trübner, 1885–94.
The Romance of William of Palerne, ed. Walter W. Skeat, EETS, ES, 1; London, Trübner, 1867.
St. Erkenwald, ed. Henry Lyttleton Savage, Yale Studies in English, 72; New Haven, Yale University Press, 1926.
The Siege of Jerusalem, ed. Eugen Kölbing and Mabel Day, EETS, 188; London, Oxford University Press, 1932.
Sisam, Kenneth, ed., *Fourteenth Century Verse and Prose,* corrected ed. London, Oxford University Press, 1955.
Solomon and Saturn, see *The Poetical Dialogues.*
Stewart, William, see *The Buik of the Croniclis of Scotland.*
The Wars of Alexander, ed. Walter W. Skeat, EETS, ES, 47; London, Trübner, 1886. (Citations, unless otherwise noted, are from MS Ashmole 44.)
William of Palerne, see *The Romance.*
Winner and Waster, see *A Good Short Debate.*

STYLE AND LITERARY HISTORY

Baugh, Albert C., "Improvisation in the Middle English Romance," *Proceedings of the American Philosophical Society, 103* (1959), 418–54.
Baum, Paull F., "Chaucer's Puns," *PMLA,* 71 (1956), 225–46.
Berry, Francis, "Sir Gawayne and the Grene Knight," in *The Age of Chaucer,* ed. Boris Ford, A Guide to English Literature, 1 (Pelican Books A290, London, 1954), pp. 148–58.

Biggins, D., "Chaucer's General Prologue, A163," *Notes and Queries*, n.s. 6 (1959), 435-36.

Bøgholm, N., *The Layamon Texts: A Linguistical Investigation*, Travaux du cercle linguistique de Copenhague, 3; Copenhagen, 1944.

Brink, August, *Stab und Wort im Gawain: eine stylistische Untersuchung*, Studien zur englischen Philologie, 59; Halle, 1920.

Brodeur, Arthur Gilchrist, *The Art of Beowulf*, Berkeley, University of California Press, 1959.

Creed, Robert P., "The *Andswarode*-System in Old English Poetry," *Speculum*, *32* (1957), 523-28.

Dunlap, A. R., "The Vocabulary of the Middle English Romances in Tail-Rhyme Stanza," *Delaware Notes*, n.s. *36* (1941), 1-42.

Ebbs, J. D., "Stylistic Mannerisms of the *Gawain*-Poet," *JEGP*, *57* (1958), 522-25.

Elliot, Ralph W. V., "Sir Gawain in Staffordshire: A Detective Essay in Literary Geography," London *Times* (May 21, 1958), p. 12.

Everett, Dorothy, "The Alliterative Revival," in *Essays on Middle English Literature*, ed. Patricia Kean (London, Oxford University Press, 1955), pp. 46-96.

Fuhrmann, Johannes, *Die alliterierenden Sprachformeln in Morris' Early English Alliterative Poems und im Sir Gawayne and the Green Knight*, Hamburg, 1886.

Gollancz, Sir Israel, "Gringolet, Gawain's Horse," *Saga-Book of the Viking Club*, *5*, Pt. I (1907), 104-09.

Greenfield, Stanley B., "The Formulaic Expression of the Theme of 'Exile' in Anglo-Saxon Poetry," *Speculum*, *30* (1955), 200-06.

Greg, Walter W., "A Bibliographical Paradox," *Library*, Ser. 4, *13* (1933), 188-91.

Jackson, Isaac, "*Gawain and the Green Knight*: A Note on 'Fade,' line 149," *Notes and Queries*, *195* (1950), 24.

Kaiser, Rolf, *Zur Geographie des mittelenglischen Wortschatzes*, Palaestra, 205; Leipzig, 1937.

Kittner, Heinz, *Studien zum Wortschatz William Langlands*, Halle, 1937.

Kullnick, Max, *Studien über den Wortschatz in Sir Gawayne and the Grene Knyȝt*, Berlin, 1902.

Loomis, Laura Hibbard, "Gawain and the Green Knight," in *Arthurian Literature in the Middle Ages: A Collaborative History*, ed. Roger Sherman Loomis (London, Oxford University Press, 1959), pp. 528-40.

Luttrell, C. A., "The *Gawain* Group: Cruxes, Etymologies, Interpretations," *Neophilologus*, *39* (1955), 207-17; *40* (1956), 290-301.

Magoun, Francis P., Jr., "Bede's Story of Cædman: The Case History of an Anglo-Saxon Oral Singer," *Speculum*, *30* (1955), 49-63.

——— "Oral-Formulaic Character of Anglo-Saxon Narrative Poetry," *Speculum*, *28* (1953), 446-67.

Mossé, Fernand, "Anthroponymie et histoire litteraire: *Le Roman de Renart* dans l'Angleterre du moyen age," *Les Langues Modernes*, *45* (1951), 22-36.

Oakden, James P., *Alliterative Poetry in Middle English: A Survey of the*

Traditions, Vol. 2, Publications of the University of Manchester, 236, English Series, 22; Manchester University Press, 1935.

―――― "The Scribal Errors of the MS. Cotton Nero A.x.," *Library,* Ser. 4, *14* (1934), 353–58.

Olszewska, E. S., *Illustrations of Norse Formulas in English,* Leeds Studies in English and Kindred Languages, 2 (Leeds, 1933), 76–84.

―――― *Norse Alliterative Tradition in Middle English I,* Leeds Studies in English and Kindred Languages, 6 (Leeds, 1937), 50–64.

Regel, Karl, *Die Alliteration im Laȝamon,* Germanistische Studien, ed. Karl Bartsch, 1 (Vienna, 1872), 171–246.

Reicke, Curt, *Untersuchungen über den Stil der mittelenglischen alliterierenden Gedichte Morte Arthure, The Destruction of Troy, The Wars of Alexander, The Siege of Jerusalem, Sir Gawayne and the Green Knight,* Königsberg, 1906.

Renoir, Alain, "Descriptive Technique in *Sir Gawain and the Green Knight,*" *Orbis Litterarum, 13* (1959), 126–32.

Savage, Henry Lyttleton, *The Gawain-Poet: Studies in His Personality and Background,* Chapel Hill, University of North Carolina Press, 1956.

Schmittbetz, Karl Roland, "Das Adjektiv in 'Syr Gawayn and the Grene Knyȝt,'" *Anglia, 32* (1909), 1–60, 163–89, 359–83.

―――― *Das Adjectiv im Verse von* "*Syr Gawayn and þe Grene Knyȝt,*" Bonn, 1908.

Seyger, Rudolf, *Beiträge zu Laȝamons Brut,* Halle, 1912.

Smithers, G. V., "A Crux in 'Sir Gawain and the Green Knight,'" *Notes and Queries, 195* (1950), 134–36.

Speirs, John, "Sir Gawayne and the Grene Knight," in *Medieval English Poetry: The Non-Chaucerian Tradition* (London, Faber and Faber, 1957), pp. 215–51.

Spitzer, Leo, "Explication de Texte Applied to Three Great Middle English Poems," *Archivum Linguisticum, 3* (1951), 1–22, 137–65.

Tatlock, John S. P., and Arthur Kennedy, *A Concordance to the Complete Works of Geoffrey Chaucer and to the Romaunt of the Rose,* Publications of the Carnegie Institution of Washington, 353; Washington, D.C., 1927.

―――― "Epic Formulas, Especially in Laȝamon," *PMLA, 38* (1923), 494–529.

Thomas, Martha Carey, *Sir Gawayne and the Green Knight: A Comparison with the French Perceval Preceded by an Investigation of the Author's Other Works, and Followed by a Characterization of Gawain in English Poems,* Zürich, 1883.

Tolkien, J. R. R., "Chaucer as a Philologist: *The Reeve's Tale,*" *Transactions of the Philological Society* (1934), 1–70.

Trautmann, Moritz, *Über Verfasser und Entstehungszeit einiger alliterierender Gedichte des Altenglischen,* Halle, 1876.

Waldron, Ronald A., "Oral-Formulaic Technique and Middle English Alliterative Poetry," *Speculum, 32* (1957), 792–804.

Wilson, Richard M., *The Lost Literature of Medieval England,* Methuen's Old English Library, Ser. C, 4; London, Methuen, 1952.

Wyld, Henry Cecil, "Studies in the Diction of Layamon's Brut," *Language, 6* (1930), 1–24; *9* (1933), 47–71, 171–91; *10* (1934), 149–201; *13* (1937), 29–59, 194–237.

LANGUAGE AND METER

Brunner, Karl, *Die englische Sprache: Ihre geschichtliche Entwicklung*, Sammlung kurzer Grammatiken germanischer Dialekte, 6; vol. 1, Halle, 1950.

Campbell, Alistair, *Old English Grammar*, London, Oxford University Press, 1959.

Crow, Charles Langley, *Zur Geschichte des kurzen Reimpaars im Mittelenglischen*, Göttingen, 1892.

Deutschbein, Max, *Zur Entwicklung des englischen Alliterationsverses*, Halle, 1902.

Donaldson, Ethelbert Talbot, "Chaucer's Final -E," *PMLA, 63* (1948), 1101–24.

Emerson, Oliver F., "Imperfect Lines in *Pearl* and the Rimed Parts of *Sir Gawain and the Green Knight*," *Modern Philology, 19* (1921), 131–41.

Fischer, Joseph, *Die stabende Langzeile in den Werken des Gawaindichters*, Bonner Beiträge zur Anglistik, 11 (Bonn, 1901), 1–64.

Kaluza, Max, *Englische Metrik in historischer Entwicklung*, Normannia, 1; Berlin, 1909.

Knigge, Friedrich, *Die Sprache des Dichters von Sir Gawain and the Green Knight, des sogenannten Early English Alliterative Poems und de Erkenwalde*, Marburg, 1885.

Kökeritz, Helge, *A Guide to Chaucer's Pronunciation*, New York, Holt, Rinehart, and Winston, 1962.

Kühl, Otto, *Der Vokalismus der Laʒamon-Handschrift B*, Halle, 1913.

Kuhnke, Bruno, *Die alliterierende Langzeile in der mittelenglischen Romanze Sir Gawayn and the Green Knight*, Studien zum germanischen Alliterationsvers, 4; Berlin, 1900.

Leonard, William Ellery, *The Scansion of Middle English Alliterative Verse*, University of Wisconsin Studies in Language and Literature, 11 (1920), 58–104.

Luhmann, Adolf, *Die Überlieferung von Laʒamons Brut*, Studien zur englischen Philologie, 22; Halle, 1906.

Luick, Karl, "Die englische Stabreimzeile im XIV., XV., und XVI. Jahrhundert," *Anglia, 11* (1889), 392–443, 553–618.

―――― "Die mittelenglische Stabreimvers," *Grundriss der germanischen Philologie, 2*, Pt. II (1905), 160–79.

―――― "Über die Betonung der französischen Lehnwörter im Mittelenglischen," *Germanisch-Romanische Monatsschrift, 9* (1921), 14–19.

McJimsey, Ruth Buchanan, *Chaucer's Irregular -E: A Demonstration among Monosyllabic Nouns of the Exceptions to Grammatical and Metrical Harmony*, New York, Columbia University, King's Crown Press, 1942.

Menner, Robert J. "*Sir Gawain and the Green Knight* and the West Midland," *PMLA, 37* (1922), 503-26.
Morsbach, Lorenz, *Mittelenglische Grammatik,* Sammlung kurzer Grammatiken germanischer Dialekte, 7; Halle, 1896.
Oakden, James P., *Alliterative Poetry in Middle English: The Dialectical and Metrical Survey,* Vol. 1, Publications of the University of Manchester, 205, English Series, 18; Manchester University Press, 1930.
Pope, John Collins, *The Rhythm of Beowulf: An Interpretation of the Normal and Hypermetric Verse-Forms in Old English Poetry,* New Haven, Yale University Press, 1942.
Pope, Mildred K., *From Latin to Modern French with Especial Consideration of Anglo-Norman,* Publications of the University of Manchester, 229, French Series, 6; Manchester University Press, 1934, repr. 1952.
Rosenthal, F., "Die alliterierende englische Langzeile im 14. Jahrhundert," *Anglia, 1* (1878), 414-59.
Serjeantson, Mary S., "The Dialects of the West Midlands in Middle English," *Review of English Studies, 3* (1957), 54-67, 186-203, 319-31.
Sievers, Eduard, *Altenglische Grammatik,* revised by Karl Brunner, Sammlung kurzer Grammatiken germanischer Dialekte, 3; 2d ed. Halle, 1951.
——— *Altgermanische Metrik,* Sammlung kurzer Grammatiken germanischer Dialekte, 2; Halle, 1893.
Skeat, Walter W., "An Essay on Alliterative Poetry," in *Bishop Percy's Folio Manuscript,* ed. John W. Hales and Frederick J. Furnivall, *3* (London, 1868), xi-xxxix.
Stewart, George R., Jr., "The Meter of *Piers Plowman,*" *PMLA, 42* (1927), 113-28.
Strandberg, Otto, *The Rime-Vowels of Cursor Mundi: A Phonological and Etymological Investigation,* Uppsala, Almqvist & Wiksell, 1919.
Thomas, Julius, *Die alliterierende Langzeile des Gawayn-Dichters,* Jena, 1908.
Trautmann, Moritz, "Zur Kenntnis und Geschichte der mittelenglischen Stabzeile," *Anglia, 18* (1896), 83-100.

General

Abrams, Meyer H., *A Glossary of Literary Terms,* revised ed. based on the original version by Dan S. Norton and Peters Rushton, New York, Rinehart, 1957.
Auerbach, Erich, *Mimesis: The Representation of Reality in Western Literature,* trans. Willard R. Trask, Princeton University Press, 1953.
Barnouw, Adriaan J., *Echoes of the Pilgrim Fathers' Speech,* Mededeelingen der Koninklijke Akademie van Wetenschappen, Afdeeling Letterkunde, Deel 55, Ser. A, 6; Amsterdam, 1923.
Bloch, Bernard, and George L. Trager, *Outline of Linguistic Analysis,* Baltimore, Linguistic Society of America, 1942.
Bloomfield, Leonard, *Language,* New York, Holt, 1933.

BIBLIOGRAPHY

Brittain, Fred, *The Medieval Latin and Romance Lyric to A.D. 1300*, 2d ed. Cambridge University Press, 1951.
Burke, Kenneth, *The Philosophy of Literary Form: Studies in Symbolic Action*, revised and abridged ed. New York, Vintage Books, 1957.
Cassirer, Ernst, *Language and Myth*, trans. Susanne K. Langer, New York, Dover Publications, 1946.
A Dictionary of American English on Historical Principles, ed. Sir William A. Craigie and James R. Hulbert, 4 vols. University of Chicago Press, 1938–44.
A Dictionary of Americanisms on Historical Principles, ed. Mitford M. Mathews, 2 vols. University of Chicago Press, 1951.
Empson, William, *Seven Types of Ambiguity*, 3d ed. Norfolk, Conn., New Directions, 1953.
Jakobson, Roman, "On Linguistic Aspects of Translation," in *On Translation*, ed. Reuben Arthur Brower, Harvard Studies in Comparative Literature, 23 (Harvard University Press, 1959), pp. 232–39.
Jespersen, Otto, *A Modern English Grammar on Historical Principles*, Vol. 1, London, Allen and Unwin, 1933.
——— "Notes on Metre," *Linguistica: Selected Papers in English, French, and German* (Copenhagen, Levin and Munksgaard, 1933), pp. 249–74.
Kökeritz, Helge, *Shakespeare's Pronunciation*, New Haven, Yale University Press, 1953.
Kurath, Hans, *A Word Geography of the Eastern United States*, Studies in American English, 1; Ann Arbor, University of Michigan Press, 1949.
Langer, Susanne K., *Philosophy in a New Key: A Study in the Symbolism of Reason, Rite, and Art*, Harvard University Press, 1942.
Lucas, Frank L., *Style*, London, Cassell, 1955.
Moore, Samuel, *Historical Outlines of English Sounds and Inflections*, revised by Albert H. Marckwardt, Ann Arbor, Wahr, 1951.
Noreen, Adolf, *Altnordische Grammatik*, Vol. 1, *Altisländische und altnorwegische Grammatik*, Sammlung kurzer Grammatiken germanischer Dialekte, 4; Halle, 1923.
Northumberland Words: A Glossary of Words Used in the County of Northumberland, and on the Tyneside, by Richard O. Heslop, Publications of the English Dialect Society, 28–29; London, Kegan Paul, Trench, Trübner, 1892–94.
Ogden, Charles K., and Ivor Armstrong Richards, *The Meaning of Meaning*, with suppl. essays by B. Malinowski and F. G. Crookshank, 8th ed. New York, Harcourt, Brace, 1956.
Olson, Elder J., "General Prosody: Rhythmic, Metric, Harmonics," dissertation, University of Chicago, 1938.
——— "Verse," *Encyclopaedia Britannica*, 1957.
——— "William Empson, Contemporary Criticism, and Poetic Diction," in *Critics and Criticism, Ancient and Modern*, ed. Ronald S. Crane (University of Chicago Press, 1952), pp. 45–82.

The Oxford Book of Medieval Latin Verse, ed. Stephen Gaselee, London, Oxford University Press, 1928.

Popular Ballads and Songs, from Tradition, Manuscripts, and Scarce Editions; with Translations of Similar Pieces from the Ancient Danish Language, and a Few Originals by the Editor, ed. Robert Jamieson, 2 vols. Edinburgh, Constable, 1806.

La Queste del Saint Graal: Roman du xiiie siècle, ed. Albert Pauphilet, Les Classiques français du moyen age, 33; Paris, Champion, 1923.

Raby, Frederic J. E., *A History of Christian-Latin Poetry from the Beginnings to the Close of the Middle Ages,* 2d ed. London, Oxford University Press, 1953.

Read, Sir Herbert Edward, *English Prose Style,* new ed. New York, Pantheon, 1952.

Richards, Ivor Armstrong, *The Philosophy of Rhetoric,* New York, Oxford University Press, 1936.

Smith, Albert H., *English Place-Name Elements,* Cambridge, Cambridge University Press, 1956.

Spitzer, Leo, *Linguistics and Literary History: Essays in Stylistics,* Princeton University Press, 1948.

Sweet, Henry, *A New English Grammar, Logical and Historical,* Pt. I, *Introduction, Phonology, and Accidence,* London, Oxford University Press, 1892.

Thomson, William, *The Rhythm of Speech,* Glasgow, 1923.

Tobler, Adolf, *Vom französischen Versbau alter und neuer Zeit,* 5th ed. Leipzig, 1910.

Ushenko, A. P., "Metaphor," *Thought, 30* (1955), 421–39.

Wimsatt, William K., Jr., *The Prose Style of Samuel Johnson,* Yale Studies in English, 94; New Haven, Yale University Press, 1941.

—— *The Verbal Icon: Studies in the Meaning of Poetry,* Lexington, University of Kentucky Press, 1954.

Wyld, Henry Cecil, *A History of Modern Colloquial English,* Oxford, Blackwell, 1953.

Index of Words

This index includes all words of the major parts of speech whose stylistic or metrical use in *Gawain* is discussed, as well as certain OE and early ME words whose history prior to their use in *Gawain* is relevant. The entry forms and subentries are, in general, based on the glossary to the GDS edition; where the entry form used by TG differs to an extent that might cause confusion, I have provided a cross-reference. Nouns have occasionally been put in the singular, and verbs in the infinitive. In cases where only one form of a word is cited—e.g. the participle or past tense of verbs—this is used as the entry form, with a cross-reference where confusion might otherwise result. Definitions, when given, are printed in italic.

abloy, 51
aboute, 157
achaufed, 167
acheue, 167
acole, 51, 167
a-corde (n.), 167
acorde (v.), 157
aghlich, 108, 112–13, 118
alder (n.), 118, 250
alle, 72, 73
al one, *alone*, 157
anamayld, 167
apert, 78
apparayl, 167
a-quoyntance, 167
arʒe (adj.), 44 (earʒh)
aryʒt, 242
armes, *armor*, 76
arwes, 76
asay (n.), 229
asswyþe, 229
aþel, 41 (æðele), 45, 58 (æðele), 65, 77, 82, 118, 225
aumayl, 167, 229
aunant, *see* auinant
aunter, 167, 254, *see also* auenture
a-vanters, 167, 229
auenture, 167, *see also* venture
auenturus, 167
a-vyse, 96, 243, 245
a-wharf, 229 (awherfe)

bay (adj.), 229, 230
bayen (v.), 229, 230
bayn, 77, 78
bayþen, 51
bak, 249
baldly, 77, 78

barayne, 269
barbe, 229
bare (adj.), 77, 192
baret, 162, 164
barlay, 51
bastel, 229, 230
batayl, 162–63
baude-ryk, 50
ba[u]leʒ, *see* boweleʒ
bench, 119–20
bene (v.), *to be*, 249 (were)
bent, 45, 76, 124, 227
bent-felde, 45
berʒ, 76
best, *see* god
better, *see* god
byden, 186 (bade)
big (adj.), 77, 82
big(g)e (v.), 50
bi-gin(n)e, 171
bigly, 77
bi-houe, 264
bilyue, 78, 83
blaste, 157
blyþe, 78, 82
blyþely, 78
blonk, 41 (blancke), 64, 67, 76, 124, 225 (blanca), 228, 237
body, 249
boʒe (v.), 41 (buʒen)
bolde, 41, 69, 77, 78, 82, 124
boldly, *see* baldly
bonchef, 166–67
borde, *table*, 44–45, 226
borelych, 78
boþe, 78
b[oue]leʒ, *see* boweleʒ
boun, 69, 78, 82

283

boweleʒ, 229
brayn, *mad*, 77
brayn-wod, 77
bredeʒ, *boards*, 228
brem, 78
bremely, 78
brent, 78
brest, 249
breþer, 101, 242
bryʒt, 77, 82, 85, 86, 88, 89
brode, 78, 186
bronde (n.), 76, 239
broþe, 77
broþely, 77
burʒe, 76
burne, 16, 42 (beorn), 53, 54, 57, 58 (beorn), 60, 64, 66, 74, 77 (beryn), 93, 118, 119, 124, 231 (berne), 236, 237
busk (v.), 39

cayre, *see* kayre
cemmed, 228
[cha]lk-quyte, 28, 263
chambre, 243, 245
chapelle, 63, 138–39, 164, 187
chef, 77, 82
chefly, 77, 82
child-gered, 117
clanly, 78 (clenely)
clene, 78, 83, 114
clere, 77, 82
cloþeʒ, 76
cofly, 77, 82
coynt(ly), *see* koynt(ly)
comaunde, *see* cumaunde
comaundement, 167
comende, 165, 263
comfort (n.), 165, 169
comfort (v.), 165, 169
comlych, 77, 82, 187, 243; comlokest, 77, 95
comlyly, 77
compaynye, 167
compas (n.), 165
compast (v.), 165
conable, 167
concience, 167
confessed, 165, 169
conysaunce, 167
constrayne, 165, 169
conueyed, 165, 169
cortayse, 77, 162, 164
cortaysly, 77
cost, 205
cote, 76
coundue, 165, 169

coundutes, 165
counsel (n.), 165
counseyl (v.), 165
countenaunce, 167
court, 74, 231, 239, 243
Cryst, 53, 231, 243
cryst-masse, 242
cropure, 187
croun, 64, 237
cumaunde, 165, 169, 263

day, 76, 156
de-bate (v.), 166
debonerté, 167
dece, 85, 118
defence, 166
de-fende, 166
degre, 166
delful, 228
delyuer, 166
de-liuerly, 165, 170
demay, 165
denayed, 166
depe, 78
de-paynt, 166
de-partyng, 165, 170
de-prece, *disemprison*, 166
deprece, *oppress*, 166
dere, 77, 82, 95; derrest, 118
derely, 77, 240
derf, 78, 82
derfly, 78
derk, 60, 262
derne, 78, 228
dernly, 78
des(s)erue, *see* disserue
destiné, 167
de-vaye, 166, *see also* denayed
deuise, 166
deuocioun, 167
diʒt, 156
dyn, 102, 248
dyngne, 160
dynt, 115
disert (n.), 166
dismayd, 165
displese, 166
dispoyled, 166
disport, 166
disserue, 165, 166, 171
doʒty, 77
do (v.), 157 (done)
donkande, 50 (donke)
doser, 50
dotʒ, *see* do (v.)
doute, 157

INDEX OF WORDS

douth, 75
dreȝ, see dryȝe (adj.)
dreȝly, 78
dryȝe (adj.), 78, 82
dryȝe (v.), 115
duȝty, see doȝty

enbaned, 167
enbelyse, 167
ende, 3
endured, 167
enfoubled, 136, 167
enker, 109-10
ennourned, 136, 253
enterludeȝ, 167
enu[ire]ned, see ennourned
erde, 70, 72, 73, 76, 106, 114, 238
erly, 78
erþe, 70, 72-73, 74, 76, 189, 238
etayn, 53, 109, 250
ex-ellently, 167

fade, 106, 108, 109, 110
fayn, 77, 157
fayre, 78, 83, 89, 95, 159
farand, 78, 90
fast, 159
feersly, 77
feye, 78
fele (adj.), 78
felle (adj.), 77, 240
felly, 77
ferde (v.), 106
fere, *companion*, 54
ferly (adj. and adv.), 35, 78
ferlyly, 78
fersly, see feersly
fetures, 249
fylter, 38
fynisment, 3, 211
fyrst, 78
flet, 95, 244-45
flone, 188
folde (n.), 70, 71, 76
fole, *horse*, 64, 69, 71, 76, 237, 239
folé, see foly
folȝande, 109, 114, 250
foly, 240 (folé)
folk, 76, 239
fonge, 159
forest, 164
forme (adj. and n.), 249
forsoþe, 155
forwonder (MS for wonder), 109, 161
for-wondered, 109

frayn, 156
fre, 77, 118
freke, 16, 53, 54-56, 57, 58 (freca), 64, 65, 66, 69, 89, 106, 111, 118, 186, 231, 236, 237
frely, 77
fryth, 75, 76, 238-39

gay, 77, 82
gayly, 77
gayn (adj.), 78, 157
game, see gomen
gate, 76
Gawayn, 17, 20, 143, 156, 157, 159, 162, 165 (Wawan)
gentyle, 77, 95, 243
gere (n.), 76
gyng, 117
glad, 77
gladly, 77; gladloker, 77
glam, 47-48, 99-100, 247
glaum, 96, 99-100, 110, 243, 247
glaumande, 96, 99
gle, 99, 100, 243
go, see ȝede
God, 53, 161, 231
god, 33, 41, 78, 83; best, 43, 78, 80, 83, 95, 103, 187; better, 78; wel, 78
godlych, 78, 83
gome, 53, 57, 58 (guma), 66, 111, 231, 236
gomen, 99-100, 118
gray, 116
grayþe (adj.), 78
grayþely, 78
graunte, 157
grene, 63, 69, 111
gret (adj.), 67, 69, 78, 83-85, 89, 95, 106, 113, 198, 249
grymme, 77
Gryngolet, 64, 236
grone, 157
grounde (n.), 63, 72-73, 74
grwe, 50

ȝede, 159, 262 (ȝod)
ȝederly, 77, 82
ȝelle, 261
ȝep, 78, 82
ȝeply, 78, 82
ȝere, 76
ȝerne, 78, 83
ȝet, 159
ȝod, see ȝede
ȝong, 78

INDEX OF WORDS

haʒer, 77
halde, 64 (hold), 244
hale, 64, 106, 108, 112, 118, 250
halle, 74, 104, 243, 245, *see also* halle dor
halle dor, 64
hap (n.), 96, 97
hapnest, 97
hard, 78
hardy, 77, 82, 95, 102–03, 119
hardily, 77
harnays, 76
hast (n.), 157
hat (v.), 271
haþel, 39, 53, 58, 60, 93, 111, 124, 231 (athel), 237
hawbergh, 167
heʒ(ly), *see* hyʒ(ly)
helme, 76
hende, 78, 82
henge (vp þyn ax), 15
here, *army*, 75, 95, 103
heterly, 50, 78
heuen, 75, 76, 95
hyʒe, 78, 83–85, 89, 101, 102, 106, 113, 185, 186, 198, 249; hyʒest, 95, 101
hyʒly, 78
hyʒt (n.), 102
hylle, 76, 95–96, 102–03, 119
hoge, 78
holde (v.), *see* halde
holde (adv.), 78
home, 76
honde, 64
honour, 164
hope, 39
hors, 41, 67, 69, 76, 124, 225, 237
houndeʒ, 161
huge, *see* hoge
hurte, 161

yʒe, 71, 72, 116
yrnes, 76

joly, 102, 248 (jolly)
jolilé, 95, 102

kay, 128
kayre, 95, 100, 243, 244 (cair)
kene, 77, 82
kenly, 77
kepe, 123
kerchofes, 167
kydde, 95, 112, 243, 245
kynde (n.), 185, 186
kyng, 53, 54, 64, 102, 118, 237, 243
knyʒt, 15, 20, 42–43 (cniht), 52–53, 54, 56 (cniht), 60–62, 64, 66, 68–69, 74, 93, 94, 96, 101, 102, 111, 118, 160, 188, 230, 231, 243
knot, 33
koynt, 77
koyntly, 77
Kryst, kryst-masse, *see* Cryst, cryst-masse

lach, 263
ladi, 102, 243
laʒande, 163
laye (n.), 143
laþe (v.), 50
launce (n.), 76 (lance)
lede (n.), 52–53, 54, 57, 58 (leod), 73, 94, 96, 101, 103, 159, 230, 231, 242 (lude)
lef, 78; leuest, 95
lende, 263 ([l]ent)
lel, 78, 262
lene, 161
lete, *let*, 161
leuest, *see* lef
lif, 243
lyft (adj.), 128
liʒt (adj.), 77
lyʒt (n.), 156
lyʒtly, 77
lyme, 114
lyndes, 109, 250
littel, 78
lodly, 78
loʒe (adj.), 78
loʒly, 78
loke (v.), 128
londe, 76
long, 78, 106
longe (adv.), 78
lorde, 53, 54, 60–61, 64, 66, 73, 93, 96, 101, 157, 159, 201, 231, 242, 243
loude, 78
lufly, 11, 77, 82, 95, 201, 243 (louely); louelokkest, 95
luflyly, 77, 120

Maré, 240
may (v.), 249 (myʒt)
mayn, 78
maynteine, 167, 263
mayster, 54, 105, 112, 118, 249, 250
make, 160 (made), 243
meʒel-mas, 159, 262
meyny, 76, 118
melle, 261
meny, *see* meyny

INDEX OF WORDS

mensk (adj.), 78
menskful, 78, 239
menskly, 78, 239
mercy, 162
mere, *splendid*, 82, 240
mery, *see* miry
meryly, 78, 87
meschaunce, 166
meschef, 166–67
mesure, 249
mete (n.), 101, 243, 247
methles, 77, 90
myȝt, *see* may
mynn (v.), 106–07
miry, 78, 82, 85, 86–88, 107, 240; myriest, 88, 106, 107, 108, 114, 205, 249
mirþe, 101, 242, 243, 247
molde, 70, 76, 106, 114, 249
mon (n.), 43, 53, 54, 60–61, 66–67, 69, 96, 106, 186, 231
mon (indef. pron.), 238
mony, 78, 89, 95, 197, 242
moroun, 76 (morne)
mornyng, *morning*, 76
most, 67, 106, 249
mote, *castle*, 95–96, 246
mote, *note on the horn*, 188
much, *see* most
muckel, 50, 109, 250

neȝ (adv.), 78
neuen, 97, 246
neuer, 64
newe, *see* nwe
nye (n.), 96
nyȝt, 76, 243
no, 72, 73
nobele, 78, 83, 89
noyce, 110–11, 118
now, 64
nwe, 111

ouer-take, 161

payne (v.), 156
payttrure, 50
palays, 50
pelures, 187
penaunce, 162
pentangel, 32
pertly, 78
place, 74, 76
plesaunt, 164
porter, 162, 164
prestly, 78, 82

prynce, 231
prowde, 78
pure, 78
purely, 78

quelle, 261
queme, 78, 82
quene, 133
quyk, 78, 83
quykly, 78
quit, *white*, 82

rad, *quick*, 78, 82
rad, *afraid*, 78, 239
radly, 78, 82, 120
raysoun, 164
rapely, 77
rasor, 187
rechate, 166 (rechated, re-chatande)
rechles, 96, 101, 102, 248
recreaunt, 167
redly, 78, 82
refourme, 166, 169
re-hayte, 165
reherced, 166
Reynarde, 157, 261
rekenly, 96, 98–99, 101, 110, 246 (re-conlice)
relece, 166, 169
remnaunt, 167
remorde, 166
renay, 166
renk, 42 (rink), 43 (rinc), 53, 58, 60, 118, 231, 232
renoun, 166, 169
repreue, 166, 169
resayt, 166, 169
re-sayue, 166
resette, *see* resayt
reuel (n.), 101, 166, 169
reuel (v.), 166, 169
reuerence, 205
rewarde (n.), 166, 169
rewarde (v.), 157
rych (adj.), 78, 83, 95, 101, 118, 160, 189, 205
rychely, 78
ryde, 80, 106, 189, 249
ryȝt (adj. and adv.), 78
roffe, 229, 230
roȝe, 78
ronk, 78, 239–40
roueȝ, *see* roffe
runisch, 77
runischly, 77

sadly, 78
sayn, *say*, 156
sayne (v.), *cross*, 161
sale, 71, 74
samen (adv.), 78, 95, 96–97, 243
schaft (n.), 76, 239
schafted (v.), 109
schalk, 53, 54, 56, 58, 231, 232 (scalc)
scharp, 76
schelde, 45 (sceld), 76
schene, 78, 82
schyre, *bright*, 78, 82
schyrly, 78
schulder, 187
segge, 53, 58, 231
selly, 77; sellokest, 77
sellyly, 77
self, 243 (seluen)
semblaunt, 164
seme (adj.), 78
semly, 78, 82, 187; semloker, 161
sere, 78, 241
serlepes, 78
seruaunt, 157, 162, 164
sesoun, 74, 76, 231
syde (n.), 76
syȝt, 71, 72
siker (adj.), 78, 118
sille, 95, 245
syre, 53, 54, 231
syþes, *times*, 76, 241
skete, 77
slade, 41
smal, 78, 106, 109, 250
softe, 78
softely, 78
solace, 162, 164
sone, 157
sore, 78
soþe, 78
spetos, 137
stalle, 104, 119
stede, *horse*, 67, 76, 80
stede, *place*, 104
stel-gere, 80, 241
stif, 78, 79–81, 82, 83, 87, 88, 104–05, 118, 119, 240, 241; stifest, 80
stifly, 78, 81
stiȝtel, 104
styþly, 78
stonde, 104, 262 (stod)
stor, 78
stounde, 76
strayne, 157
stubbe, 50
sturne, 106, 108, 114, 160, 249

swange, 108, 110
sware, 109, 250
swete (adj.), 78, 81
swete (n.), 228
swetely, 78
swyre, 106, 107–08
sworde, 76, 239

table, 85
take, 157 (tone)
tale, 59
talk(k)e, 232
talkyng, 163
tappe, 160
telde, 76
tene (adj.), 78
tyde, 76
til, 185
tyme, 76
tole, 76
tone, *see* take
tor, 78
toruayle, 167
tote, 50, 127–28
toune, 76
trauayl (n.), 167
trauayle (v.), 167
trecherie, 205
tryst, 185
Troye, 270
trwe, 78
tulk, 25, 53, 58–59, 63, 94, 96, 100, 101, 231, 232

þede, 76
þer-inne, 156
þik, 69, 78, 106, 188, 249
þynkes, *see* þoȝt (v.)
þoȝt (n.), 241
þoȝt (v.), 189, 243
þonk (v.), 157, 262
þryȝt, 50 (þrycche)
þrynne, 160
þryue, 35
þro, 78, 82, 241
þrowe (n.), 76

vmbe-kesten, 38
vmbe-lappeȝ, 38

venture, 167, 254
verdure, 187

way (n.), 76
wale (adj.), 78, 82
walke, 89

INDEX OF WORDS

war (adj.), 78
warly, 78
waþe, see woþe
Wawan, see Gawain
wede, 76
wel, see god
wele, 96, 101, 102, 243
welkyn, 75
wene, 78, 82
weppen, 76
[w]eterly, 77
whider-warde-so-euer, 161
whyle (n.), 76, 133
whyte, see quit
wyȝe, 53, 57, 58, 64, 65, 69, 111, 186, 231 (wye), 237
wyȝt (adj.), 78, 82
wiȝt (n.), 112, 250
wyȝtly, 78
wylde, 78
wynne (adj.), 77, 82
wynne (n.), 156
wynne-lich, 77
wynter, 76
wlonk, 77, 82, 157, 262
wod (n.), 76
wodwos, 53
wombe, 109, 249
won (n.), 76
wonder, 109, 161
wone (v.), 96, 243
worch, see wroȝt
worlde, 64, 70, 72, 74, 76, 231, 237, 239, 243
worth, 78
worþy, 106; worþyest, 205
worthily, 106
woþe, 155
wrast (adj.), 78
wroȝt, 142, 271

Index of Lines and Passages

Italicized numbers are of lines in *Gawain*. Lines exemplifying scansion patterns or the use of single words have not been included here. The latter may be found through the Index of Words.

37–42: 100–01
37–59: 94–103
41–42: 25
50–54: 113
58–59: 103
50–129: 103–05
93–95: 118
122–25: 123
136–50: 105–14
137–41: 113–14
196–98: 71
201–02: 115
224–25: 117
224–27: 208–09
241: 65
246–49: 119
252–55: 208–09
259–60: 79–80
265–66: 219
280: 118
301 ff.: 116
330 ff.: 116
332–33: 126
333: 114
339: 22
366–69: 121
366–71: 120
375: 125
387–89: 35
417 ff.: 117
427–28: 121
432: 124–25
465–66: 118
495–99: 3
674–75: 125–26
732: 128
742–48: 124
748: 125
785: 125
817–30: 121–22

842–50: 207–08
853: 125
894–96: 121
945: 126
1141: 188
1172: 124–25
1179–94: 92
1204–07: 126
1312: 123
1315–16: 69
1366–67: 125
1433: 124–25
1438: 124–25
1452–53: 122
1460–63: 122
1476: 127–28
1508–15: 208
1582: 124–25
1586–88: 122
1592–96: 209–10
1594–95: 122
1616–18: 125
1705: 71–72
1723: 124–25
1963: 22
1979–88: 121
2006: 125
2047: 125–26
2047–49: 123
2061–63: 123
2065: 124
2074–76: 125
2263–64: 125–26
2265–67: 126–27
2278–79: 115
2293–94: 23
2309 ff.: 127
2338: 124
2441–42: 23

Index of Subjects and Authors

This index is selective. Citations limited to bibliographical data and description of content have for the most part been omitted, as have references to authorities on historical phonology, when not concerned specifically with *Gawain*, and references to ME alliterative poems other than *Gawain* which illustrate verbal parallels. Authorities consulted in the interpretation of particular words in *Gawain* may be found through the Index of Words.

Abrams, Meyer H., *Glossary of Literary Terms*, 217
Accentuation of OF loan words. *See* Old French loan words
Adjectives: in ME alliterative poetry, 77-90; use in *Gawain*, 95, 106, 113. *See also* Vocabulary
Alexander of Macedon, 90
Alliterative long line: participation of OF loan words in alliterative patterns of, 164-67; accentuation of OF loan words in, 167-71; patterns of alliteration in, 170-71, 233; four- and seven-stress theories concerning, 172; final -*e* in, 182-89; feminine ending in, 188-89, 269. *See also* Meter
Alliterative phrases in ME, 62; stylistic differences among, 64-65
Alliterative rank, 52-53, 76-77
Ambiguity, 214
Aphaeresis, 136
Arthur, characterization of in *Gawain*, 104, 117
Auerbach, Erich, *Mimesis*, 218

Baugh, Albert C., "Improvisation in the Middle English Romance," 235-36
Beowulf, 57-58
Berry, Francis, "Sir Gawayne and the Grene Knight," 221
Bloomfield, Leonard, *Language*, 213
Bøgholm, N., *Layamon Texts*, 40-41
Brink, August, *Stab und Wort im Gawain*, 51, 230, 232, 239; alliterative rank, 52-53; groups of synonymous nouns, 53-60, 70-76; adjectives (adverbs), 77-89
Brittain, Fred, *Medieval Latin and Romance Lyric to A.D. 1300*, 258
Brodeur, Arthur G., *Art of Beowulf*, 241-42

Brut. *See* Lawman
Burke, Kenneth, "Semantic and Poetic Meaning," 215-16

Cassirer, Ernst, *Language and Myth*, 215
Cheuelere Assigne, 89
Chief syllables defined, 66, 144
Common (frequently used) words, 31, 33
Compound meter: general description, 173-74; in first half-lines of *Gawain*, 193-98. *See also* Meter
Connotation, 217. *See also* Meaning
Context, 11-12; contexts, classification of, 30-31. *See also* Meaning
Creed, Robert P., "*Andswarode*-System in Old English Poetry," 225
Criticism of style, 4-5; based on opinion, 10-11; aim of, 91
Crow, Charles L., *Zur Geschichte des kurzen Reimpaars im Mittelenglischen*, 259
Cursor Mundi, 144, 222-23; Northern vocabulary of, 36-38; orthography of, 142, 148-49; final -*e* in rhyme, 142; meter of, 146-48; accentuation of OF loan words in, 150-54; suffix-accent in rhyme, 151-52; final -*e* in intralinear position in, 154-55

Day, Mabel, introduction to *Sir Gawain and the Green Knight*, 233
Denotation, 217. *See also* Meaning
Descriptive style, 20; in *Gawain*, 92-93, 120-28. *See also* Style
Destruction of Troy, 59, 61-62, 122, 183-84, 233
Details. *See* Descriptive style
Dialect words, 30-31, 32. *See also* Vocabulary

291

Donaldson, E. Talbot, "Chaucer's Final -E," 256, 260-61, 270
Double meaning. *See* Meaning

Ebbs, J. D., "Stylistic Mannerisms of the *Gawain*-Poet," 236-37
Elliott, Ralph W. V., "Sir Gawain in Staffordshire: A Detective Essay in Literary Geography," 220
Emerson, Oliver F., "Imperfect Lines in *Pearl* and the Rimed Parts of *Sir Gawain and the Green Knight*," 262
Emotive language, 216-17
Empson, William, *Seven Types of Ambiguity*, 214
Epithets, 82, 105
Everett, Dorothy, *Essays on Middle English Literature*, 220-21
Expressive value, 3, 23, 211
Extended first half-lines, 180, 192-204

Figurative meaning, 13-15, 17, 214-15; implications of, 21; use in the alliterative line, 89-90. *See also* Meaning
Final *-e:* in OF loan words, 134; sources of, 140; evidence for loss of, 141-42; in rhyme in *Cursor*, 142; in intralinear position in *Cursor*, 154-55; in rhyme in Chaucer, 155-56; in intralinear position in Chaucer, 260-61; in rhyme in *Gawain*, 155-58; in intralinear position in the wheels of *Gawain*, 159-60; in the long lines of *Gawain*, 182-89. *See also* Orthographic
Final *-es, -ed:* sources of, 142-43; in *Cursor*, 148-49; in the wheels of *Gawain*, 161; in the long lines of *Gawain*, 205. *See also* Orthographic
Fischer, J., *Stabende Langzeile in den Werken des Gawaindichters*, 262-63, 266
"Foot, reversed." *See* "Reversed foot"
Formality and informality in language, 5-8, 29-30; determined by mode of reference, 21-23. *See also* Style
Formulas, 33; in ME alliterative poetry, 60-63; originated by the *Gawain*-poet, 63-64. *See also* Style
Four-stress theory, 172. *See also* Seven-stress theory
Fuhrmann, Johannes, *Alliterierenden Sprachformeln . . . im Sir Gawayne and the Green Knight*, 235

Gawain. *See Sir Gawain*
Gollancz, Sir Israel, "Gringolet, Gawain's Horse," 236
Gordon, E. V. *See* Tolkien
Green Knight: entrance of, 110-15; description of, 113-14, 116-17
Greg, W. W., "Bibliographical Paradox," 220

Half-lines, extended first, 180, 192-204. *See also* Meter
Higden, Ranulph, *Polychronicon*, 223
Hupe, H., "On the Filiation and Text of . . . *Cursor Mundi*," 223

Implication, 8-9, 21, 23, 24, 212, 216-17. *See also* Meaning
Informality in language. *See* Formality
Intermediate syllables defined, 66, 144
Isochrony, tendency toward in meter, 191-92. *See also* Meter

Jakobson, Roman, "On Linguistic Aspects of Translation," 214
Jespersen, Otto, "Notes on Metre," 237-38, 271-72

Kaiser, Rolf, *Zur Geographie des mittelenglischen Wortschatzes*, 36-40
Kittner, Heinz, *Studien zum Wortschatz William Langlands*, 227-28, 232
Klaeber, Friedrich, glossary to *Beowulf*, 225
Kühl, Otto, *Vokalismus der Laȝamon-Handschrift B*, 225
Kullnick, Max, *Studien über den Wortschatz in Sir Gawayne and the Grene Knyȝt*, 48-51, 228

Langer, Susanne K., *Philosophy in a New Key*, 212-13
Langland, William, *Piers Plowman*, 232
Language. *See* Vocabulary
Latin accentual verse, 145
Lawman's *Brut*, 40-45, 224-25, 226
Leonard, William Ellery, "On the Scansion of Middle English Alliterative Verse," 172-73
Long line. *See* Alliterative long line
Loomis, Laura Hibbard, *Arthurian Literature in the Middle Ages*, 220
Lucas, F. L., *Style*, 212
Luick, Karl, "Englische Stabreimzeile im XIV., XV., und XVI. Jahrhundert," 183-88, 261-62, 269-70, 273

INDEX OF SUBJECTS AND AUTHORS 293

Luttrell, A. C., "*Gawain* Group: Cruxes, Etymologies, Interpretations," 229

Magoun, Francis P., Jr., "Oral-Formulaic Character of Anglo-Saxon Narrative Poetry," 61, 233-34

Meaning: defined, 9-10; interpretation of, 10-19; double or multiple, 13, 14, 17, 214; operative, 17; suggested, 17-19; symbolistic, 212-13. See also Connotation; Context; Denotation; Figurative meaning; Implication; Qualitative meanings

Menner, Robert J.: glossary to *Poetical Dialogues of Solomon and Saturn*, 225-26; introduction to *Purity*, 220, 267; "Sir Gawain and the Green Knight and the West Midland," 219

Meter in English: general description, 144-45; native tradition in, 145; simple and compound, 173-75. See also Alliterative long line; Half-lines; Isochrony; Rhyme; Seven-stress theory; Suffix-accent; Syllables; verse; Wheels

Middle English alliterative poetry: vocabulary of, 46-48; formulaic style of, 60-65; use of tags in, 63, 70-71; use of adjectives in, 81-83; narrator of, 93-94. See also *individual stylistic and metrical headings*

Morte Arthure, 62, 63, 100-01, 103-04, 123-24, 127

Multiple meaning. See Meaning

Narrator: importance in study of style, 91-92; in ME alliterative poetry, 93-94; in *Gawain*, 115-29. See also Speaker

Neologisms, 34-35

Northern words in ME, 36-40. See also Vocabulary

Oakden, J. P., *Alliterative Poetry in Middle English*, 46-48, 62, 63, 219, 220, 227, 233, 266, 269

Occasion as element of style, 4, 6, 8, 23. See also Style

Offord, M. Y., introduction to *Parlement of the Thre Ages*, 270

Ogden, Charles K., and I. A. Richards, *Meaning of Meaning*, 214, 216

Old French loan words: accentuation in ME, 134-39; accentuation in *Cursor*, 150-54; accentuation in the wheels of *Gawain*, 161-63; participation in alliterative patterns of the long line, 164-67; accentuation in the long line, 167-71. See also Vocabulary

Old French verse, 145

Old Norse words in *Gawain*, 227. See also Vocabulary

Olson, Elder J.: *General Prosody*, 257; "Verse," 257; "William Empson, Contemporary Criticism, and Poetic Diction," 212

Operative meaning. See Meaning

Orthographic evidence, 133, 138-39, 141-42, 148-49, 154. See also Final -e; Final -es, -ed; Reduction of Suffix-vowels; Reversed spellings

Parlement of the Thre Ages, 103

Pearl, 260

Periphrasis, 15, 22, 33

Piers Plowman. See Langland

Pleonasms, 70-73, 95, 102

Poetic words, 30; in ME alliterative poetry, 52, 57-58; use in *Gawain*, 94-95, 106. See also Vocabulary

Point of view in *Gawain*, 126-28. See also Narrator

Polychronicon. See Higden

Pope, John Collins, *Rhythm of Beowulf*, 271

Pope, Mildred K., *From Latin to Modern French*, 253

Purity, 59, 220

Qualitative meanings, 83-85, 86, 89; use in *Gawain*, 101-02. See also Meaning

Rank, alliterative, 52-53, 76-77

Rare words, 31-33; in *Gawain*, 49, 50-51. See also Vocabulary

Read, Sir Herbert, *English Prose Style*, 212

Realistic technique: in *Morte Arthure*, 100-01; in *Gawain*, 113-15

Reciprocal actions in *Gawain*, 121-23

Reduction of suffix-vowels in ME, 138-40. See also Orthographic

Reference: subject of, 12; mode of, 15-17; stylistic effect of, 21-23; in ME alliterative poetry, 56-57; a problem of, in *Gawain*, 110-12. See also Subject of reference

Regel, Karl, "Alliteration im Laȝamon," 226

Reicke, Curt, *Untersuchungen über den Stil der mittelenglischen alliterierenden Gedichte Morte Arthure*, 235
Renoir, Alain, "Descriptive Technique in *Sir Gawain and the Green Knight*," 251
"Reversed foot": in *Cursor*, 146; in *Gawain*, 158, 159
Reversed spellings in *Gawain*-MS, 138-39. See also Orthographic
Rhymes as evidence for loss of *-e:* in *Cursor*, 142; in *Gawain*, 156-58. See also Meter; Orthographic
Richards, Ivor A., *Philosophy of Rhetoric*, 212-13, 215. See also Ogden
Romance words. See Old French loan words

St. *Erkenwald*, 59, 232-33
Savage, H. L., *Gawain Poet*, 219, 221
Schmittbetz, Karl Roland: "Adjektiv in 'Syr Gawayn and the Grene Knyȝt,'" 239, 241; *Adjektiv im Verse von "Syr Gawayn and þe Grene Knyȝt*," 239
Serjeantson, Mary S.: "Dialect of MS. Cotton Nero A.x.," 218-19; "Dialects of the West Midlands in Middle English," 218
Seven-stress theory, 172, 177-78, 190; tested on the long lines of *Gawain*, 178-82. See also Meter
Simple meter. See Meter
Sir Gawain and the Green Knight: vocabulary of, 48-51; traditional alliterative style in, 50-90; stylistic artistry of, 92-129; narrator of, 115-29; metrical form of, 155-63 (the wheels), 164-206 (the long lines); metrical artistry of, 207-10; dialect provenience of, 218-20; MS of, 218, 220; date of composition, 220; style praised by critics, 220-21. See also Arthur; Green Knight; *and individual stylistic and metrical headings*
Sisam, Kenneth, *Fourteenth Century Verse and Prose*, 222, 266
Space, treatment of, in *Gawain*, 123-24
Speaker: importance in study of style, 4, 6, 7-9; as narrator in fictional works, 91-92; in ME alliterative poetry, 93-94; in *Gawain*, 115-29. See also Narrator
Speirs, John, *Medieval English Poetry: The Non-Chaucerian Tradition*, 221
Spelling. See Orthographic
Spitzer, Leo: *Linguistics and Literary History*, 218; "Three Great Middle English Poems," 218
Stewart, George R., Jr., "Meter of *Piers Plowman*," 266
Stock words and expressions, 33. See also Vocabulary
Strandberg, Otto, *Rime-Vowels of Cursor Mundi*, 222-23
Style: general definition of, 3; as choice among alternatives, 3, 6, 8-9, 19-20; historical study of, 4, 27-29; critical study of, 4-5, see also Criticism; formality and informality, 5-8, see also Formality; broader definition, 19-20; partly determined by meanings, 24-26; in narrative works, 91-92. See also Descriptive style; Formulas; Middle English alliterative poetry; Occasion
Stylistic values: how determined, 30; evidence for, 34-36
Subject of reference, 12, 15-17, 216. See also Reference
Suffix-accent in rhyme: in *Cursor*, 151-52; in the wheels of *Gawain*, 161-62. See also Meter; Rhyme
Suggested meaning. See Meaning
Syllables, chief and intermediate, defined, 66, 144. See also Meter
Symbolistic meaning. See Meaning
Synonyms, 3, 5, 11; in ME alliterative poetry, 53-76. See also Vocabulary

"Tags" in ME alliterative poetry, 63, 70-71. See also Meter
Tatlock, John S. P., "Epic Formulas, Especially in Laȝamon," 226
Technical terms, 31. See also Vocabulary
Thomas, Julius, *Alliterierende Langzeile des Gawayn-Dichters*, 262-63, 267-68
Thomson, William, *Rhythm of Speech*, 174, 257, 259, 265
Tobler, Adolf, *Vom französischen Versbau alter und neuer Zeit*, 258
Tolkien, J. R. R., and E. V. Gordon, introduction to *Sir Gawain and the Green Knight*, 232
Trautmann, Moritz, *Über . . . einiger alliterierender Gedichte*, 235

Ushenko, A. P., "Metaphor," 214-15

Value. See Expressive value; Stylistic values

Verbal style, 20. *See also* Style
Verse, Latin accentual and Old French, 145
Vocabulary: of ME alliterative poetry, as studied by Oakden, 46–48; of *Gawain*, as studied by Kullnick, 48–51. *See also* Adjectives; Dialect words; Northern words; Old French; Old Norse; Poetic words; Rare words; Stock words; Synonyms; Technical terms

Waldron, Ronald A., "Oral-Formulaic Technique and Middle English Alliterative Poetry," 234, 236, 237
Wars of Alexander, 59, 62, 63, 73, 233

Wheels: metrical structure of, 66, 155, 158–61; final -*e* in rhymes of, 155–58; reversed foot in, 158, 159; final -*e* in intralinear position in, 159–60; final -*es*, -*ed* in, 161; suffix-accent in rhyme in, 161–62; accentuation of OF loan words in, 161–63. *See also* Meter
William of Palerne, 59, 63, 233
Wilson, R. M., *Lost Literature of Medieval England*, 222
Wimsatt, William K., Jr.: *Prose Style of Samuel Johnson*, 211; *Verbal Icon*, 211, 215
Winner and Waster, 59, 233
Wyld, H. C., "Studies in the Diction of Layamon's *Brut*," 40, 41–42, 226